BUCKNER

The Buckners of Virginia

and the allied families of

Strother and Ashby

Edited by

William Armstrong Crozier, F.R.S., F.G.S.A.

Editor of

The American General Armory; The Use and Abuse of Coat Armor;
Records of Spottsylvania County; Virginia Colonial Militia;
Williamsburg Wills, etc.

Published Privately for

William Dickinson Buckner

by

The Genealogical Association

New York

1907

Notice

In many older books, foxing (or discoloration) occurs and, in some instances, print lightens with wear and age. Reprinted books, such as this, often duplicate these flaws, notwithstanding efforts to reduce or eliminate them. The pages of this reprint have been digitally enhanced and, where possible, the flaws eliminated in order to provide clarity of content and a pleasant reading experience.

*The Buckners of Virginia
and the allied families of
Strother and Ashby*

Originally published
New York
1907

Reprinted by:

Janaway Publishing, Inc.
732 Kelsey Ct.
Santa Maria, California 93454
(805) 925-1038
www.janawaygenealogy.com

2012

ISBN: 978-1-59641-196-8

Made in the United States of America

MR. WILLIAM DICKINSON BUCKNER

"You writ them Sir, at my request."
—Two Gentlemen of Verona.

Preface

THE following pages have been written, that the records of an old and well known Virginia family might be preserved in true and simple form, not only as a reference book, but as a fraternal bond of good fellowship among the different branches of the family.

For sixteen years, William Dickinson Buckner, Esq., has gathered in a systematic manner, notes, manuscripts and records pertaining to the family, with the ultimate intention of printing them in suitable form. The accumulation of this data having assumed such formidable array, and the exigencies of his business precluding the actual compilation of the work by Mr. Buckner himself, the task of pruning the old, and gathering additional material was placed in my hands. To Mr. Buckner, however, the thanks of the members of the family should be rendered, for it is entirely owing to his determination to accomplish that which he had set out to do, and the furnishing of the necessary finances that this work has been brought to a successful completion.

The family chronicler is prone to set forth in glowing colors the good deeds of one's ancestors, and to gloss over those of more doubtful lustre. It can, however, be truthfully said, that a painstaking examination of old records in America and England has failed to reveal a "hidden Buckner skeleton."

We have standards of excellence which we never attain, and if some of our own flesh and blood have reached the higher ideals which we have set for ourselves, it should serve as an incentive for us to press forward in healthy emulation of noble traits.

We frequently read about family traits and family characteristics. How for generations one family has been a race of soldiers; another of clergymen; another of statesmen; another of lawyers, and another of merchants. A perusal of these pages will show that the Buckners are a combination of all of the above. It will show that the first of the name in America was one of the most respected merchants and progressive colonists. That his son as a Major of militia did his duty in repelling the attacks of blood thirsty Indians.

That another descendant was a fellow soldier with the great Washington. That in the defence of "a cause" they believed to be just and right, the Buckner blood was freely shed. That other descendants gave to Virginia, Kentucky and Missouri some of the ablest lawyers and staunchest statesmen that those states have ever known. It will show that they were "makers of men."

In preparing this history of the family, so many members have rendered help and encouragement that it would be impossible to enumerate them all by name. To Howard Randolph Bayne, Esq., most grateful acknowledgments are due for his assistance on the Ashby and Strother families. To the late Dr. James H. Buckner of Cincinnati, whose interest in the family history was most profound. To Mrs. Simon Bolivar Buckner; Mrs. Murray F. Tuley of Chicago; Mrs. Mildred Buckner McCay of Baltimore; Thomas Aylette Buckner, Esq., of New York; William Buckner McGroarty, Esq., of Washington, and Alvaro F. Gibbens, Esq., of Parkersburg, W. Va., our thanks are especially rendered.

The Buckner coat of arms depicted on the frontispiece is the one ascribed by Papworth and Burke to the Buckners of Berkshire, England. While there is no documentary evidence to show that the early Buckners of Virginia used armorial bearings, yet the records prove that they as descendants of the Berkshire family had a just right to use it had they valued such insignia.

No claim is made that the following pages are free from errors. The book aims to present a faithful record of the history of a family, and wherein it fails, the fault is not always to be imputed to the compiler, who may have been misled by incomplete information. Genealogy is a history of ourselves, and as CHAUCER truthfully says—"T'is not renomee of auncestres, but gentil dedes that make ye gentil man."

WILLIAM ARMSTRONG CROZIER

Contents

The English Buckners	1
The Buckners of Chichester	16
John Buckner of Gloucester Co., Va.	20
William Buckner of York Co., Va.	25
John Buckner, Jr., of Gloucester Co., Va.	31
Richard Buckner of Essex Co., Va.	34
Philip Buckner of Louisa Co., Va.	41
Thomas Buckner of Spottsylvania Co., Va.	56
Thomas Buckner of Caroline Co., Va.	87
John Buckner of Caroline Co., Va.	91
Philip Buckner of Kentucky	91
William Buckner of Caroline Co., Va.	112
Francis Buckner of Caroline Co., Va.	122
Richard Buckner of Westmoreland Co., Va.	125
George Buckner of Caroline Co., Va.	132
Thomas Buckner of Gloucester Co., Va.	153
Ann Buckner of Gloucester Co., Va.	164
Thomas Buckner of Gloucester Co., Va.	167
Philip Buckner of Stafford Co., Va.	169
Thomas Buckner of Caroline Co., Va.	171
Buckners of West Virginia	190
Lewis and Washington Families	201
Stith Family	206
Thruston Family	210

Dickinson Family	217
Strother Family	219
Ashby Family	241
Thornton Family	280
Claiborne Family	283
Unidentified Buckner Families	284
Buckners of South Carolina	284
Buckners of North Carolina	285
RoBards Family	295
Bucknors of New York	299
Bucknors of Pennsylvania	300
Buckners of New England	301
Addenda	302
Index	303

Illustrations

Buckner Arms	
William Dickinson Buckner	
Arms of the Buckners of Chichester	2
Chart of Anne Family, Oxford, England	4
Chart of Smyth Family, Lancashire, England	6
Chart of Barry Family, Oxford, England	10
Facsimile of Buckner Seal	12
"The Lawn," Sittingbourne, Kent, England	14
Arms of the See of Chichester	16
Mrs. Augusta Plimley Buckner Gascoyne	18
Chart of Buckner Family of England and Virginia	20
Richard Buckner's Survey	35
General Simon Bolivar Buckner	44
General Simon Bolivar Buckner in 1885	50
Mrs. Simon Bolivar Buckner	53
Mrs. Murray F. Tuley	56
John Buckner's Survey	76
Edmund Garnett Buckner	80
Judge Murray F. Tuley	83
Lake Farm	85
Fitzhugh Arms	87
William I. Dickinson	88
Spring Hill	90
Marengo	92
Grave Yard—Chestnut Valley	94
Nottingham	96
Chestnut Valley	98
House on the Neck Farm	112
Commission of Major Colin Buckner	114
George O. M. Buckner and Family	116
Moss Neck	118
Court House, Bowling Green, Caroline Co.	123
William Fitzhugh Thornton Buckner	124
Mrs. William Fitzhugh Thornton Buckner	127
Family of Charles Madison Buckner	128
Residence of Charles Madison Buckner	130
Lieutenant Bailey Buckner	133
Mildred Strother Buckner	134
Honl. Aylette Hawes Buckner	136
Major Caldwell Calhoun Buckner	139
Louisa Fitzhugh Dickinson Buckner	141
Marshall Dulany Buckner	143
Louise Dickinson Brown	144
Edith Hamilton Brown	146
Island View	149
Tomb of Captain George Buckner	150
Braynefield	152
Cooke Arms	164
Marlfield	168
Mill Hill	170
Judge Benjamin F. Buckner	175
Sarah Martin Buckner	176
Samuel Buckner	178
Louisa Malvina Dodge Buckner	180
Thomas Aylette Buckner	182
Thomas Aylette Buckner, Jr.	184
Walker Buckner	186
Colonel John A. Buckner	188
Dr. James H. Buckner	190
Thruston Arms	212
Ormesby	218
Chart of Strother Family, Northumberland, England	220
Madison Arms	222
Mary Wade Strother	225
Colonel William Menefee	226
Wadefield	228
Wadefield, Front View	231
Strother Arms	233
John Strother	234
Chart of Ashby Family	241
Howard Randolph Bayne	270
General Turner Ashby	273
Thornton Arms	279
Chart of Thornton Family	281
Fairfield	282
Claiborne Arms	284
Rev. A. G. Buckner, D.D.	286
Rev. Robert Cook Buckner, D.D., L.L.D.	297
William Heald Buckner	301

PRINTED BY
GEORGE HARJES CO.,
NEW YORK

" People will not look forward to posterity, who never look backward to their ancestors."
—Edmund Burke.

The English Buckners

IT is always true that honorable ancestry only aggravates the blame for a degenerate present. It is also true, that it is at all times wise and proper to illuminate and study the virtues of past ages, if we purpose in so doing, to set them before us as a model to imitate for the future.

In such a spirit, and with such a purpose we have endeavored to trace the history of John Buckner of Virginia, who, like a patriarch of old, with his children and children's children around him, became part of that band of empire builders, who carved out of the primeval wilderness the cornerstone, on which is still being upreared the temple of the best civilization of the nations.

The earliest mention of the name Buckner, in the existing records of Virginia, is that of John Buckner of York County, who patented 1,000 acres of land in Gloucester County in the year 1667. The latter county was formed from York in 1642, but its records previous to 1820, have been destroyed by fire, so that any clue they may have contained is forever lost.

The next of the name is Philip Buckner, a brother of John. His name is first mentioned in the records of Gloucester County in 1669. Then comes Nathaniel Buckner of Stafford County in 1680, and Anthony Buckner of Stafford in 1678, who patented land in Rappahannock in 1672-3.

In an endeavor to establish the identity of these Buckners, an exhaustive search of the English records was made, and the result has been the unearthing of various wills, and entries in Parish Registers, pertaining to the family.

As a matter of fact, the main object of the English search has been to ascertain, what connection, if any, John Buckner of Virginia had with a certain Thomas Buckner, who was a member of the "Raleigh Expedition," in the unsuccessful attempt to establish a settlement on the Western Continent in the year 1585.

What became of this Thomas Buckner after the failure of the expedition, whether he was one of the unfortunates of the colony, who died on the soil of what is now the State of North Carolina, or whether he lived to return to England, and tell of the attractions of the New World beyond the Atlantic Ocean, has hitherto been a matter of conjecture.

Until the production of this present work, the only detailed account of the Buckners consisted of a skeleton outline of the family which appeared a number of years ago in the *Richmond Critic*. This slight sketch was not only incomplete, but recent original research shows it to have been erroneous in several important particulars.

The article in the *Critic* makes mention of a work entitled "*A Royal Descent*," by Miss Thomasine Elizabeth Sharpe, and published by her in London in 1875. A copy of this work is in the Library of the British Museum. Amongst the many pedigrees given therein, is one of a Buckner family, which the author states had its origin in Westphalia. The first of the name, Richard Buckner, was born there in 1695, came to England, and died an Alderman of Chichester in 1772.

As a tradition is prevalent amongst some of the American Buckners that the immediate forefathers of John Buckner, the immigrant, were of German descent, it may be remarked *en passant*, that the ancestors of John Buckner are now known to have been in England 150 years before Richard Buckner of Westphalia was born. This fact does away with any surmise as to the close kinship of John and Richard.

It will readily be seen by the veriest tyro in the study of genealogy, that an attempt to find the parent stem of an American family, settled in this country since the middle of the seventeenth century, was a stupendous task.

The only clue to work upon was the fact, that Thomas Buckner of the "Raleigh Expedition," was believed to have been born in, or contiguous to the City of London. The search commenced, therefore, amongst the Middlesex records, and from thence to the surrounding counties. It was not, however, until the counties of Berks and Bucks were approached that anything tangible came to light. Then was unearthed what was thought to be the earliest will of an English Buckner—that of Richard Buckner of Cumnor, Berks, whose will is dated as far back as 1548. This Richard may

be styled the founder of the American family, for beyond him we have been unable to go, although there is little doubt that the family had been living in the neighborhood of Cumnor for several generations previous to 1548. The phraseology of the will, and the amount of property bequeathed by the testator is conclusive that he was no immigrant from Germany, but rather that he and his ancestors had belonged to the class of stout English yeomanry for many years.

The County of Berkshire may justly be considered as the home of the Buckners. From thence they spread to picturesque Oxfordshire, and as the parent stem gradually dwindled in the mother country, its transplanted branches settled in the beckoning West, there to become in the fullness of time makers of men and history.

As we have stated before, of the first Buckners who came to Virginia, at least two of them were brothers—John and Philip. Of the other two—Nathaniel and Anthony—nothing is known, although it is extremely probable that there was some degree of consanguinity between all of them. The christian names of John, Philip and Anthony are found in the English records.

Richard Buckner of Cumnor

In the S. W. of the County of Berkshire, and three and one-half miles from the City of Oxford, nestles the quiet little village of Cumnor. Possibly from its settlement, until the time of the Parliamentary Wars, its handful of inhabitants had pursued the "even tenour of their ways," and then as now, when the day's work was o'er, would gaze across the valley and descry in the distance, silhouetted against the evening sky, the "City of towers and spires," which from the days of King Alfred in 879, had been noted as a seat of learning.

It was this modest little hamlet that was the home of the Buckners, and from it in later years went forth the sons, some to rise to high emolument and honor in the Church of England, others to forsake husbandry for the more exciting life of barter and commerce in the Metropolis of the Old World, which finally ended in their migration to the Colony of Virginia.

The founder of the family was Richard Buckner, and unfortunately we know but little about him. It is evident from his will that he was a man of some considerable property, and of high standing in the community, for a son, daughter and granddaughter married into the best of the county families. The date of his birth is unknown, but it was most likely previous to 1500, as he died in 1548, at which time he was a grandfather. His will, which is on file in the Prerogative Court of Canterbury, is as follows:

Will of Rychard Buckner

"Rychard Buckner, of Cumnor, Co. Berks., Sept. 4, 1548.

"Thomas my eldest son to kepe the oldeman Thomas and Elizabeth his sister. To Thomas and John my sonnes the (e) state at Raccote for my yeres answering the lorde his rente.

"John my son to occupy the third part of Whiteley in the parish of Cumnor.

"To Mr. Bery, to Johan my doughter, to Johan's two doughters, to my doughter Mary and her sister Elizabeth my house of Lechlade.

"My children Thomas, John, William, Mary and Agnes my lands in Whiteley, and to be executors.

"Mr. Laurence Berry, Mr. Richard Ruffin and William Secole to be overseers."

Witnesses: Thomas Woode.
  Robert King.
  William Buckner.

Proved March 1, 1548-9, by Thomas Buckner.

(F. 27 Populwell) Prerogative Court of Canterbury.

We come to the conclusion that Richard Buckner was a widower, as there is no mention of his wife. It is also interesting to note that his son Thomas signs his name—Bukener. The first clause in the will, "the oldeman Thomas and Elizabeth" probably refers to two old servants, for in those days the surname of a dependent or retainer was rarely used, and he evidently requests his son to keep them in his service.

Thomas, the eldest son, mentioned in the above will, married Dorothy, one of the daughters of William Anne, Esq., and Anne Denton, his wife, of North Aston, Oxfordshire. This information we learn from the Herald's Visitation of Oxfordshire, made by Richard Lee in 1574.

Thomas Buckner inherited a portion of the estate of Whiteley.

His wife Dorothy died in 1586, as her estate was administered upon by her husband in that year. He soon followed her, as his will is dated March 10, 1587-8. Proved April 11. In it he leaves his estate to his daughter Dorothy, and makes his brother John Buckner, executor. She was evidently the only living child, and is probably the Dorothy Buckner whose estate at Cumnor is administered upon in 1598.

As Richard Buckner names on two occasions his son John immediately after Thomas, it is natural to suppose that he was the second son. There are no entries in the Parish Register of Cumnor of a sufficiently early date, to denote the marriages of the children of Richard Buckner. It is quite likely that the marriages did not take place in Cumnor, as that of the eldest son Thomas occurred at the seat of his wife's parents at North Aston, Oxford.

John Buckner, the second son, died in 1599 (Will dated Nov. 26. Proved Dec. 30. Book (J. P. C. C.). He leaves "portion of my lands at Whitely left me by my father, to my nephew William Buckner of Chawley, and my nephew John Buckner of Botley; my nephew Francis Barry; my sister Mary."

William Buckner of Cumnor, third son of Richard Buckner, died in 1558. His will is as follows:

Will of William Buckner

William Buckner of Cumnor, Co. Berks, yeoman. Dated 12 May 1558. Prob. 24 May 1558. E. 19. (P. P. C.)

"To be buried in churchyard of Cumnor. Wife Martha lease of my lands in Whiteley, which I rente of my brother Thomas. To my sones John and William to occupy the third part of Botley: my sones Hugh and Richard my tenements of Oxford; my daughters Rose Smith and Elizabeth my lands in Whiteley after the death of Martha my wife." Executors: Mr. Thomas Smyth and Andrewe Carpenter. Overseers: Mr. William Harris and William Penne in Oxford.

Witnesses: Edmund Herne.
Henry Keene.
Thomas Buckner.

Hugh Buckner, a son of the above William of Cumnor, resided in the City of Oxford. According to the "Registrum Universitatis, Oxon," he took the oath as Bailiff, Oct. 2, 1592; and on Nov. 25,

1596, appeared before the Vice-Chancellor for examination in a claim that he had presented of the amount of £20. His sister Rose had married in 1553, Thomas Smyth, gent., who was Mayor of the city at the time of his death in 1601. Agnes Smyth, a daughter of Rose Buckner, married Ralph Flexney, who also became Mayor of Oxford, and who died in 1624.

If Hugh Buckner left a will, no record of it has been found, but in the Parish Registers of St. Aldates, and of the Church of St. Mary, Oxford, there are various entries pertaining to his children and grandchildren, and the issue of his sister Rose.

St. Aldate's Parish Register

May 24, 1553. Rose Buckner and Thomas Smyth, married.
Dec. 24, 1560. Peter, son of Thos. Smyth, was baptised.
Apl. 16, 1562. John, son of Thos. Smyth, was baptised.
July 6, 1566. Thomas, son of Thomas Smyth, was baptised.
June 2, 1596. William, son of Thomas Smyth, buried.
Sept. 11, 1569. Katherine Smyth and Thomas Mysson, married.
Aug. 4, 1577. Peter, son of Thomas and Rose Smyth, buried.
Sept. 7, 1582. Rose, wife of Thomas Smyth, buried.
Apl. 4, 1583. John Smyth and Eliz. Zarcheade, married.
June 8, 1579. Agnes Smyth and Ralf Flexney, married.
July 18, 1580. Agnes, wife of Ralf Flexney, buried.
Apl. 22, 1589. Joan Smyth and Robert Jones, married.
Jan. 1, 1591. Margaret Smyth and John Furnes, married.
July 9, 1601. Thomas Smyth, Mayor of Citie, buried.
July 12, 1624. Ralf Flexney, sometime Mayor, buried.
Jan 6, 1575. Anthony, son of Hugh Buckner, baptised.
Mch. 12, 1581. Dorothy, daughter of Hugh Buckner, buried.
Feb. 20, 1590. Thomas, son of Hugh Buckner, baptised.

St. Mary's Parish Register

Aug. 12, 1598. William, son of Hugh Buckner, buried.
Nov. 2, 1605. William, son of Hugh Buckner, baptised.
Feb. 12, 1622. Richard, son of Thomas Buckner, baptised.
June 19, 1624. Elizabeth, daughter of Thomas Buckner, buried.
Aug. 16, 1628. Thomas, son of Thomas Buckner, baptised.
Feb. 2, 1631. John, son of Thomas Buckner, baptised.
Oct. 29, 1634. Lawrence, son of Thomas Buckner, baptised.
Mch. 19, 1639. Philip, son of Thomas Buckner, baptised.
May 6, 1645. Thomas Buckner, buried.
July 19, 1650. Jane Buckner, buried.
Feb 13, 1666. William, son of William Buckner, baptised.

It is from the above Parish Registers that we get strong evidence as to the parentage of John and Philip Buckner, the Virginia immigrants. In none of the English records do we find

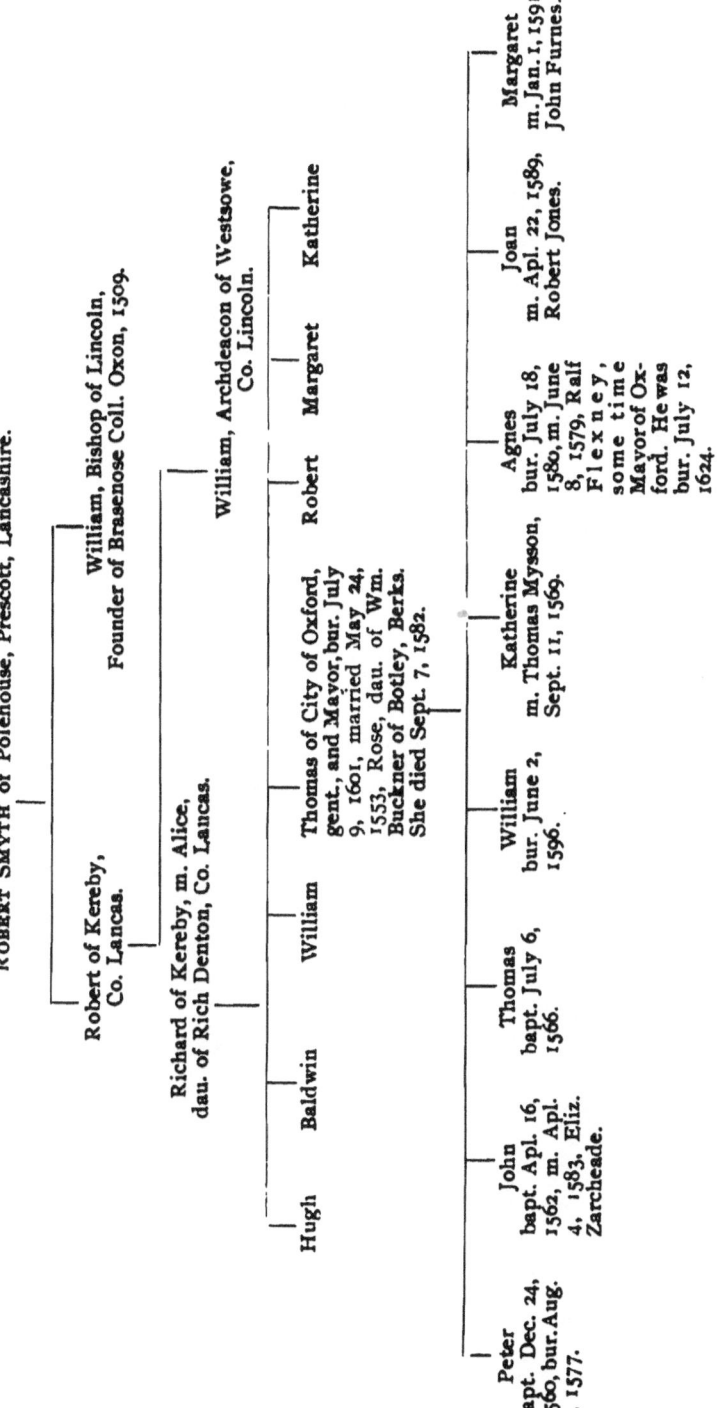

the slighest mention of their habitation in Virginia, with the possible exception of a Thomas Buckner, Alderman of London, of whom we will speak later.

The names John, William, Thomas and Richard occur in every generation of the Buckner lines in England, and also in the first generation in Virginia. It is true that they were common in all families, but we do not observe any deviation from this rule until we find that of Hugh Buckner of Oxford, which name seems to have ended with him. In his son Anthony we get a name that is next found in Virginia, viz.: Anthony Buckner, who patented lands in Rappahannock County in 1672. In the Canterbury records there are letters of administration on the estate of Anthony Buckner of Cumnor, Berks, in 1643. This is probably the Anthony who was son of Hugh, and who was baptized in 1575. The Anthony Buckner of Virginia may have been his son.

There is little doubt that John Buckner of Virginia was a well educated and progressive man. This may be accounted for from the fact that he was born and presumably educated in Oxford, although we find no evidence that he was ever at the University. The environments of the seat of learning, must have had some effect upon his character as he was the first man to introduce the printing press into the Colony of Virginia.

John Buckner was in Gloucester County, Virginia, as early as 1667, and in 1669 his brother Philip had a "headright" in the same county. We find no trace of the name Philip in any of the English records after the year 1667, and there is not a scrap of evidence to show that either of them married after they came to Virginia. There seems to be, however, *prima facie* evidence that they married in England. Let us see what this is.

John Buckner was born in Oxford in 1631. During his life in Virginia he was the agent of various London merchants, so that it is probable he was a resident of London for a time at least, previous to his leaving England. In the "Registry of the Vicar General of Canterbury" is the following entry:

"July 10, 1661. John Buckner of St. Sepulchre's, citizen and salter of London, Bach. about 31, and Debora Ferrers of West Wickham, Bucks, about 19; with consent of her mother, now wife of Andrew Hunt of the same, at West Wickham."

If the above John and Debora Buckner resided in London and had issue, it is natural to suppose that some record of their births would be found. On the contrary, this is the first and last that we hear of them, which tends to the conclusion that this is the John Buckner of Virginia, and that he and his wife went there very soon after their marriage.

Other evidence in favor of this theory, is the age of the male applicant, which is given as "about 31." This agrees with the birth of John Buckner in 1631, which would make him about 31 years old at this time—1661. Again, the residence of the bride is stated to be "West Wickham," Bucks. The County of Buckingham adjoins that of Berkshire, and West Wickham and Cumnor are but a few miles apart, and it is not unreasonable to imagine that John Buckner would find a bride in the vicinity in which he was born, and his ancestors had lived and died.

We now turn to the presumed marriage of Philip Buckner. If he married in England it probably took place before 1669, in which year he is on record as being in Gloucester County, Va.

Outside of the entry of his baptism in 1639 at St. Mary's, Oxford, the name of Philip does not appear in any records until 1667, and after that not at all. The name Philip was unique at this period in the Buckner family in England, but in Virginia it has been carried down for generations, since the first Philip went there.

In the Parish Register of St. James, Clerkenwell, is the following entry: "July 15, 1667, Philip Buckner and Elizabeth Sadler, married."

From this issue also, no records of birth can be found in England. So that we may conclude that this was the Philip Buckner who was in Virginia in 1669.

We have unfortunately no evidence in the Virginia records to strengthen our supposition as to these two marriages. For when John Buckner died in 1695, he left no will, and at the death of Philip Buckner in 1700, although he left a will, there is no mention of his wife, in fact, the phraseology of the document is proof that he was a widower.

Having shown the descent of John and Philip from Richard Buckner of Berks, we turn to the Thomas Buckner who was a member of the "Raleigh Expedition" in 1585.

He was without doubt one of the Berkshire family of the name, but his exact identity is not quite clear. He was certainly not a son of Richard Buckner of Cumnor, as his eldest son

Thomas was dead in 1587. It is possible that he may have been a nephew.

In further confirmation that he was a member of the Berkshire Buckners, is the marriage of his daughter Mary Buckner to Rowland Holt of Berks and London. The issue of this marriage was a son Thomas, doubtless named after his grandfather.

Thomas Holt became Recorder of Reading, Berks, and was Knighted at Windsor Castle, April 16, 1680. Sir Thomas Holt, married Susan, daughter of John Peacock, of Cumnor, Berks, and the eldest son of this marriage was Sir John Holt, Knt., who became Lord Chief Justice of the King's Bench in 1699. He purchased the manor of Redgrave in Suffolk, from Sir Robert Bacon. Sir John died in 1709 and was buried at Redgrave. He married a sister of Sir John Cropley. His will dated in 1709, leaves to Lady Holt £700 per annum, £3,000 in money and all jewels and household goods. He leaves £200 per annum to his sister, and to his brother Rowland Holt, £1,000 per annum, and his real estate to his nephews, John, Thomas, Rowland and Henry, and £7,000 to be divided between his brother's younger sons and daughters. It will, therefore, be seen that the grandson of Mary Buckner was an extremely wealthy man.

Thomas Buckner resided in Threadneedle Street, near the Royal Exchange. He married Jan. 24th, 1590, Elizabeth Crackplace. He was an influential merchant and an Alderman of the City and a staunch friend of the celebrated Thomas Harriot, with whom he had been a companion in one of Raleigh's first expeditions to Virginia in 1585.

Thomas Harriot was born at Oxford in 1560. He was a mathematician and astronomer, and was for a time tutor to Sir Walter Raleigh, who appointed him to the office of geographer in the second expedition to Virginia. He published in 1588 an account of his travels.

In 1621, Harriot resided with his friend Thomas Buckner, at whose house he died July 2 of that year. He made Thomas Buckner one of the executors of his will. After a lengthy preamble, it recites, "I give unto Mrs. Buckner wife unto Thomas Buckner, Mercer, at whose house being in St. Christopher's Parish I nowe lye, and hereafter nomenate one of my Executors, the some of fifteene poundes, towards the repacons of some damagues that I have made, or for other uses as shee shall thincke convenient. Item: I give unto Mr. John Buckner their eldest sonne, the some of five poundes."

In the "Accomptes of the Church Wardens of the Paryshe of St. Chrystofer's, in London," are the following entries:

"For Anno 1622. Received of Mr. Thomas Buckner, being the gift of Mr. Harriot, £4, paid to the poore."

"For Anno 1626. Received of Mr. Thomas Buckner for the erecting of Mr. Herriot, his monument in the Chauncell, the some of one pound."

Thomas Buckner died intestate in 1634. His children were:

I. John Buckner.
II. Thomas Buckner, matriculated at Magdalen Coll, Oxford, graduated B. A., Dec. 15, 1614; M. A., June 28, 1617; B. D., July 7, 1627; D. D., March 15, 1638-9. (Incorporated at Cambridge 1621). Prebendary of Winchester 1635; Chaplain to Archbishop Abbott; Rector of Mersham, Surrey, 1632, and of Chevening, Kent, from 1633 until his death Jan. 21, 1644-5.
III. William Buckner, born 1605; matriculated Oct. 13, 1621, at Christ Church, Oxford. B. A., Oct. 21, 1623; M. A., June 13, 1626. Rector of Hertingfordbury, Herts, 1630.
IV. Mary Buckner, baptised Nov. 15, 1609, married Rowland Holt, Gent., of London, and had issue, Sir Thomas Holt, Recorder of Reading.
V. Elizabeth Buckner, baptised July 12, 1612, buried July 17.

Going back to the first Richard Buckner of Cumnor, he mentions in his will his daughter Jane, or as it is written, "my doughter Johan and her two doughters."

Jane Buckner married Lawrence Barry of Ensham, County of Oxon, gent., and owner of Hampton Gay. In the Herald's Visitation in 1574, no mention is made of the two daughters, nor are their names given in the Visitation of 1634. It is evident the daughters died previous to 1574, but were alive in 1548 at the time of their grandfather's death. From Jane Buckner's second son, Francis, descended her grandson, Vincent Barry, of Thame, Oxon, 1634, who married Elizabeth, daughter of Robert Scroope of Wormesley, County of Oxon. She was a descendant of Lord Scroope of Bolton.

Sir Richard Scroope (or Scrope), first Lord Scrope of Bolton, was a participant in the celebrated controversy with Sir Robert Grosvenor in 1385-90, concerning his right to bear the same arms as Scrope.

In the year 1385 an English army, under the King in person, invaded Scotland. Among the banners displayed on this occasion

Barry of Eynesham, County of Oxford, Visitation of 1634

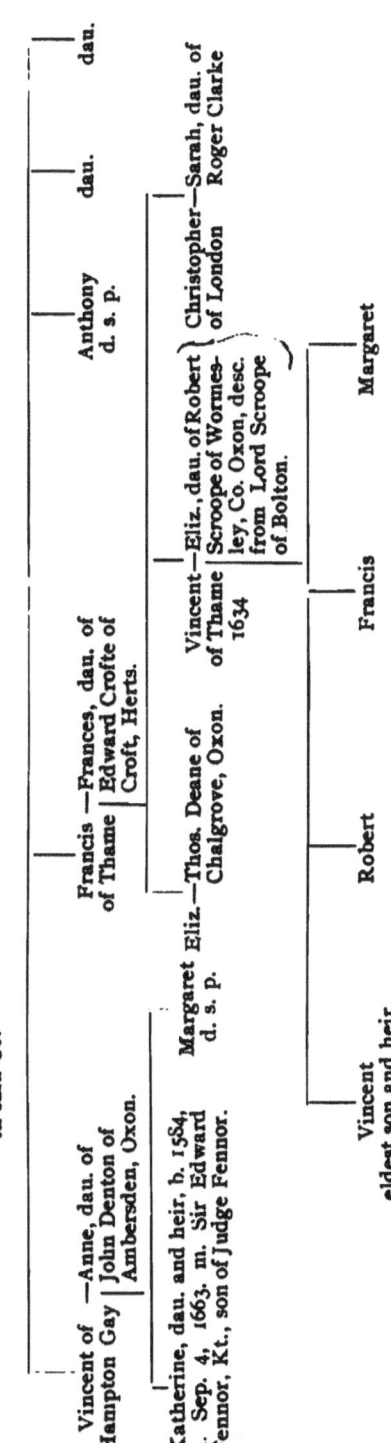

LAWRENCE BARRY of Eynesham Co.—JANE, dau. of Richard Buckner, of Whitley, Co. Berks. Oxon, gent., owner of Hampton Gay in said Co.

- Vincent of Hampton Gay — Anne, dau. of John Denton of Ambersden, Oxon.
- Francis — Frances, dau. of Edward Crofte of Croft, Herts. of Thame
- Anthony d. s. p.
- dau.
- dau.

Katherine, dau. and heir, b. 1584, d. Sep. 4, 1663. m. Sir Edward Fennor, Kt., son of Judge Fennor.

Margaret d. s. p.
Eliz. — Thos. Deane of Chalgrove, Oxon.
Vincent of Thame 1634 — Eliz, dau. of Robert Scroope of Wormesley, Co. Oxon, desc. from Lord Scroope of Bolton.
Christopher of London — Sarah, dau. of Roger Clarke

Vincent eldest son and heir
Robert
Francis
Margaret

In the North Chancel of Hampton Gay Church is the monument of Vincent Barry and his wife, Anne Denton, with their arms impaled.

ARMS OF BARRY—Per pale azure and gules, two lions passant guardant or.

ARMS OF DENTON—Argent, two bars gules, in chief three cinquefoils sable. (Originally of Denton Hall, Co. Cumberland, settled there *temp* WILLIAM I.)

ARMS OF CROFTE—Quarterly, per fesse indented azure and argent, in the first quarter a lion passant guardant or.

ARMS OF SCROOPE—Azure a bend or.

was that of Sir Richard Scrope, a distinguished soldier and statesman, who, besides being present at several of the greatest battles of his time, had held the office of treasurer, steward of the King's household, and twice chancellor of England. His arms were, "*asure a bend or*." To his high indignation he found in the camp a knight, Sir Robert Grosvenor, bearing the same coat. A dispute followed, when Grosvenor maintained his right; and the matter was referred to a court of chivalry, composed of the constable and marshall of England, with other nobles, knights, and learned clerks, the Duke of York and the Earl of Salisbury among them. Many sittings were held; much evidence collected and heard on either side. Scrope brought forward the more numerous and distinguished array, leading off with John of Gaunt. Other deponents on his part were *Le Counte de Derby*, afterwards Henry IV.; the Earl of Northumberland and a Sir Henry de Percy, in whom we recognise the Harry Hotspur of history and ballad; and if not most noble, most famous of all—Geffray Chaucere, *esquier*. At length, in 1389, the Duke of Gloucester, as constable, gave sentence in favor of Scrope. The controversy became the most notable in heraldic history in regard to the right of two families to the same arms.

Richard Buckner's eldest son, Thomas, married Dorothy Anne, and by this alliance the Buckners were connected with a very ancient Oxfordshire family. His wife being descended from the Giffords, Fosters and Dentons, all families of great antiquity, and long settled in Oxon and Berks.

It must not be thought that the Buckners strayed no further afield than their home counties, for in the Rrerogative Wills of Ireland, there is recorded the will of John Bucknor, gent., of Limerick, 1671; and William Buckner of Coolefin, County Waterford, Esq., 1700. Who they may be, we have not endeavored to ascertain, as the dates of their demise are not early enough for our purpose.

The name Buckner can be traced in the English records to a period anterior to 1548, although we might have considerable difficulty in making satisfactory connections. To cite the words of Ashmole, "in our public Records lye matter of Fact, in Full Truth, and therewith the Chronological part, carried on, even to days of the month; so that an industrious Searcher may thence collect considerable matter for new History, rectifie many mistakes in our old, and in both gratifie the world with unshadowed verity."

In what are known as the "Close Rolls," we find that a fief was divided in 1309 between Joan and Margaret, daughters and co-heirs of Hugh de Mortimer, descended through an heiress from Osbern Fitz Richard, lord of the fief in Domesday Book, to whose father, a Norman favorite of Edward the Confessor, a castle called "Richards' Castle" derived its name. Joan de Mortimer was the wife at this time of Thomas de Bocknor—or as we call it now—Buckner. His arms were "Argent on a chevron azure, three lions rampant of the first." *Crest:* A pheon erm.

There is also a Sir Thomas de Bukenore, Kt., whose seal is affixed to his grant of the manor of Bredhurst, Kent. It is without date, but from collateral evidence, we conjecture it to be late Edward I., or early Edward II., *i. e.*, about A. D., 1300.

In the Surrey records there is a rent of nine marks in the parish of St. Olave's in Southwark, by deed sealed. It is dated "Ffolkestane, on Tuesday on the morrow of St. John the Baptist, in the fifth year of the reign of the Lord the King Edward III, (A. D. 1331) to Durandus de Wydmerpole and John de Bykenore, son and heir of Sir John de Bykenore, Kt., and their heirs forever."

Oldest Buckner Will

The most ancient of the Buckner wills that has been discovered is that of a Robert Buknore who died in 1365. His will is recorded at the Court of Hustings, London, and is as follows:

Robert Buknore of the parish of Derteford. Dated at Derteford, April 8, 1365, Probated May 6, 1365.

Bequests to St. Edmund's Chapel at Derteford; the high altar of the church at Derteford, its chaplains, etc.

To Agnes, daughter of Alice his late wife, he leaves a tenement in the lane of St. Martin Ongar; his growing crops in the manor of Northcraye, and a pair of swans in the water of Northcraye.

To Robert de Louthe a pair of swans swimming at Portebrugge, and to Edmond Lambyn and Richard Stone, a pair of swans swimming in Stoneham Ree.

To William de Kyrkeby he leaves his big horse "Bayard" and three quarters of barley.

To John Boch six quarters of the same, his new rayed cloak and his rayed tunic.

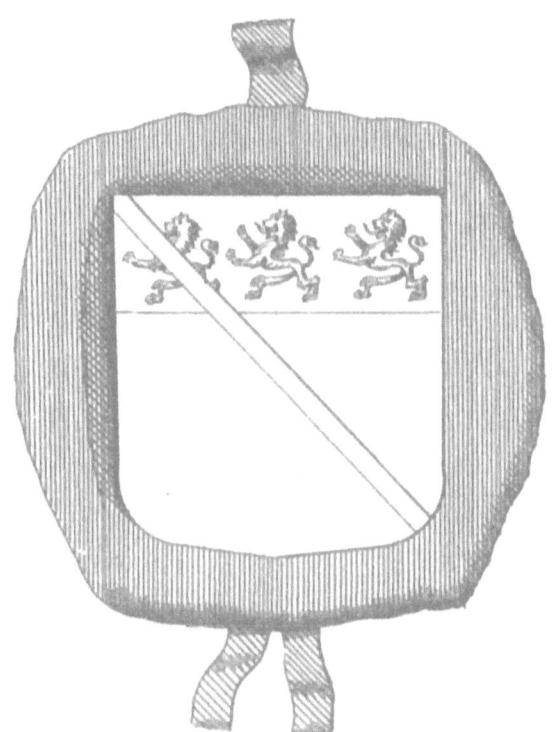

To William Hunte two quarters of barley and a cloak of bluet (*sic.* blue).

To John Cook, William Claydon and others he leaves divers measures of the same barley.

To Margaret his late wife's servant, a sum of money, a curtepy of morre with hood, and a green tunic with hood."

Buckner Names in the English Records

Middlesex Sessions Rolls

March 15, 1657-8. Walter Buckner of Bartholomews the Great, London. "Recognizance in the sum of £50, for his appearance as a witness."

Register of St. Peter, Mitcham, Surrey

Nov. 13, 1595. William Buckner, proctor of Milend hospitall, dyinge in the streat, att ye may poole, near Cat poole, against Batte his house. Buried ye 13th.

Parish Register of Cumnor, Berks

May 20, 1558. William Buckner, buried.
April 1, 1579. George, son of Thomas Buckner, buried.
June 10, 1580. John, son of John Buckner, christened.
Jan. 9, 1586. Dorothy, wife of Thomas Buckner, buried.
March 20, 1587. Thomas Buckner was buried.
Jan. 22, 1588. Elizabeth Buckner, baptized.
Nov. 29, 1599. John Buckner, buried.
May 3, 1605. Mary Buckner, buried.

St. Mary's, Reading

April 12, 1619. Thomas Buckner and Alice Page, married.
Sept. 10, 1672. John Buckner, buried.

Parish of Soulsbury, Bucks

July 16, 1624. Elizabeth Buckner and Thomas Stevens, married.
June 13, 1677. John Buckner and Elizabeth Savage, married.
Nov. 9, 1691. Alice Buckner and Richard Scarborow, married.
June 10, 1703. Jonathan Buckner, widower, and Anne Goss, widow, married.

Parish of Ivingboe, Bucks

Oct. 13, 1586. Richard Buckner and Winifred Williams, married.
Jan. 23, 1607. Frances Buckner and Robert Raunce, married.

London Parish Registers

St. Botolph Bishopsgate

Nov. 15, 1609. Mary, daughter of Thomas Buckner, christened.

St. Mary's

Sept. 27, 1653. William Buckner, batcheler, to Mrs. Sarah Chitts, virgin, both of ye parish of Queen-hith.

St. Saviour's, Southwark

July 24, 1623. Margerie Bucknor and Henry Hughes, married.

St. Thomas the Apostle

Jan. 8, 1603. John, son of John Bucknar, christened.

Kensington Parish

Oct. 18, 1666. Dorcas, daughter of Mr. Humphrey and Mrs. Dorcas Buckner baptised.

Dec. 8, 1666. Margaret, daughter to Mr. Humphrey and Mrs. Dorcas Buckner, buried.

St. James, Clerkenwell

July 4, 1608. John Buckner and Susan Staples, married.
Feb. 7, 1609. John Buckner and Joane Nichols, married.
July 12, 1612. Elizabeth, daughter of John Buckner, christened.
July 17, 1612. Elizabeth, daughter of Mr. John Buckner, buried.
July 15, 1667. Philip Buckner and Elizabeth Sadler, married.

St. Michaels, Cornhill

Jan. 24, 1590. Thomas Buckner and Elizabeth Crackplace, married.

Licenses Granted by the Bishop of London

Mar. 19, 1638-9. William Buckner, gent., of Mestham, Co. Surrey, bachelor 30 years, and Jane Wood of the same, widow, 32 years, at St. Bennet's or St. Peter's, Paul's Wharf.

Registry of Vicar General of Canterbury

July 10, 1661. John Buckner of St. Sepulchre's, citizen and salter of London, bachelor, about 31, and Debora Ferrers of West Wickham, Bucks, about 19, with consent of her mother, now wife of Andrew Hunt of the same, at West Wickham.

"THE LAWN"
SITTINGBOURNE, KENT, ENGLAND
RESIDENCE OF MRS. AUGUSTA PLIMLEY (BUCKNER) GASCOYNE

Dec. 4, 1662. William Buckner of St. Botolph, Aldgate, London, apothecary, bachelor, 21 and upwards, and Isabel Rountree of the same place, aged 26, at own disp. alleged by Leonard Rountree of same place, dyer.

Sept. 13, 1667. Richard Buckner of St. Martin's in the Fields, Middlesex, bachelor, about 22, and Deborah Nelson of same place, spinster, about 26, at own disp. Gray's Inn Chapel, Middlesex.

Registry of the Bishop of Winchester

May 29, 1742. Thomas Buckner of Portsmouth, 29, bachelor, and Mary Mackeen, 22, spinster, of the same place.

" He from John of Gaunt doth bring his pedigree."
—I. Henry VI.

The Buckners of Chichester

ACCORDING to Miss Sharpe, in her work, "A Royal Descent," Richard Buckner, the first one in England of this line, was born in Westphalia in 1695; came to England and died an Alderman of the City of Chichester in 1772, aged 77 years. He married Mary Saunders, born 1701; died in 1772. Both of whom are buried at St. Andrew's, Chichester. According to a pedigree in the Herald's College, Mary Saunders was the daughter of —— Saunders of Boxgrove, County Sussex, Yeoman. Richard and Mary Buckner had issue two sons:

I. JOHN BUCKNER, D. D., born 1734. Consecrated Lord Bishop of the See of Chichester in 1798, one of the oldest Bishoprics in England. The See was transferred from Selsea to Chichester in the year 1083, by Stigand, 23d Bishop of Selsea. The Bishop's Palace stands to the west of the Cathedral Church, both of which suffered greatly on the capture of the city by Sir William Waller in 1642, when Bishop King was sent a prisoner to London, and the Parliamentary troops took possession of the Palace. He found it on his return to the See nearly reduced to ruin, and his own fortunes were probably at too low an ebb to permit him to undertake its restoration. This was partially effected in the following century by Bishop Waddington, who recast the whole of the main building, and this was again repaired in 1800 by Bishop Buckner. The Bishop married a Miss Heron, who died in 1789, aged 49 years. His Lordship died at the age of 90, leaving no issue, and is buried in Chichester Cathedral.

II. CHARLES BUCKNER, R. N., of Clewer Villa, Clewer, Berks, Vice-Admiral of the White, was instrumental in suppressing the mutiny at the Nore in 1797, and was offered a Baronetcy for his services, but declined in favor of the next

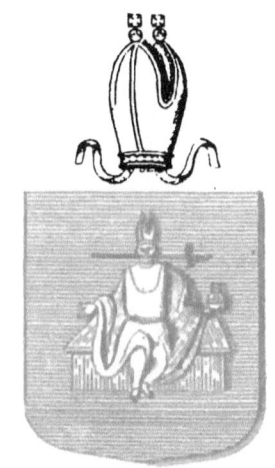

Arms of the
See of Chichester.

in command. Admiral Buckner died in 1811. He was twice married, but by his second wife, Anne, daughter of Thomas Frewen, Esq., of Northiam, and widow of her cousin, Charles Frewen, he had no issue. During her first widowhood, she was with her nephew, William Jenkin, in France at the time of the great Revolution. They were incarcerated for eight months in the Château of St. Germain, and escaped by the aid of a false passport on the death of Robespierre. She died in 1826, and is buried at Northiam.

Admiral Buckner's first wife was Mary, daughter of the Rev. John Parke, Vicar of Amport, and Prebendary of Chichester. He graduated at St. John's College, Cambridge, in 1707; M. A., 1711; B. D., 1718, and married Ann, only daughter of Thomas Jenkin, Esq., Barrister-at-Law. Issue by first wife:

1. Richard Buckner, C. B., of Wyke House, Chichester, died March 13, 1837, and is buried in Chichester Cathedral. He was Lieutenant-Colonel of the Royal Artillery and a Commander of the Bath. Served and was wounded in the Peninsula War. Married Nov. 15, 1802, at St. James's, Westminster, Mary Marsh Pierce, died Dec. 24, 1852, and is buried in Chichester Cathedral. She was born in 1775, and was the daughter of John Pierce, Esq., of Canterbury, who was the son of Sampson Pierce, Esq., of Doddington, Kent, and descended from Gabriel Pierce, Esq., of Charing, died 1669. Issue:
    A. Charles Buckner of Wyke House, born April 3, 1807; B. A. of Wadham College, Oxford, 1828; M. A., 1831; B. D., 1842; Rector of West-Stoke, near Chichester, 1849. He married first, Oct. 26, 1837, Georgina, daughter of the Rev. George Maximilian Bethune, Rector of Worth, Sussex. Said to be of the same family as Maximilian de Béthune, Duc de Sully, the Minister of Henry IV., King of France. She died 1858. He married secondly, Oct. 25, 1861, his cousin, Emma Roberta Pierce. He died s. p. May 28, 1871.
    B. John Buckner, of whom presently.
    C. Richard Buckner, born Oct. 25, 1812. Associate of the Royal Academy; formerly in the 60th Rifles.
    D. Mary Buckner, the only daughter, married March 3, 1840, the Rev. Walter Kelly, M. A., Cambridge, 1830; Vicar of Preston-Cum-Hove, Sussex. Issue:
        aa. Rev. Walter William Kelly, M. A.
        bb. Mary Kelly.
        cc. Rev. Edward Emilius Kelly, M. A., Oxford, 1871.

John Buckner; born Feb. 26, 1809, of St. John's College, Cambridge; B. A., 1840; M. A., 1843. Vicar of Bapchild,

Sittingbourne, Kent, 1855; formerly in the Rifle Brigade; married April 16, 1830, at Florence, Italy, Eliza, daughter of General the Hon. William Henry Gardner, Royal Artillery, third son of Admiral Lord Gardner, who was engaged with Admiral Buckner in the suppression of the mutiny at the Nore in 1797. Issue:

- A. Charles Goddard Buckner, born 1836; served in Cape Mounted Rifles; in H. M. 56th Regiment, and in United States Artillery. Died unmarried Sept. 21, 1874, at Omaha, Neb., U. S. A.
- B. Capt. John Alan Gardner Buckner, R. N., died 1885.
- C. Richard Edward Herbert Buckner, late R. N., now in Canada.
- D. Commander William Henry Pierce Buckner, R. N., Totnes, Devonshire.
- E. Mary Eliza Buckner, married at Cape of Good Hope, John Henry Sale, Commissary General. He died 1869, leaving issue, two sons and a daughter.
- F. Georgiana Buckner, married 1856, the Rev. Thomas Augustus Firminger of Edmonton, son of the late Thomas Firminger, LL. D., and had issue, three sons and four daughters.
- G. Augusta Plimley Buckner, born at Bognor, Sussex, June 14, 1840; married June 30, 1857, William Whitehead Gascoyne, Esq., J. P., of Bapchild Court, Kent, born Dec. 13, 1825; died March 18, 1887. Issue:
    - aa. Augusta Helen Gascoyne, born June 18, 1859; married 1888, Major ——— of "The Buffs."
    - bb. William Walter Gascoyne, born Jan. 24, 1861; married 1881, Edith Wood of San Francisco.
    - cc. George Gascoyne, born Aug. 27, 1862; married July 14, 1900, Ethel Slade.
    - dd. Marian Louisa Gascoyne, born July 2, 1864; married Aug. 3, 1893, Arthur W. Gordon.
    - ee. Edith Eliza Gascoyne, born May 25, 1866; married Nov. 5, 1895, Arthur S. Webb.
    - ff. Gertrude Sarah Gascoyne, born Jan. 16, 1869.
    - gg. Edward Buckner Gascoyne, born Oct. 9, 1870; married Winifred Price Miles.
    - hh. Frederic Kelly Gascoyne, 20th Hussars.

Mary Buckner, only daughter of Admiral Charles Buckner, married Nov. 13, 1813, Rev. Henry Plimley. She was co-heir of her uncle, Dr. John Buckner, Bishop of Chichester. The Rev. Henry Plimley and his wife are buried at Cuckfield, Sussex, where upon a tablet in the north aisle of the church is this inscription:

"In a vault in this church are deposited the remains of the Revd. Henry Plimley, M. A., Chancellor of the Diocese of Chichester; Vicar of St. Leonard's, Shoreditch, London, and 24 years Vicar of this Parish, where he lived universally respected and beloved.

MRS. AUGUSTA (PLIMLEY) BUCKNER GASCOYNE

"Also in the same vault are the remains of Mary, wife of the above and daughter of Admiral Buckner. She departed this life at Cowfold, Jan. 27, 1842, aged 70 years."

Buckner Arms

The Coat of Arms granted to John Buckner, Bishop of Chichester, and his brother, Admiral Charles Buckner, are as follows:

"Gules, a book open or, between three bucks' heads erased ermine."

Crest: A buck courant erminois, in front of a beech tree, issuant from a mount p. p. r.

Motto: Fide surgimus ad spem.

" From ancestors who stood equivalent with mighty kings."
—Pericles.

The Virginia Buckners

John Buckner of Gloucester County

THE earliest mention of the name of Buckner in Virginia is that of John Buckner, to whom was granted in 1667, a land patent of 194 acres in Gloucester County. In 1668 he was granted additional land, and from then on, to the time of his death, he was constantly adding to his landed estate.

John Buckner, who may be regarded as the head of the family in America, was a member in 1671 of the vestry of Petsworth Parish, Gloucester. It is evident that he soon became prominent in the civil affairs of the Colony, as he was a Member of the House of Burgesses in 1683, as well as being Clerk of Gloucester County.

It is certain that he was a man of progressive ideas, and his name will always be remembered in connection with the introduction of the first printing press, which he was instrumental in bringing to Virginia. His efforts in this line were not appreciated by the Council, as the following extract from the Minutes will show:

"Feb. 21, 1683.

"John Buckner was summoned before the Council for his presumption in printing the Acts of Assembly made in Nov. 1682, without a license.

"He made answer, that he had given the printer orders to print nothing without the Governor's license, and had only struck off a couple of sheets for His Excellency's approbation. The Board was satisfied therewith, but ordered Buckner and William Nulhead the printer, to enter into bond for £100, to print nothing further until the King's pleasure was known. Recorded Sept. 29, 1684."

(Signed) NICHO. SPENCER, *Secretary*.

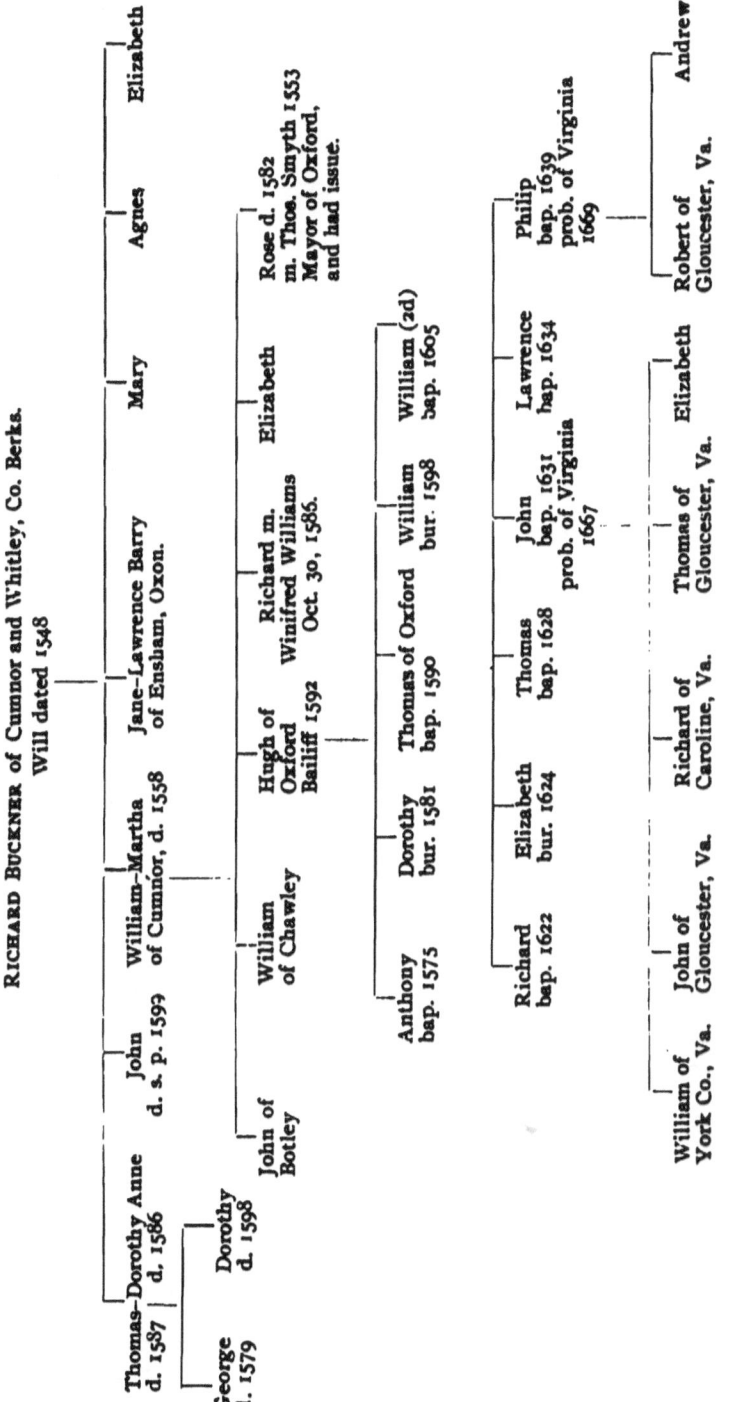

The following abstracts of letters, taken from the Fitzhugh MSS. and written by Col. William Fitzhugh to John Buckner, are of more than passing interest, and upon perusal, one must perforce agree with the gallant Colonel that a "dumb negro, who was bad at work, and worse at talking," was but a poor bargain.

Dec'r 3rd, 1681.

Mr. John Buckner

Sir: I was intended the last general court to have waited on you, in order to have taken care for your payment what I am indebted to you, but in my going was straitened in time and my coming home earnest to be here. I have now taken this opportunity by Mr. John Withers to send you bills of Major Robert Beverlys for £20, 5, 0, which I suppose before this time he has taken care with you about his promised payment in your hands at the passing of the bills. Esqr. Wormley likewise at the same time assured me that he would take care to pay you £20 more upon my account, which I doubt not but before this he has done; what remains I will hereafter take care honestly to pay, but hope you will make me some abatement for your Dumb Negro that you sold me; had she been a new Negro, I must have blamed my fate not you; but one that you had two years, I must conclude you knew her qualities which is bad at work and worse at talking and took the opportunity of the softness of my Messenger to quit your hands of her. I will freely give you the £3, 5, 0 overplus of £20 that he gave for her to take her again and will get her conveyed to your hands or hope if my offer be not acceptable you will make me some abatement of so bad a bargain. * * * * *

Sir, Your Obdt.

WILLIAM FITZHUGH.

The next letter seems to indicate that John Buckner had met with some loss, either of a business or family nature. It may refer to the death of his wife, but its precise meaning, of course, we will probably never know.

March 14, 1686-7.

Mr. John Buckner

I three days since, received yours of the 7th of March last, and do as truly condole your present affliction and past losses therein mentioned, as I heartily thank you for your Kindness and trouble therein expressed both in the preventing Sir Robert's note and the return of the £3 bills inclosed. I wish both yourself and family perfect health and full Recovery. Sr. the inclosed protest will speak its own business. I have been already so often troublesome to you, and yet continue, that I want expressions to beg pardon and have no other refuge left than to assure you if any of your business lies this way, I shall court all occasions to assure you, I am sincerely

Your servant
WILLIAM FITZHUGH.

Beyond fragmentary mention in the county records, we know but little of John Buckner's life in Virginia. We gather that he was factor or attorney for various London merchants, and that his business relations with the best families in the Colony were of an intimate and extensive nature. He was a large property holder as the following abstracts show:

Land Grants

Gloucester

Feb. 19, 1667. Mr. John Buckner, 194 acres in Gloucester County adjoining the plantation whereon he now resides, adjoining Mr. Bernard's and Mr. Taliaferro's land.

June 16, 1668. Mr. John Buckner and Mr. Thomas Vickers, 122 acres.

Feb. 19, 1669. Mr. John Vickers and Mr. John Buckner, 517 acres in Gloucester County. Philip Buckner a headright.

Oct. 12, 1669. Mr. John Buckner and Thomas Royston, 1000 acres. John Buckner a headright.

Sept. 18, 1681. Mr. John Buckner, 300 acres in Petsworth Parish, Gloucester, lying between 200 acres surveyed for Mr. John Smith, April 1, 1665.

Dec. 22, 1682. Mr. John Buckner and Major H. Whiting, 2673 acres.

Oct. 30, 1686. Mr. John Buckner and Major Henry Whiting, 280 acres in Ware Parish, Gloucester County.

Oct. 30, 1686. Mr. John Buckner and Major Henry Whiting, 2400 acres in Gloucester County, on northmost river of Mabjack Bay, escheated and granted to Henry Waring, by order of General Court, Oct. 16, 1686, and by him assigned to Buckner and Whiting.

Rappahannock County

May 2, 1671. Mr. John Buckner and Mr. Thomas Royston, 2000 acres in Rappahannock County, on south side of the Rappahannock River, and adjoining the land of Mr. Lawrence Smith in the freshes.

Sept. 9, 1671. Mr. John Buckner, Mr. Robert Bryan and Mr. Thomas Royston, 3553 acres in Rappahannock adjoining the land of John Prosser, called Golden Vale.

As stated in a previous chapter, it is believed that John Buckner was married in England in 1661, and that his wife was

Debora Ferrers of West Wickham, Bucks. It is quite likely that most of his children were born in Virginia, and as he was a vestryman of Petsworth Parish the records of their baptism would naturally be entered in the Church Register of that parish. Only the vestry book in a very dilapidated condition remains, containing the vestry-meetings from 1677 to 1793, and it is from its worn and faded pages that we learn of the official position that John Buckner held in the church. In the Land Grants of Rappahannock County there is a grant to Mr. Richard Buckner, son of Mr. John Buckner. It is quite likely that Richard was the eldest son, for if he was born in 1662, he would be 20 years of age at the time of the grant, which was in 1682. John Buckner's son, John, Jr., obtained a grant in 1691, eleven years after his brother Richard, so he was presumably a younger brother.

In addition to his four sons, it is believed that John Buckner had a daughter named Elizabeth. She married James Williams, a lawyer, who was born in England. Their daughter Mary, born Dec. 25, 1695, married first, Orlando Jones, who d. s. p. She married secondly, June 23, 1720, John James Flournoy, born Nov. 17, 1685. He died March 23, 1740, and his wife died one or two days later. They had issue:

I. Elizabeth Julia Flournoy, born Dec. 5, 1721; married Thomas Spencer.
II. Gideon Flournoy, born March 19, 1723; married in 1748 Jane Frances Sabourin.
III. Samuel Flournoy, born Oct. 4, 1724; married April 9, 1748, Elizabeth Harris.
IV. John Flournoy, born Dec. 9, 1726; married Sept. 2, 1755, Camilla Bailexserd.
V. David Flournoy, born Sept. 3, 1728; died Oct. 18, 1757, d. s. p. He was Captain of Militia, and first Sheriff of Prince Edward County.
VI. Rachel Flournoy, born Sept. 25, 1730; died Aug. 28, 1741.
VII. Mathew Flournoy, born June 21, 1732.
VIII. Mary Flournoy, born Feb. 23, 1735; married William Booker.
IX. A daughter, born Nov. 25, 1736; died in six weeks, unbaptised.
X. Thomas Flournoy, born Nov. 20, 1738.

We find from the records, that the known issue of John Buckner consisted of four sons and one daughter. They are treated under separate headings, and as the date of birth is conjectural, two of the sons, Richard and Thomas, are placed last, as their descendants are more numerous than are those of William and John Buckner, Jr.

Issue of John Buckner

I. William Buckner.
II. John Buckner, Jr.
III. Richard Buckner.
IV. Thomas Buckner.
V. Elizabeth Buckner.

John Buckner the immigrant died about 1695, for although we can find no will, there is an inventory of his estate recorded in Essex County under date of Feb. 10, 1695.

" A gentleman well bred and of good name."
—Henry V.

William Buckner of York County

ILLIAM BUCKNER, one of the sons of John Buckner, was for many years a prominent merchant of Yorktown, in addition to being an important man in the civil and military affairs of the Colony of Virginia. It is impossible to give the primogeniture of any of the sons of John Buckner. Neither has it been possible to ascertain with any degree of certainty whether they were born in England or in Virginia. In the present history of the family, William Buckner has been placed first amongst the sons, for the reason that the direct male line ends with his own two sons, the descendants of his daughter Elizabeth being the only ones distinctly traceable.

From existing records, we learn that William Buckner was Deputy Surveyor for Stafford County in 1691, and a Justice of the Peace for York County in 1694. He was also an officer of Militia, for at a meeting of the Court of Claims for York, Oct. 11, 1697, he is called Captain William Buckner, and in subsequent years is given the rank of Major. In the years 1698 and 1699 he was a member of the House of Burgesses, and during these sessions he took an active part in the revision of the laws of the Colony. He was a member of the Assembly in 1714, and from 1708 to 1716 held office as Deputy Surveyor-General for the College of William and Mary.

It is evident from the important positions that he held that he was a man of superior attainments, and we can get some slight idea of his character from the fact, that he refused to take the prescribed oaths to King William and Queen Mary, alleging that he had previously taken the oath of allegiance to King James II.

The following entries from the first Order Book of Stafford County are of interest:

"At a Court held for the County of Stafford at the house of Mr. Thomas Elsey, November 14th, 1690. Present—Col. Wm.

Fitzhugh, Mr. Samuel Haward, Capt. George Mason, Mr. John Withers, Mr. Edward Thomason, Mr. Wm. Buckner, and Mr. Matthew Thompson, Justices.

Buckner
vs.
Thomason.

Wm. Buckner, Attorney of Thomas Starke and Nicholas Haward, merchants in London, complains against Edward Thomason of this County, gentleman, in a plea of debt for that the said Edward Thomason stands indebted to the plaintiff in the qualification afsd the sum of Four Hundred and Eighty pounds of tobacco as by the audit between Mrs. Mary Massey and the plaintiff will appear for which the plaintiff hath brought his action against the said Edward Thomason this cost of suit and etc."

"At a Court held for the County of Stafford at the house of Thomas Elsey, August 12th, 1691. Mr. Wm. Buckner, being by this Court desired to take the oaths appointed instead of the oaths of allegiance and supremacy and likewise the oath of a Justice of Peace for this County, he refused it alleging that whereas he had formerly taken the oaths of allegiance and supremacy to King James the Second, in this county cannot now, in his conscience think himself fairly discharged from the said oaths in the life of King James, and therefore humbly desires to be excused from his being obliged to take the said oaths until hereafter he may in his conscience be better satisfied concerning the same."

"At a Court held for Stafford County October, 7th, 1691. Ordered, that Mr. Wm. Buckner, Deputy Surveyor of this County, shall on Thursday next, being the 15th of this inst., October, 1691, repair to the Malachy Peale Neck, being the place allotted by Act of Assembly for the towne and Port of this County, and shall then and there survey and lay out the said towne or Port according to law to the intent that all the gentlemen of, and all other of the inhabitants may take up such lots or lot as he and they desire, that the houses and Port may proceed and goe on effectually according to the true intent and meaning of the Act in that case made and provided, at the last session of the assembly held at James City."

"At a Court held for Stafford County, November, 11th, 1691. Wm. Buckner complains against Jonah Revet in a plea of debt for that is to say, that he stands indebted to the plaintiff in the sum of

Four Hundred and Twenty pounds of tobacco due bill under hand and seal, wherefore the plaintiff brought his action against the said Revet the defendant and prays judgment against him for his said debt with costs. And the said Jonah Revet the defendant by Henry Merest his attorney, came into Court and confessed judgment unto John Withers the then appointed attorney for the said Wm. Buckner for the said sum of Four Hundred and Twenty pounds of tobacco due as aforesaid."

In the York County records we find the following entry in regard to the building of a windmill:

"John Lewis, Esq., and Madam Elizabeth Lewis, wife of said John Lewis, Esq., sell to William Buckner one acre of land at a point near Yorktown, on York River, just below a small creek formerly known as Townshend's Creek, and sometimes it is called in ancient patents Martue's Creek, but now it is called Yorktown Creek, one chain and a half on the river bank, for a windmill, to enter if the mill is not kept up, to grind for the donors 12 bbls. of Indian corn without toll."

Dated July 16, 1711.

Major William Buckner is believed to have married Catherine Ballard. She may have been a daughter or sister of Col. Thomas Ballard of York County, who was born 1630; died 1689. Col. Ballard was Clerk of York County for many years after 1652, was Burgess for James City, 1666, member of the Council in 1675, and Speaker of the House of Burgesses in 1680 and 1682. He was also High Sheriff of York County.

Major William Buckner died at Yorktown, and his will was proved there May 1, 1716. He left three children, two sons and a daughter, the sons being under legal age at the time of their father's death. Issue:

I. William Buckner.
II. John Buckner, Jr.
III. Elizabeth Buckner.

I. Of the two sons of Major William Buckner, but little is known. William died young, leaving his share of the estate to his brother John. His will is in the York Court records. After a brief preamble, it reads—"I give unto my loving brother John Buckner all ye estate I die possessed of real and personal, and doe appoint my sd. loving brother my whole and sole exr. of this my last will and testament." Dated Dec. 17, 1722. In the parish register of St. Paul's, Stafford County (now King George), is the entry of death of a William Buckner under date of Nov. 14, 1729. On the same day and year is also recorded the death of Elizabeth Buckner. This Elizabeth could not, however, have been the daughter of Major William Buckner, who married Col. Drury Stith, as she bore her husband children after the year 1729.

II. JOHN BUCKNER, JR., was a Justice of York County from 1729 to 1741, and Burgess in 1736. During the latter part of his life he resided in King George County, where he died about 1748.

The inventory of his estate was recorded in Stafford County Oct. 11, 1748. The total value of the personal property being £805. Not included in the appraisement were, "two negroes at Drury and Griffin Stith's; about 80 hogs in Stafford; seventeen silver spoons, and eighty volumes of books." His nephew, John Stith, was executor.

There is recorded in Northumberland County a deed from Griffin Stith, conveying certain land in York, which his uncle, John Buckner, had left to him in his will, which is stated to be on record in King George County. As the will books of King George—which was originally part of Stafford County are missing, it is impossible to say if John Buckner left direct issue or not.

III. ELIZABETH BUCKNER, daughter of William and Catherine (Ballard) Buckner, married Colonel Drury Stith of Brunswick County, who died in 1770. Colonel Stith, married secondly, Elizabeth, widow of Thomas Eldridge, by whom he had issue, Edmunds Stith, who died in 1789. Issue by first marriage:

I. Griffin Stith, of whom presently.
II. Buckner Stith of Brunswick County. (For issue see Stith Family.)
III. John Stith, born March 20, 1724; died May 29, 1773, s. p.
IV. Drury Stith, married Fanny Love.
V. Bathurst Stith, born Sept. 19, 1729.
VI. Thomas Stith, born Dec. 29, 1731. He was a Burgess in 1771.
VII. Dudley Stith.
VIII. *Elizabeth Stith, born June 23, 1754; married (1st) Henry Fitzhugh of Fitzhughburg; (2d) Henry Fitzhugh of Bellair.

---

* It seems hardly possible that she could have been the daughter of Elizabeth Buckner, as the latter is believed to have been born about 1698 or 1700, which, if correct, would make her 56 years of age at the time of her daughter's birth. She was either born about 1734, or if 1754 is the proper date, then she was more likely to have been a daughter by Col. Drury Stith's second wife, Elizabeth Eldridge.

GRIFFIN STITH, eldest child of Colonel Drury and Elizabeth (Buckner) Stith, was born Nov. 28, 1720. He resided in Northumberland County, where he died in 1784. Married Aug. 19, 1743, Mary, daughter of William and Catherine Blackley of Williamsburg. William Blackley died in 1736, and is buried in Bruton Churchyard. Mrs. Catherine Blackley died Oct. 25, 1771, aged 73 years, and is also buried at Bruton. Issue:

1. Catherine Stith, born Aug. 5, 1744; died Aug. 23, 1744.
2. Elizabeth Buckner Stith, born July 16, 1745; married John Stringer.
3. John Buckner Stith, born Jan. 3, 1747; died Dec. 22, 1766, and was buried in Bruton Parish Churchyard.
4. Griffin Stith, born Aug. 24, 1753; died 1794; married and left issue.
5. Drury Stith, born Jan. 19, 1755; died July 16, 1789; married Mary Jacob.
6. William Stith of Northumberland County, died 1794; married Sarah Smith.
7. Susanna Stith, of whom presently.
8. Lucy Stith, married Mark W. Pringle.
9. Janet Carson Stith, d. s. p.

SUSANNA STITH, daughter of Griffin and Mary (Blackley) Stith, was born 1759; died March 31, 1838; married 1779, Christopher Johnston of Baltimore, Md. He was born 1750; died March 6, 1819, and had issue:

1. Maria Stith Johnston, born March 6, 1781; died Aug. 8, 1875.
2. John Johnston, born Feb. 11, 1783; died young.
3. Janet Johnston, born Sept. 4, 1784; died Sept. 2, 1816; married Nov. 25, 1802, Rev. James Hughs.
4. John Griffin Johnston, born Nov. 7, 1786; married ——— Price.
5. Robert Neilson Johnston, born Oct. 29, 1788; died Sept. 3, 1845; married Maria Pringle.
6. Susanna Johnston, born Jan. 6, 1791; died Nov. 18, 1871.
7. Elizabeth Johnston, born April 16, 1793; died young.
8. Elizabeth Johnston, born July 31, 1795; died Nov. 1, 1864; married April 14, 1818, John Muir Hepburn.
9. Christopher Johnston, born May 18, 1800; died Sept. 2, 1835; married Nov. 20, 1821, Eliza Gates, daughter of Capt. Lemuel Gates, U. S. A., died Nov. 12, 1887, and had issue:
   A. Christopher Johnston, of whom presently.
   B. Maria Stith Johnston, born Dec. 1, 1823; died young.
   C. William Hyde De Neuville Johnston, born Feb. 13, 1825.
   D. Isabella Marr Johnston, married Hugh McBirney.
   E. Henry Morris Johnston, married (1st) Frances Fuller; (2d) Mary Leidy.
   F. Maria Stith Johnston.

CHRISTOPHER JOHNSTON, born Sept. 27, 1822, at Baltimore, Md. Graduated M.D., University of Maryland, 1844; Professor of Anatomy and Physiology, 1864; Professor of Surgery, 1869. Died Oct. 11, 1891; married at Washington, D. C., Sept. 26, 1855, to Sarah Lucretia Clay Smith, born Jan. 12, 1835, at Loudoun County, Va.; died July 7, 1879; daughter of Benjamin Price and Matilda Rebecca Price Smith. Issue:

1. Christopher Johnston, of whom presently.
2. Benjamin Johnston, born June 5, 1858; married Oct. 10, 1888, Jane Elizabeth Halliwell—address, Whistler, Mobile County, Ala.
3. Eliza Yates Johnston, born Nov. 3, 1859; died Oct. 13, 1867.
4. Matilda Price Johnston, born July 8, 1861; married Dec. 13, 1892, Rev. Percy St. Michael Podmore—address, London, Eng.
5. Robert Clapham Johnston, born Dec. 31, 1863; married Sept. 4, 1889, Lucille Mitchell Gorham—address, Owings Mills, Md.
6. Susan Stith Johnston, born Aug. 15, 1865; died young.
7. Harry Morris Johnston, born May 29, 1867—address, Asheville, N.C.

CHRISTOPHER JOHNSTON, son of Christopher Johnston, M.D., and Sarah L. C. Smith, was born Dec. 8, 1856, at Baltimore. He is Associate Professor of Oriental History and Archæology at Johns Hopkins University; M.A., University of Virginia, 1879; M.D., University of Maryland, 1880; Ph.D., Johns Hopkins University, 1894. Married June 2, 1897, Madeline Tasker Tilghman, born June 10, 1863; daughter of Capt. Richard Lloyd Tilghman, U. S. N., of Talbot County, Md., and Agnes Riddell Owen, his wife. Issue:

1. Agnes Riddell Owen Johnston, born April 18, 1898.
2. Sarah Clapham Smith Johnston, born Aug. 12, 1899.
3. Christopher Johnston, born Dec. 7, 1901.
4. Madeline Tasker Tilghman Johnston, born April 12, 1904.

The Johnstons are of Scotch ancestry, being descended from John Johnston of Moffat, Scotland; born 1720; died 1790. His son Christopher, born at Moffat, 1750; died at Baltimore, March 6, 1819, being the first of the family in this country.

" Our ancestors are very good kind of folks."
—The Rivals.

John Buckner, Jr., of Gloucester County

F all the children of John Buckner, the immigrant, we know the least concerning his son, John Buckner, Jr.

Unlike his brothers, he does not seem to have aspired—or at all events, does not appear to have occupied any high civil or military position in the affairs of the Colony, but evidently contented himself with more peaceful avocations, and the supervision of his estate.

We know that his estate must have been quite extensive. On Oct. 20, 1691, he was granted 3125 acres in old Rappahannock County, "on the south side of Golden Vale creek," adjoining his land, and the lands belonging to himself, Bryan and Royston. In this grant he is alluded to as "John Buckner, Jr., of Gloucester County."

In April, 1702, he was granted 3080 acres of land on Herring Creek, in Pamunkey Neck, King and Queen County.

On Dec. 23, 1714, "John Buckner of Gloucester, gent., and Robert Ballard of King and Queen County, are granted 400 acres of land on the south fork of the Mattapony, in King and Queen County.

There is a tradition that his wife was Ann Ballard, but nothing certain is known about this. That her Christian name was Ann is ascertained from a deed which she made in Essex County, dated July 17, 1727, in which she mentions two of her sons—John and William—as well as her husband, John Buckner.

There is some doubt as to the number of children of John and Ann Buckner. There may have been only the two sons mentioned in the above deed, but if his son William is the William Buckner of Gloucester County, Va., who removed to Maryland, it is evident that he had six other children. The records of Baltimore County, Md., show that William Buckner received deeds from Thomas Todd and William Todd, trustees of Thomas Todd, deceased, late of Baltimore County. This William Buckner married Patience Colgate Sept. 20, 1724, but died Aug. 17, 1731, leaving one daughter, who died young. (Register of St. Paul's Parish, Baltimore County.) His widow married George Eliott, June 12, 1732. In 1733, Thomas and Philip Buckner, Ann, Elizabeth and Mary Buckner, and Charles Debrois and Christian, his wife, of Virginia, brothers and sisters of said William Buckner, petition against George Eliott and Patience, his wife.

If they are the children of John Buckner, Jr., it is probable they were of legal age in 1733, and it is also evident that their father was dead at that time.

There is a deed in Essex County dated July 17, 1727, in which John Buckner of St. Paul's Parish, Stafford County, gives "500 acres in St. Mary's Parish, Essex County, to my son, William Buckner, being part of the tract given me by my mother, Ann Buckner." This William is thought to have been the William Buckner who died in St. Paul's Parish, Stafford, Nov. 14, 1729 (see Parish Register), and that he left no issue.

The names of the children are strongly in favor of their being the offspring of John Buckner, Jr., as it is quite probable that he called them by the names of his near relatives. His son William for his uncle William of York; son Thomas for his uncle Thomas of Gloucester; son Philip for his great-uncle Philip of Stafford; daughter Ann for her own mother; Elizabeth after her aunt Elizabeth, wife of Richard Buckner of Essex.

We have no records to show the time of death of John Buckner, Jr. There is in Stafford County the inventory of the estate of a John Buckner, which was recorded Oct. 11, 1748, the value of the estate being £805. This may refer to John Buckner, Jr. Although, if he died previous to 1733—as it seems reasonable from the evidence to conclude that he did—it is strange that 15 years elapsed before an inventory of his estate was recorded. Yet, on the other hand, such instances of delay are found to have been fairly frequent in those days.

Taking the stand, therefore, that John Buckner, Jr., and Ann, his wife, had eight children, the line of descent would be as follows :

 I. John Buckner of St. Paul's Parish, Stafford County. In 1727 he gave to his son William Buckner 500 acres in St. Mary's Parish, Essex County, "part of the tract given me by my mother Ann Buckner."

It is believed that this son William is the William Buckner who died in St. Paul's Parish Nov. 14, 1729. (St. Paul's Parish Register.) He was probably not alive at the time of his father's death, as the will of the latter specifically mentions his only daughter, Susanna, and his wife, Elizabeth, to whom he leaves all his estate.

The will of John Buckner is dated Jan. 24, and was proved in Stafford County Oct. 10, 1752. His widow, Elizabeth, evidently married a second time, as there is on record a marriage contract under date Nov. 3, 1759, between Captain Zachariah Brazier and Elizabeth Buckner, widow.

II. William Buckner removed to Maryland, where he was a Justice of the Peace for Baltimore County in 1729. He married Patience Colgate Sept. 20, 1724, and died Aug. 17, 1731, leaving issue a daughter, who died young. His widow married George Eliott, June 12, 1732. In 1733, Thomas, Philip, Ann, Elizabeth and Mary Buckner, and Charles Debrois and Christian, his wife, of Virginia, brothers and sisters of said William Buckner, petition against George Eliott and Patience, his wife.

III. Thomas Buckner, believed to have resided in Caroline County, 1732.
IV. Philip Buckner.
V. Ann Buckner.
VI. Elizabeth Buckner.
VII. Mary Buckner.
VIII. Christian Buckner, married Charles Debrois.

"It is indeed a desirable thing to be well descended, but the glory belongs to our ancestors."
—Plutarch.

Richard Buckner of Essex County

RICHARD BUCKNER, probably the eldest son of the first John Buckner, was the owner of 500 acres of land in Rappahannock County on Sept. 22, 1682, it being part of a tract called "Golden Vale." Either he, or his son, also named Richard, patented lands in King and Queen County, viz.: 70 acres to Richard Buckner of Essex, Feb. 1, 1720; and 4500 acres in Drysdale Parish, Oct. 28, 1723. His residence was in Essex County, as a grant dated 1709, gives to him an island containing 20 acres on the north side of the Rappahannock River in Richmond County, lying near the plantation where said Buckner resides, about two miles below Taliaferro's Mount. On Aug. 17, 1715, he patented 179 acres in St. Mary's Parish, Essex, "adjoining the two tracts belonging to said Buckner of 1000 and 300 acres."

Essex County was formed from old Rappahannock in 1692, and Richard Buckner was Clerk of the new County of Essex in 1703 and again in 1712. Whether he was Clerk continuously during that period is not definitely known, as the records of the county are incomplete, but the recorded dates of his appointment are still on file. He was also Clerk of the House of Burgesses in 1714.

Of the four sons of John Buckner, Richard stands out prominently, from the fact, that his descendants were more conspicuous in the affairs of the colony and afterwards of the republic.

Richard Buckner is said to have married Elizabeth Cooke of Gloucester County, but there is no documentary evidence to prove this assertion. It is believed that Richard's daughter, Elizabeth Buckner, also married a Cooke, viz.: Mordecai Cooke—son of Mordecai Cook the immigrant—who was Sheriff of Gloucester in 1698,

and Justice and Burgess in 1702 and 1714. The traditions of the Cooke family are, that Mordecai married a Miss Buckner and left at least one son.

Richard Buckner's will was proved in Caroline County March 4, 1733, by Elizabeth (probably his wife), and Richard Buckner his executors. His known issue being:
  I. Richard Buckner.
  II. Philip Buckner.
  III. John Buckner.
  IV. William Buckner.
  V. Elizabeth Buckner, who presumably married Mordecai Cooke (2d).

The above named sons were the founders of the Caroline County branch of the family, their descendants now being settled in nearly every Southern and Western state. Major Richard Buckner (2d), the eldest son, was Justice in 1732, Sheriff of Caroline County in 1753, and Major of Militia in 1777. He died in the latter year, his will being proved in Caroline County Dec. 14. He married Elizabeth Aylett, a daughter of William Aylett, and sister of John Aylett of King William County, and had issue:
  I. Aylett Buckner.
  II. Francis Buckner.
  III. Richard Buckner (3d).

I. AYLETT BUCKNER was born in Caroline County in 1745, and afterwards removed to Fauquier County. He married Judith Presley Thornton a daughter of Anthony Thornton of "Ormesby" Caroline County, and Sarah Taliaferro, his first wife.

Aylett Buckner was commissioned Major of Militia for Fauquier County in May, 1778; Justice of the Peace 1791; Sheriff 1794. He was alive in 1802, as there is on record a deed of gift of certain negroes to John T. Taylor on Dec. 2d of that year. Aylett and his wife, Judith Buckner, had issue:
  I. Richard Aylett Buckner.
  II. Colonel Thornton Buckner, who was member of the House of Delegates from Fauquier County from 1815 to 1818. According to a deed of gift on record Oct. 30, 1801, his wife's name was Sally.
  III. John Buckner.

JUDGE RICHARD AYLETT BUCKNER, born in Fauquier County Feb. 5, 1784; died in Greensburg, Ky., in 1849; married Elizabeth Lewis Buckner, daughter of William Buckner of Taylor

County, Surveyor-General of the State of Kentucky, and nephew of President James Madison. She died in 1868 at Memphis, Tenn. Issue:

1. Aylett Buckner, born in 1804; died unmarried. Was Member of Congress and a distinguished lawyer of Lexington, Ky.
2. William Buckner, married Jane Du Tois RoBards who was born Dec. 29, 1805. Had issue, Mary Buckner, who married ——— McElroy.
3. Richard Aylett Buckner, born 1810; died unmarried. Judge of the Fayette District in Kentucky.
4. Arthur Presley Buckner.
5. Maria Lewis Buckner, of whom presently.
6. Anthony Thornton Buckner.
7. Luther Arthur Buckner, died in California.
8. Elizabeth RoBards Buckner, married Dr. John R. Allen of Lexington, Ky., and Keokuk, Ia.
9. Dr. George R. Buckner, born May 16, 1823, at Greensbury, Ky.; died 1897; married Harriet Ann Creel, born 1828; died 1878. Issue:
A. Richard Aylett Buckner, of whom presently.
B. Charles C. Buckner, born Oct. 17, 1852; died 1891.
C. Elizabeth Buckner, born Aug., 1855, of Kansas City, Mo.
D. Luther A. Buckner, born Aug., 1857, of Dermott, Ark.

RICHARD AYLETT BUCKNER, lawyer and jurist, was born Jan. 21, 1849, in Owenton, Ky. At the early age of fourteen years he was elected Captain of the Governor's Guards, a gallant young company of Kentuckians of some renown, and took part in the defence of Frankfort in the latter part of 1863. In 1876 he was admitted to the bar at St. Charles, Mo., and since 1884 has practiced his profession at Dermott, Ark., after having lived several years in the states of Missouri and Kentucky. In 1880 and 1884 he was a delegate to the National Republican Conventions from Missouri and Kentucky respectively. In 1895 he was nominated by the Republicans for State Senator from the 15th Senatorial District, and in 1898 he was nominated by the Democrats and elected as Senator from the 15th Senatorial District of Arkansas. Senator Buckner married Oct. 28, 1878, Miss Anna Crenshaw, who was born in 1853 at St. Louis, Mo., and has issue one daughter, Nanna Richard Buckner, born May 28, 1880, at Greensburg, Ky.

MARIA LEWIS BUCKNER, daughter of Richard Aylett, Sr., and Elizabeth Lewis Buckner, was born Jan. 5, 1815; died Jan. 5, 1875, at St. Louis, Mo.; married Oct. 15, 1832, to Dr. Richard Farril Barret, born Feb. 27, 1804, at Rock Castle Farm, Greene

County, Ky.; died at Burlington, Ia., April 16, 1860. Dr. Barret was President of the Burlington Land Co., Fund Commissioner of the State of Illinois in 1839; banker in St. Louis, Mo., and Professor of Materia Medica and Physiology at the Missouri Medical College in 1841. One of his sisters, Anna Barret, married Brig. General James Allen of the War of 1812. Issue:

1. Richard Aylett Barret, of whom presently.
2. Arthur B. Barrett, born Aug. 21, 1835.
3. Julia Allen Barret, born Nov., 1838; married Dr. C. T. Alexander, U. S. A.
4. William Lee Barret, born March 5, 1843; died in 1886 at St. Louis in the zenith of a brilliant medical fame and a lucrative practice of $20,000 a year. His three daughters reside at Woodmere, Long Island, N. Y.
5. John Allen Barret, born 1846, resides at Bloomfield, Mo.
6. Winston Lee Barret, born Aug., 1858, resides in New York City.

RICHARD AYLETT BARRET of St. Louis, Mo., was born June 21, 1833, at Cliffland, Greene County, Ky. Studied at Phillips Exeter Academy, Exeter, N. H., and entered Harvard June, 1848, matriculating in the Class of 1851. Graduated in medicine in 1854, and then went to the University of Heidelberg, Germany. Admitted to the St. Louis Bar in 1859, and was Government Attorney during the Civil War; President of the Rhodes-Barret Lead Mine, Webb City, Mo., also Park Commissioner of St. Louis. Married Feb. 27, 1862, to Mary Finney, born 1837, daughter of William and Jane Finney of St. Louis. Issue, one child—Mary Lee Barret, born Dec. 20, 1862; died April 30, 1870. A handsome memorial window is erected to her memory in the Episcopal Church, Burlington, Ia., where she attended Sunday school.

II. FRANCIS BUCKNER, son of Richard (2d) and Elizabeth Aylett Buckner of Caroline, was born in that county about 1747. He married Martha, the daughter of Colonel James Upshur, a noted officer during the Revolution. Issue:

I. Susan Buckner, born 1780.
II. James Buckner, of whom presently.
III. George Buckner.
IV. Richard Upshur Buckner.
V. Lewis Buckner.
VI. Elizabeth Aylett Buckner, married (1st) Henry Garnett of Essex County, a grandson of James Garnett, Gent., of St. Anne's Parish, Essex County, whose will was proved Aug. 19, 1765. By agreement made Sept. 28, 1771, the land left in Spottsylvania County to Henry and Augustine Garnett, grandsons of James, was equally divided. After the death of Henry Garnett, his widow removed to Christian County, Ky., and married William Murrell.

By her second marriage she had a son, Samuel Murrell, who married Mary E. Grymes. Their daughter, Elizabeth Murrell, married James M. Buckner. Issue:

1. Pearl Buckner, born 1874; married Arthur Cary of Paducah, Ky., who died in 1900, leaving issue:
   A. Lucele Cary.
   B. Arthur Cary.
   C. Bessie Cary.
2. Murrell Buckner, Dallas, Texas.
3. James M. Buckner, Jr., Louisville, Ky.
4. Mary Aylett Buckner, Louisville.
5. Blanche Randolph Buckner, Louisville.
6. Garnett Upshur Buckner, Louisville.
7. Paul C. Buckner, Louisville.
8. Frank M. Buckner, Louisville.

VII. Martha Jones Buckner, married John Buckner, son of Philip and Tabitha Buckner of Bracken County, Ky.

VIII. Mary Amiss Buckner, married John P. Campbell.

JAMES BUCKNER, son of Francis and Martha Upshur Buckner, was born in Caroline County in 1782; died Feb. 4, 1832; married in 1807 Lucy Madison Buckner, born 1787; died Aug. 28, 1831, a daughter of Francis and Lucy Thornton Buckner of King William County. Issue:

1. James Francis Buckner, born in Caroline County Sept. 1, 1813; died in Louisville, Ky., 1889; married to Gabriella Lewis Hawkins, born Feb. 5, 1819; died 1900, and had issue:
   A. Gabriel Lewis Buckner, born July 17, 1838; died Oct. 20, 1896; married in 1888 to Jeanette Davies. No issue.
   B. Lucy Madison Buckner, born in Louisville, Feb. 19, 1846; married Dec. 7, 1870, to Thomas Speed, died Jan. 31, 1905. Issue:
      aa. James Buckner Speed of Berkeley, Cal., born Oct. 13, 1871; married Sept. 26, 1900, to Mary Martin Craik.
      bb. Mary Whitney Speed, born Oct. 20, 1876.
   C. James Francis Buckner, Louisville, Ky., born May 6, 1849; married Feb. 1, 1887, to Susan Yandell. No issue.
2. Edward Madison Buckner of Hopkinsville, Ky., born 1818. Left one daughter, Jennie, who married ——— Clark.
3. William Taylor Buckner, lived and died in Hopkinsville; born 1826. Issue:
   A. Lucy Buckner, who died young.
   B. Threshley Berryman Buckner, now residing in Nebraska.

III. RICHARD BUCKNER, third son of Richard and Elizabeth Aylett Buckner, was born at Hazel Grove, Caroline County. He married Feb. 27, 1772, Judith Edmonds, of Fauquier County. She was the daughter of Elias Edmonds. The will of Elias Edmonds of Leeds Parish, Fauquier County, is dated Oct. 30, 1782, probated June 28, 1784. He mentions in it as legatees, "his wife Elizabeth; son Elias, and daughters, Ann Hubbard, Judith Buckner and Elizabeth Bruin." Elias Edmonds, the son, was a Colonel in the Revolutionary Army.

Richard and Judith Edmonds Buckner had at least two sons and five or six daughters, the names of all, however, cannot be ascertained. Known issue:

1. Col. Richard Buckner, moved to Missouri and died there in 1837. He was the father of eighteen children. The names of those known are:
   A. Richard Buckner.
   B. Ellen Buckner.
   C. Sarah Buckner.
   D. Thomas Buckner, Colonel of 33d Virginia Infantry. Killed at Battle of Spottsylvania Court House.
   E. Cuthbert Buckner.
   F. Elias Buckner.
   G. Virginia Buckner, married ——— Semple, and had known issue: Prof. Robert B. Semple, of William Jewel College, Liberty, Mo.
2. Dr. Elias Edmonds Buckner was born at Hazel Grove, Caroline County, Feb. 14, 1792; died Jan. 11, 1865, at Boonville, Mo.; married at Moratico Hall, Richmond County, Va., Maria Henrietta Smith, Oct. 14, 1818; born 1793; died March 31, 1875. Dr. Buckner was Sergeant in Lieut. Benj. Clark's Company, 16th Regiment, during the War of 1812. Issue:
   A. Nathaniel Chapman Buckner, born Aug. 16, 1819; died at Versailles, Mo., Sept. 26, 1841.
   B. Charles Smith Buckner, born March 2, 1821, at Frank Town, Northampton County, Va.
   C. Judith Ann Buckner, born at Moratico Hall, Va., Dec. 12, 1822; died Feb. 19, 1882; married Capt. James Thompson, Booneville, Mo.
   D. Edmond Sneed Buckner, born March 21, 1825; died Aug. 3, 1833.
   E. Virginia Teackle Buckner, born at Moratico Hall, Jan., 1827; married July 13, 1847, to Rev. Almon D. Corbyn, born April 19, 1810, at Woodstock, Conn.; died Nov. 18, 1855, at Jackson, Miss. Issue, five children, of whom are living:
      aa. Mrs. John T. Boone, Kansas City, Mo.
      bb. Mrs. Nellie Corbyn Ragland, Booneville, Mo.
   F. Maria Elizabeth Buckner, born Jan. 18, 1829; died March 2, 1855; married John Kelly Ragland of Cooper County, Mo.
   G. William Gilmore Buckner of Sweet Springs, Va., born Oct. 18, 1830, in Richmond County, Va.; married 1854, Sarah Julia Brown, born Aug. 4, 1835. Issue:
      aa. Mary Virginia Buckner, born Oct. 7, 1854; died.
      bb. Edward Chapman Buckner, born Oct. 4, 1855; died.
      cc. Charles Brown Buckner, born Jan. 6, 1857; died.

  dd. Henry Willard Buckner, born Jan. 2, 1859; died.

  ee. Frances Gilmore Buckner, born Dec. 20, 1861; married Dr. R. Martin, Gainsville, Texas.

  ff. John Lee Buckner, born Dec. 19, 1863, of Chicago, Ill.

H. Sallie Smith Buckner, born Richmond Court House, Va., Nov. 5, 1833; died Aug. 27, 1888, at Lamar, Mo.; married William Harper Finney, born Feb. 14, 1832; died June 15, 1900. Issue:

  aa. Jane Lee Finney, born Sept. 25, 1858, at St. Louis, Mo.; married (1st) James B. Adams of Booneville, Mo.; married (2d) Jerome S. Boarman, Springfield, Mo., Issue:

    1. Washington Adams, born June 19, 1880, at Booneville.
    2. Frank B. Boarman, born Oct. 11, 1883, at Foster, Mo.
    3. Richard Keith Boarman, born June 4, 1885, at Clinton, Mo.

  bb. Maria Ragland Finney, born June 4, 1860, at St. Louis; died Dec. 21, 1896, at Rich Hill, Mo.; married Thomas M. Colbert of Cooper County, Mo., died 1895. Issue:

    1. Thomas Reuben Colbert, born June 3, 1881, at Pilot Grove, Mo.
    2. Mary Lee Colbert, born March 22, 1883, at Pilot Grove.
    3. William Cecil Colbert, born June 10, 1885 at Pilot Grove.
    4. Jennie Finney Colbert, born March 9, 1889, at Rich Hill.

  cc. Sallie Buckner Finney, born Oct. 7, 1861, at St. Louis; married Cecil B. Rhodes of Kansas City. Issue:

    1. Charles Ross Rhodes, born Sept. 15, 1887, at Lamar, Mo.
    2. Mark Finney Rhodes, born May 1, 1890, at Lamar, Mo.

  dd. William Barrett Finney, born Dec. 13, 1863, in St. Louis; died Feb. 10, 1866.

  ee. Mary Ann Finney, born April 16, 1866, at Booneville; died in Chicago, Ill., Feb. 26, 1900; married (1st) Herbert Trowbridge; (2d) Albert Gottschalk of Chicago. Issue by 1st husband:

    1. Alfred Trowbridge, born Rich Hill, Mo.
    2. Sallie Trowbridge, born Rich Hill, Mo.

  ff. Thomas Finney of San Antonio, Texas, born March 7, 1871, at Boonville; married July 29, 1900, Jennie Sutphen McConnell.

I. Marianna Buckner, born Oct. 10, 1835; died March 31, 1873; married Jan. 31, 1854, at Fayette, Mo., to John Bullock Clark, Lawyer, Member of Congress and Brig. General of C. S. A., who died Sept. 7, 1903. Issue:

  aa. Charles Buckner Clark.
  bb. Elias Buckner Clark, Washington, D. C.
  cc. Augusta Clark, married —— Gray.
  dd. Kate Pearson Clark, married Paul White, April 19, 1899, and has Harriet Buckner White, New Franklin, Mo.

ee. Marianna Buckner Clark, married —— Hale, of Earl Court, Baltimore, Md.

J. Augusta Buckner, born Oct. 10, 1835, twin sister of Marianna Buckner.

Philip Buckner of Louisa County

PHILIP BUCKNER was the second son of Richard Buckner, Clerk of Essex County, and Elizabeth, his wife, and the grandson of John Buckner the immigrant. His residence was in Louisa County where he died in 1762. He married Jane Aylett, widow of Christopher Robinson and sister of John Aylett of King William County. This connection is proved by a deed dated 1767 from Jane Buckner of Orange County to William Hughes of Louisa, conveying part of a tract of land formerly belonging to Mr. John Aylett of King William County, and by him left to Jane Buckner his sister.

Philip Buckner's will is dated July 14, 1761, and was proved Aug. 10, 1762. In it he mentions his wife Jane; son William, to whom he leaves land in Orange County; daughter Ann; son Thomas; daughter Mary; son Philip; daughter Elizabeth; son Aylett. It is probable that his children are given in the order of their birth:

I. William Buckner of Spottsylvania County.
II. Ann Buckner.
III. Thomas Buckner.
IV. Mary Buckner.
V. Philip Buckner.
VI. Elizabeth Buckner.
VII. Aylett Buckner.

The following is a list of the Births, Marriages and Deaths as taken from the family Bible of Aylett H. Buckner and his wife, who was Elizabeth Ann Morehead.

Births

Philip Buckner, son of Philip Buckner and Jane Aylett, was born January 13, 1753.

Aylett Hartswell, son of Philip and Elizabeth Buckner, was born the 13th of January 1793, in Albermarle County, Va.

Elizabeth Ann, daughter of Turner and Mary Morehead, was born 9th of August 1801, in Fauquier County, Va., three miles from Warrenton.

Turner H. Buckner, son of Aylett H. and Elizabeth A. Buckner, was born Tuesday at 10 o'clock p. m. on the 5th of September 1820, in Hart County, Ky.

Emily Morehead Buckner, daughter of Aylett H. and Elizabeth A. Buckner, was born on Monday at 2 o'clock p. m., 22d of October 1821, in Hart County, Ky., at Walnut Hills.

Simon Bolivar Buckner, son of Aylett H. and Elizabeth A. Buckner, was born on Tuesday at 9 o'clock p. m., 1st of April 1823, at Walnut Hills, Hart County, Ky.

Caroline Jane Buckner, daughter of Aylett H. and Elizabeth A. Buckner, was born Sunday at 6 o'clock a. m., 26th December 1824, at Walnut Hills, Hart County, Ky.

Morelos Aylett Buckner, son of Aylett H. and Elizabeth A. Buckner, was born on Friday at 10 o'clock a. m., 7th July 1826, at Walnut Hills, Hart County, Ky.

Mary Elizabeth Buckner, daughter of Aylett H. and Elizabeth A. Buckner, was born on Friday at 6 o'clock p. m., 27th June 1831, at Walnut Hills, Hart County, Ky.

Aylett Hartswell Buckner, son of Aylett H. and Elizabeth A. Buckner, was born on Sunday at 10 o'clock p. m., 12th May 1833, at Clay Furnace, Hart County, Ky.

Aylett Hartswell Buckner, second son of that name, of Aylett H. and Elizabeth A. Buckner, was born on Thursday at 11 o'clock a. m., 10th September 1835, at Clay Furnace, Hart County, Ky.

Morelos Aylett Buckner, second son of that name, of Aylett and Elizabeth A. Buckner, was born on Friday 30 minutes past 12 o'clock a. m., 27th October 1837, at Muhlenburgh Iron Works, Muhlenburgh County, Ky.

Aylett Buckner Tooke, son of John A. and Mary E. Tooke, was born at Beechland, Arks., on the 17th day of November 1848, at 7 o'clock a. m.

Edwin Arthur Tooke, son of John A. and Mary E. Tooke, was born at home in Union County, Arks., on the 3rd day of August, 1850.

Marriages

Philip Buckner, son of Philip Buckner, was married to Elizabeth Watson on the 27th October 1789.

Aylett H. Buckner, son of Philip Buckner and Elizabeth Watson, was married to Elizabeth A. Morehead on Wednesday, the 8th of December 1819.

Mary E. Buckner, daughter of Aylett H. and Elizabeth A. Buckner, was married on the 22d day of February 1848, to John A. Tooke, late of Georgia.

Deaths

Philip Buckner, son of Philip Buckner and Jane Aylett, died on the 15th March 1819.

Elizabeth Watson, wife of Philip Buckner, died on 1st March 1828. Elizabeth Watson was daughter of William Watson.

Emily Morehead Buckner, daughter of A. H. and E. A. Buckner died 1st March 1827.

Morelos Aylett Buckner, son of A. H. and E. A. Buckner, died on the 15th of September 1828.

Caroline Jane Buckner, daughter of A. H. and E. A. Buckner, died on the 29th June 1834.

Aylett Hartswell Buckner, second of that name, son of A. H. and E. A. Buckner, died on the 14th March 1838.

Morelos Aylett Buckner, second of that name, son of A. H. and E. A. Buckner, died on the 13th March 1838.

The two last of scarlet fever.

Aylett Hartswell Buckner, who was born 13th January 1793, died at Beechland, Columbia County, Arks., on 11th December 1851.

Turner Hartswell Buckner, who was born 5th September 1820, was drowned in the Arkansas River, near Fort Gibson in the Cherokee Nation, while attempting to save a companion from a similar fate, on the 5th day of June 1854.

Elizabeth Ann Buckner, wife of Aylett H. Buckner, died in Union County, Arks., on the 7th day of March 1861.

Mary Elizabeth Tooke, wife of John A. Tooke and daughter of Aylett H. and E. A. Buckner, died at the place of her birth on the 3rd day of October 1883.

John Arthur Tooke, husband of Mary E. Tooke, died at Gaines Landing on the Mississippi River, on the 10th day of August 1858.

From the above records we learn that Philip Buckner was born Jan. 13, 1753. He removed to Hart County, Ky., and died at Bacon's Creek March 15, 1819. His wife was Elizabeth Watson, a daughter of William Watson of Virginia. She died at "Glenlily," Hart County, March 1, 1828. Issue:

1. John Buckner, born 1791.
2. Aylett Hartswell Buckner, born 1793.
3. Henry Watson Buckner, born 1800; died 1871.
4. Jane Buckner.
5. Nancy Buckner, born 1802, married her cousin, Simeon Buckner, son of Thomas and Hannah (Burton) Buckner.
6. Ann Buckner.

AYLETT HARTSWELL BUCKNER, was born in Albermarle County, Va., Jan. 13, 1793, and removed when quite young to Kentucky, with his parents. He was successively an iron manufacturer and planter, but like so many of his ancestors, he was to the front in the time of war, being with the Kentucky troops under General Harrison at the Battle of the Thames, in the War of 1812. He married in 1820, Elizabeth Ann Morehead, at Bowling Green, Ky., his wife being the daughter of Turner and Mary Morehead of Fauquier County, Va., in which county she was born on the 9th of August, 1801, dying at Beechland, Arks., in 1862, her husband having predeceased her in 1851. Issue:

1. Turner H. Buckner, born Sept. 5, 1820; died June 5, 1854.
2. Emily Morehead Buckner, born Oct. 22, 1821; died March 1, 1827.
3. Simon Bolivar Buckner, of whom presently.
4. Caroline Jane Buckner, born Dec. 26, 1824; died June 29, 1834.
5. Morelos Aylett Buckner, born July 7, 1826; died Sept. 16, 1828.

6. Mary Elizabeth Buckner, born June 27, 1831; died Oct. 3, 1883; married Feb. 22, 1848, to John A. Tooke, who died Aug. 10, 1858. Issue:
A. Aylett Buckner Tooke, born Nov. 17, 1848.
B. Edwin Arthur Tooke, born Aug. 3, 1850.
7. Aylett Hartswell Buckner, born May 12, 1833; died ——.
8. Aylett Hartswell Buckner, born Sept. 10, 1835; died March 14, 1838.
9. Morelos Aylett Buckner, born Oct. 27, 1837; died March 13, 1838.

GENERAL SIMON BOLIVAR BUCKNER of Rio, Kentucky, soldier and statesman, was born in Hart County April 1, 1823. His first wife was Mary Kingsbury of Connecticut, born Feb. 24, 1831, died Jan. 1873, and by whom he had one child, Lily Buckner, born June 1858, died 1893. She married Morris B. Belknap of Louisville, by whom she had Gertrude, Walter, Lily and Morris Belknap.

General Buckner married secondly, June 10, 1885, Delia H. Claiborne of Richmond, Va., by whom he has issue an only son, Simon Bolivar Buckner, Jr., born July 18, 1886, at Glenlily, Hart County, and who is now a cadet at the Military Academy at West Point.

General Buckner was appointed a cadet at West Point, June 1840; graduating in 1844, when he was appointed 2nd Lieutenant of the 2nd Infantry. From Sept. 1845 he was Assistant Professor of Ethics at West Point, until his assignment as 2nd Lieutenant of the 6th Infantry, May 9, 1846. He joined the Army in Mexico, Aug. 1846, and participated in the seige of Vera Cruz, also taking part in the following battles: Cerro Gordo, San Antonio, Cherubusco, Molino del Rey, Chapultepec, Garita de Belen, the skirmish of Amazoque, and the final capture of the City of Mexico. He was breveted 1st Lieutenant for gallant and meritorious conduct at the battle of Cherubusco, August 20th, in which engagement he was wounded, and on Sept. 8, 1847, was breveted Captain for gallant conduct at the battle of Molino del Ruy.

At the close of the Mexican War, he was appointed Assistant Instructor in Infantry Tactics, a position he occupied for two years until his promotion as 1st Lieutenant in the Line in 1850. In 1851 he was in command of Fort Atkinson, Indian Territory, and in 1852 was Captain of the Staff in the Subsistence Department stationed in New York City, until 1855, in which year he resigned from the army.

In 1860, General Buckner was Inspector General of Kentucky,

GENERAL SIMON BOLIVAR BUCKNER
1861

during which period he organized the Kentucky State Guard. At the breaking out of the Civil War, he was offered by President Lincoln the commission of Brigadier General in the United States Army, which he declined, and casting his fortunes with the Confederacy was appointed Brig. Gen. C. S. A., Sept. 1861, occupying Bowling Green, Ky., with the Confederate forces on the 18th of that month. Ordered by Gen. Albert Sidney Johnston to reinforce Generals Floyd and Pillow at Ft. Donelson, Tenn., both of whom were his senior commanders, he participated in the different actions at Ft. Donelson, and on the surrender of that garrison, which was deemed inevitable by every member of the council of war, was sent as a prisoner of war to Ft. Warren in Boston Harbor where he remained until July 30th when he was exchanged, and coming to Richmond was immediately promoted to the rank of Major-General.

General Buckner then reported to Gen. Bragg at Chattanooga and was assigned to the command of a division in Hardee's corps. He made the campaign in Kentucky under Gen. Bragg and was selected by the latter to receive the surrender of the U. S. garrison at Munfordville. At the battle of Perryville he commanded a division and returned with Gen. Bragg's army to middle Tennessee. In December, 1862, he was ordered to Mobile to command the Department of Southern Alabama, and in May, 1863, held command of the Departments of East Tennessee and South West Virginia with headquarters at Knoxville. Joining his forces with those of Gen. Bragg in December, he participated in the campaign of '63; commanding a corps composed of the divisions of Gens. Stewart and Preston in the battle of Chickamauga. Early in the spring of '64 he reported to Gen. Longstreet, and was directed to join the army of Gen. Lee. In Sept., 1864, he was promoted to Lieutenant General and assigned to the command of a corps in the Trans-Mississippi Department, remaining there till the close of the war, when he located temporarily in New Orleans and entered commercial and editorial life. In 1868 he returned to Kentucky and for sometime was chief editor of the Louisville *Courier*, but in 1872 he returned to his native county and old home.

In 1887 General Buckner was elected Governor of the Commonwealth of Kentucky for a term of four years. During his term as Governor, he was chosen by the people of his county without opposition, a member of the Constitutional Convention, and in

1896 was nominated by the Indianapolis Convention for Vice-President on the ticket of the Gold Democracy.

Possibly, no better estimate of the life and character of General Buckner could be given than the one penned by Mr. Morton M. Cassedy, whose father, General Cassedy, served on General Buckner's staff during the Civil War. This sketch was written during the campaign of 1896, but was never published.

"Gen. Simon Bolivar Buckner, the candidate of the National Democracy for Vice-President of the United States, perhaps typifies more completely than any other individual the principles of Democracy as they are understood in his native State, Kentucky, where those principles have ever been cherished in their purity. A sketch of this hero of Kentuckians would be incomplete without some reference to the history of the State which has delighted to honor and be honored by him; and such a reference is the more appropriate in view of the foremost position taken by, and most gracefully accorded to Kentucky in the present struggle for the preservation of the integrity of the Democratic party. Not only are both National candidates natives of Kentucky, but at the recent Indianapolis convention the recognition given to the Kentucky delegation was out of all proportion to its size and the electoral vote it represented. One of the delegates was modestly expressing to an Eastern delegate his appreciation of and surprise at this honor, when the gentleman whom he addressed said:

"Yes; that is as it should be. In this country we have Democracy everywhere; but it is a Democracy with a dialect. In Kentucky the accent is pure.'

"The compliment was the more deserved that in the present crisis Kentucky had been the first State to protest in indignant, unequivocal terms against the debauchery of Democracy attempted at Chicago, and presented to the country, as the white-plumed bearer of the unstained standard of a militant Democracy, the name of Simon Bolivar Buckner—a name accepted with acclaim the country over. Democracy is but the expression for individual manhood in its political relation; and no more dignified embodiment of this idea can be found than in the person of Gen. Buckner.

"Kentuckians may reflect with pride that in every great national crisis their State has stood boldly forth to preserve the Constitution, to declare the majesty of the law, and equally to insist on the Constitutional limitations of the powers of the general

Government, leaving to the State and to the citizen a responsible freedom that shall not be surrendered so long as the spirit of Jefferson and Jackson shall animate the minds of men. The Kentucky Resolutions of 1798, offered by John Breckinridge, but believed to have been written by Jefferson himself, directed against the 'alien and sedition laws' then recently passed, were really an interpretation of the Federal Compact, declaring that the Constitution was the measure of the powers of the General Government. Many of the men who shaped the political thought of Kentucky had been students under Jefferson and were in close touch with him. His writings disclose that he was nearly concerned for the political welfare of the young Commonwealth. The seed they planted still bears fruit in the Buckners of to-day.

"At the outbreak of the Civil War Kentucky's position, however chimerical and impractical, was strictly within the Constitutional lines, and was a dignified assertion of State autonomy. At the close of the war she was the first to proclaim: 'The war is over; let us have peace.' Who but a Kentuckian formulated the expression: 'A tariff for Revenue only?' And is not the Star-Eyed Goddess native there? Who presented her image in maiden panoply as a better object for the view than the bloody shirt of the evil days of Reconstruction? And, of all Kentuckians, who more manfully accepted the verdict of the war, recognizing defeat without complaint and meeting in the fullest measure the duties imposed by the new order, than Simon Bolivar Buckner?

"In the formation of so fullrounded a character as his, many influences work; and in such a man we may see the epitome of a people. It is in this view that an account of his surroundings and antecedents must be considered. Among these is an early experience in the history of Kentucky, which offers an instructive parallel to the present political madness. Prior to 1818 there was only one bank in the State, its early commerce having been conducted by barter or the use of Spanish money. The period following the war of 1812 and 15 was one of remarkable commercial activity, and the Legislature in 1818 chartered forty-six banks, with a capital of nearly nine millions. In two years nearly all of these were wrecks, and the one sound bank suspended payment. In 1820 the bank charters were annulled, the people being left under a great burden of debt. To relieve this condition the Legislature chartered the Bank of the Commonwealth, after a long and bitter debate, in which the debtors contended that the State could by some mysterious power, restore their fortunes. So the Commonwealth Bank was allowed to issue notes not payable in specie. It put out three millions of circulating paper, which was made a legal tender for all debts. Of course this paper fell to less than its face value. Creditors refused to receive it; and then the courts were appealed to, they decided that the Legislature could not impair the obligations of a contract, and such notes could not be made a legal tender for payment of debts already existing. Then came a fierce outcry, 'the will of the people' had been set at naught. The judiciary was threatened; the judges barely escaped impeachment. In 1824 a Governor was elected by the Radicals, who secured control of the Legislature and repealed the laws creating the Supreme Court. It was very like what it is proposed to do in 1896. A furious campaign ensued, with the result that common honesty and common sense carried the day. Fiatism, an attack upon the Supreme Court, the fatuous assertion of popular power had been arrayed against honesty and good citizenship. But the heart of the Commonwealth was sound.

"Gen. Buckner was born April 1, 1823, before this experiment in finance was finished. Its bitter lesson was fresh in the minds of men while his own mind was forming. His birth-place was the log house where he now lives, in Hart County, Ky., near Munfordville. His father was a farmer and iron manufacturer, operating one of the early furnaces in Kentucky. The family was of English descent, having come into Kentucky from Virginia. Young Buckner received his early education in an excellent school in Munfordville. His father having removed to Muhlenburg County, he was appointed to a cadetship at West Point. At the military academy he met his old friend and schoolmate, Thomas J. Wood, who became a Major General in the Federal Army. Gen. Grant was also a cadet with Buckner. Upon his graduation in 1844 young Buckner was assigned to the 2nd Infantry. In August of the following year he was made assistant professor of ethics at West Point. Upon the breaking out of the Mexican War he asked for a transfer to the field, and being commissioned Second Lieutenant in the 6th Infantry, spent the winter of 1846 on the Rio Grande. He was at the siege of Vera Cruz; at Cherubusco he was brevetted First Lieutenant, Captain at Molino Del Rey, both brevets being won by gallantry on the field. He served in Mexico till the close of the war, when he was ordered to West Point as Instructor of Infantry Tactics. His next service was on the Western frontier, where, in 1852, he was commissioned Captain. He was afterwards sent to New York, where he remained till 1855. He resigned his commission and devoted himself to business affairs, his wife having large interests in Chicago. He also superintended the construction of the Custom House there. In 1858 he moved to Louisville, Ky.

"His military training had given this large-minded man strength, self-reliance, and self-control. He had not become a mere part of a military machine, but a man of the strongest personality, which made itself widely felt upon his return to Kentucky. He was elected Captain of the Citizens Guards, a company of the best men of Louisville, and in 1860 was appointed by the Governor, Inspector General of the Kentucky State Guard, with the rank of Major General. He framed the admirable militia law of Kentucky, greatly increased the efficiency of the State troops, and at the commencement of hostilities between the North and South was actively engaged in trying to maintain Kentucky's pronunciamento that her soil must not be invaded by either side. This position was, of course, impossible, and when the State's neutrality had been disregarded, Gen. Buckner, in September 1861, went where his sympathies called him and cast his lot with the South, being appointed a Brigadier General. It is proper to state a similar appointment in the Union Army had been offered to him.

"On Sept. 17, Gen. Buckner, under orders from Gen. Albert Sidney Johnston, occupied Bowling Green, Ky., around which point he was for several months engaged in checking Buell. Having been ordered to reinforce Pillow at Fort Donelson, Gen. Buckner arrived there with about 5000 men on the night of February 12, 1862. Gen. Floyd arrived the next day, when the battle commenced.

"This battle made Buckner a hero of the war. He was third in command, but the brunt of the fighting, the odium of the surrender and the hardship of imprisonment fell upon him. After two days' of incessant fighting, it was determined to try on the third day, to open a way for the garrison to fall back on Nashville, and thus avoid the danger of surrender due to the increasing

Union force. On the morning of the third day the attack was made by the Confederates, and the way of escape was opened after the severest fighting. Then the superior generals ordered Gen. Buckner to retire with his men into the intrenchments. It was a complete reversal of the plan agreed upon and already partly executed, and it resulted in the surrender of the garrison. Gen'ls. Floyd and Pillow, the former with some of his command, escaped from the fort on a steamer, but Buckner refused to escape, saying he would share the fate of the men who had fought so bravely for three days. Gen. Buckner, on the morning of February 16, surrendered to Gen. Grant. His generalship and his loyalty to his men increased the esteem in which he was held by his people.

"The distinguished prisoner was conveyed first to Indianapolis and soon afterward to Ft. Warren in Boston Harbor. Although harshly treated by order of the Federal Government, and kept in close confinement, Gen. Buckner did not allow his misfortune to disturb the dignified equanimity of his bearing, the calmness of his mind, making a sort of triumph of defeat. On July 30, he was released, and coming to Richmond he was exchanged Aug. 16, and immediately promoted to a Major Generalship. He reported to Gen. Bragg at Chattanooga, where he was heartily welcomed by the troops. He was assigned to the command of a division in Hardee's corps, the army moved into Kentucky, and Gen. Buckner was assigned to the organization of new troops in the State, but was recalled to his command, which he rejoined just before the battle of Perryville. In this battle, and in the operations around Perryville, Buckner displayed generalship of the highest order. He urged Gen. Bragg to concentrate his forces at Perryville, overwhelming Buell at that point, intercepting him from Louisville, and fighting him in detail. Instead of following this counsel, Gen. Bragg scattered his army and threw away an opportunity that would, if availed of, have changed the result of the campaign in Kentucky.

"Gen. Buckner was next placed in charge of the defenses at Mobile, where he remained four months, having converted an open town into a formidable fortress. His next duty was the command of the Department of East Tennessee, where the preponderance of Union sentiment rendered the position one of great delicacy and difficulty. His duties were discharged with prudence,

GENERAL SIMON BOLIVAR BUCKNER
1885

firmness, and with admirable regard for law and justice, which, during his whole public career, military as well as civil, he has held constantly in view.

"In the fall of 1863 Gen. Buckner was ordered to join Gen. Bragg in Georgia. He commanded his corps in the battle of Chickamauga. Here again he showed the superior character of his military genius by his apprehension of the disposition and movements of the opposing forces, a clearness of view not shared by the General in command. Buckner's conduct in this battle is thus described by the Rev. Dr. Cross, an army chaplain who was at the scene of action:

"He rode through the fiery tempest as calmly as if he knew himself invulnerable, and seemed as thoughtless of danger as if he were out on an equestrian pleasure excursion. He was every where among his troops, in front and flank and rear, directing their movements and cheering them on to victory. To his cool courage, in connection with Longstreet's superior strategy and heroic resolution, more than to the management or energy of their compeers, is attributable the triumph of the Confederate arms on the field of Chickamauga.'

"Upon the opening of the campaign of 1864, Gen. Buckner was assigned to the charge of the district of Louisiana, and commanded a corps of the Trans-Mississippi army with the grade of Lieutenant General. Here there were but few active operations after Buckner took charge. Upon the surrender of Lee and Johnson, Gens. Buckner and Price negotiated their surrender with Gen. Canby.

"The Rev. Dr. Cross, in closing his sketch of Buckner's military career, says:

"'His moral character is irreproachable. During the months of my intimacy with him, I never saw in him an act, nor heard from him a word, which would not become the purest Christian on earth. Though not a communicant of the Church, his Bible and his prayer-book are his constant companions. In short, he is the most perfect gentleman I have found in the Confederate army; and of all the distinguished men, civilians or soldiers, whose acquaintance I have enjoyed, I have never known one whose private character was altogether so unexceptionable as that of Lieut. Gen. Simon Bolivar Buckner.'

"Under the terms of the surrender Gen. Buckner was not permitted to return to Kentucky. He therefore remained in New

Orleans, becoming a writer on one of the daily papers there, and also engaging in commercial pursuits. No man ever exhibited greater equipoise of character, more moderation of thought and action, and finer self-control than did Gen. Buckner, both during the war, when more than his share of ungrateful duties fell to him, or than afterward, when he proceeded to retrieve his fortunes from the wreck of war.

"Through his wife, a Miss Kingsbury, whom he married in 1850, Gen. Buckner had become possessed of an ample fortune. When he went into the Southern army he deeded his property to his brother-in-law, Lieut. Kingsbury, of the United States army. The latter was mortally wounded in battle, and though he made a nuncupative will restoring the property to Gen. Buckner, it required several years of tedious litigation to recover the estate. Barely had this been accomplished, when the Chicago fire destroyed a greater part of the property. Ultimately, however, the General's efforts were successful and his fortune was fully restored.

"In 1870 or '71, Gen. Buckner retired to his farm in Hart County, dwelling in the old log house in which he was born. Here he lived the life of a country gentleman, seeing little of the world, but occupied with his books, and with the resources he finds so abundant within himself. His daughter, to whom he was devoted and who has since died, was his companion. The people of Kentucky, though they saw him seldom, still retained for him the highest respect and most affectionate regard. In 1883 his friends and neighbors urged him to make the race for Governor of the State. He had not sought this honor or preferment. In 1883 his name was presented too late, and the gubernatorial nomination of the Democrats went to J. Proctor Knott, who was elected. But four years later Gen. Buckner was nominated almost without opposition, and was elected by 17,000 plurality over W. O. Bradley the present Governor of the State.

"As Governor, Gen. Buckner gave the people a business administration. Being himself a fine Constitutional lawyer, he used the veto power with good effect, and his fearlessness in its exercise won the admiration of all disinterested citizens. Had his veto of the tax reduction bill not been over-ridden, the treasury of the State would not be empty, as for a year it has been. Upon one occasion when the State was in need of funds with which to

MRS. SIMON BOLIVAR BUCKNER

meet its obligations, he himself advanced to the treasury $50,000. When he left office, a great meeting of citizens was held in Louisville to testify the popular approval of his administration. Republicans united with Democrats in this remarkable testimonial to a retiring executive. While in the office of Governor, Gen. Buckner's friends wanted to present his name as a candidate for the United States Senate, and though, no doubt, he would have been gratified at an election to that body, he absolutely refused to allow his name to go before the Legislature, declaring that his position as Governor rendered such a course improper. In Sept., 1891, Gen. Buckner retired to private life, but upon the urgency of his friends, was elected a delegate to the Constitutional Convention, in which he took a prominent part.

"No amount of public applause has ever seemed as grateful to Gen. Buckner, as the quiet of Glen Lily, as his Hart County farm is called.

"Just before his election as Governor, he married a second time, his wife being Miss Claiborne of Richmond, Va. They have one son. From the seclusion of his home, the Sage of Glen Lily makes occasional excursions into the world, and wherever he goes, honors and plaudits greet him. Before the death of Gen. Grant, he and Gen. Buckner had resumed their old friendship, and at the great soldier's funeral his aforetime foe was a pall bearer. At the Grant memorial celebration in New York he was the most remarked of all the guests. At Indianapolis admiring crowds surrounded him. Yet, withal, he bears himself so modestly and gently, that he seems unconscious of his popularity and his power over men.

"Always alert when duty calls, though hidden from public view in his secluded home, he was first in Kentucky to sound the alarm when danger threatened in the form in which it has now come upon the people. May 6, 1895, through the medium of the press, he addressed the Democracy of his State, declaring that 'local self-government, sound money and free trade—the latter, subject only to the wants of government to collect Revenue to defray its legitimate expenses—is the shiboleth of the Democratic party.' He entered into a convincing discussion of the money question, showing the disaster that would follow the free coinage of silver. This position was taken at a time when he was prominently advanced as a candidate for the United States Senate, and when the position was thought to be a dangerous one in Kentucky.

"In his home, to which he is so deeply attached, Gen. Buckner leads a life of the utmost simplicity. A few books satisfy him, but he reads those constantly. He knows Shakespeare by heart, and has a fine Shakespearian library. He reflects much, is an accomplished scholar and most of his reading is of a serious character, but says that no man more than he loves a pretty love story. In his learning he is unobtrusive as in all other matters, and he once let a couple of young visitors engage in a heated and unsatisfactory dispute over the meaning and pronounciation of a French phrase without giving them the slightest intimation that to him French was a familiar language. He afterwards said he thought it would have been impertinence on his part. With his neighbors Gen. Buckner is on terms of the closest friendship, and is as approachable by the poorest of them as he is by any man whom he meets in the big world. His farm lies in a hilly and rough district, but he has improved it to its utmost capacity, except such part of it that is still in virgin forest. He has also improved the roads of his neighborhood, and to the work of road overseer brought as much earnestness of purpose as to any larger vocation.

"Gen. Buckner is as straight at 73 as he was at 40. He is tall and broad and strong, his step elastic, though his abundant hair is snow-white. His corn-cob pipe is an ever present part of the picture, whether on the 'verandah' at home or in the streets of a great city. It's a well smoked, Democratic looking sort of a pipe, too.

"When the Kentucky Democracy met on Aug. 20, 1896, to declare the faith in protest against the heresies of Chicago, the Kentucky delegation was instructed to present at Indianapolis, for the Vice-Presidential nomination, the name of Simon Bolivar Buckner. How the country took up the call and cheered on the Kentuckians, and how the Democrats of the Union named Buckner of the South, with Palmer of the North, and thus declared there was no longer either North or South, are incidents too recent to need repeating."

ANN BUCKNER, daughter of Philip and Elizabeth (Watson) Buckner was probably the eldest child, she married —— Hoskins. Issue:

1. Judith Elizabeth Hoskins, born 1808; died Dec. 17, 1863; married Jan. 7, 1830, at Tappahannock, Va., George Henry Dobyns, son of Abner Dobyns. He was born 1799 and died Sept. 27, 1857. Issue:
A. Thomas Abner Dobyns, born at Tappahannock, April 15, 1831; died Dec. 26, 1870; married March 3, 1858, at "May Fair," King William County, to Lucy Ellen Sizer, born Oct. 10, 1838. Issue:
   - aa. Annie Baylor Dobyns, born Feb. 26, 1859, at Tappahannock; married Oct. 12, 1881, John Sizer Exall of Danville; born July 21, 1848, at Richmond; died April 29, 1893. Issue: Douglas Exall, born April 7, 1883; Alice Buckner Exall, born Oct. 15, 1884; Colin Stuart Exall, born Sept. 24, 1888; Le Roy Randolph Exall, born May 31, 1891.
   - bb. George H. Dobyns, born April 8, 1860.
   - cc. Thomas A. Dobyns, born Sept. 3, 1862, of Washington, D. C.
   - dd. Dr. Frederick Dobyns, born Jan. 28, 1865, of Baltimore, Md.
   - ee. Lucy Robinson Dobyns, born Aug. 6, 1868.
B. Mrs. Ella Dobyns Derieux, Tappahannock, Va.

HENRY WATSON BUCKNER, son of Philip and Elizabeth (Watson) Buckner, was born in Virginia—probably Albemarle County—in 1800. He went with his parents to Kentucky and died at Munfordville, July 19, 1871. He married Mary Bowman, by whom he had issue:

1. Joseph Buckner.
2. Watson Buckner.
3. John Buckner.
4. Philip Buckner.
5. Murphy Buckner.
6. Phebe Buckner, married —— Bolton.
7. Mary Buckner.
8. Richard Buckner.
9. Simon B. Buckner.
10. Alfred Buckner, born at Munfordville, Ky., June 4, 1831; died at Franklin, Ill., Jan. 15, 1896; married (1st) Dec. 30, 1852, Martha Hawkins, died 1863; married (2d) Oct. 8, 1865, to Narcissa Hawkins; born Feb. 5, 1840. Issue by first marriage:
    A. Amanda J. Buckner, born Dec.—1853; resides at Farmville, Ill.
    B. Mary E. Buckner, born April 10, 1855; died Dec. 8, 1902; married Sept. 21, 1875; James T. Owen.
    C. Richard H. Buckner, born Aug. 23, 1856; died Jan. 17, 1877.
    D. Virginia F. Buckner, born Oct. 23, 1858; married March 1, 1877, David W. Durham.
    E. Andrew H. Buckner, born April 25, 1860; died Feb. 4, 1877.
    F. James W. Buckner, born Feb. 19, 1862; died Dec. 4, 1880.

    ISSUE BY SECOND WIFE.

    G. Melvina E. Buckner, born Jan. 16, 1867; died Oct. 23, 1871.
    H. Phebe B. and Clara H. Buckner, (twins), born Dec. 15, 1869.
    I. Robert W. Buckner, born Aug. 20, 1873; died Sept. 1, 1903; married May 17, 1900 to Nellie F. Rawlings.

Thomas Buckner of Spottsylvania Co.

TO Mrs. Priscilla Aylette Reardon, and Mrs. Katharine Edmondson Tuley, wife of the late Judge Murray F. Tuley of Chicago must be ascribed the credit of putting in booklet form a partial history of the Buckner family, with especial reference to the line of Thomas Buckner, from whom both of these ladies are descended.

The data given in the little *brochure*, " Reminiscences of the Buckner Family," is in great measure traditionary. In a recent search of the County records it has been proved that the traditions are in the main correct. The "Reminiscences" were prepared in the first instance solely for the entertainment of Mrs. Tuley and her husband, with no thought of publication. Amplified, and placed in chronological order by Mrs. Tuley, they have been incorporated in this volume, together with certain additional information inserted in the form of editorial notes.

Mrs. Reardon's narrative is as follows:

A Story of the Past
For my Children and Grandchildren

"My children have often urged me to write what I can remember of my own early days and the stories told me by my grandmother, Hannah Burton Buckner, and by my own father and mother. My father, Simeon Buckner, was the seventh child of Thomas Buckner, who was born in Virginia, probably about 1765 or '66, I think, since he married Hannah Burton in 1787, who was also a Virginian by birth. Eight years later, in 1795, they gathered together their little ones and goods and chattels and emigrated to Kentucky. Other children were born to them, twenty in all. They owned a fine farm in Jefferson County, not far from Louisville. I remember grandmother as a beautiful old lady, always dressed in black, wearing spotless white cap, with

MRS. MURRAY F. TULEY

high crown and ruffles around the face, sitting by the open fireplace, with its tall, brass andirons and red-painted hearth, and I remember the reflection of my face in the shining brass of the andirons and fender. I remember, also, the 'Love Apples,' or tomatoes, which grew in her garden, and later, it was at her table that I first ate them cooked—and what a dainty and well furnished table she kept. At the time of which I speak grandfather Buckner was dead, and the three youngest children, Aunt Louisa, Uncle Eliphalet and Aunt Helena, were living with her, and Uncle Eliphalet was studying law.

"I was her oldest grandchild, and, I think, a favorite one, for I was an absorbed listener to her stories. You can fancy us sitting round the fire, while she told this story, which was, as nearly as I can remember, about as follows:

Grandmother's Story

"When our family emigrated from Virginia to this country, we traveled in emigrant wagons; those big covered things sometimes called 'Schooner' wagons. The country was full of Indians, most of them hostile to the whites, who were taking possession of the hunting grounds, and some of them had old grudges to settle after their encounters with Simon Kenton and Rogers Clark, and so the men of our party were well armed and constantly on guard. When we camped at night the wagons were arranged in horseshoe form, the wheels chained together, the cattle in the centre, and the men standing guard by night, taking turns, two at a time. The roads were awful, and we crawled along, the feet of the horses and oxen sticking in the mud at every step. Sometimes we would hear the whoops and yells of the Indians, which terrified the women and children almost to death, for there were several families of us traveling together for mutual protection. We had been within the borders of Kentucky some time when, at one of our camping places, a poor, frightened, hungry woman came into camp, with her clothes hanging in rags and tatters, with bare and bleeding feet, and a wild look in her eyes, which made us afraid of her. We gave her food and some articles of clothing, and allowed her to take a good sleep before she told her story.

"She said she had been captured by the Indians the year before, who kept such close watch on her that it was impossible to escape. During that time she had to perform the hardest labor, and was often beaten when her strength failed. A few days previous the Indian braves had gone on a big hunt, leaving her guarded by an old Indian, who kept close watch on her. To put him off his guard she pretended to be cheerful and contented. When he finally fell asleep, she made her escape noiselessly and in all haste. She had no idea which way she should go to reach the nearest settlement, but ran on in frantic haste to escape pursuit. For several days she subsisted on roots and berries, and was growing very weak when she came to a swamp; there hearing the whoops of the Indians in pursuit she crawled inside of a big, hollow log, lying in the swamp, and prayed fervently for deliverance. She heard the Indians running, and one of them stood on the log within which she was concealed, whooping and calling. At last she heard them going away, and after a long time, when all was quiet, she crawled out, and walked for hours till she came to a road, which she followed till it parted in two directions. Fearing that one of them might lead her to the Indian camp, she hid in the bushes and prayed to be directed. Soon a little bird came chirping and fluttering about her, then flew off up one of the roads. Believing that God had sent the bird to guide her, she followed that road till it brought her to our camp. We were the first white people she had seen for a year, and she cried for joy, poor thing! For awhile she journeyed with us, then, with our assistance, she finally reached her home and kindred.

"The farm which Thomas Buckner owned was in a beautiful and fertile region, twenty miles from what is now the city of Louisville, but which must have been a small town then, as it was founded in 1778, only seventeen years before grandfather emigrated to Kentucky. On that farm his children were raised, and later I myself was born there. I have heard some of the aunts and uncles say it was a busy community, where besides the farm work—in which grandfather and the bigger boys took part, as well as the negroes—there was the weaving, spinning, dyeing, knitting and sewing to be done for that large family of whites and blacks. The shoemaker in those days traveled from farm to farm, making and repairing shoes for the family, for his board and

The Buckners of Virginia

wages, and he must have found the Buckner farm the most profitable one in that region. Uncle Ben, one of the youngest sons, used to tell of how the mischievous ones, of whom he was the leader, would beg the shoemaker to put 'squeaks' in father's, mother's and grandmother's shoes, that the children might have warning of their approach when they were in mischief. For all that, they grew up a fine-looking, energetic and capable set of men and women, much respected in the communities in which they lived. After my father and mother had settled in Louisville, a distant cousin of the family called 'Colonel Nick,' or Nicholas Buckner, used to come to our house, and he told us many stories about the Indians. He was a great Indian fighter, and hated the 'red devils,' as he called them, and we children were spell-bound listeners to his tales. He had a dramatic way of acting them out, taking aim with his gun at an imaginary foe in a way which thrilled us to the marrow. One of these was about the

Chineworth Spring Massacre

"Not far from the Buckner farm was a beautiful spring of water called the 'Chineworth Spring,' from the family who owned the place. One day a report reached Col. Nick that a party of Indians had been seen near the Chineworth place. In great haste he started with his company of Indian fighters, armed with shot guns and rifles, for the Chineworth farm. No Indians were found at the spring, but when they reached the cabin, seeing no signs of life about they pushed open the door, and there, to their horror, saw Mr. Chineworth on the floor dead, and his murdered children around him—all had been scalped. One child only had escaped death. Pursuing their search they found in another room this child, a little girl, trying to kindle a little flame by blowing on a few coals left in the fireplace. With sobs she told of hearing the dreadful cries and blows, and knew that the Indians were killing them all, and had slipped out of bed on the side next the wall and hid behind the bed curtain, by which means she escaped the tomahawk and scalping knife of the Indians, who passed through the room without seeing her. Being asked about her mother she said, 'They are all dead but me!' Pursuing their search they found in the yard traces of blood, following which they reached the spring house, a rude cabin built over the outlet to the spring, in which milk and butter were kept. Here they found Mrs. Chineworth, covered with blood from a wound in the body, and her head scalped. She said the Indians drove a spear through her body as she ran, which pinned her to the earth, and taking her scalp, left her for dead. Bye and bye she returned to consciousness and managed to pull the spear from her body, then swooned again; but finally crawled on hands and knees to the spring, bathed her wounds, and with a piece of her skirt managed to bind them up, and waited for help.

"About forty years later there passed through Little Rock a lady missionary bound for the reservation of the Indian Nation, where she was going to devote herself to the civilization and conversion of the Indians. She stopped at Mrs. Roswald Beebe's house, where she told them the gruesome story of the massacre at Chineworth Spring, as told by Col. Nick B. She was the child who escaped the fate of the rest of the family, going in the spirit of Christian love and forgiveness, to help the race that had killed hers.

"How little Col. Buckner could have imagined such a finale to his story!

"Grandfather Buckner died in 1827, when I was only six years old, so I remember nothing very distinctly about him, except his death. When his children were grown, and most of them married, he sold his farm to a man named Hoffman, and moved into Louisville. I remember that my mother and Aunt Priscilla Tuley once took me with them to the old farm, to visit the family who bought it. The house was a two-story brick, and the farm was large and well cultivated. I remember more distinctly the town house, however, with its garden and fruit trees. The soldiers' barracks were not far away, and I had a wholesome terror of the soldiers, and ran away when I saw them, as I had been told they were bad men. I remember distinctly when Lafayette was in Louisville, which I think was not long after grandfather's death, so I must have been between six and seven years old. I remember as he passed our house how my mother caught me up in her arms and held me so that I could see the great man for whom all good Americans felt such gratitude and love.

"I think my grandfather must have lived rather handsomely for those times—for I remember he kept a carriage and horses and that my mother and I were upset in it once going to camp-meeting at Bear Grass Creek, which has made me timid to this day about riding in a closed carriage. After grandfather went to Louisville he was elected High Sheriff of Jefferson Co., a very honorable position in those days, for which the best men were sought; you may be sure he filled it worthily, for he had a high sense of honor and justice. He was a tall man with a red head and a quick temper, but a just man when his temper was over, in illustration of which I will tell you a story told by Uncle Ben which I had from Cousin Kate Tuley, who heard it from his own lips."

Uncle Ben's Story

"One day, said Uncle Ben, my father got into a heated discussion with a man on the streets of Louisville, and for some insulting remark made by the latter, my father knocked him down and punished him severely. Whereupon the man sued him for assault and battery. I was present and saw the whole thing, and was summoned by my father to testify in his defence, without any previous examination as to the character of my testimony. Greatly to his surprise my testimony went dead against him as the first aggressor. So the other man won his suit, and father had to pay the fine and costs. I thought I saw fire in the old man's eyes as I told my story, and I tell you as soon as I stepped down off that witness stand I got out of there in a hurry, and was cutting around a corner to escape the thrashing I expected when I felt a slap on my shoulder, and turned to face my father. And what do you think he said? *'Ben, my son! I'm proud of you! I'm proud of you!* You told the truth and shamed the devil, if you did beat your father in that suit, you dog you! Now, sir, you go straight to my tailor, and tell him to make you a fine broadcloth suit and charge it to me, do you hear?' With a hearty handshake we separated, and away I went, thanking my stars I had missed the thrashing, and mighty glad to get the present. I won't say but what the water got into my eyes, too, as I turned away."

The Tragic Wedding Feast

"In 1834, seven years after grandfather's death, a dreadful tragedy was enacted in the Buckner family, which shook the whole city of Louisville; it was at the wedding of Helena, the youngest daughter of grandfather, who was married to a Mr. Clark at her mother's house, rather quietly. Among the refreshments served was 'Floating Island' or custard, of which there were two large kettles. One of these was set away in a cool place, and was not used at the wedding. Next day, however, it was partaken of by the family, and portions were sent to the houses of several of grandmother's married children. That night grandmother was taken ill, and shortly after Aunt Adeline Foster, then Aunt Emily Fontaine, also a son of Uncle Milton Buckner, and some others—I don't know how many—were affected. The symptoms grew so alarming that doctors and friends were running to the aid of the sufferers, and the wildest alarm prevailed. The night was dark and the dogs of the neighborhood set up a doleful howling, and as the death of first one member of the family and then another was announced a terror seized that part of the city, and spread like wild-fire. The wildest rumors prevailed—'It was cholera.' 'The wells were poisoned by the negroes!' 'An uprising of the negroes would follow,' it was said, but finally, as no more deaths followed, it simmered down to the statement that 'the custard was poisoned by the negroes.' Aunt Louisa, however, who was present and knew all the facts (she was then unmarried and living with her mother) says that the kettle containing the custard which caused the tragedy was of brass, and it was supposed had corroded in the twenty-four or more hours in which it had been set away. It is to her I am indebted for a description of the horrors of that night which laid low dear old grandmother and all the others who had eaten of it, save one cousin, now living in St. Louis, who merely tasted it. Long was that night of terror remembered by the old citizens of Louisville.

"My father was at this time owner of a line of boats and captain of one of them. He was absent from home at this time; his boat had been aground in the Arkansas river for three months, and he had heard nothing from home. After he got off the sandbar he was one day hailed by one of his old pilots on another boat. This man was named Shaddock. When the boats were landed Shaddock said, 'Captain Buckner, when did you hear from home?' 'Not for three months,' said my father. 'Come ashore then, I have something to tell you.' They seated themselves on a big log, facing the boats, and Shaddock began hesitatingly, 'So you have not heard about your sister Helena's marriage?' 'No!'

'Then, Captain, prepare yourself for bad news! At the wedding, poison was put in the food, and your mother, your sisters (Mrs. Foster and Mrs. Fontaine) are dead, several children and a servant, and—and—your wife and children—all dead!' At that my father fell to the ground as if struck by a cannon ball, and never knew the truth till he got home some time later and clasped us all in his arms, the truth being that none of our family were there, else I might not have been here to tell the story.

"Some time before this tragedy, my father having gone into the mercantile business in Louisville had failed, along with many others. It was at the time when so many of the United States Banks broke; in 1832, I believe. He and my mother were Whigs, and ardent admirers of Henry Clay. They thought that the failure of the banks and the misfortunes of the country were due to General Jackson and the Democratic Party. My mother was a woman of a great deal of character and of very pronounced views—political and otherwise. She had a kind heart and cheerful disposition, and was idolized by her nephews, and nieces who considered 'Aunt Nancy' their refuge from parental displeasure, and their best friend. She was a Buckner before marriage, and she and my father were cousins. She was a daughter of Philip Buckner and Elizabeth Watson Buckner, his wife, both born in Virginia, where my mother herself was born in 1803. I do not know the date of Elizabeth Watson's marriage to Philip Buckner. The Bible of the latter which was given to my mother, and contained such entries, was unaccountably lost when we moved to Clark Co., Arkansas. They had four children—Aylette, Jane, Harry, and Nancy Watson Buckner, my dear mother. Aylette, the eldest, became guardian to my mother on the death of grandfather Philip. All of our branch of this family were fond of the name of Aylette; the boys were apt to have it for the first name, the girls for a middle name; hence my mother called me Priscilla for my Aunt Priscilla Buckner, and Aylette for the middle name. It seems that at an early period *Judith Aylette* (whose first husband was a Hawes (daughter of Wm. Aylette, living in King Wm. Co., Va., married *Wm. Buckner* of 'the Neck,' in Caroline Co., and after that, there were many marriages between the Aylettes and Buckners. There are some of the Aylettes in Virginia now, for I have seen in the New York Herald a notice of a fancy ball in Richmond where a Miss Mary Aylette appeared in the dress and jewels of her ancestress, Mary Aylette, the wife of one of the Governors of that period."

My Mother's Story

"My mother used to tell me this story of the old days in Virginia during the Revolutionary War, told her by *her* mother, who was Elizabeth Watson before she married Philip Buckner. It was something like this:

"The family was living on a plantation in the eastern part of the State, in what county I know not—it may have been Spottsylvania Co., since Thomas Buckner is said to have come from there, and Philip, my grandfather, was related to him—but it was certainly in the eastern part of Virginia. There were a few Tories in that county, though most of the people were ardent supporters of the cause of Independence. You remember that Virginia was the first colony, even before Massachusetts, to enter her protest against the levying of unjust taxes on the Colonies by Parliament. John Fiske, in his 'Virginia and Her Neighbors,' makes this clear. You will find it also in Howe's 'Historical Collections of Virginia.' There had been rumors of a probable descent of a detachment of the British army on that locality, and the people were uneasy and troubled. About this time a report spread that some British soldiers had been seen in the neighborhood. Greatly excited, immediate preparations were made to save their property from the depredations of the enemy, and her father, Mr. Watson, hastily gathered together his stock of cattle; taking one or two servants with him, and leaving the rest to protect the family, he hastened to find some safe place among the mountains. He had not been gone long when a British officer in full uniform rode up to the gate and dismounting, was seen talking earnestly to one of the negroes. Presently he approached the house and demanding admittance, was shown into the best room, where her mother awaited him. She rose and greeted him with cold civility. He stated that he wished to see the owner of the plantation. She replied that her husband was absent and could not be seen. He said he had urgent business with him—what time would he return? She, believing he meant to capture him or do him some harm, replied somewhat evasively. 'Then,' said he, 'I will wait till he comes;' and pleading great fatigue threw himself on a sofa and covered his eyes with his hand. My grandmother left the room with as much dignity as she could command, though sorely troubled as to the meaning of this strange visit. The news penetrated to the negro quarters, and an old darky, whom his master had charged with the special care of his young mistress, suddenly appeared in the doorway of the room with his master's drawn sword in his hand. Believing the stranger was able at any moment to rise and slay the household, (as he observed he was only feigning to sleep,) he never took his eyes from him. The hours dragged on wearily and still the officer slept, or feigned to, and the faithful servant stood guard, till at length the master arrived, and was soon closeted with the intruder. He at once avowed that the uniform he wore was a disguise, assumed for the purpose of learning how many Tories there were in that vicinity. That he was an officer in the *Continental* Army, acting under orders of his superior officer, and was in fact on a secret mission. He mentioned also that he had been talking with one of Mr. Watson's servants, and that he, believing him to be a British officer, had revealed to him the place where he, Mr. Watson, had concealed his stock, also their number and value. 'But there is *one* old fellow you can certainly trust,' he added; 'the one who stood guard over me with a drawn sword. I was afraid to close my eyes'—he laughed—'for fear he'd chop my head off.' Being assured of the truth of his story, Mr. Watson pressed him to stay all night, and my grandmother made ample amends for her former lack of hospitality.

"There used to be a number of mother's branch of the Buckners living in Greensburg, Elizabethtown, and adjacent parts of the interior of Kentucky. In the summer of 1837, when I was sixteen, I spent my vacation visiting among them. Judge Richard Aylette Buckner of Greensburg was one of them. He was a United States Senator in Andrew Jackson's time, and was distinguished both as a lawyer and judge. His wife was a Miss Taylor, and their eldest son was named Aylette B., his second son, Richard Aylette Buckner, both lawyers. Richard Aylette Buckner was afterwards a judge, and lived in Lexington, Kentucky. There were two other sons, Arthur and Luther B., and two daughters, the eldest of whom married Mr. Barrett, and lived in St. Louis, Mo. The youngest daughter was named Betty. They were a charming family.

"The sister of Judge Richard Aylette Buckner, senior, married, a Taylor also, and her eldest son, Richard Aylette Taylor, was my mother's first lover when she was going to school, and boarded at their house. Years after this, Richard A. Taylor, having moved to Arkansas, rode 40 miles to see my mother when she was in her last illness at our house, in 1851. But she was too ill to be seen, and died shortly afterward. Judge Buckner told me after he moved to Arkansas that he had a perfect record of the Buckner and Aylette families, and the coat of arms of the latter. His granddaughter, living in Little Rock, furnished me with this record of the births and deaths in the family of my mother's old sweetheart:

RICHARD AYLETTE TAYLOR, born 1802; married Rebecca W. Williamson 1824. Issue:

    John Young Taylor, born 1826; died 1846, unmarried; 20 years old.
    Daniel White Taylor, born 1828; died 1846, unmarried; 18 years old.
    Sally McGee Taylor, born 1830; died 1862; married B. J. Emby, 1847; married at 17; died at 32 years.
    Richard Aylette Taylor, Jr., born 1833; died 1862; married Juliet A. Dowdle, 1853.
    Catherine Buckner Taylor, born 1835; died 1852; married Geo. W. Vaden, 1852; married and died same year.
    Rebecca Aylette Taylor, born 1840; died 1858; married Robert A. Dowdle, 1858; died same year.

"My mother's brother Aylette married Miss Morehead of Tennessee, and they had three children—Turner, Simon Bolivar, and a little girl. I remember the first visit I made in company with my mother to Uncle Aylette's. We travelled by stage. The house, I remember, was on a knob or hill near Green river, Hart county, Kentucky. It was a substantial and commodious log house. In the front room hung the portraits of Uncle Aylette and Aunt Elizabeth. They had an old house servant, Uncle Jerry, who had a superstitious awe of those portraits, for whenever he moved, their eyes watched him. I can hear him say now: 'Ye needn't tell *dis* child dat dem pictures ain't alive! Don't ye see how dem eyes follows me ev'y place I go! Fore God! I'se afeard ov' em I is!' There was a loom in one of the back rooms, and I remember seeing my mother weaving a counterpane to take home with her. I remember the great forest trees about the house and how Uncle Aylette lifted up Cousin Bolivar and put him on a tall stump, telling him to make a speech. He was a little fellow then, about my age, and when he recited 'You'd scarce expect one of my age,' etc., I looked at him with admiring eyes.

"The last time I was there was in 1837, and then my uncle's home was in the valley. He had a large house, and owned an iron foundry, and was considered a rich man for the time. The boys had grown tall, were well educated, and refined in manner. I was charmed with Cousin Bolivar's pigeons, which would come flocking about him when he fed them, as tame as chickens. When I left, Cousin Turner, who was the eldest, was my escort to Elizabethtown, Kentucky, and Cousin Bolivar from there to Louisville. This was the last I saw of the boys for many years. Later Cousin Bolivar entered West Point, and remained till he graduated. He was afterwards in the Mexican war and was at the capture of the City of Mexico.

" His father, mother and sister were with me in Little Rock at the time, for I was then married, and they used to read his letters to me, which I found very interesting. After the war was over he visited me on his way to West Point. Cousin Bolivar afterwards married a Miss Kingsbury of Chicago, who was, I believe, well off, and some years after her death he married a Miss Claiborne of Virginia, who I hear is a devoted wife. His public career is part of the history of our country, as General Buckner, on the Confederate side in the Civil War, then as Governor of Kentucky, and later as candidate for the Vice-Presidency of the United States, nominated by the Gold Democrats and defeated by Republicans—of which defeat he and the Presidential candidate had a full assurance before they consented to run. He continues to live in his father's old log house I have heard, though probably this is only in the summer, as I believe he has also a residence in Louisville. A reporter who visited him in the old family home describes it as tastefully adorned with many interesting old relics, and there he smokes his corn-cob pipe in peace. It is many years since we have met, and it is not likely I shall ever see him again.

"Cousin Turner grew to be one of the tallest men I have ever seen. He had to stoop in entering any ordinary door. Though born in the backwoods of Kentucky he had a good knowledge of Latin, and knew some Greek. His voice was pleasant and his manner gentle; but he was a man of strong and independent ways of thinking—quite original. When his brother Bolivar was stationed at West Point he invited Turner to make him a visit. Turner said as this was his first visit North, he wanted to see the country, and he preferred to walk. And so he did, every step of the way from Hart County to West Point, where the officers received him with open arms.

"When Uncle Aylette Buckner moved at length to southern Arkansas he sent the cattle and servants on foot, but he and his family went by carriage or stage, with the exception of Cousin Turner; he put his servant on his horse, a fine blooded one, preferring to walk the whole way, 'and see the country.'

"When he reached Little Rock he was detained some weeks; meantime his servants encamped near town, and he set them to work making charcoal, and was sometimes seen driving the charcoal wagon into town himself. His maxim was, 'all work is honorable,' and he lived up to that principle. I think Cooper might have taken him for one of his heroes in his novels. He made more than one trip to California on foot with servants and cattle. At length, when crossing the Arkansas river at Fort Smith, though an expert swimmer, in attempting to rescue one of his herdsmen, both were drowned together. The officers at the Fort buried him there with their own dead. So perished a noble hearted man in his prime.

"I have spoken of spending my summer vacation with my mother's relatives in Elizabethtown in 1837. It was while I was there that an unexpected summons came for me to return home at once. My dear mother wrote that my father had been awarded the contract by the United States Government to remove the Cherokee and Seminole Indians to the large tract assigned them, known afterwards as Indian Territory. Vicksburg was to be the point of debarkation, and he thought the time required might be about three years; so, as he wanted his family near him, we were to remove to Little Rock, Arkansas. Cousin Bolivar escorted me home, and I remember my father was greatly surprised to see how rapidly I was developing. 'Almost a young lady, Nanny!' I heard him say to my mother. He charged her to fit me out with everything I required, and accordingly I had all, and more than I needed given me. Our family then consisted of three children besides my mother and father. I, Priscilla, being the eldest, next my brother Perry, then 14, and my sister, Josephine Preston, the youngest. My mother was very busy for some weeks making preparations for our journey, while my father was engaged in purchasing boats for the removal of the Indians. He bought six steamboats. I remember only the names of three—*The Kentucky, The Cin-*

derella and *The DeKalb*. The names of the others can be found in Pope's book. I had once before had a perilous ride on one of my father's boats, the *Daniel Boone*, purchased about 1825 or 1826, when my father started to New Orleans with my mother and myself, and I was not anxious to try another. These boats were very different from our boats of the present day. They were very slow, and it took one month to go to New Orleans and return to Louisville. The ladies' cabin was in the hull of the boat, and in the gentlemen's cabin the staterooms resembled our sleeping cars when the births are made up at night. They were concealed by curtains which were let down at night, and looped back in the daytime. We got safely down the Ohio, but after we entered the Mississippi the *Daniel Boone* ran on a snag somewhere, I don't remember the place, and sunk. I remember they had to tie the boat up to some trees on the shore, to keep her head out of water, while the passengers were got on shore, the women and children first of course. Tents were pitched for our accommodation, and we had to stay there several days till a boat came along and took us back to Louisville. I remember we were devoured by mosquitoes in our tents.

"It was on *The Cinderella* that we travelled leisurely and safely to our new home, having abundance of time to cultivate the acquaintance of many Little Rock people going home after their summer '*in the north*,' as St. Louis and Louisville were called. There were the Johnsons, Ashleys, Peays, Cunninghams, Fultons, Trapnells, Beals, Clendennings, Reardons, Waits, Nolands and Hempsteads, besides Mr. Cook, Col. Fowler, Capt. Pike and others. We went to the hotel kept by Major Peay and wife, old friends of my father. We were visited and cordially treated by many delightful people, both at the hotel and at our next home, which was with Dr. Watkins. The population of Little Rock then was somewhere between three and five thousand, and strangers were coming from Missouri, Kentucky, Maryland and Virginia.

"After my father had fulfilled his contract with the Government, for which he received $80,000, with $40,000 more for the demurrage of his boats, he purchased a large cotton plantation called 'The Rich Woods,' not far from Archidelphia on the Ouachitah (or Washita river), or rather 7 miles from there. On the high ridge, running through the center, he built our house. On this ridge also were the garden, orchard, negro cabins, and the cotton gin. A lane a mile long led from the woods to the house, and another back of the house led to Archidelphia. The country folks travelled this road, and often stopped to get a meal or to beg for a little coffee, sugar or medicine, which my father with his open-handed ways never refused.

"I have a vivid remembrance of our first arrival at the plantation. We made the journey from Little Rock, a distance of one hundred miles, by stage, till we were within fifteen miles of Rich Wood. There the overseer met us with saddle horses for the party, and we proceeded on our journey much interested in the new scenery. When we reached the place we found the colored folks lined up on each side of the lane, the men on one side and the women on the other, dressed in their Sunday clothes, the latter with gay bandanas on their heads. As we rode down the lane the men doffed their hats, and the women ducked a courtesy, with cheerful salutations, 'Howdy Marster,' 'Howdy Mistus,' and to me with broad smiles, 'Pooty little Mistus!' The overseer had arranged this spectacle I suspect, though it was quite in consonance with negro ways. My father and mother were kind to their slaves, and I think the negroes probably found no reason to regret the change of masters. Here I looked for the first time on the cotton fields, stretching on both sides the lane.

"On this plantation a few years later I was married to your father, Lambert Jeffries Reardon, of Little Rock, formerly of Baltimore, Md. Mr. Reardon was a tall, handsome man, with soft brown eyes, and of good family, and we loved each other dearly. My father gave me five negroes for my marriage portion. By this time our means were becoming restricted, my father in his lavish way having loaned 30,000 dollars to the Vice-President of the United States, Col. Richard Johnson, and later he had to pay a security debt for $6,000 and another for $30,000, with various gifts to the family, and other like matters, and it was not long before he became bankrupt.

"Before this came to pass my brother Perry had been sent to Mr. Hallowell's school in Alexandria, and my sister Josephine to an expensive school in Washington. There Col. Washington was made her guardian. He was very kind to her and claimed kin with her. I have since learned that a granddaughter of Wm. Buckner of 'The Neck' married a John Washington in 1770, and that there have been several intermarriages between the two families since then. My brother Perry, who was always a good student, and stood high in mathematics and Latin at his school, was able to enter the Naval Academy at Annapolis in 1841. His first cruise was on the *Marion* to the West Indies; then he was transferred to the *Bainbridge*, and went to the coast of Africa; after that he was for three years on the old *Constitution*, where he made the tour of the world. During all this time he was studying while the necessary buildings were being erected at Annapolis, at the end of which time he graduated with honor. This was the *Constitution's* last cruise and my brother's last voyage. For nine years after this he acted as teacher, and after awhile as Professor of Mathematics. He had spent much time on the coast of Africa and at the Philippine Islands, and I have a large package of most interesting letters sent me by him from these and other points, also many curiosities from foreign parts. He was considered one of the best navigators in the Navy at that time. During the Civil War he remained in the service of the United States. He thought secession wrong, but his heart was with his kindred and friends in the South, and I think the struggle between duty and love broke his heart. He was Captain in the Navy when he died in 1869, and was put on the retired list about two months before that event.

"After my marriage to Mr. Reardon we built a comfortable two-story house, commanding a beautiful view of the Arkansas river, and the green woods, crowning the hills, with an occasional house in view. The long howl of the wolves and the song of the whipporwill lulled us to sleep at night. Four children came to keep us company in time—my two boys, Buckner and Walter, and my two girls, Annie and Lallie, who were to be my unspeakable comfort and stay in old age. We were very happy in each other and our children. About 1843 my dear father, while on a visit to Louisville, died at the home of Aunt Louisa Hughes, aged forty-six years. This was the beginning of many partings for me. Between the years of 1843 and 1855 I had lost father, mother, sister and husband; none left of our immediate family but my brother Perry, myself and my husband's brother, and they left me some years later. Some time before Mr. Reardon's death in 1846, he assumed editorial charge of a newspaper in Little Rock, called the 'Banner,' which he continued to edit for some years. He was considered a fine writer. Afterward the name of the paper was changed to 'The True Democrat.' Later Mr. Reardon accepted the office of Commissioner of State Swamp Lands, which he filled till his death. My two boys, Buckner and Walter, died in 1892, my darling, Annie Raleigh, died in 1895, leaving six sons. Lallie, my youngest, was married to Dr. J. A. Dibrell, eminent as surgeon and physician in many States, and beloved and revered wherever known, who died November 1, 1904, a great loss to the community as well as to his family and friends. He was kindest and truest of men, to whom and to her two sons, John and James, she was the tenderest of wives and mothers, like my dear Annie. She, too, has now withdrawn her sweet face from the home which she blest with her presence. What a meeting there will be in the sweet-bye-and-bye.

"I neglected to say that my dear mother remained at 'Rich Wood' some time after Pa's death, then went back to Louisville, her old home, but at last consented to make my home her own.

"But now I want to tell you something about

Slavery Times

"In Louisville, Ma hired by the year a young colored girl named Mary, who had a little girl named Susan, Mary's husband being owned by someone else. When Ma was about to break up housekeeping and come to me, Mary's master offered to sell Mary and her child to her, but Ma refused, saying that she did not want to part husband and wife. When Mary was consulted, however, she seemed to be perfectly willing to belong to Ma and to go South with her, *provided Ma would buy her husband and take him along*. But the husband stoutly refused to leave Louisville unless forced to do so. This refusal made Mary angry, and as she was really attached to my mother she went without a murmur. Afterwards she became my property, and I always found her a trusty and loyal servant, a good cook, and kind hearted, though hot-tempered.

"And here I want to say that I often ask myself whether freedom and education have made the negro morally better. I confess that they disappoint me greatly when I find that the educated ones can't be trusted as we used to trust our servants in slavery times. When my mother was living alone on the plantation with the negroes she could sleep securely, with neither bolt or bar on the door; and she used to drive in safety many miles along lonely roads to visit me, alone with her negro coachman. What white woman in the South would *dare* to do such a thing *now?* If slavery is a wrong, which I do not deny, yet it bred in our colored people such loyalty, such unselfish devotion to the families of their masters, such trustworthiness as I have never found in those of their race born in freedom. No race could have behaved better than they did during the Civil War. No insurrections, no outrages, but the most extraordinary fidelity to the women and children left to their care while sons and fathers were away on the battlefield.

"One Christmas I remember Mary came to me to ask a favor. She wanted to have a dance in my kitchen, and to have the house servants on some of the neighboring plantations, 'none o' yo' common low down niggers,' and she 'wouldn't give me no trouble,' and 'Wheeler (her brother) would bring her the eggs and sugar, etc., she needed.' I gave my consent willingly, and Mary went to work with a will. When we built the house I planned for a fine, large kitchen, and Mary soon had that floor and the tables snowy white, and the tin and copper vessels shining brightly among the bunches of holly evergreen stuck here and there. I had given her permission to use the dining-room and my best linen and silver, knowing she would take good care of everything. Perhaps I had a little pride in having *our* servants outshine those on the other plantations. When the table was set Mary, proud and delighted, called me to come and see it, and I must say it was beautiful. In the middle of the table there seemed to be the largest cake I had ever seen, from the center of which sprang a branch of evergreen, sprinkled with flour, which looked as if powdered with snow. 'Why, Mary!' I said, 'what a *big* cake! They can't eat all that!' 'Laws, Miss P'rcilla! that aint no cake! 'taint nothin' in the worl' but *cawn bread!* an' them niggers is goin' to eat ever' single mossel of it, cause it's aig-bred an' I got some *little* cakes for 'em 'sides that!' Away into the night I heard the strains of the fiddle, the calls of the fiddler, the thumping of feet on the floor and the hearty laughter. Next morning Mr. Reardon said to me, 'Priscilla, I wish some of those Northern abolitionists who are so concerned about the down-trodden negroes South could have looked into this dining-room and that kitchen last night!' A few more Christmases came and went, and then the old home where we had spent such happy years together was broken up, and we went to Little Rock to live. Susan (Mary's daughter) had grown to be a smart, handy girl, and I kept them both, though only one was needed. After my husband's death one day Mary said to me, 'Miss P'scilla I wish you'd please ma'am let me go an' hire myself out? You can get along with Susan, and I might as well be gittin' some wages and bringin' it to you.' So I told her she could be looking around and if she could find a good home I was willing. A few days afterwards she came and told me that old Mr. Fenne, an old bachelor, wanted her to work for him. She said he had no one to work for him and he was 'liven' like a hog,' but she said she would clean the house up and make things look decent and comfortable, and he offered her good wages, and she thought he would treat her well. She went, and after awhile he wanted to buy Mary of me, and as Mary was willing I sold her, but kept Susan. He gave Mary her freedom, and she lived with him as his wife till his death —and no wife could have taken better care of him. This went on for some time, till he was taken with a severe illness, and Mr. Fenne sent for a lawyer, who was also a friend. He had a large amount of property for the times, and he wanted a will drawn in Mary's favor. The lawyer remonstrated and asked if he did not want to leave some to his relatives. No! he did not! He had left home when he was a boy, had worked hard and saved, with no help from his relatives. Mary had done more for him than anybody else, and she should have it. She was the only person in the world that cared for him. The lawyer was preparing to obey when Mary entered her protest, 'Look here Old Marse! where that brother o' yourn you tol' me about? Didn't you say he helped you oncet? 'Tain't right for you to give *all* that money to me. What I goin' to do with all that money? Now jist you give *him* some of it, please Sir?' 'Well, all right, Mary, I reckon you're right!' And then she mentioned someone else who had claims on him, and prevailed on him to divide with them also, and it was done as she said. After his death she still had more than enough for herself and her two children (for she had one child by him, named Mary Fenne). She bought her a home in Little Rock, and when Susan and Mary married she built homes for them in her own yard. Mary married Rector, an educated negro, who went to West Point, but failing in his examination, got a place in the Post Office.

"Mary used often to tell me that she had never known a happy day since she came into her property, and that she was happier when she belonged to me than at any other time of her life. She died suddenly, of heart disease, one day, in going from a neighbor's home to her own. I was sent for, but found she was past help.

"Before I stop to-night I want to tell you of another instance of the fidelity of our slaves—one owned by my dear mother, who called himself Joe Buckner. She bought him in Kentucky, after my father's death, and after her death he became the property of my sister Josephine. My health being bad, Mr. Reardon thought a change would do me good, and we went together to Annapolis to see my brother Perry, then stationed there. On leaving home my last charge was 'Joe, take good care of Miss Josephine and the children!' 'I'll take *good* keer of 'em Miss 'Scilla sho!' And he did till unfortunately poor Joe got into a fight with another darky and was struck on the head with a hoe. He was sick for several days, and sister called in our family physician. While she was talking with him Joe became suddenly and violently insane. His screams were so loud and terrifying that it was not long before at least a hundred people were gathered in the yard. My sister and children fled in terror to a neighbor's house, and Joe was put into a straight-jacket and confined. A few days afterward Mr. Reardon and I returned home. Somehow Joe managed to make his escape after he had quieted down, and came straightway home, and for a long time we were kept in a constant state of fear and anxiety about him. But at length, on sister's marriage to Mr. Clements of Maryland, her husband sold him down the river. Though Joe seemed to have recovered and only had occasional spells, he always made his way home after them; he said he wouldn't be contented any other place. It was during the Civil War, and after Joe had been gone a long time, and the Federal troops had taken possession of our place, one day as we all stood talking I said to the children, 'I wonder if poor Joe is alive! if he is, I'm afraid he will come back to us.' A few minutes later who should enter the gate but Joe, with a big bag of something over his shoulder. He came with a broad grin on his face, and a 'Howdy, Miss 'Scilla!' and set down the bag at my feet. 'Here I is at last!' he said. 'I done heerd dat Mass Lambert was daid, and Miss Josephine too, so I's come home to help you, I is! an' here's some sweet-taters I brought yer!' So he staid, and all that winter he chopped my wood and made my fires, and did not want me to pay him a cent. He worked in the hospital the rest of the time. When the war was ended, Joe got his back pay to the amount of several hundred dollars. He brought it straight to me and wanted me to accept it. 'No, Joe,' I said, ' I can't take your money, you have earned it and you must keep it yourself.' 'Well Miss 'Scilla, if I was to *die* an' *leave* it to ye, would ye be too proud to take it *then?*' I replied 'No Joe, of course not, but I think you'll *need it all.*' Not long after that Joe bade us good-bye and left town with a white man, and we never saw him again. We always believed he had been murdered for his money. Poor Joe, so good hearted and loyal to our family; he deserved a better fate.

The Genealogical Line of Thomas Buckner*

I. JOHN BUCKNER, the immigrant, Essex Co., 1667.

II. RICHARD BUCKNER, son of above, Clerk of Essex Co., 1703; afterwards of Caroline Co.; married Elizabeth Cooke. Richard Buckner's will was proved March 4, 1733. Issue:
1. Richard, of Caroline Co.
2. William, of "The Neck," Caroline Co.
3. Philip.
4. Elizabeth.
5. John.

III. The Philip above named, date of whose birth is unknown, lived in Louisa Co., where his will was proved in 1762. He married Jane, sister of John Aylette of King William Co., by whom he had issue seven children, viz.:
1. William, of whom presently.
2. Ann.
3. Thomas.
4. Mary.
5. Philip.
6. Elizabeth.
7. Aylett.

In the records of Louisa Co., there is a deed dated Oct., 1767, from Jane Buckner of Orange Co., to William Hughes of Louisa, conveying part of a tract of land formerly belonging to Mr. John Aylett of King William Co., and by him left to the said Jane Buckner, his sister.

The will of Philip Buckner is dated July 14, 1761, and is proved in Louisa Co., Aug. 10, 1762. In it he mentions his wife Jane; son William, to whom he leaves land in Orange Co.;

---

* EDITORIAL NOTE.—According to family tradition, Thomas Buckner belonged to Spottsylvania Co. His father's name was William, and his grandfather's Philip. A careful examination of the records of Gloucester, Essex, Louisa and Orange counties enables us to carry the pedigree back to the original immigrant, John Buckner. The oft-recurring names of Thomas and William are apt to be confusing, but the recorded evidence, combined with family tradition, shows the line of descent to be as above.

JOHN BUCKNER'S SURVEY—1765

daughter Ann; son Thomas; daughter Mary; son Philip; daughter Elizabeth; son Aylett.

From the above will, it is probable that the names of the children are given in the order of their birth. There is also no doubt but that William was the eldest child. In confirmation of this supposition, we turn to a deed of conveyance, which is in Deed Book 14, of the Orange Co. records:

"27 June, 1765. Jane Buckner (late Jane Robinson), to her "eldest son and heir-at-law, William Buckner. Whereas, sd. "Jane Buckner, while sole being possessed in her own right of "sundry negro slaves, together with Christopher Robinson, after-"wards her husband, did make a certain deed of trust dated 28 "Feby. 1740, whereby sd. Christopher and sd. Jane did convey "the sd. slaves to Ann Aylett of King William Co., in trust for "the sd. Jane (in case she survived the sd. Christopher) during her "life, and after her death, in trust to and for the heirs lawfully "begotten of the body of the sd. Jane forever, and whereas the sd. "Jane having survived the sd. Christopher and intermarried with "Philip Buckner, by whom she hath issue the said William "Buckner, her eldest son and heir-at-law, who is now of the age "of 21 years and married, conveyance of sd. negro slaves, etc., etc."

Here we have evidence that William was the eldest child of Philip and Jane Buckner, and as William was of the age of 21 years in 1765, he must have been born about the year 1744. William's brother Philip was born in 1753, and from the latter is descended General Simon Bolivar Buckner of Kentucky.

Tradition has it, that Thomas Buckner's father (ancestor of Mrs. Tuley) was named William, and that the latter's parents were Philip and Jane Buckner. The before-mentioned Philip and Jane Buckner are the only ones found bearing those Christian names who were living at that time. The family tradition states William to have been of Spottsylvania Co. The records of the latter county contain but two references to William Buckner. He was a witness to a deed in 1769, and again in 1775. In 1789 Thomas Buckner of Spottsylvania Co., is mentioned as one of the executors of the will of Francis Purvis. This Thomas, born 1765 or '66, may have been the son of William Buckner.

William Buckner of Orange and Spottsylvania counties married Sally Thomas, a daughter of Edmund, Jr., and Sally (Pendleton), Thomas. Both the Pendleton and Thomas families were very prominent in the above-named counties. In 1767 Sarah Buckner was witness to a deed in Spottsylvania, and it is extremely probable that she was then the wife of William Buckner, as the eldest child of the latter was born about 1765.

There is a deed in the Spottsylvania records dated Dec., 1739, in which "Joseph Thomas, Gent., and Sarah his wife convey to Zachary Lewis part of a tract of land in Spotts. Co., which was granted by patent 16 June, 1727, to Rowland Thomas, father of said Joseph."

No evidence has been found as to the parentage of Hannah Burton, wife of Thomas Buckner. The only record of Burton in the Spottsylvania records is of one Thomas, who was witness to a deed in 1730. It is possible he may have been the father of the above-named Hannah.

The line of descent of Thomas Buckner as prepared by Mrs. Tuley is given below, together with certain additions and corrections which have been forwarded by members of the family since Mrs. Tuley's record appeared in print.

This is the Thomas Buckner pedigree as far as known to his grandchildren. Mrs. Unetta Childs of Frankfort, daughter of Thos. Buckner's sister, Sally Buckner, who married Mr. Sutton, gives this account obtained from her mother, long deceased. In Spottsylvania Co., Va., Wm. Buckner married a Miss Sally Thomas; her mother's maiden name was Sally Pendleton, who married Edmund Thomas, Jr., son of an eminent lawyer, Edmund Thomas, Sr. This Wm. Buckner was the father of Thomas Buckner. Mrs. Unetta Child's record is as follows:

WM. BUCKNER married Sally Thomas. Issue 10 children:
- Thomas Buckner, born about 1765 or '66, married Hannah Burton, 1787; died 1827.
- Wm. Buckner, Junior, "went to Nashville."
- George.
- Robert.
- John, "died in Bolivia Expedition."
- Ambrose.
- Betsy, married Mr. Grant.
- Sally, married Wm. Sutton, who lived in Shelbyville, Ky., and died there.
- Kate Buckner.
- Fanny Buckner, married Henderson.

Of these brothers and sisters of Thomas Buckner who were born, and presumably raised in Spottsylvania Co., Va., we know nothing, except in the case of his sisters: Betsy, married to Mr. Grant; and Sally, married to Mr. Sutton; Fanny married a Henderson, and the fact that the brother next to Thomas "went to Nashville." He probably emigrated to Kentucky with his brother Thomas, then went farther south to Tennessee. There is a Mr. Matt Buckner living in Nashville now, with his son, Dr. Matt Buckner, who may be descendants of Thomas Buckner's brother William. The following is the record of Thomas Buckner's children, obtained from Mrs. Adelaide Defrees of South Bend, Indiana, who had it from her mother, Louisa Buckner, one of the youngest daughters of Thomas Buckner, who married Mr. Jesse Hughes of Tennessee. If the date of the emigration to Kentucky is correct, 1795, the five eldest children of Thomas Buckner must have been born in Virginia, and the rest in Jefferson County, Kentucky. This is Mrs. Defrees' record of the names and order in which Thomas Buckner's children were born. The dates of births of a few being known, together with the date of marriage of Thomas and Hannah Buckner, the date of birth of the other children is completed by allowing one and a half years between each child, as tradition asserts.

SECOND GENERATION FROM WM. BUCKNER AND SALLY THOMAS.

THOMAS BUCKNER, born 1766; married Hannah Burton, 1787; died 1827. Issue:

    William, born 1788; married Nancy Bridges; two children, Emily and Leander Buckner.

    Ambrose, born 1790; died a young man.

    Katy, born 1791; died early.

    Robert, born 1792; married twice. Thomas, son of first, died unmarried; Malinda, child of second married—?

    Malinda, born 1794; married twice; first Bridges, second Crockett. No issue.

    Hiram, born 1795; died unmarried.

    Simeon, born 1797; married *Nancy W. Buckner; died 1843. Issue: Priscilla, Perry and Josephine Preston.

BENJAMIN, born 1798; married Cordelia Sutton; one child, Mary Ellen.

MILTON, born Feb. 22, 1803, in Jefferson Co., Ky., died 1853, in Knox Co., Mo., married three times, (1) Amanda Dimmet. Issue:

    1. William Thomas, born June 17, 1825; died June, 1831.

    2. Mildred Ann, born Dec. 30, 1826; died June 27, 1905; married Judge Samuel Taylor Glover, June 28, 1842, at Knox Co., Mo.,. Judge Glover was born March 13, 1813; died Jan. 22, 1884. Issue:

---

* Nancy W. Buckner was a daughter of Philip and Elizabeth Watson Buckner of Va. and afterwards of Hart Co., Ky.

Fanny D., born Oct. 17, 1847.
Samuel Taylor, born March 11, 1850; died June 6, 1855.
John Milton, born June 23, 1852.
Joseph Albert, born May 29, 1855.
James L., born Feb. 24, 1857; died Dec. 19, 1896.
Mildred B., born March 11, 1858; married (1) Prosser Ray; (2) R. H. Ken.
Betty Moore, born July 11, 1859; died Dec. 22, 1884.
William P., born April 26, 1861; died Aug. 4, 1861.
Robert Griffith, born Jan. 9, 1864.

FANNY D. GLOVER, eldest child of Mildred Ann and Samuel T. Glover; married June 12, 1873, James Clark Way of St. Louis, who was born Aug. 27, 1845. Issue:

Samuel G., born April 13, 1874.
Mildred G., born Aug. 7, 1875.
Clark Harrison, born Dec. 12, 1876.
Betty G., born Nov. 10, 1885.

3. James Milton Buckner, born Dec. 22, 1828; died June, 1834.
4. Luminous Buckner, born April 2, 1830; died May 26, 1898.
5. Eliphalet F. Buckner, born March 27, 1832; died July, 1832.

MILTON BUCKNER, married (2) Juliet Puryear. Issue:

William, died.
Robert, died.
Juliet, died.

MILTON BUCKNER'S issue by third wife, Mrs. Johnson:

Dora.
Milton.
Saml. Glover.
Mary.
Amanda.

SECOND GENERATION FROM WM. BUCKNER AND SALLY THOMAS.

PRISCILLA PENDLETON, born 1803; married twice; first Coatney Melmouth Tuley. Issue, Virginia; second, Murray Floyd Tuley; third, Theodore, and fourth, Isadore twins (died 1886); married second Col. Richard J. Hamilton. No issue.

EMILY, born 1804, married Messina Fontaine; died 1834. Issue, Martha; married Jones; three children.

ELIZA, born 1806, married Francis Henry Edmondson; six children, four died. Katherine E., married Murray F. Tuley, living; Louisa E., married Wilson; died 1898, left three children—Murray, Harry E., Kate M.

ADELINE, born 1807; married Foster; died 1834.

THOMAS, born 1809; died unmarried.

ELIPHALET, born 1810; married; one child, Betty; married De Gress of Texas.

VIRGINIA, born 1812; died young.

MARY LOUISA, born Jan. 29, 1814; died Oct. 22, 1888; married Jesse Hamilton Hughes, born April 14, 1807, at Robertson Co., Tenn.; died 1856. Issue:

1. Geo. Buckner Hughes, born Aug. 3, 1836; died March 4, 1843.
2. Amelia Eliza Hughes, born April 27, 1838; died 1863.
3. Virginia Adelaide Hughes, born May 13, 1842.
4. Richard Dallas Hughes, born Aug. 16, 1843; died same day.

EDMUND GARNETT BUCKNER

5. George Richard Dallas Hughes, of Jeffersonville, Ind., born Nov. 3, 1846; married April 11, 1872, Elizabeth C. Rose, born Dec. 23, 1855. Issue:
   1. Lola Amelia, born Feb. 7, 1873; married Joseph Ewing, July 28, 1897.
   2. Adelaide Virginia, born Aug. 20, 1875.
   3. Anne E., born June 4, 1877; married July 15, 1895, John B. Field, of St. Louis.
   4. Clara Louisa, born Nov. 5, 1880; died Jan., 1886.
   5. Jennie Priscilla, born July 7, 1885.
   6. Joe Ewing McDonald, born July 28, 1883.
   7. Charles Richard Thomas, born April 2, 1888.
   8. Donald Buckner, born April 11, 1891; died in infancy.
   9. Georgie Marie, born June 17, 1893; died in infancy.
   10. Edgar Hunter, born March 8, 1896.
   11. Mabel Lee, born May 16, 1899.

VIRGINIA ADELAIDE HUGHES, born May 13, 1842; died Oct., 1904; married March 11, 1868, Archibald De Frees, born July 13, 1835, of So. Bend, Ind. Issue:
   1. Lola Amelia, born Aug. 10, 1869.
   2. Jane L., born Nov. 26, 1871; married Oct. 4, 1899, John C. Birdsell, born June 23, 1859, of So. Bend, Ind., and have issue.
   3. John C. Birdsell, Jr., born July 15, 1900.

HELENA BUCKNER, born 1816, married first, Clark; second, Hoard; one child, Helena Hoard, married.

THIRD GENERATION FROM WM. BUCKNER AND SALLY THOMAS.

EMILY (daughter of Wm. Buckner), married Wm. Granger; died about 1879. Issue:
   1. Sarah, married —— Mandeville, Louisville, Ky.
   2. Kate A., married Dr. Octerlong, President of Louisville Medical College; died 1899.
   3. Andrew F.
   4. Walter C.
   5. Albert H.
   6. Charles F., married Jennie Cooke. Has been twice Mayor of Louisville.
   7. Ida M., married —— Parsons; died shortly after her marriage.
   8. Mary M., married —— Anderson, and has issue.
   9. Joseph M., married Miss Smith.
   10. Jane F., married —— Wilthite.

LEANDER BUCKNER, son of Wm. Buckner, married Miss Amanthus Shipp. Issue:
   Ewell E. Buckner, married Miss McDearmon; lives in St. Louis, Mo.
   Edmund Garnett Buckner, married Miss Mary Murdock, of Owensboro, Ky., has been cashier and executive head of National Deposit Bank for twenty-four years. Has lately accepted the position of President of the Marsden Manufacturing Co., with headquarters in Philadelphia, at a large salary. A great tribute to his energy, integrity and business ability. Has one living child, Louisa Ewing Buckner.

SIMEON BUCKNER, born 1797; died 1843; son of Thomas and Hannah (Burton)

Buckner; married Aug. 3, 1820, Nancy Watson Buckner in Kentucky; died 1851. They had :
1. Priscilla Aylett.
2. Wm. Perry.
3. Josephine Preston, born Oct. 14, 1826; married Robert Clement, May 20, 1854.

PRISCILLA AYLETT BUCKNER, born May 6, 1821; married March 7, 1839, in Clark Co., Ark., Lambert Jefferies Reardon, born in Talbot Co., Ind., 1813; died Oct. 24, 1854, and has issue :
1. Simeon Buckner Reardon, born April 12, 1841; died April 25, 1892.
2. Annie Lavinia Reardon, born Nov. 23, 1843; died Feb. 23, 1895; married July 30, 1867, Patrick Raleigh, and had issue six sons.
3. Lambert Walter Reardon, born Feb. 18, 1846; died Nov. 18, 1892.
4. Lallie Reardon, born Sept. 21, 1850; died March 4, 1899; married Oct. 3, 1876, Dr. James A. Dibrell, Dean of Faculty of Arkansas University, Little Rock, and had issue two sons.

WM. PERRY BUCKNER, son of Simeon B., born 1823, United States Navy; married Mary Mezick; died 1869. Issue :
Aylette Buckner, died unmarried 1877, in Chicago.
Joseph Buckner, died.
William Buckner, living.

Perry Buckner entered the Naval Academy in 1841, after spending some years on board different vessels, where he became proficient in navigation; was for nine or more years Professor of Mathematics at Annapolis Navy Yard; was promoted to be Captain, and two months before his death was put on the retired list. He died at Brooklyn Navy Yard 1889, an able officer and a man of high character. His letters, in the possession of his sister, Mrs. Priscilla Reardon, of Little Rock, from South Africa, the Philippines and other places, are racy and trenchant, and full of interesting facts about the country and people, showing that he was a keen and intelligent observer.

MILDRED, daughter of Milton Buckner, married Samuel T. Glover. Issue :
Fanny D. Glover, married Clark Way of St. Louis. Issue: Glover, Clark, Mildred, Betty, all living.
Samuel Glover, died young.
John Milton Glover, Attorney-at-law.
Joseph Albert Glover, Bloomfield, Mo.
James Lawrence Glover, born 1857; died 1898.
Mildred Buckner, born 1857, married first Prosser Ray. Issue: Prosser, Sam Glover ; second, Robert Kern, Attorney-at-law.
Betty Moore Glover, born July, 1859; died 1884.
Wm. Pike Glover, born 1861; died 1861.
Robert Griffith Glover of Bloomfield, Mo., born 1864; married Marion Rhodes, daughter of the Rev. Dr. Rhodes. Issue : Clara, Mildred.

I cannot refrain from a few words here in regard to the husband of my cousin, Mrs. Glover, herself a woman of strong char-

JUDGE MURRAY F. TULEY

acteristics. She was helpmeet to such a man as one may not meet once in a lifetime; like a Damascus blade—fine, strong, keen, incisive, supple; only one of his own type and level could describe and interpret him. From his well stored mind treasures of knowledge poured forth in conversation with unfailing memory, and one left his presence enriched and stimulated to new and higher thought. Never ponderous or tiring, but flashes of humor and drollery made him irresistibly charming. True and tender as husband and father was he; loyal, upright, good and kind. As a lawyer he was recognized as one of the greatest in Missouri, if not in the entire West. He died January, 1884, and we shall not see his like again. Mrs. Glover died June 27, 1905.

VIRGINIA, daughter of Priscilla (Buckner) Tuley, married Carlton Holland of Milwaukee, Wisconsin. Issue:
    Dora Holland, died young.
    Kate Holland, married James Egan, attorney and judge. Issue: two boys, Floyd Carlton and Frank Egan.
    Helen Irene, married Edward Mawson, of New York City.
    Isadore and Theodore, twins (children of Priscilla Buckner-Tuley), Isadore married Clark; died 1900, no issue; Theodore married ———, died 1901.

MURRAY FLOYD, son of Mrs. Priscilla Pendleton-Tuley (*née* Buckner), married Katherine Edmondson, his cousin on Buckner side. No issue.

Murray F. Tuley, born in Louisville, Kentucky, 1827, came to Chicago 1843; admitted to the bar 1847; same year went as Lieutenant of Fifth Regiment of Illinois Volunteers to Mexican War; resigned on treaty of peace 1848; remained in Santa Fé to practice law; became Attorney General of Territory in 1849 and 1850; member of the territorial legislature in 1851 and 1852; returned to Chicago in 1854; was Corporation Counsel in Chicago from 1869 to 1873; member of the City Council 1878; elected Judge of Circuit Court 1879, and has now served on the bench for over twenty-two years. Has refused nomination for State Supreme bench; has twice refused appointment on Appellate bench; and three times refused to run for Mayor under strong party pressure. Is a Democrat and is known far and wide as one of the ablest Chancellors on the bench. He is called "the Great Chancellor" and "the Grand Old Man of Chicago." [EDITOR'S NOTE: Judge Tuley died in 1906.]

MARTHA A., daughter of Emily (Buckner) Fontaine, widow of Albert Jones of South Bend, Indiana. Issue:
    Emma Jones, married Simon Lantz, Lansing, Michigan. Issue: Florence Lantz.

Fontaine Jones, married —— Attorney-at-law, Rosedale, Mississippi; several children.

Alberta Jones, Principal of a South Bend public school; died March, 1904.

A few descendants of Benjamin Buckner's daughter, Mary Ellen Ferguson, live at Independence and Kansas City. She had two daughters and a son. The eldest daughter married Mr. Bryan, the Principal of a Ladies' Seminary, and they have a married daughter, Mrs. Georgean, living at Kansas City.

THOMAS BUCKNER'S SISTER'S FAMILY.

SALLY BUCKNER, married Wm. Sutton, of Shelbyville, Kentucky. Issue: eleven children;

Demetrius, married Caroline Grant.
Paulina Virginia, married, first, McWilliam; second, Hardin.
Pendleton Lane, no issue.
Cordelia Frances, married Benjamin Buckner, son of Thomas Buckner.
Ellen Jane, married Alvin Lightburn.
Sarah Elizabeth, married Richard P. Lightburn.
James Monroe, married three times, first Margaret Patterson.
Temperance Reubena, married Thos. B. Caldwell.
Willamette, married Wm. Ready.
Unetta Smith, married Walter Carr Childs, now of Frankfort, Kentucky.
Juliet, married Dr. Wm. Norton.

SISTER OF THOMAS BUCKNER AND SALLIE [BUCKNER] SUTTON.

BETSY BUCKNER, married Grant. Issue:

Caroline Grant, married Demetrius Sutton, cousins, son of her Aunt Sally Sutton.
Bernard Grant, died.
Oscar Grant, died.

SECOND SUTTON GENERATION.

DEMETRIUS SUTTON, married Caroline Grant. Issue:

William, died.
Ruth Ellen.
Henry.
Juliet.
John.
Elizabeth.
Mary, married a Todd.
Philip.

CORDELIA FRANCES SUTTON, married Benjamin Buckner, first cousins. Issue:

Mary Ellen Buckner, married Ferguson of Montana, three children; Maggy, eldest, married Mr. Bryan, Principal of Young Ladies' Seminary, Independence, Missouri.

LAKE FARM—FORMERLY THE RESIDENCE OF
THOMAS AND LUCY (FITZHUGH) BUCKNER

SARAH ELIZABETH SUTTON, married Richard P. Lightburn, of Louisville.
Issue:
    Anna T. Lightburn, married, first, Mr. Peters; second, Wm. S. Caldwell, first cousins.
    Richard P. Lightburn, married, first, Lute Speed; two children: Dick and Mamie; second, Sallie Speed. No issue.

(NEPHEW OF THOMAS BUCKNER.) SECOND GENERATION OF SUTTONS.

JAMES MONROE SUTTON, married, first, Margaret T. Patterson.

(NIECE OF THOMAS BUCKNER)

TEMPERANCE REUBENA SUTTON, married Thomas B. Caldwell. Issue:
    Wm. S. Caldwell, married Anna T. Lightburn, of Louisville.
    Mary, married Geo. B. Macklin.
    Monroe, married Anna Ferguson.
    Nettie, married Jno. R. Boyd.
    George, married Rebecca Glascock.
    Sally, married Wm. Harbison.
    Ellen, married Jas. Gray.
    Ben, married Laura Hardin.
WILLAMETTE SUTTON, married Wm. Ready. Issue:
    Wm. Ready, Jr.

(NIECE OF THOMAS BUCKNER.)

UNETTA S. SUTTON, married Walter Carr Childs. Issue:
    Sally, married John L. Scott.
    Richard, married Sally Sanders.
    Edward, married Lizzie Waterman.
    Louisa, married Sam'l Thomas.
    Ellen.
    William, died in infancy.
    Emily.
    Walter.
JULIET SUTTON, Married Dr. Wm. Morton. Issue:
    Wm. Morton, married.
    Sallie Morton, married Mr. Greenup Bird.
    Emma.
    Mary Morton married Sandusky.
    Fanny, married Thomasson.
    Netty.
    Ella.

    To you of the rising generation of our family I wish to say that you come of a good, sound stock, not titled or particularly brilliant perhaps, but so far as I can learn they have for the most part belonged to that sturdy middle class which is always and everywhere the backbone of the social system and the bulwark of national greatness. See that you keep the name clean, and make it revered. A few Buckners have distinguished themselves here and there, and there are doubtless those who have disgraced their kin, but on the whole they have been a self-respecting and honest people, with proper pride of character, which would not let them do a mean thing, doing their duty in the station to which they are called as private citizens or public officials, for

> "How e'er it be it seems to me
> 'Tis only *noble* to be *good;*
> Kind hearts are more than coronets
> And simple faith than Norman blood."

One of your kin,

KATHERINE EDMONDSON TULEY.

Thomas Buckner of Caroline County

THOMAS BUCKNER, son of Philip and Jane (Aylett) Buckner of Louisa County, resided in Caroline County. His wife's name is unknown to his descendants, and only the name of one of his children can be definitely determined, namely Thomas Buckner, who was born July 26, 1771.

Thomas Buckner (2d) resided at "Lake Farm," Caroline County, He married Sept. 2, 1800, Lucy Fitzhugh, born Feb. 1, 1781, a daughter of Henry Fitzhugh of "Bell Air," born Feb. 9, 1747, and Elizabeth, widow of Henry Fitzhugh of "Fitzhughburg," who was a daughter of Colonel Dudley Stith of Brunswick County, her mother being Elizabeth, daughter of William Buckner of York County, who was a son of the first John Buckner. Thomas and Lucy Buckner had issue:

I. William Henry Buckner born July 8, 1801, in Caroline County, and died in Lauderdale County, Tenn. He married in Caroline County in 1833, Maria Madison, born June 14, 1811. Issue:
  1. John Archer Buckner, born May 27, 1834.
  2. Maria Louisa Buckner, born Jan. 12, 1836.
  3. Jane White Buckner, born Nov. 17, 1837.
  4. Mary Madison Buckner, born April 5, 1839; married May—, 1830, to John M. Sapp of Arp, Tenn., who died March 9, 1897, leaving issue:
    A. Bessie Sapp, born March 3, 1871; married 1888 to Edwin Thornley.
    B. Lucy Sapp, born 1876.
    C. C. J. Sapp, born 1879.
  5. William H. Buckner, born Sept. 8, 1842.
  6. Benjamin A. Buckner, born Oct. 28, 1844.
  7. Lucy Fitzhugh Buckner, born July 17, 1846; died 1900.
  8. Ellen Carmichael Buckner, born Dec. 17, 1849.
  9. Eugene Tunstall Buckner, born May 29, 1854.
II. Eliza Stith Buckner, born Nov. 12, 1803; married William Peake of Fredericksburg, afterwards of California, and had issue:
  1. William Buckner Peake.
III. John Bolling Buckner, born April 9, 1806, d. s. p., in Florida.
IV. Jane Richard Buckner, born Nov. 12, 1808; died Jan. 4, 1883; married April 16, 1829, to William I. Dickinson of "Chestnut Valley," Caroline County, who was born Feb. 9, 1801; died March 25, 1874. William I.

was the son of James and Sally Dickinson. James Dickinson died June 1, 1826, and his wife Sept. 20, 1821. Issue:

1. Sarah Elizabeth Dickinson, born March 2, 1830, in Caroline County; married April 26, 1855, at Nottingham, Spottsylvania County, to Charles William Ashby, who died Feb. 15, 1863. Issue:
   A. Lucy Dickinson Ashby, born March 27, 1856, at Alexandria married Nov. 15, 1892, at Fredericksburg, to Charles Carter Carmichael, born Oct. 29, 1839; died March 28, 1905. Issue:
      aa. Mary Spottswood Carmichael, born March 8, 1894.
      bb. Charles Ashby Carmichael, born June 14, 1895.
      cc. Lucy Ashby Carmichael, born Oct. 16, 1897.
   B. Jane Pollock Ashby, born Oct. 6, 1857, at Culpeper; married Jan. 18, 1900, at Fredericksburg, to Henry Burns Coghill of King George Court House; born 1857. Issue:
      aa. William I. Dickinson Coghill, born March 3, 1901.
   C. Mary Louisa Ashby, born July 16, 1859, at Culpeper; married Oct. 26, 1881, at Fredericksburg, to William Henry Camp of Petersburg; born March 23, 1848. Issue:
      aa. Mary Jeffery Camp, born Nov. 15, 1882.
      bb. Ashby Pendleton Camp, born Oct. 5, 1885.
      cc. William Henry Camp, Jr., born Sept. 14, 1889.
      dd. Charles Ashby Camp, born Jan. 13, 1894.
      ee. Harriotte Peltier Camp, born July 12, 1897.
   D. Alice Royall Ashby, born July 1, 1861, at Culpeper; married Jan. 25, 1887, at Fredericksburg, to Lawrence Lloyd Coghill; born Nov. 14, 1859; died July 4, 1901. Issue:
      aa. Elizabeth Ashby Coghill, born May 8, 1889.
2. Louisa Fitzhugh Dickinson, born June 14, 1831; married Calhoun C. Buckner, of Orange Co.
3. Jane Hipkins Dickinson, born March 7, 1834, in Caroline County; married July 19, 1860, at Nottingham, to Thomas Pratt Yerby of "Belle Voir," Spottsylvania Co. Issue:
   A. Alice Dickinson Yerby, born 1861; died May 28, 1882; married Jan. 10, 1882, to Samuel Gordon, Jr.
   B. William Dickinson Yerby, born ——; died June 23, 1889.
   C. Thomas Pratt Yerby, Jr., born July 9, 1864; married (1st) April 19, 1887, at Fredericksburg, to Lucilla Wallace, born Oct. 16, 1862; died July 22, 1895; by whom he had Jennie Dickinson Yerby, born April 3, 1890, and Gordon Wallace Yerby, born Oct. 24, 1892. By second wife, Patsy Gordon, born May 2, 1876; died Feb. 28, 1902, he had issue, Patsy Gordon Yerby, born April 4, 1900.
   D. Lelia Fauntleroy Yerby, born April 23, 1866, at "Belle Voir."
   E. Arthur Bernard Yerby, born Dec. 12, 1867; died Oct. 15, 1891.
4. William Bolling Dickinson, born April 12, 1836, in Caroline County; married (1st) Nov. 24, 1860 in Stafford County, to Margaret Atchison Gray, born April 8, 1839; died Feb. 7, 1863. Issue:
      aa. Margaret Gray Dickinson, born Jan. 25, 1863.
   By (2d) wife, Emma Yerby, born April 23, 1850; died Jan. 5, 1888, William Bolling Dickinson had issue:

WILLIAM I. DICKINSON

  aa. William Bolling Dickinson, Jr., born Oct. 9, 1873; died 1886.
  bb. John Yerby Dickinson, born Dec. 8, 1875, in Caroline County; married June 8, 1898, Anne Mason Dickinson, born July 4, 1874.
  cc. James Cooper Dickinson, born May 5, 1879.
  dd. Carrie May Dickinson, born July 21, 1880; died 1886.
  ee. Emma Yerby Dickinson, born Dec. 4, 1887.
5. James Cooper Dickinson, born Feb. 20, 1838, in Caroline County; married (1st) July 11, 1867, at Fredericksburg, to Anne Mason Smith, born May 11, 1844; died July 25, 1874. Issue:

A. Harriet Mason Dickinson, born Aug. 24, 1868.
B. Thomas Buckner Dickinson, born Oct. 1, 1869.
C. William I. Dickinson, born Nov. 30, 1871.
D. Anne Mason Dickinson, born July 4, 1874. (For marriage see pedigree above).

 James Cooper Dickinson married secondly, Feb. 28, 1883, at "Lessland," in Orange County, Fannie Halsey, born Nov., 1848. Issue:

A. Fannie Halsey Dickinson, born Jan. 6, 1884.
B. Abram Halsey Dickinson, born May 22, 1885.
C. James Morton Dickinson, born Sept. 16, 1889.
6. Caroline May Dickinson, born May 19, 1840, in Caroline County; married May 24, 1866, at "Chestnut Valley," to Charles Bruce Morton, of "Soldiers Rest," Orange County, born Sept. 3, 1835. Issue:

A. William Jackson Morton, born May 8, 1867, at "Soldiers Rest;" married at Fredericksburg, April 11, 1893, to Dora Ashby Moncure, born Aug. 13, 1870, at "Oakenwold," Stafford County. Issue:
  aa. Charles Bruce Morton, Jr., born Jan. 10, 1900, at Tappahannock.
  bb. William Jackson Morton, born Sept. 2, 1901, at Harrisburg.
  cc. Powhatan Moncure Morton, born Dec. 10, 1903, at Alexandria.
7. Lucy Fitzhugh Dickinson, born March 14, 1844, in Caroline County; married at "Chestnut Valley," Oct. 4, 1877, to Charles Herbert Pierson, of Summit, Va., born in Leeds, England, Sept. 19, 1847. Issue:

A. Leonard Forster Pierson, born July 12, 1878.
B. Anne Fitzhugh Pierson, born Dec. 1, 1880.
C. John Bolling Pierson, born Aug. 13, 1882.
D. Victor Randolph Pierson, born April 28, 1884.
8. Alice Johnston Dickinson, born March 14, 1844, in Caroline County; died Aug. 26, 1860.
9. Thomas Buckner Dickinson, born April 8, 1846, in Caroline County; died Sept. 10, 1861.

V. Caroline Matilda Buckner, born July 8, 1811, in Caroline County; married in 1832 to her cousin, William Spence Buckner, who died in 1875, in Audrain County, Missouri. Issue:

 1. Letitia S. Buckner of McCune, Kansas, married —— Leach.

2. Elizabeth Jane Buckner, born Feb. 1, 1843; married March 11, 1873, to John T. Willis of Paris, Ky., born June 17, 1836. Issue:
A. James Morrison Willis, born Dec. 13, 1873; married Sallie B. Taylor. Address Paris, Ky.
B. Lucy Woodford Willis, born 1876; married Steele Marsh of Paris, Ky.
C. John T. Willis, born Sept. 14, 1885, Paris, Ky.

VI. Mary Madison Buckner, born Jan. 23, 1814; married Aaron Thornley, member of an old Georgia family, who moved first to Missouri and afterwards to Tennessee. Issue:
1. Thomas Thornley.
2. Francis Thornley.
3. Allen Thornley.
4. Mary Thornley.
5. Ella Thornley.
6. Lewis Thornley.
7. Edwin Thornley.
8. Charles Thornley.

VII. Frances Fitzhugh Buckner, born June 14, 1816; married Robert Wade, July 4, 1837, of Bourbon County, Ky., and had issue:
1. Ida Wade, married —— Bratton, and had issue three children.
2. John B. Wade.
3. Thomas B. Wade.
4. Robert Wade.
5. Melia Wade, married John Lambert, Dec. 18, 1870, of Centralia, Boone County, Mo. Issue:
A. William B. Lambert.
6. Nannie P. Lambert.

SPRING HILL—HOME OF JOHN WASHINGTON
FIRST HOME OF THOMAS AND LUCY (FITZHUGH) BUCKNER

John Buckner of Caroline County

JOHN BUCKNER, third of that name, was a son of Richard and Elizabeth Cooke Buckner. His wife's name was Sarah, and she is believed to have been a Buckner before her marriage. We know, positively, that the above John and Sarah Buckner had a son Philip, and there is a tradition that they had other children. It has been impossible, however, to find any trace of them; neither can anything be ascertained regarding John Buckner and his wife, owing to the destruction of the court records.

Philip Buckner of Kentucky

Philip Buckner was born in Caroline County, Va., on May 13th, 1747. Early in life, being fond of travel and adventure, he engaged in commercial pursuits and frequently crossed the Atlantic to England, the home of his ancestors. The scraps of history and anecdote concerning his life in England that have been handed down in the family have led some persons to suppose that he was the immigrant ancestor, but such is not the fact. On Sept. 9th, 1772, he married Tabitha Ann Daniel, the daughter of Captain William and Elizabeth Daniel, of Port Royal, Caroline County, a lady of culture and of fine family.

During the Revolutionary War, Captain Buckner's patriotism was unswerving, and he expended his energies and his private fortune in the cause of Virginia. He held the position of Commissary, and in payment for the supplies which he furnished the army from his own means, he received numerous Land Office Treasury Warrants from the Commonwealth of Virginia, which was then poor in money but rich in prospective lands.

By virtue of these Warrants he obtained, at different periods, large grants of Kentucky and Ohio lands, consisting of many thousands of acres. One grant alone was for seven thousand acres situated in what is now Fayette County, Ky., and which at that time included a vast territory.

It will be remembered that at the close of the Revolution Kentucky was a part of Virginia, and known as Kentucky County. It was provided that lands to satisfy the Warrants issued should be located in Kentucky County, and when suitable lands were no longer available there, they could be located on the north of the Ohio River between the Sciota and Big Miami rivers.

Captain Buckner made his first visit to Kentucky in 1783, and at least one more trip prior to 1793, in which year he brought out his family and servants, forty negroes, and a party of his neighbors. He had located a large tract on the South bank of the Ohio, the site of the present city of Augusta. He had originally selected this land for a home when the party was traveling down the Ohio in keel boats, and it was his intention to land at this point; but finding that the Indians were giving trouble, Captain Buckner continued on down the river to Bear Grass Station, then a frontier military post, and now the site of the city of Louisville, Ky.

Leaving his family there in safe quarters, he returned to Virginia and inducing other families to enter into the expedition, he piloted them down the river, and they, with others who rapidly followed, established a colony at Augusta; and soon the cabins of civilization sprang up in place of the Indian wigwam. The colony having in due course become a safe place of habitation, Captain Buckner removed his family to his own land.

His services were also demanded at Fort Washington, now Cincinnati, Ohio, and through this post of duty he received a large grant of land in Ohio.

Being an enterprising business man and equipped with these Treasury Warrants from Virginia his transactions in land were extensive; and through various manipulations, as shown by land office records in Virginia, and in Frankfort, Maysville, Lexington and Brooksville, Kentucky, and also in Ohio, he acquired enormous possessions of land.

In 1795 he built for his family the first brick house in the town of Augusta, the foundation of which has now disappeared. On the 2d day of October, 1797, Captain Buckner gave six hundred acres of land to the town of Augusta and vested the title in Trustees appointed by the County Court, thus founding the present city of Augusta.

A portion of the plot being divided into city lots and sold at auction, the proceeds of which were to be devoted to the improve-

"MARENGO"
THE HOME OF THE LATE JAMES C. DICKINSON

ment of the site, Captain Buckner purchased a large proportion of them, and thus again acquired possession of a part of the city which he again donated at different times to public institutions— one being the College Lot, where the present magnificent school building stands; another, the old Court House lot, which is now the city park.

The officers of the first court held in Bracken County were his sons-in-law; John Blanchard, Judge; Willis Hord, Clerk; John Pickett, Attorney and Dickinson Morris, Sheriff.

Captain Buckner represented the County of Bracken as Representative, in which capacity he served for two terms, and as Senator for four years. Among the names appended to the second Constitution of Kentucky, adopted 1799, is that of Philip Buckner.

In 1799 the General Assembly of Kentucky, of which Captain Buckner was a member, donated six thousand acres of land to educational purposes. This land was sold and the proceeds were vested in Trustees who fixed the seat of the institution in Augusta, upon a lot donated by Captain Buckner. By this act the first college in the United States west of the Alleghenies, was located in Augusta.

On the 21st of December, 1821, the Ohio and Kentucky Conference of the Methodist Episcopal Church entered into a contract with the trustees and established "Augusta College," the first college in the world to be established under the care and patronage of the Methodist denomination. From this great school of learning was graduated a host of distinguished men. Thus the public career of Philip Buckner speaks for itself, showing his influence towards the education and development of his fellow men.

That he was a man of originality and courage is self-evident. His philanthropy and generosity are shown by the official records, still preserved in the archives of Bracken and Mason counties, of farms given away to poor men for such considerations as "Fifty cents," "A spotted calf," or "A sorrel colt."

His home was noted far and near for its hospitality. It was a place of feasting for his friends and neighbors, and a harbor of refuge for the poor and needy. Simon Kenton was a frequent and welcome visitor, and on one occasion was there nursed through a serious illness.

As Captain Buckner grew older his love of retirement asserted itself. He wanted more space in which to live, to hunt and fish and follow the chase, and, still having the pioneer spirit, he went fourteen miles into the wilderness, where he built another home.

For years it was a great hunting seat, where game was plentiful and sport fine. Many anecdotes have been handed down of the quaint humor and entertaining wit of this eccentric old gentleman.

On the day preceding his death, feeling the premonition of its approach, he ordered a feast prepared for his friends, according to his old custom. At its close, in bidding them farewell, he told them to go to their homes and he, too, would go to his last resting place.

Heroically and calmly he fell asleep that night, and true to his word passed into the great "Beyond." His death occurred October 24th, 1820. His wife survived him a number of years and died at the home of her daughter, Mrs. William Orr, Sr., near Augusta, Ky., Sept. 19th, 1838. She was born Jan. 15th, 1756.

On the second day of October, 1897, the city of Augusta celebrated its centennial when due honor was paid to its founder, Philip Buckner, "Who," in the words of Governor W. O. Bradley, at that time Governor of Kentucky, and the orator of the day, "had one hundred years before rode his gallant steed over the Virginia hills to the beautiful river and marked the spot forever for his home." Thousands of people assembled for the occasion from far and near, and appropriate addresses were made giving the history of the early settlers; and an Original Centennial Ode was recited by Mrs. Mary Armstrong Bayless, a great granddaughter of Philip Buckner.

Thus after many years a just and merited tribute was paid by a grateful community to the memory of a truly good and great man.

Land Grant to Philip Buckner

EDWARD RANDOLPH, ESQ.,
GOVERNOR OF THE COMMONWEALTH OF VIRGINIA,

TO ALL TO WHOM THESE PRESENTS SHALL CONCERN; GREETING:

KNOW YE, that by virtue and in consideration of seven Land Office Treasury Warrants, numbers 7798, 7797, 7803, 7799, 7800, 7801, 7802, issued the

GRAVE YARD—CHESTNUT VALLEY
WILLIAM I. AND JANE BUCKNER DICKINSON
WERE BURIED HERE

first day of November, 1781, there is granted by the said Commonwealth unto

Philip Buckner

a certain Tract or Parcel of Land, containing SEVEN THOUSAND ACRES by survey bearing date the 30th day of November, 1785, lying in the County of Fayette, on the waters of Locust and also the waters of the North Fork of the Licking joining and bounded as followeth, To Wit: Beginning in S. Taylor's line three miles above his Beginning corner at a black walnut, white hickory and sugar tree thence up Locust creek according to the meanders thereof and binding on the same 480 poles on a reduced line to the head of the creek at a hickory and red oak corner to Wm. Taylor and Benjamin Taylor surveys thence S40 W1280 poles to a black walnut, hoop ash and sugar tree, thence N50 W1160 poles to two hickories and a poplar, thence N60, E1660 poles to the Beginning. With its appurtenances: To Have And To Hold the said Tract or Parcel of Land, with its appurtenances, to the said PHILIP BUCKNER and his heirs forever.

In witness whereof, the said Edward Randolph, Esq., Governor of the Commonwealth of Virginia, hath hereunto set his hand, and caused the lesser Seal of said Commonwealth to be affixed at Richmond on the twentieth day of March, in the year of our Lord, one thousand seven hundred and eighty-eight, and of the Commonwealth the twelfth.

(Signed) E. RANDOLPH.

A copy Teste:
(Sig.) Austin P. Cox, DRLO.,
for John M. Foster, RLO.

Philip and Tabitha Ann Daniel Buckner were the parents of nine children, all of whom grew to maturity, married, and raised families. Their names in order of birth were:

I. Samuel Buckner.
II. Elizabeth Buckner.
III. Polly Buckner.
IV. William Buckner.
V. Fanny Buckner.
VI. Sarah Buckner.
VII. Susan Buckner.
VIII. John Buckner.
IX. Thomas Buckner.

I. SAMUEL, the eldest son, and first child, of Philip and Tabitha Buckner, was born Oct. 25th, 1773; died in 1851. Married Susan Evans, Jan. 2d, 1793. Issue:

1. Coleman Buckner, born May 18th, 1797. Married Lucy Curd (?), July 14th, 1820. They left several children, sons and daughters, living in, or near Louisville, Ky.

II. ELIZABETH BUCKNER, the second child of Philip and Tabitha Ann. Buckner, was born April 29th, 1776; died in 1830. She was married to John Blanchard, January 2d, 1793. The Blanchards moved to Warren County, Mississippi, and died there. Issue:

1. Molly Blanchard.
2. Betsey Jane Blanchard.
3. Tabie Blanchard.
4. Sarah Blanchard.

5. Samuel Philip Blanchard.
6. John Blanchard.
7. Lee Blanchard.
8. Nelson Blanchard.

III. POLLY BUCKNER, the third child and second daughter of Philip and Tabitha Ann Buckner, was born at Port Royal, Va., Feb. 16th, 1778, and was married to Willis Hord, January 2d, 1793. It is interesting to note that on the same day occurred the marriage of her brother Samuel to Susan Evans, and also that of her sister Elizabeth, to John Blanchard. Willis Hord was born April 17th, 1769, in Caroline County, Va. They were married in Bracken County, Ky. Polly Hord died in 1865. In 1816 they removed to a farm on Little Sandy river, Carter County, Ky., at what is still known as "Hord's Ford." This farm is still in the family, the property of Mr. W. T. Hord of Greenup, Ky., and his two brothers.

Willis Hord was the first Clerk of the first Court held in Bracken County. He was a man of influence, strong intellectually and physically. Polly Buckner Hord was a proud, aristocratic woman and lived to be eighty-seven years old, retaining her full faculties till her death. They had ten children, viz.: William, died in infancy; John Taylor, died in infancy; Thomas Todd, Lucy Norrell Taylor, Robert Craddock, Philip Buckner, John Nicholas, Betsey Taylor, Laura Agnes and Polly Willis.

1. Thomas Todd Hord was born Dec. 15th, 1796; died Sept. 11th, 1851; married Clarinda Kibbey, March 16th, 1823, she died Jan. 26th, 1869. He was a successful farmer and trader, and amassed a large fortune. Issue:
    A. Mary Ann Hord, married Dr. A. J. Lansdowne, a Virginian. He was a brilliantly educated man of great wealth. His home, "Luck Enough," near Grayson, Carter County, Ky., was known far and wide for its hospitality. His wife was a woman of marked social qualities, and fit mistress for such an establishment. Issue:
        aa. Lucy Lansdowne, married Louis Goble and had one child, Annie Louise Goble.
        bb. Daisy Lansdowne, married George Osenton. Issue: Blanche, who married H. H. Case; Charles, who married Kate Capella, and Juliet, who married F. O. F. Harbeson and lives in Kansas City, Mo., and the youngest son, Lansdowne Osenton, who married Clara Givens.
        cc. George Lansdowne, married Helen Bayless, daughter of the Rev. John C. Bayless. Issue: Andrew Jackson, Wallace, John C., Geo. Underwood, Rosa, Herman, Mary, Helen, Therese.
        dd. Juliet Lansdowne, a brilliant conversationalist and a charming woman, married Frank Power of Ohio. They now live in Grayson, Ky.
    B. Mildred Lewis Hord, married Dr. Wm. D. Jones of Pennsylvania. She was a woman of agreeable and charming manner. They had two children, Thomas Hord, who married Martha Virgin, and Sallie Mildred, who married John G. Ault of West Virginia.
    C. Moses Pendleton Hord, brother of Mary Ann and Mildred L. Hord, married Mary Frizzell, moved to Flemming County,

"NOTTINGHAM"
FORMERLY OWNED BY WM. I. DICKINSON, NOW THE RESIDENCE OF
HIS SON-IN-LAW, DR. CHARLES BRUCE MORTON

Ky., and died there Feb. 27th, 1871. Their children were Lizzie, Lyde, Sallie, Mildred, Moses.

D. Sarah Thomas Hord, daughter of Thomas Todd Hord, married Lafayette Burroughs, and after his death married Hugh Nelson Richards. She left one son, who died in his youth.

2. Lucy Norrell Taylor, daughter of Polly and Willis Hord, born Aug. 28th, 1798; married Jefferson Bell. Lived first in Jefferson and afterwards in Oldham Counties. Many of her descendants live now in Oldham and Shelby Counties. Children were Mary, Willis, Agnes.

3. Robert Craddock, son of Polly and Willis Hord, born Oct. 15th, 1803; died July 18th, 1848. Married his cousin, Julia Ann Pickett. Lived in Jefferson County, Ky. Their children were Mildred Lewis, Lucy Mary, Hancock Taylor and Robert Craddock, Jr. (See further record under Buckner-Pickett.)

4. Philip Buckner, son of Willis and Polly Hord, was born Dec. 22d, 1804; married Catherine England, and died in Carter County, Ky., April 10th, 1886. Issue:

A. William Taylor Hord.
B. Hebe Susan Hord, married John Z. Duly, of Carter County. Issue: Florence, Jennie, Aurora, John, Schuyler, William.
C. Mary Catherine Hord.

5. John Nicholas, son of Willis and Polly Hord, born Feb. 3d, 1806; married Ann Lewis Beckwith, who was a granddaughter of Councilor Carter of Virginia. John Nicholas died June 26th, 1878. Issue:

A. Lewis Beckwith Hord, died.
B. Mary Willis Hord, died.
C. Bainton Matilda Hord, married Wm. C. Mitchell of Massachusetts, and had issue, Lewis B., William H., both living in Pulaski County, Ky.; Annie, married H. G. VanArsdell; Mary S., married John H. Carter, Jr., and Hebe Hilton. The home of the last three is in Lexington, Ky.
D. Arthur Almerine Hord, died.
E. John Willis Hord, son of John Nicholas, married Edith Spangler of Virginia. They live on the Willis Hord farm in Carter County, Ky.
F. William Thomas Hord, son of John Nicholas, married Margaret Jane Geiger of Boyd County, Ky. He is President of the First National Bank of Greenup, Ky.
G. Frank Joyce Hord, son of John Nicholas Hord.

6. Betsey Taylor Hord, daughter of Willis and Polly Hord, was born Aug. 30th, 1808; married George Roberts of Carter County; had one daughter, Lucy Mary, who married Geo. Vincent.

7. Laura Agnes Hord, daughter of Willis and Polly Hord, was born Nov. 27th, 1810. We have no further record.

8. Polly Willis Hord, daughter of Willis and Polly Hord, was born Jan. 17th, 1814; married (1st) a Mr. England; (2d) James Clark. She had a large family.

IV. WILLIAM BUCKNER, the fourth child, and second son, of Philip and Tabitha Ann Buckner, was born at Port Royal, Caroline County, Va., June 19th,

1780; he was married on June 26th, 1799, to Lucy Mary Taliaferro, the daughter of Capt. Nicholas and Ann Taliaferro. She was born August 6th, 1782. William Buckner died January 27th, 1854, at Georgetown, Ohio.

Nicholas Taliaferro was an officer in the War of the Revolution, and in "The Historical Register of the Officers of the Continental Army," by T. B. Heitman, is mentioned as follows:

"Taliaferro, Nicholas, (Va.) Ensign 10th Virginia 15th August, 1777; 2d Lieutenant, 15th November, 1777; Regiment designated 6th Virginia 14th September, 1778. Taken prisoner at Charleston 12th May, 1780. Exchanged ———. First Lieutenant, 18th February, 1781, and served to the close of the war."

William and Lucy Mary Buckner had five children: Philip Johnson, Ann Whitaker, Nicholas Taliaferro (died young), Jane Champe, and William Thornton Taliaferro. All were born in Bracken County, Ky.

1. Philip Johnson Buckner, was born August 8th, 1800. He was a physician and surgeon of international reputation and commenced his practice in Georgetown, Ohio, where he married, Oct. 8th, 1822, Sophia Hewitt, by birth a Pennsylvanian. He died in Cincinnati at the height of his fame, August 23d, 1853. The children of Philip and Sophia Buckner were Elizabeth Jane, William, Lucy Mary, and Matilda Battaille Marshall.

   A. Elizabeth Jane Buckner married Patrick McGroarty, a native of Ireland, and a scholar and lawyer of renown. Their children were, Charles Neil, Philip Buckner, Stephen Battaille, William Buckner and Alma Letitia.

      aa. Charles Neil McGroarty, married Evangeline Tweed. Issue: Catherine Elizabeth, Lucina Frances, Charles Neil, 2d, Mary Evangeline, Nellie Battaille (deceased), Robert Buckner (deceased), and Stephen Patrick. Home, Washington, D. C.
         1. Lucina Frances McGroarty, married John Franklin Bethune.
         2. Catherine Elizabeth, married Frederick Eickhoff, Denver, Col.
      bb. Philip Buckner, died in infancy.
      cc. Stephen Battaille, died unmarried.
      dd. William Buckner McGroarty, fourth child of Elizabeth and Patrick McGroarty, married Georgiana Fee Pease, daughter of Granville and Fanny Louisa Keeler Pease of Clermont County, Ohio, and had issue, Robert-Ryan, Stephen Buckner (deceased), Kathleen Fee and Alma Georgina. They live in Washington, D. C.
      ee. Alma Letitia McGroarty (deceased), sister of above, only daughter and youngest child, married I. L. Ronsheim. They had one child, a daughter, Tirsa Julia. Home, Middletown, Ohio.
   B. William, the second child of Philip and Sophia Buckner, was also a physician and surgeon; married Charlotte Reed. Their only adult child, Sophia Mary, became the wife of the Rev. Samuel Herbert Boyer and had issue, Herbert Morton, Charlotte Buckner and Francis Buckner. Their home is in Philadelphia.

CHESTNUT VALLEY
W. I. DICKINSON'S OLD HOME

C. Lucy Mary, the third child of Philip and Sophia Buckner, married Dr. Thomas Melancthon Tweed. Their children were Lizzie Jane Buckner, Lewis Taliaferro, Evangeline and Thomas Stanley.
- aa. Lizzie Jane Buckner Tweed, married Rev. John McCurdy Robinson (deceased). Their only living child is a son, James Raymond. Their home is in Denver, Col.
- bb. Evangeline Tweed, married Charles Neil McGroarty. A record of their children is given above.
- cc. Lewis Taliaferro Tweed (deceased), married Louisa Caroline Lewis; their only adult child is a son, Charles Lewis Tweed, who married Mrs. Deen Stafford. They live in Minneapolis.
- dd. Thomas Stanley Tweed, was massacred by the Indians while serving with General Custer, June 25th, 1876. He was unmarried.

D. Matilda Battaille Marshall Buckner, the youngest child of Philip and Sophia Buckner, married Captain Robert Hetrick Higgins (deceased), a nephew of General Thomas Hamer, and himself a soldier of distinction. They live in Georgetown, Ohio. Their children are:
- aa. Henry Buckner Higgins, married Ann Louisa Turner. Issue: Henry Buckner 2d, and Louisa Turner Higgins. Home, Denver, Col.
- bb. Robert Hetrick Higgins 2d, married Laura Alwilda Prescott. Issue: Ruth, Robert Hetrick 3d, Nellie and Howard. Home, St. Louis.
- cc. Laura Battaille Higgins (deceased) married James Richmond Nunnelley. No surviving issue.
- dd. Martha Elizabeth Higgins, married Marion Lee Richards (deceased). Issue: Joseph Percy, Robert William and Henry Buckner. Home, Georgetown, Ohio.
- ee. Beatrice Jane Higgins, married William Hutter. Home, Centralia, Ill.
- ff. Sophia Buckner Higgins, married John Walgamon McTamany. Issue: John Russell (deceased), Beatrice Battaille and Tirsa Doniphan (twins), and Mary Margaret. Home, Georgetown, Ohio.
- gg. William Taliaferro and Ita Blanche, children of Robert H. and Matilda Battaille Marshall Higgins, died young.

2. Ann Whitaker Buckner, second child of William and Lucy M. T. Buckner, was born January 8th, 1803; died in January, 1885. She was married to William Orear Blackerby, October 20th, 1819. Their adult children were: John Marcus, William Buckner, Jeduthan Orear, George Washington, Martin Marshall, Eliza Jane, Philip Nicholas and Franklin Buckner.

A. John Marcus Blackerby, eldest son of above, married Sarah A. Holton and at this writing is still living at Germantown, Ky., past 82 years. He was a physician of note. Issue:
- aa. Kate K. Blackerby, married N. J. Bradford. Issue, one son, Eugene, who married Ida Holmes. Their children are Charles, Alice and Florence. Home, Newport, Ky.

Kate K. married a second time, Alex. P. McClanahan, and had issue, Birdie (deceased), Perrine, Kirby (deceased), and Kathleen.

    bb. Perrine M. Blackerby, son of John Marcus, married Nora ——. Home, Versailes, Ky.

    cc. Clifford L. Blackerby, son of John Marcus, married Mary Peddicord. Home, Paris, Ky.

B. William Buckner Blackerby, second son of Ann W. Blackerby, married Malinda Fishback. Issue, one daughter, Matilda Battaille, who married Geo. K. Cole, and had two children, Wm. C. and Jas. K. Home, Vanceburg, Ky.

C. Jeduthan Orear Blackerby, third son of Ann W. Blackerby, also a successful physician, married Sarah J. Linn. Issue:

    aa. William Orear Blackerby, married Louise Gilmore. Issue: Verna, Ethel, Sydney, Irene, William F., Louise. Home, Brooksville, Ky.

    bb. Clara Blackerby, sister of William Orear, married Jas. H. Barrett, M. D. Issue: Edith (deceased), Ernest. (Ernest married a Miss Dietz). Home, Mt. Auburn, Ky.

    cc. Jeduthan Orear Blackerby, Jr., M. D., married Effie Redden. Issue: Lynn R. and Doris. Home, Montgomery, O.

    dd. Emma L. Blackerby, married Edward Woolfolk. Issue: William Roper and Pearl Buckner. Home, Ashland, Va.

    ee. Julia Blackerby, married U. S. G. Pepper. Issue: Jennie Marie, Christine. Home, Paris, Ky.

    ff. Eb., brother to Julia, married Emma Bay. Issue: Corinne, Roma and Pearl Linn. Home, Los Angeles, Cal.

D. George Washington Blackerby, fourth son of Ann W. and Wm. Orear Blackerby, married Harriet Fishback. Issue, Thornton Taliaferro (deceased).

E. Martin Marshall Blackerby, fifth son, married Elizabeth Pickett. One daughter, Mary O., married L. H. D. Freeman, and had issue: Archie, Susan, Ella, Elizabeth, Lemuel and Corinne. Home, Joplin, Mo.

F. Eliza Jane Blackerby, sixth child of Ann W., married Oliver R. Straube (deceased). Issue: Frank R., J. William, Charles N., Earl P., Ida, Minnie. Live in Indiana.

G. Philip Nicholas Blackerby, seventh child of Ann W., married Carrie B. McDonald. Issue: James F., Robert M., Philip Earl, Mabel J. Home, Berlin, Ky.

H. Franklin Buckner Blackerby, eighth child, married Mary O'Neal. Issue: Anna, James, William F., Cliff L., Thomas O., Battaille, Emma, George P., Leota. Home, Versailes, Ky.

3. Jane Champe Buckner, daughter of William and Lucy Mary T. Buckner, was born Aug. 20th, 1807; died March 21st, 1874. She married William Musgraves Barker, Sept. 10th, 1823. He died Sept. 15th, 1863. Their children were Joseph Nicholas, Lucy Mary Taliaferro, William Buckner, Matilda Charity, Malvina Ann and Eliza Jane.

A. Joseph Nicholas Barker, eldest son of the above, was an eminent lawyer, and for many years a resident of Chicago. He was an authority on Marine Law, and at the time of his death, May 13th, 1902, was in point of years at the Bar the oldest practicing Attorney in Chicago. He married Frances M. Long. Their adult children were:

    aa. Frank William Barker, married Julia Shumway. Issue: Sherman Bouton (deceased), Margery, Joseph Shumway and Ellen Gould. Home, Chicago.

    bb. Josephine Barker, married George Tisdale Williamson (deceased). Issue: Florence Barker, Frances (deceased), Harold Long. Home, Chicago.

    cc. Mary Barker, married Dr. Wm. Noble Hibbard (deceased). Issue: Robert Barker (deceased). Home, Chicago.

B. Lucy Mary Taliaferro Barker (deceased), daughter of Jane C. and Wm. Barker, married Dr. Adamson Bently Newkirk (deceased). Issue:

    aa. Laura Matilda Bentley, married Henry Jacob Shepherd (deceased). Married a second time to Andrew Kinkead Shepherd. Issue, second marriage, Lucy Ethel and Adamson Clare. Home, San Diego, Cal.

    bb. John Naylor Bentley, married Alice Parker. Issue: Juliet Cullum and Lucy Barker. Home, San Diego, Cal.

    cc. Adamson Bently, married Eva May Ingram. Issue: William Bently. Home, Los Angeles, Cal.

    dd. Joseph Thornton Bentley, married Mrs. Mary Elizabeth Robinson Auer. Home, Los Angeles, Cal.

    ee. Jane Champe Bentley, married Charles Edwin Smith. One son, died in infancy. Home, Jerusalem, Palestine.

    ff. Clara Barker Bentley. Home, Los Angeles.

    gg. Malvina Ann Bentley. Home, Los Angeles.

C. William Buckner Barker (deceased), son of Jane C. and Wm. Barker, married (1st) Ellen Stephens; (2d) Mary E. Hurd. No issue. Lived in Higginsport, Ohio.

D. Matilda Charity Barker (deceased), daughter of Jane C. and Wm. Barker.

E. Malvina Ann Barker, daughter of Jane C. and Wm. Barker, died Dec. 15th, 1904.

F. Eliza Jane Barker (deceased), daughter of Jane C. and Wm. Barker, married Dr. James Hollister (deceased). Issue:

    aa. Otis Champe Hollister, M.D., married Katherine Kearney. Issue: Florence Virginia. Home, Portland, Oregon.

    bb. Antoinette Belle Hollister. Residence, Chicago.

    cc. Matilda Grace Hollister, married Joseph H. Smalley. Issue: John Hollister. Home, Chicago.

    dd. Bertram Keats Hollister, married Gertrude Tilford. Issue: Bertram Keats, Jr., and John James. Home, Chicago.

    ee. Effie May Hollister.

4. The fifth and last child of William and Lucy Mary Buckner, was William Thornton Taliaferro, who was born at Augusta, Ky., May 14th, 1813, and died at Farmington, Iowa, January 16th, 1848. He was a physician of note. Married Margaret Newell

Thome of Augusta, Ky., who was born February 9th, 1817, and died May 29th, 1870, at Walnut Row, near Athens, Mo. Issue:
A. Arthur James Buckner, M.D., married Florence Virginia West. Home, Peakesville, Mo. Issue:
   aa. Margaret May Buckner, married Linzy M. Dawson. Home, Stronghurst, Ill.
   bb. William West Buckner, born Feb. 27th, 1872; died Feb. 25th, 1896, both leap years, and was interred on the 24th anniversary of his birth.
   cc. Charlie Thome Buckner.
   dd. Florence Audrey Buckner, married Orval M. Lucas. Issue: Thelma Letta. Home, Peakesville, Mo.
   ee. Arthur James Buckner, Jr. (died in infancy).
   ff. George Verckler Buckner.
B. William Thornton Buckner (died in infancy).
C. Charlie Philip Buckner, M.D., married Mary Elizabeth Pruitt. Issue:
   aa. Margaret Hannah Buckner, married A. W. Harter. Issue. Lola May. Home, Pasadena, Cal.
   bb. Mary Ensley Beaman Buckner, married Mr. Gray Little. Issue: Vera and Ariel. Home, Troy, Texas.
   cc. Hattie May Buckner, married Theodore Lamber. Home, St. Louis, Mo. Several children.
D. William Dalzell Buckner (deceased).
E. George Adams Buckner (deceased).

V. FRANCES (FANNY) BUCKNER, the fifth child of Philip and Tabitha Ann Buckner, was born December 8th, 1782, in Virginia. The date of her death is not known. She married October 23d, 1799, Dickinson Morris, the son of Elijah and Mary Morris, who was born in Delaware, August 8th, 1763. He died October 1st, 1849. Issue: Buckner Stith, Mary (Polly), John P., Elizabeth, Philip Buckner and Susan M.

1. Buckner Stith Morris, first child, was born in Augusta, Ky., Aug. 19th, 1800; died in Chicago, Dec. 16th, 1879. He was married Aug. 21st, 1832, in Mason County, Ky., to Evelina Barker, who was born Aug. 17th, 1809, and died in Chicago, March 15th, 1848. Issue:
A. Malvina C. B. Morris, born Aug. 26th, 1837; died Nov. 6th, 1892; married Nov. 15th, 1855, to Robert H. How. Mr. How died Oct. 13th, 1866. Home, Chicago. Issue:
   aa. Letitia E. How, married Wm. G. Farrar; no issue.
   bb. Buckner Morris How, Robert M. How and Jas C. How, died, infants.
   cc. Juliet Turner How, daughter of Malvina and Robt. H. How, married Daniel B. Hansen. Issue: Mary Louise, Letitia (deceased), Frederick Philip, Daniel Joseph, Jas. Hagan, Joseph Jasper, Malvina Cecelia, Anthony Buckner.
   dd. Fred. J. How, born in Springfield, Ill.; married Eliza Leona Reese, daughter of Jacob P. Reese of Augusta, Ky. Issue: Elizabeth, Ruth. Home, Chicago, Ill.
B. Laura Evelina Buckner, daughter of Buckner S. and Evelina Barker Morris, married Frederick Hudson. One child, died in infancy.

Buckner Stith Morris married, secondly, Eliza G. A. Stevenson of England, Aug. 1st, 1850. They had two children, both died in infancy.

He was married a third time to Mrs. Mary Blackburn Parish of Kentucky, on Nov. 21st, 1855. No issue.

2. Mary (Polly) Morris, second child of Frances Buckner and Dickinson Morris, born Aug. 30th, 1802; died ———. Married May 5th, 1819, in Kentucky, to Amos O. Hanson. Their children were, Avarilla, Fanny Buckner, John, Jay, Sarah Maria and Wm. Amos.

We have no account of any of the children of Polly and Amos Hanson, excepting their daughter, Sarah Maria. She married John Wesley Ross. They had one child, Mary Buckner Ross, (a) who married Jefferson Helm Claypool. Their only child is a son, Benjamin F. Claypool. Home, Indianapolis, Ind.

3. John P. Morris, third child of Frances Buckner Morris, born Sept. 29th, 1805; died ———. Married May 21st, 1827, to Mary Webster. No issue.

John P. Morris married, secondly, Mary McClanahan, and had issue: Champe Taliaferro Morris (P. O. Morris, Bracken County, Ky.), Thornton M. and George Pickett Morris. (Home, DeFuniack, Fla.). Thomas M. (lives in Indiana), Robt. A. Morris (Carntown, Pendleton County, Ky.), Samuel and Minnie (deceased); Minnie married a gentleman named Dix. Have no further account of the descendants of John P.

4. Elizabeth Morris, fourth child of Frances Buckner Morris, born Feb. 13th, 1808; died ———; married Nov. 17th, 1825, in Kentucky, to William Dora. Issue: Penelope, William N. Thomas (Germantown, Ky.), Frances Ann (deceased), Mary Susan, Robert Craddock, Clara E. Isabel (deceased). No further record of the descendants of Elizabeth Morris Dora.

5. Philip Buckner Morris, fifth child of Frances Buckner and Dickinson Morris, born July 12th, 1810; died Jan. 26th, 1884, near Powersville, Ky.; married June 23d, 1842, to Nancy Fishback who was born March 1st, 1821. They were the parents of twelve children.

A. Jas. Henry Morris, eldest child of Philip and Nancy Morris, married Kate Kenton Hart. Issue: Henry Raymond, Frederick Lancing.

B. Nicholas Dickinson Morris, second child of Philip and Nancy Morris, married Sarah Bell, and had issue:

aa. Callie Morris, married Joseph Callahan, and had issue: Bessie, Hayden and Sallie Callahan.

Nicholas D. Morris married, secondly, Sarah Bratton, and had issue:

bb. Lillie May, married Wm. Webb. Issue: Clyde and Thelma Webb.

cc. William N. Morris, son of Nicholas D. and Sarah Morris. Home, Powersville, Ky.

C. Frederick Alexander Morris, third child of Philip and Nancy Morris, born 1846; died 1881.

D. Benjamin Franklin Morris, fourth child, married Jane Jett. Issue: William, Ray, Mary, Henry B. Morris. Home, Catawba, Ky.,

E. George Philip Morris, fifth child of Philip B. Morris, married

Mollie Corwin. Issue: Franklin Corwin, Chas, Philip (deceased). Home, Morgan, Ky.

F. Willis Young Morris (deceased), sixth child of Philip and Nancy Morris, married Fanny Bourbon Hart. Issue: Edna Earl, Nina M. The latter married Joseph Reeves, and has one son, Morris Hart Reeves. Home, Lexington, Ky.

G. Chas. Orr Morris, seventh child of Philip and Nancy Morris, lives in Morgan, Ky.

H. Nelson Morris (deceased).

I. Mary Jane Morris (deceased).

J. Marcus Morris, tenth child of Philip and Nancy, married Emma Craig, and has one child, Nancy. Lives at Morgan, Ky.

K. Martha Ann Morris (deceased).

L. Buckner Stith Morris, last child of Philip and Nancy Morris, is an eminent lawyer of Henderson, Ky. He married Edna Earl Agnew, and had issue: Walter Agnew, Julia How (deceased).

6. The sixth and last child of Frances Buckner and Dickinson Morris, was Susan Morris, born March 30th, 1831, in Kentucky; married Joseph Fishback, who died Aug., 1871. They were married Dec. 15th, 1842. Joseph Fishback was the brother of Philip B. Morris' wife. Susan and Joseph Fishback had issue: Maria Louisa, Laura B. and Philip. Maria Louisa married Adolphus Aulick and lives at Falmouth, Ky. Philip lives in Texas.

VI. SARAH BUCKNER, the sixth child of Philip and Tabitha Ann Buckner, was born April 7th, 1786; died Nov. 25th, 1851; married January 28th, 1801, to Gen. John Pickett, who died March 11th, 1817. They had one child, Julia Ann, who was born April 15th, 1811; died Aug. 21st, 1845.

1. Julia Ann Pickett, as already shown, married her cousin (the son of her Aunt Polly), Robert Craddock Hord. They were married Nov. 28th, 1825. This bride of 14 years had the unique experience of being escorted on her wedding day, by her husband and her mother, to a select boarding school for young ladies where she remained for a year. Julia and Robert Hord had five children, Mildred Lewis, Hancock Taylor, Robert C., Jr., Laura Pickett and Lucy Mary.

A. Mildred Lewis Hord married Edward Gibson Taylor, a cousin. They had seven children, as follows:

aa. Julia Taylor, married Richard Isaacs. Issue: Edward Gibson Isaacs, who married Lulie Monks, and had two children, Edyth and Edward Gibson Isaacs, Jr.

bb. Minnie Louise Isaacs, married Herbert Jackson Stone. No issue.

cc. Nancy Clay Isaacs, married John Alfred Beckley. Issue: Julia Ann, Maud Louise and Richard Isaacs Beckley.

dd. Coates Lane Isaacs.

B. Florence Vane Taylor, married Edward Polk Johnson. Issue: Albert Sidney (deceased), Harry Gibson and Florence Pickett, who married Garnett Zorn of Louisville, Ky.

C. Thomas Pickett Taylor, married Achsah Miller. Issue: Horace A. and Thomas Pickett, Jr.

D. Carroll Granger Taylor, deceased.

E. Harry C. Taylor, married Fanny Melone. Issue, one daughter, the wife of the Rev. A. R. Love of Hendersonville, N. C.
F. Mattie B. Taylor, married Richard T. Collins. Issue: Alfred and Lula.
G. Cora M. Taylor, married Logan Russell. Issue: Lewis, Carroll and Jane.

2. Hancock Taylor Hord, married Mary Eliza Shanks. Issue:
A. Lou Emma Hord, married Parks Avery.
B. Thomas Hord, married Mary Basler.

Hancock Taylor Hord married, secondly, Sarah Sedbolt, by whom he had two children.

C. Amos Hord.
D. Maurice Hord, married Pearl Ehlers of Little Rock, Ark.

3. Robert C. Hord, Jr., married Lucy Able. Issue: George Hord. Married a second time to Mahaley Marcum. No issue.

4. Laura Pickett Hord, married James S. Johnson (brother of Mr. E. Polk Johnson mentioned above). Six children, as follows:
A. Minnie Johnson, married Geo. Sedbolt.
B. Julia Johnson, married Patrick Henry Mussulman. Issue: Johnson Mussulman.
C. Eva Johnson, married Julius Arteburn. Issue: Covington and Shelton Arteburn.
D. Fanny Johnson, married Edward Ragland. Issue. Minnie Ragland.
E. Edward P. Johnson, married Adaline Cassady. Issue: John DeJarnett; married a second time to ———. Issue: Edward P., Jr.
F. Thomas S. Johnson.

5. Lucy Mary Hord, married Dr. Norrell Taylor, of which marriage five children were born, viz.:
A. Melville Francis Taylor.
B. Jennie Taylor, married Fennell Harris. Issue: Lucy, Iloff (a physician), and Maurice (a lawyer).
C. Julia Taylor, married Geo. Dixon. Issue: Robert Dixon, who married Miss Posey; Taylor and Mary Dixon. After Mr. Dixon's death Julia married Mr. Munroe McKinley, and had one child, a daughter, Wille McKinley.
D. Ellen Taylor, married Fred. Alloway. Issue: Nannie and Fred., Jr.
E. Mollie Taylor, married Theodore Denton. Issue, three sons, Harry, George and Chester; and five daughters, Ula, Lena, Jennie, Myrtle and Ellen.

Lucy Mary Hord, after the death of Dr. Taylor, married the Rev. W. W. Cooke, of the Louisville Conference, by whom she had one son, Sevilla Dayton Cooke, now a prominent citizen of Madisonville, Ky. His wife was Emma Hall.

After the death of Gen. Pickett, his widow, Sarah Buckner, married, on May 20th, 1819, Cates B. Mayfield. Two children were born of this marriage, Emily and William Nicholas.

1. Emily Mayfield, married Dr. Catlett Taylor (brother of Dr. Norrell Taylor). Issue: Bettie Sue and Fannie.
A. Betty Sue Taylor, married Hiram Jesse Wallace. Issue: Carroll T., Minnie, Jennie, Jesse and Herbert Francis.

B. Fannie Taylor, married Thos. Alloway. Issue: Murray A., Sue A., Eulah A. and Emma A.

2. William Nicholas Mayfield, born July 4th, 1822; died April 8th, 1903; married January 1st, 1846, to Harriet Newell Bliss, in Louisville, Ky. She was born in Massachusetts, Feb. 25th, 1823, and died January 25th, 1880. They had three children.

A. Helen Maria (died, infant).

B. Wm. Henry Mayfield, a prominent physician of Louisville, born Jan. 25th, 1849; married Jan. 11th, 1882, to Laura Gerstenberger. Issue: Harriet Newell Mayfield, who married T. F. House, Nov. 21st, 1903, and Arthur Paul Mayfield.

C. Virginia Sarah Mayfield, married F. J. Franz.

William Nicholas Mayfield married a second time, on May 5th, 1881, to Mrs. Louisa Kate Hauser. Issue, one son, Samuel Avery.

D. Samuel Avery Mayfield, born May 21st, 1883; married May 21st, 1902, to Bessie O. Morris. Issue: Frank Avery Mayfield. Home, Louisville, Ky.

It has been shown that Julia Ann Pickett Hord died in 1848. Later, Mr. Hord married Mrs. Helena Buckner Clark, daughter and twentieth child of Thomas and Hannah Burton Buckner. By this second marriage Mr. Hord had one child, a daughter, Helena, who married Walker A. Howard.

VII. SUSAN BUCKNER, the seventh child of Philip and Tabitha Ann Buckner, was born March 29th, 1789, and died Nov. 11th, 1852. She married, May 3d, 1808, John Champe Taliaferro, the son of Nicholas and Ann Taliaferro, and brother of the Lucy Mary Taliaferro who was the wife of her brother, William Buckner. Susan and John Champe Taliaferro had two children, Tabitha Ann and John Champe.

1. Tabitha Ann Taliaferro, married Wm. H. Gibbons. Issue: William and Mary Lucy.

A. William Gibbons, married Virginia Morgan. Issue:

aa. William Morgan Gibbons, married Mary McAtee; one child, Elizabeth.

bb. Alice Gibbons, married Matthew Harbison. No issue. Home, Covington, Ky.

B. Mary Lucy Gibbons, daughter of Tabitha Ann Taliaferro, married Louis Philip Knoedler. Issue:

aa. Anna Louise Knoedler, married Frederick Warren McKinney. Issue: Lois, Frederick Knoedler, Mary Buckner, Frances. Home, Chicago.

bb. Philip Knoedler, married Fanny Bentley. Issue: Anna Louise.

cc. Eva Bauer Knoedler, married Augustus Robbins. Issue: Augustus, Mary Bauer and Ada Frazier (twins). Home, Augusta, Ky.

dd. Wm. Gibbons Knoedler, married Eva C. Reynolds. Issue: Mary, Alice Louise. Home, Augusta, Ky.

ee. Louis Stevens Knoedler, married Anna May Stanhope. Issue: Louis Philip. Home, Elgin, Ill.

2. John Champe Taliaferro, the second child of Susan and John Champe Taliaferro, married Adaline Lyles. Issue: James T., and John Champe T., Jr., who died in Texas, June 22d, 1838.

John Champe Taliaferro, Sr., was born Oct. 12th, 1784, and died February

26th, 1811. Susan Buckner married secondly in June, 1820, to Wm. Orr. Lucy Mary, William Wilson and Philip Buckner Orr were the adult children of this second marriage.

 1. Lucy Mary Orr, married Thos. S. Orr of Virginia. There were two children from this marriage, John Stevens and Susan Buckner Orr. The former married, first, Mary Knoedler, second, Julia Mentz. No issue. Susan is unmarried. Their home is in Augusta, Ky. Thos. S. Orr died in June, 1856. Mrs. Lucy Mary Orr married secondly, A. C. Armstrong of Pennsylvania. They had one child, a daughter, Mary Armstrong.

  A. Mary Armstrong, married Dr. Herman Bayless. Issue, one son, Herman Armstrong Bayless. Home, Cincinnati, O.

In this connection it is eminently fitting to record that the descendants of Philip Buckner owe a debt of gratitude to Mrs. Lucy Mary Orr-Armstrong. She was a woman of the highest education and most brilliant mind. Her family pride was great, and her knowledge of family history even greater. For many years she was totally blind, but, to the end, her strong individuality and mental superiority won her the reverence and love and admiration of the Buckner tribe, to its most distant connection.

 2. William Wilson Orr, the second child of Susan Buckner and Wm. Orr, married Amanda Lyons. They had two children, John and Sadie Orr, who died without issue.

 3. Philip Buckner Orr, third child of Susan Buckner and Wm. Orr, married Pamelia Robertson. They had seven children who grew to maturity and died without issue. They had a son, Philip, who married Elizabeth Lyons. Issue, one son, Philip Henry Orr. Home, Dayton, Ohio.

VIII. JOHN BUCKNER, the third son and eighth child of Philip and Tabitha Ann Buckner, was born Dec. 31, 1791, in Port Royal, Caroline County, Va. He was married to Martha Jones Buckner, March 6th, 1817. She was born Dec. 4th, 1795, the daughter of Francis and Martha Upshur Buckner, and the granddaughter of Richard 2d, and Elizabeth Aylett Buckner. John Buckner, her husband, was the grandson of John Buckner 3d, a brother to Richard 2d. John and Richard were the sons of Richard 1st, noted as "The Clerk of Essex," and his wife, Elizabeth Cooke. Richard 1st was the son of John Buckner 1st, the immigrant. Therefore, it is shown that the grandfathers of John Buckner and his wife were brothers. Martha Jones Buckner died August 28th, 1843; John Buckner died March 1st, 1878. Their home was in Hopkinsville, Ky., where many of their descendants reside.

The children of John and Martha Buckner were, Martha Virginia, Susan Frances, Robert William, Mary Elizabeth, Francis Philip, Martha Margaret Berryman Upshur, Octavia Allison, Clementina.

 1. Martha Virginia Buckner, was born Dec. 6th, 1817, and died Aug. 8th, 1897. She married, Oct. 13th, 1835, Clement Stewart of Yazoo, Miss. Married, secondly, to Stephen E. Trice of Hopkinsville, Ky., May 15th, 1845. Issue of second marriage:

  A. John Buckner Trice, married Jeanie Mallary Dagg of Lafayette, Ala. Issue: William Waller, Stephen Edward, Jr. (deceased), Francis Dagg, Rollin Mallary, John Buckner, Jr., Walter Graham, Annie Virginia. Home, Hopkinsville, Ky.

B. Annie Mallory Trice. Home, Hopkinsville.
2. The second child of John and Martha Jones Buckner was Susan Frances Buckner, born Oct. 26th, 1821; died Aug. 6th, 1856; married July 8th, 1846, to Dudley Jeffries: Issue: Martha (deceased), and Francis.
A. Francis Jeffries married Barbara A. Barter of Kerrville, Texas. Issue: Frank Buckner, Walter Burnett, Hazel Lucile (deceased), Grace Darling. Home, San Antonio, Tex.
3. Robert William Buckner, third child of John and Martha Jones Buckner, born Oct. 7th, 1823; died July 19th, 1855; married Dec. 15th, 1846, to Ann M. Ratcliff. She died April 17th, 1857. Their children were Edward M. (deceased); Mary, who married Edwin W. Steger, and has one daughter, Jennie Louise. Home, Beverly, Ky., and Martha, who married Cincinnatus Douglas Bell. Home Hopkinsville, Ky.
4. Mary Elizabeth Buckner, fourth child of John and Martha Jones Buckner, married Wm. Wallace Ware, Nov. 25th, 1846. She was born April 11th, 1826. Issue:
A. James Dudley Ware, married Antonia B. Clardy, and had one child, Antonia C. Ware. Married a second time to Bettie A. Massie, and had issue, Mary E. (deceased), and Bettie Massie Ware. Was married a third time, to Fannie S. Fairleigh, and had issue, Robert Fairleigh and William Wallace Ware, Jr. Home, Hopkinsville, Ky.
B. Martha Julia Ware (deceased).
C. Mary Elizabeth Ware, third child of Mary E. and Wm. W. Ware, married Robert B. Withers, and had issue: Mary E., Robert V. (deceased), John Buckner, Julia W., Bessie B. and James D. Home, Reidsville, N. C.
D. Lelia Parish Ware, fourth child, married M. F. Crenshaw. Issue: Elizabeth, Mary Eliza and Martha Buckner. Home, Hopkinsville, Ky.
5. Francis Philip Buckner, the fifth child of John and Martha Buckner, was born Feb. 11th, 1829. No further record.
6. Martha Margaret Berryman Upshur Buckner, sixth child of John and Martha Buckner, was born Aug. 4th, 1830; married Jas. Richardson of Pembroke, Ky., Dec. 12th, 1858. Issue:
A. Frank Buckner Richardson (deceased), married Carrie D. Pendelton. No surviving issue.
B. Annie Payne Richardson (deceased), married Charles Herschell Porter. No children.
C. Martha Buckner Richardson, third child, married Robert Graham of Hadensville, Ky. Issue: Annie Bell (deceased), Mary Irene (deceased), William George, Martha Buckner, Robert Ferguson, John Trice (deceased), and Virginia Richardson Graham.
D. Mary Withers Richardson, fourth child, married James Walter Williams. Issue: Jas. Richardson, Thomas Herschell (deceased), Annie Porter, Walter Jameson and Frank Buckner Williams. Home, Hopkinsville, Ky.
E. Virginia Trice Richardson, fifth child of Martha and Jas.

Richardson, married William Francis Shaffner. Home, Winston-Salem, N. C.

F. Octavia Allison Buckner and (G) Clementina S. Buckner, daughters of John and Martha Buckner, died unmarried.

John Buckner was married, secondly, to Mrs. Catherine Payne, September 28th, 1848. She died in 1856. He was married a third time, to Mrs. Mary P. Allensworth, March 13th, 1861. She died February 24th, 1876. There were no children of either marriage.

IX. THOMAS BUCKNER, the ninth and last child of Philip and Tabitha Buckner, was born January 8th, 1796, and died the 13th of October, 1833. He married Matilda Hanson, August, 1819. She was born September 16th, 1789, and died October 10th, 1884. They had four (adult) children, viz.: Martha A., John Philip, Sarah A. and William N. All married and raised families. Home, Brooksville, Ky.

1. Martha A. Buckner, was born July 23d, 1820; married Wm. Ambrose. They had four children:
    A. Matilda Ambrose, married Joseph Hamilton. They had six children:
        aa. William Hamilton, died young.
        bb. Comma L. Hamilton, married David King. Issue: Edmon B., Imogene and Naomi.
        cc. Josie Hamilton, married Edmon King. Issue: Marie.
        dd. Grace Hamilton, married Edmon King after the death of her sister, Josie. Issue: Leonard, Mabel and Pauline. Home, Brooksville, Ky.
        ee. Clay Hamilton, died young.
        ff. Charlie Hamilton.
    B. Sarah Ambrose, married Robert Breeze. One child, Mattie.
        aa. Mattie Breeze, married W. H. Duncan. Issue: Bernice, Carroll and Paul Duncan.
    C. Isabel Ambrose, married Adolphus Hamilton. Issue:
        aa. Louis Hamilton, married Miss Browning. Issue: Charles.
        bb. Laura Hamilton, married James B. King. Issue: Birdie King.
    D. William T. B. Ambrose, died young.
2. John Philip Buckner, second child of Thomas and Matilda Buckner, was born May 23d, 1822; died February 4th, 1896. He married Mary Jane Asbury, and had five children, of whom we have the following account:
    A. Willis Buckner, married Miss Harber; four children, viz.:
        aa. John Buckner, married Miss Tilton.
        bb. Willy Buckner, married Miss Tilton.
        cc. Martha Buckner, married Mr Newman.
        dd. George Buckner, unmarried. The home of this family is at Mt. Olivet, Ky.
    B. Thomas Buckner, son of John Philip Buckner, married Anna Rigg. Six children were born to them, four of whom are living at this time, viz.:
        aa. Orla Buckner, married Frank Jacob.
        bb. Miss "Bob" Buckner, married H. Anderson.
        cc. Miss "Dick" Buckner, married Gus Fowler.

dd. Mabel Buckner, unmarried. The home of this family is at Mt. Olivet, Ky.
C. John Buckner, son of John Philip Buckner, married Amanda Hitt. They had two children, viz.:
    aa. Cora Buckner, married a Mr. Arn.
    bb. Claud Buckner, married a Miss Reaves. Home, Mt. Olivet, Ky.
D. Mary Martha Buckner, daughter of John Philip Buckner, married Leander Berry. Three children:
    aa. John Buckner Berry, married ——.
    bb. Ira Buckner Berry, married a Miss Moneyhon.
    cc. Ida Buckner Berry. Home, Bridgeville, Ky.
E. James Buckner, son of John Philip Buckner, married Vi. Insko. They had six children:
    aa. Ida Buckner, married Wm. Colvin.
    bb. Martha Buckner, married a Mr. Bell.
    cc. John Philip Buckner, Jr.

The names of the other children are unknown. Home is at Mt. Olivet, Ky.

3. Sarah A. Buckner, daughter of Thomas and Matilda Buckner, born October 6th, 1825; died January 2d, 1902; married James Milton Gill of Ripley, Ohio, on Sept. 11th, 1844. He was born Sept. 10th, 1823. Their children were Susan Francis, Thomas (these two died young), Mary Lucy, Adaline Buckner, Sarah Belle, Anna Matilda, William Watson and Minerva Jane. Of these we have the following account:

A. Mary Lucy Gill, married Ben. Craig. Issue:
    aa. Ira Craig, married Bessie V. Barnes. Issue: Omer Ellsworth. Home, Pittsburg, Pa.
    bb. Bertha Craig.
    cc. Lena Craig. Home, Augusta, Ky.
B. Adaline Buckner Gill, married James E. Mefford. Issue, seven children, as follows:
    aa. Noah Clifton Mefford.
    bb. Fay Edgar Mefford, married Daisy Belle Lyman. Issue: James T. and Lillian B.
    cc. Elmo Franklin Mefford.
    dd. Leo Kirk Mefford.
    ee. Roy Weaver Mefford (died young).
    ff. Lula Ethel Mefford.
    gg. James Vern Mefford. The home of this family is Lexington, Ky.
C. Sarah Belle Gill, married William G. Martin. One adult child, a daughter, Nelly, who is married. Home, Ripley, Ohio.
D. Anna Gill, married William A. Shinkle; four children, viz.:
    aa. Wilbur Shinkle, married Maggie May McCoy.
    bb. Francis Shinkle, married Frankie Wilson.
    cc. Archie Shinkle, married Lillie Belle Wagner.
    dd. Jennie May Shinkle, married Geo. W. Pophan. The home of this family is in Cynthiana, Ky.
E. William Watson Gill, married ——. Eight children, viz.:
    aa. Nora Gill.
    bb. James Gill.

       cc. Bertha Gill.
       dd. William Watson Gill, Jr.
       ee. Anna Bell Gill.
       ff. Thomas Buckner Gill.
       gg. Henry Clay Gill.
       hh. Alice Gill. The home of this family is Ripley, Ohio.
F. Minerva Jane Gill, married Giles Day.
4. William N. Buckner, son of Thomas and Matilda Buckner, was born Sept. 15th, 1828; died October, 1903; married January 16th, 1851, Millie Yelton. Their home was in Bluffton, Indiana, where in 1901, they celebrated their Golden Wedding. They had nine children, viz.:
A. John T. Buckner, married Laura Pribble.
B. Charles N. Buckner, married Josephine Newkirk.
C. Millie J. Buckner, married Joseph Thralkill.
D. Martha H. Buckner, married Byron Pribble.
E. Marion E. Buckner, married Stella Doster.
F. George W. Buckner, married a Mexican lady.
G. Mamie M. Buckner, married Louis Beerbower.
H. Benjamin F. Buckner, married Mary Gavin.
I. Ellen Buckner. The home of this family is at Bluffton, Ind.

William Buckner of Caroline County

WILLIAM BUCKNER of "The Neck," Caroline County, was a son of Richard and Elizabeth (Cooke) Buckner of Essex, and afterwards of Caroline County. He is believed to have married a widow—Judith Hawes, who was the daughter of William Aylett of King William County.

William Buckner may be considered as the founder of the branch of the family located at "The Neck," but owing to the destruction of family records, little can be ascertained as to his life, or even the date of his death. It is possible he may have been the William who is mentioned in the court records as a Justice of Caroline County in June, 1768. His son, William, was a Justice, and in August, 1768, we find a record of William Buckner, Jr., serving in that capacity.

Judith Hawes Buckner was noted for her ungovernable temper, and family pride. It was no unusual occurrence for her to horsewhip her negro coachman, when she thought the occasion demanded such treatment; in consequence of which, she was universally known as—*Lady Buckner*. Her dying request was, that she be buried beneath the pavement of the aisle of the old wing of Rappahannock church—of which she had become a member—which was occupied by the poor; as an act of self-abasement for the pride she had manifested, and the contempt she had exhibited towards the common people during her life, alleging that—"she wanted those she had looked down upon, to walk over her when she was dead."

William and Judith Hawes Buckner had known issue:
I. William Buckner.
II. Francis Buckner.
III. Richard Buckner, afterwards of "Albany," Westmoreland County.
IV. George Buckner.
V. Thomas Buckner.

I. Although William Buckner has been placed first amongst the above named children, no authority can be given for his right of priority. He is known, however, to have inherited

THE PRESENT HOUSE ON NECK FARM
OCCUPYING SITE OF OLD BUCKNER RESIDENCE
DESTROYED BY THE U. S. GUNBOATS

his father's estate at "The Neck," although that fact alone, is not to be considered as conclusive evidence of his primogeniture; as it was of frequent occurrence in those days for a younger son to inherit the family estate. If he was the eldest son, he must have married rather late in life, as his first child was not born until 1766.

William Buckner, 2nd, married Dolly Roy, who is said to have been of the Roy family of Spottsylvania County. In the records of this county we find a Dolly Roy, who was the wife of John Roy of St. Mary's Parish, Caroline County, in 1733, but there is no mention of a daughter by that name. William and Dollie Roy Buckner of the "The Neck," had issue:

1. William Aylett Buckner.
2. Colin Buckner.
3. Roy Buckner.
4. Richard Buckner.
5. Judith Buckner.
6. Lucy Buckner.
7. Elizabeth Buckner.
8. Anne Roy Buckner.

WILLIAM AYLETT BUCKNER was born at "The Neck," Caroline County, Feb. 13, 1766; died June 2, 1830, and was married June 23, 1797, to Charlotte (Hawes) Buckner, widow of Richard Henry Buckner, who was the son of George Buckner of "The Neck." William was a Justice of Caroline County in 1804. By her second marriage, Charlotte Buckner had issue three children:

1. William Smith Bickley Buckner of "The Neck," born April 16, 1798; died March 21, 1836; married Mildred Hawes, and had issue:

A. Ann Hawes Buckner, born March 17, 1820; died Nov. 19, 1880; married William Aylett, son of Richard and Catherine (Hawes) Buckner.
B. Elizabeth Pollard Buckner, died unmarried, aged about 60 years.
C. Mary Susan Buckner, died 1892; married Major William H. Thornton of Prince William County, died Oct. 24, 1884; and had issue:
  1. Mildred Hawes Thornton, married James J. Davis, attorney-at-law, a native of England.
  2. James Bankhead Taylor Thornton, attorney-at-law, married Fannie Case Bander of Port Royal.
  3. Bickley Buckner Thornton of Manassas, unmarried.
  4. William Willis Thornton, married Adrienne Dessez, Spokane, Wash...

5. Richard Ewell Thornton, Fairfax, Va., born Jan. 7, 1865; married Sue Plummer, June 25, 1891.
6. Nannie Ratcliffe Thornton, married J. Boyd Washington.
7. Mary Susan Thornton, Washington, D. C., unmarried.
D. Jane Walker Buckner, died unmarried.
E. Catharine Bickley Buckner, died unmarried.
2. Emily Buckner, daughter of William Aylett and Charlotte (Hawes) Buckner, was born Oct. 27, 1804; married Colonel John Ashby. (For descendants see Ashby excursus).
3. Jane Buckner, daughter of William Aylett and Charlotte (Hawes) Buckner, was born July 27, 1808; married (1st) to Thomas Hawes, by whom she had one son, Thomas Martin Hawes, who inherited a large fortune, most of which he had run through at the time of his death, which occurred when he was a young man. Jane (Buckner) Hawes married (2d) Henry Anderson of Kentucky, and had issue:
1. Clarence Anderson, married and had issue.
2. Lelia Anderson, married —— Trabue of Kentucky, and had issue, Helen, Kate and Henry. It is believed that one of the daughters married Governor Foraker of Ohio.

COLIN BUCKNER, son of William and Dollie (Roy) Buckner, was a Major in the 20th Infantry, U. S. Army, and served with distinction in the War of 1812. He was one of the principals in two duels, one with a French officer, and the other with General Bankhead, U. S. A. Some years after the war he removed to Lynchburg, Ky. He married Martha Doswell of Nottoway County, Va. Issue:

1. John William E. Buckner, born 1819, at Lexington, Va.; died Dec. 25, 1857; married Oct. 13, 1846, Rachel Eleanor Paxton, born 1825; died at Vicksburg, Miss., July 25, 1865, and had issue:
   A. Colin Buckner, deceased.
   B. William E. Buckner, deceased.
   C. Martha Buckner, deceased.
   D. Elisha Paxton Buckner, born at Lexington, Va., April 4, 1848; died May 24, 1903, at Madison, Mo.; married May 11, 1884, Lulu V. Walker, born Jan. 5, 1864. Issue:
      aa. Edwin Paxton Buckner, born at Madison, Mo., April 7, 1885.
      bb. Rachel E. M. Buckner, born at Madison, Mo., June 25, 1887.
2. Dr. Beverley Buckner, married (1st) Laura Reagan, by whom he had one son—Beverley who died in infancy. Married (2d) —— and had one son, H. Beverley Buckner.
3. Mary Eppes Buckner of Lynchburg, married William Henry Langhorne, born near Cumberland Court House, Va., son of Maurice and Elizabeth (Allen) Langhorne of Prince Edward County. Issue:
   A. Maurice Buckner Langhorne, died in infancy.

COMMISSION OF MAJOR COLIN BUCKNER
1812

B. Fannie Beverley Langhorne, married Hugh W. Fry of Botetourt County. No issue.
C. William Archer Langhorne, died aged 26 years. Unmarried.
D. Devereux Alexander Langhorne, died in 1889. Unmarried.
E. Betsey Allen Langhorne, died young.
F. Martha Doswell Langhorne, married Alexander F. Anderson. Issue:
    aa. Mary Langhorne Anderson, died young.
    bb. Laurice Alexander Anderson.
    cc. Beverley Doswell Anderson.
G. Robert Colin Langhorne, died in infancy.
H. Beverley Reagan Langhorne, died young.
I. Mary Potter Langhorne, married Thomas B. Bond of Petersburg. Issue:
    aa. Minnie Bond, died in infancy.
    bb. Thomas Allen Bond.
    cc. William Langhorne Bond.
J. Sallie Carey Langhorne.
K. Daniel Allen Langhorne, married Effie Brabham. Issue:
    aa. Devereux Langhorne.
    bb. Ogarita Brabham Langhorne.
    cc. Mary Anderson Langhorne.
    dd. Daniel Allen Langhorne.
L. Kent Langhorne, married D. Clay Talbot. Issue:
    aa. Langhorne Worthington Talbot.
M. Lucy McGavock Langhorne.
N. Maud B. Langhorne, married William J. Nelson of Staunton.
O. Harry Holmes Langhorne, died in infancy.

4. Fannie Buckner, married A. Alexander of New Orleans, La. Issue:
A. Mattie Doswell Alexander.
B. Robert Alexander, deceased.
C. Kate Alexander.
D. Lulu Alexander.
E. Irby Alexander.

5. Robert Henry Buckner, married Cornelia Leftwich of Bedford County. Issue:
A. Daisy Buckner, deceased.
B. Patty (Martha) Buckner, died in infancy.
C. Cornelia Otey Buckner, deceased.
D. Robert Buckner of Raleigh, N. C., married Inez ——. No issue.
E. John Buckner, deceased.
F. Beverley Buckner, married Hollis Augustus Lockridge. Issue:
    aa. Cornelia Lockridge.
    bb. Robert Lockridge (daughter).
    cc. Elizabeth Lockridge.
G. William Langhorne Buckner.

ROY BUCKNER, son of William and Dollie (Roy) Buckner, of "The Neck," was born about 1770, and married Nancy Moore of Stafford County, Va. Issue:

1. Edward Buckner, d. s. p.
2. George A. Buckner, d. s. p.
3. William Moore Buckner.
4. Helen Buckner.

I. William Moore Buckner was born in Stafford County, Va., in 1799; died at Greenfield, Ohio, Nov. 11, 1856; married 1839, at Flemingsburg, Ky., Jane Elizabeth Morrison, born 1813; died May 21, 1894. He was a lawyer by profession, a man of broad and liberal ideas, and an uncompromising opponent of slavery. Issue:

A. Edward M. Buckner of Peoria, Ohio, born Oct. 11, 1841, at Richmond, Va.; married Oct. 31, 1878, at Marysville, O., to Elizabeth Clegg, born Oct. 15, 1846. Issue:
   aa. William Moore Buckner, born Nov. 16, 1879.
   bb. Mary Roberta Buckner, born March 8, 1881.

B. Helen A. Buckner, born Jan., 1844; died Oct., 1899; married Oct., 1864, John N. McElwain. Issue:
   aa. Dessie McElwain, married Wm. Ryan, Washington, D. C.
   bb. Edward McElwain.

C. William Thomas Buckner, Attorney-at-Law, of Wichita, Kansas. Served in 73d and 175th Regiments, Ohio Volunteers, during Civil War. Judge of Probate Court of Sedgwick County from 1889 to 1893. Born Jan. 2, 1846, at Washington Court House, Ohio; married June 6, 1883, to Mary J. Wadsworth, born Oct. 4, 1851. Issue:
   aa. Dora Adaline Buckner, born June 22, 1884.
   bb. Susan Elizabeth Buckner, born Nov. 6, 1889.

D. Adaline V. Buckner, born April, 1848; married Oct., 1869, to William P. Cleveland of Wichita, Kansas. Issue:
   aa. Carl Cleveland.

E. George O. M. Buckner of Buffalo, N. Y., born March 3, 1850, at Washington Court House, Ohio. Educated at the Public Schools and employed in the U. S. Treasury, Bureau of Engraving and Printing, 1866-69. Removed to Buffalo, N. Y., 1873. Studied law in the office of Hon. Grover Cleveland and was admitted to the New York bar June, 1881, and since 1891 has been connected with the *Buffalo Daily Courier*. Married March 12, 1889, Emily H. Paddon, born Jan. 16, 1856, in New York City. Issue:
   aa. Alice Buckner, born Nov. 30, 1892.
   bb. Robert William Buckner, born Feb. 3, 1895.

II. Helen Buckner, daughter of Roy and Nancy (Moore) Buckner, born 1802; died July 9, 1871; married Dr. Robert Briggs of Richmond, Va., born 1785; died 1838. Issue:

A. Robert Moore Briggs, born 1831; died Feb. 11, 1869; married Nov. 30, 1852, Catherine Robinson. Issue:
   aa. William M. Briggs of Spokane, Washington.

B. Jean Briggs, born July 21, 1836, Richmond, Va.; married Oct. 15, 1861; Charles Anthony Palmer, Attorney-at-Law, of Washington Court House, Ohio, born 1838. Issue:
   aa. Robert B. Palmer, born Aug. 23, 1862; married 1896, Mary Irwin, Washington Court House.

GEORGE O. M. BUCKNER AND FAMILY

bb. Margaret Marie Palmer born July 30, 1864; married 1887, Herbert B. Maynard, Washington Court House.
cc. Paul Palmer, born Oct. 22, 1866; married 1886, Emma Burris, Salina, O.
dd. Helen Virginia Palmer, born Nov. 13, 1868; married June 3, 1893, Rufus C. Dawes, President of Union Gas Co., Chicago, Ill., born July 30, 1867. Issue:
    1. William Mills Dawes, born Dec. 27, 1894.
    2. Robert Rufus Dawes, born June 21, 1896; died April 16, 1897.
    3. Charles Cutler Dawes, born March 30, 1899.
    4. Jean Palmer Dawes, born June 7, 1901.
ee. Luther Saxton Palmer, born Oct 9, 1870.
ff. William Moore Palmer, born Nov. 15, 1873; married 1897, Elizabeth Davis, Cleveland, O.
gg. Alice Palmer, born Dec. 21, 1875; married 1896, W. R. Wood, Cincinnati, O.
hh. Harrison Buckner Palmer, born Nov. 10, 1879.

RICHARD BUCKNER of Caroline County, son of William and Dollie (Roy) Buckner of "The Neck," was born Dec. 7, 1775; died May 8, 1864, at Oakland; married Dec. 23, 1801, to Catherine E. Buckner, born Jan. 25, 1785; died Sept. 16, 1850. She was the daughter of Richard Henry Buckner and Charlotte Hawes. After the death of Richard Henry Buckner, Charlotte (Hawes) Buckner married William Aylett Buckner of "The Neck," brother of her son-in-law. By these two marriages, Richard became brother-in-law to his mother-in-law, and William Aylett Buckner was both uncle and stepfather to his niece. Richard Buckner was Sheriff of Caroline County in 1837. Issue:

1. Colin Buckner, born Dec. 20, 1802; died 1803.
2. Charlotte Buckner, born 1803; died 1805.
3. Rev. Richard Henry Washington Buckner, born Dec. 9, 1810; died Feb. 25, 1895; married (1st) Judith Boulware of Caroline County, who died without issue. Married (2d) Maria Slaughter of Rappahannock County, by whom he had issue:
  A. Mary Dorothy Buckner, born March 1, 1820; married Robert Moseley Wright of Caroline County, and had issue:
    aa. Ella Wright, married James Campbell of Caroline County, and has issue:
      aaa. Minnie Washington Campbell.
      bbb. Preston Campbell.
      ccc. Anna Campbell.
      ddd. Luola Campbell.
      eee. Robert Hawes Campbell.
      fff. William Campbell.
    bb. Richard Buckner Wright, died young.
    cc. William Lewis Wright, unmarried.
    dd. Katie Wright, unmarried.

  ee. Mildred Wright, died young.
  ff. Judith Wright.
  gg. Robert Burton Wright.
  hh. Moseley Wright, married Silas Goulden, and has issue:
   (1) Robert Goulden; (2) Silas Goulden.

4. Ann Eliza Buckner, married Summerfield Fitzhugh of Prince William County, and had issue, one daughter—Kate Fitzhugh, who married Aylett Hawes Conway of Fredericksburg.

5. William Aylett Buckner, was born at Oakland, Caroline County, May 14, 1814; died Aug. 2, 1865; married Oct. 17, 1837, Ann Hawes Buckner, the daughter of William S. B. and Mildred Hawes Buckner. Ann Buckner was born March 17, 1820; died Nov. 19, 1880. William Aylett Buckner was a prominent lawyer and politician. He was for several years a member of the House of Delegates, and was one of the State Delegates to the Charleston Convention when Virginia seceded from the Union. Issue:

A. William Smith Bickley Buckner, born April 11, 1839; died 1841.
B. Mary Smith Buckner of New London, born at "The Neck," Feb. 2, 1844; unmarried.
C. Richard Henry Washington Buckner, born Oct. 24, 1845. Joined the Confederate Army and was killed at the battle of Brandy Station, June 9, 1863, giving up his life at the early age of seventeen.
D. William Aylett Buckner, Jr., born Nov. 11, 1847; died Dec., 1902. Entered the C. S. A. before he was sixteen, becoming 1st Lieutenant of his company. A few years after the war he removed to Mexia, Texas. Married Jennie Corbet and had issue:
  aa. William Aylett Buckner, married a Miss Tuckner and has issue:
   aaa. George Aylett Buckner, Mexia, Texas.
   bbb. William Warthon Buckner, Mexia, Texas.
  bb. Henry Benjamin Buckner.
E. Mildred Charlotte Buckner, born Oct. 19, 1849; died April, 1897; married C. L. Jones.
F. Walker Hawes Buckner, born Sept. 24, 1851; married M. B. Goulden, resides at Rappahannock Academy. Issue:
  aa. Walker Hawes Buckner, Jr.
G. Catherine Elizabeth Buckner, born Aug. 4, 1853; died June 1, 1854.
H. Annie Buckner, born July 10, 1855; died Aug. 4, 1855.
I. John Breckenridge Buckner, born June 18, 1856; moved to Mexia, Texas, but returned to Caroline County in 1896. Married Allie White, Nov. 1885. Issue:
  aa. John B. Buckner, born Oct. 30, 1896, at Mexia.
  bb. Richard Campbell Buckner, born Oct. 24, 1889, at Mexia.
  cc. Mary V. Buckner, born March 15, 1892, at Mexia.
  dd. Mildred Hawes Buckner, born Dec. 19, 1894, at Mexia.
  ee. Sarah Buckner, born Sep. 1, 1899, in Caroline County.
  ff. Henry Aylett Buckner, born June 6, 1902, in Caroline County.
J. Ann H. Buckner, born May, 1858; died June, 1858.

MOSS NECK, ADJOINING "THE NECK FARM"
AT ONE TIME HEADQUARTERS OF GENERAL JACKSON
DURING THE CIVIL WAR

JUDITH BUCKNER, daughter of William and Dollie (Roy) Buckner, married William Smith Bickley, an Englishman. He was the possessor of a large fortune, and for some time was engaged in business in Alexandria. He afterwards returned to England with his family, which consisted at least of two sons, but all trace of this line has been lost.

LUCY BUCKNER, daughter of William and Dollie (Roy) Buckner, married George Catlett of Port Royal, a descendant of Col. John Catlett of Rappahannock. Issue:
1. Harriet Catlett, died unmarried.
2. Anna Catlett, died unmarried.
3. William Catlett, died unmarried.
4. George Catlett, died unmarried.
5. Colin Catlett, married Ellen Rootes Thornton, and had issue:
A. George William Catlett, married a Miss Brooke, and had issue:
 aa. Ellen Catlett.
 bb. Lucy Catlett.
 cc. Hattie Catlett.
B. Nannie Gordon Catlett, died unmarried.
C. Lucy Catlett, married —— Brooke of Essex; d. s. p.
D. Hattie Catlett, married Alexander Brooke of Essex; d. s. p.
E. Robert Morris Catlett.
F. Alice Catlett.

ELIZABETH BUCKNER, daughter of William and Dollie (Roy) Buckner, married Robert Gaines Beverley of Caroline County. He is believed to have died about 1797.

There is a deed in Spottsylvania County dated June 16, 1784, in which Robert G. Beverley and Elizabeth, his wife, "convey to George Stubblefield 828 acres of land in said county for £1656; reversion in the estate of his grandfather, Robert Beverley." The father of Robert Gaines Beverley was Robert Beverley of Spottsylvania, his widow Ann, marrying secondly, June 21, 1738, William Waller.

Another deed executed Sept. 10, 1784, by Robert Gaines Beverley and Betsy his wife, conveys 115 acres, part of a tract called "Newlands," in Spottsylvania County, for the sum of £1700, to Thomas McKenney.

Robert Gaines Beverley and his wife, Elizabeth Buckner, had issue:
1. William Beverley.
2. Harry Beverley.
3. Maria Beverley, married John Hooe of Prince William County, and had issue:
A. Maria Hooe, married (1st) a Dr. Mason; (2d) William McLean. By her first husband she had:

aa. Maria Mason, married Philip Leigh of Fairfax, and left issue.
   bb. Osceola Mason, married a Tebbs, who served under Mosby; afterwards removed to Texas and was there killed by the Indians. He left one daughter named Jane.

Issue of Maria (Hooe) Mason by second marriage.
   aa. William McLean of "Yorkshire," Prince William County.
   bb. Lula McLean, married James Blackwell of Fauquier County, and left issue, two sons.
   cc. Nannie McLean, married a son of Judge Spellman of Fauquier County.
   dd. Jennie McLean, unmarried, of Prince William County.

ANNE ROY BUCKNER, daughter of William and Dolly (Roy) Buckner of Caroline County, was born in 1782; died Sept. 10, 1802, and is buried in St. Paul's churchyard, Norfolk, Va. She married James Thorburn of Norfolk, who was born Dec. 27, 1769, at Dumfries, Scotland, and died at Fredericksburg, Va., Dec. 29, 1838. He was a son of John Thorburn of "Barnkin," Dumfries, died April 18, 1792, aged 43 years, and Isabella Donaldson, who was the daughter of John Donaldson, died Jan. 12, 1767, and Margaret Tate, his wife.

James and Anne Roy (Buckner) Thorburn had issue:
   1. James Donaldson Thorburn, who lived but ten days, and was afterwards re-interred with his mother.
   2. James Donaldson Thorburn (2d) born June 1, 1802; died June 11, 1835, and is buried in Norfolk. He married Jan. 5, 1826, Anne Moore Howison, daughter of Samuel Howison and Helen Rose Moore. Issue:
   A. Isabella Donaldson Thorburn, of whom presently.
   B. Helen Moore Thorburn, born Aug. 2, 1829; married Oct. 19, 1848, Lieut. Edward Lloyd Winder, U. S. N. and C. S. N., and died Dec. 7, 1891, d. s. p.
   C. Col. Charles Edmondson Thorburn, U. S. N. and C. S. A., of New York City.

Isabella Donaldson Thorburn, born June 28, 1827; married Dec. 4, 1849, Commander Charles Fleming McIntosh, fourth son of George McIntosh and Elizabeth Mason Walke. He was born in Norfolk, Oct. 24, 1813. Entered the U. S. Navy in 1828, and participated in the Mexican War, at which time he was a Lieutenant on the U. S. S. "Saratoga." When the war between the States broke out, he was a Commander, but resigned his commission and was given the same rank in the C. S. N. On the 10th of March 1862, he went to New Orleans and assisted in preparing the C. S. Ram "Louisiana" to go down and meet Admiral

Farragut's fleet, below Forts St. Philip and Jackson. During the engagement of April 20, 1862, Commander McIntosh was severely wounded in the knee, and lost his right arm; the "Louisiana" was blown up, and the Federals proceeded to New Orleans. He lingered in the hospital until May 13, when he expired at 6 p. m. His remains were removed in 1866, and brought to Cedar Grove Cemetery, Norfolk. Issue:

1. George McIntosh, born Oct. 21, 1850; died Dec. 7, 1902; married June, 1873, Mary Saunders, daughter of Commander John Loyall Saunders, U. S. N. She was born Aug. 10, 1852. Issue:
A. Mary Saunders McIntosh, died young.
B. Charles Fleming McIntosh, born Feb. 7, 1876, Attorney-at-Law, Norfolk, Va.
2. Anne D. McIntosh, married Dr. Alexander Tunstall.
3. Isabella Thorburn McIntosh, married Richard Baylor, both living, with issue.
4. Helen Winder McIntosh, died young.
5. Elizabeth Walker McIntosh, died young
6. Charles Fleming McIntosh, died young.

Francis Buckner of Caroline County

ACCORDING to family tradition Francis Buckner was a son of William and Judith (Hawes) Buckner of "The Neck." We have, unfortunately, no documentary evidence to support it; but in the Spottsylvania records there is a deed under the date of Jan. 23, 1793, in which "Benjamin McWilliams and Letitia his wife of Spottsylvania County, convey to Francis Buckner of Caroline County for £192 currency, 320 acres, a part of a tract of land given the said Benjamin by his father, William McWilliams."

It is also claimed that the above named Francis was a cousin of the Francis Buckner who married Martha Upshur; their respective fathers being William Buckner 2d, and Richard Buckner 2d, two of the sons of Richard Buckner who was Clerk of Essex.

There is some conflicting testimony in regard to the name of the wife of Francis Buckner. One tradition states that she was Elizabeth Thornton, and another, that she was named Lucy Madison. The names of both Thornton and Madison were used by Francis Buckner as given names for three of his children. It is possible that Francis Buckner was married twice; his first wife being a Thornton and his second a Madison. We can find no data concerning his life, and the time of his death is unknown. He had, however, the following issue:

    I. THORNTON BUCKNER, who married and had a daughter, Mrs. Ellen Cox, of Greensburg, Ky.
    II. GEORGE MADISON BUCKNER.
    III. CHARLES BUCKNER.
    IV. LUCY MADISON BUCKNER, born 1787; married James Buckner, son of Francis and Martha (Upshur) Buckner.
    V. MARY BUCKNER.
    VI. MILDRED BUCKNER.
        1. George Madison son of Francis Buckner was born in Va., April 15, 1783; died at Paris, Mo., Feb. 1857; married in Va., in 1807 to Malinda Minor, who was born Feb. 4, 1785; died 1844. Issue:
            A. Elizabeth M. T. Buckner, born June 3, 1808; married 1831; Thomas B. Ragland.

COURT HOUSE AT BOWLING GREEN
CAROLINE CO., VA.

The Buckners of Virginia

B. Francis T. Buckner, born Nov. 10, 1810; married 1829, Sally Ann Vivion.
C. Mary Hill Buckner, born Jan 26, 1813; married 1834, William B. Giddings.
D. Louisa A. M. Buckner, born May 6, 1815; married Jan. 1837, Martin Sidner.
E. Mildred Matilda Buckner, born Nov. 17, 1817; married (1st) Oct. 8, 1839, John G. Caldwell; married (2d) March 7, 1861, J. C. Fox. Issue by 1st marriage:
    aa. James N. Caldwell, born Jan. 25, 1841; died May 14, 1848.
    bb. George Buckner Caldwell, Paris, Mo., born March 11, 1843; died Feb. 12, 1885; married May 1, 1867, Katharine Marshall Robinson; born Feb. 6, 1846 at Paris, Mo.; died Jan. 8, 1883. Issue:
1. John G. Caldwell, born March 29, 1868; died Sept. 24, 1869.
2. Clara Buckner Caldwell, born July 6, 1870 at Paris; married Nov. 18, 1891; Frederick Thomas Bristor, born June 8, 1868, of Mansfield, Ohio. Issue: Katherine Caldwell Bristor, born Dec. 15, 1895; Thomas Goodrich Bristor, born Nov. 9, 1898; Miriam Buckner Bristor, born Nov. 14, 1902.
    cc. Mollie F. Caldwell, daughter of Mildred M. Buckner and John G. Caldwell, was born April 4, 1850; married Nov. 22, 1871, W. D. Blakey of Paris, Mo; Issue:
        1. James Fox Blakey, Fayette, Mo.
        2. George C. Blakey, Paris, Mo.
        3. Nellie May Blakey, San Francisco, Cal.
        4. Carrie Leslie Blakey, Paris, Mo.
        5. Kathleen Blakey, Paris, Mo.
        6. Mildred G. Blakey, Paris, Mo.

Mildred M. (Buckner) Caldwell, by her second marriage to J. C. Fox, had issue:
    1. Annie May Fox, born Sept. 13, 1862; married Oct. 16, 1884, Robert O. Osborn of San Francisco, and has issue: Dixie Gage Osborn.

2. Charles Buckner, son of Francis Buckner, born near Fredericksburg, Virginia, Sept. 19, 1785; died at Paris, Mo. April 4, 1834; married April 20, 1815, Susan Elizabeth Thornton, daughter of Thomas Griffin Thornton and Ann Harrison Fitzhugh, of Ormsby, Caroline County, Va.; born Oct. 29, 1797; died Feb. 2, 1875. Issue:
A. Ann Eliza Buckner, born March 11, 1816; died June 17, 1835; married Dec. 14, 1834, Captain David Willock.
B. Mary Mildred Buckner, born June 15, 1818; died ——; married Feb. 25, 1834, Dr. John W. Bowen.
C. Lucy Thornton Buckner, of whom presently.
D. Sallie Diggs Buckner, born Dec. 3, 1821; died ——; married Sept. 17, 1839, Dr. J. S. Cunningham.
E. Francis Buckner, unmarried, Lake County, Cal.
F. Thomas Griffin Thornton Buckner, born Feb. 15, 1826; died 1827.
G. Wm. Fitzhugh Thornton Buckner, of whom presently.
H. Harriet Griffin Thornton Buckner, born April 18, 1830; married March 12, 1854, Courtney Campbell, Independence, Mo.

I. Malinda Madison Buckner, born Oct. 27, 1832; died Sept. 3, 1834.

Lucy Thornton Buckner, daughter of Charles and Susan E. (Thornton) Buckner, born Feb. 6, 1820; married Jan. 28, 1836, Judge John Heard of Ky. Issue:
- aa. Mary Eliza Heard, San Francisco, Cal.
- bb. Charles Buckner Heard, deceased.
- cc. Susan Virginia Heard.
- dd. Sally Cunningham Heard, deceased.
- ee. Thomas Reynolds Heard, deceased.
- ff. Jennie Heard, married Edward Yorke, C. E., and has issue:
    1. Irma Thornton Yorke, deceased.
    2. Edwina Yorke.
- gg. John Heard, deceased.
- hh. Lucy Thornton Heard, Sacramento, Cal.

William Fitzhugh Thornton Buckner, of Paris, Mo., son of Charles and Susan E. (Thornton) Buckner, born Jan. 27, 1828 in Caroline Co., Va.; married Elizabeth M. Woods, born July 6, 1832, and has issue:
- aa. Elizabeth Buckner, born Jan. 7, 1854; died Aug. 12, 1862.
- bb. Susan Buckner, born March 18, 1856; married June 15, 1876, Frank V. Ragsdale, Paris, Mo.
- cc. Sallie Thornton Buckner, born May 26, 1858; married Nov. 17, 1880, A. S. Houston, Mexico, Mo.
- dd. Charles Madison Buckner of Marshall, Mo., born Sept. 14, 1860; married June 2, 1887, Daisy Potter; born May 26, 1865. Issue:
    1. William Fitzhugh Buckner, born Oct. 26, 1888.
    2. Frances Buckner, born Oct. 23, 1890.
    3. Mary Buckner, born Jan. 29, 1893.
    4. Daisy Buckner, } twins born June 10, 1896,
    5. Dorothy Buckner, } died in infancy.
    6. Charles Madison Buckner, Jr.; born Sept. 12, 1898.
- ee. Anderson Duncan Buckner, born Oct. 6, 1862; Paris, Mo.
- ff. Mary Elizabeth Buckner, born Feb. 17, 1866; married 1887, C. R. Gibbs, Mexico, Mo.
- gg. Emma Tabitha Buckner, born Sept. 18, 1871. Paris, Mo.
- hh. Frances Fitzhugh Buckner, born June 18, 1874, Paris, Mo.

NOTE.—That Francis Buckner was one of the sons of William and Dollie (Roy) Buckner, is amply confirmed by the will of Richard Buckner of "Albany" on page 125, wherein he mentions "My brother Francis Buckner's estate," etc., Francis Buckner evidently being deceased at that time—1793.—(EDITOR.)

WM. FITZHUGH THORNTON BUCKNER
PARIS, MO.

Richard Buckner of Westmoreland County

RICHARD BUCKNER of "Albany," Westmoreland County, son of William and Judith (Hawes) Buckner of "The Neck," Caroline County, was born probably about 1730-5. He was one of the signers of "The Westmoreland Protest," which Richard Henry Lee wrote and presented against the Stamp Act in 1765. He married Eliza Ariss, only child of Spencer Ariss and Sarah Ataway, and granddaughter of Richard Ariss.

From certain deeds, we learn that Sarah (Ataway) Ariss married one Pierce, and that her first husband died previous to 1792.

Will of Richard Buckner

In the name of God, Amen. I, Richard Buckner of the County of Westmoreland, being sick and weak of body but of sound mind and memory, thanks be to God for the same, do make and ordain this to be my last will and testament, in manner following, viz:

Imprimis, my will and desire is that a double tombstone be sent for to Great Britain nine months after my death, value about thirteen pounds sterling, with this humble inscription. "Underneath this stone lies the bodies of Richard and Elizabeth Buckner, who lived to a good old age, and then dropped like ripe fruit from the stock."

Item. I desire that my brother Francis Buckner's estate shall not be liable for any part of my Father's debts to Robert Giterest; property being left in my hands for that purpose.

Item. I desire that my Executors shall advertize in nine months after my death for Alexander Conntee to bring his account against me, so it may be paid, amounting as I suppose to about fourteen pounds.

Item. I give and bequeath to my son Ariss Buckner, the four following negroes at the death of his grandmother. Jenny, Milly, Betty and Billy.

Item. I give likewise to my son Ariss Buckner my two guns, and confirm to him all the articles I have before given by letter.

Item. I give and bequeath to my grandson James Richard Miller, two negro boys, Jack and James.

Item. I give to my granddaughter Lucy Roy Miller, two negro girls, Les and Dinah and their future increase. These two bequests not to take place until after the death of my wife Elizabeth Buckner.

Item. It is my desire that a certain Mr. Scott a joiner who worked on a vessel of mine, shall receive out of my estate, one hogshead of tobacco, and Mr. Thomas Miller to see it paid.

Item. All the rest of my estate of what kind soever not already given, I give and bequeath to my loving wife Elizabeth Buckner, such as negroes with their future increase, also all the stocks of cattle, sheep, horses and hogs, with all the household and kitchen furniture, and all the crops of corn and wheat, tobacco, etc., with all debts due and demands of whatsoever kind or nature; to be disposed of by her in any manner she thinks proper, only subject to this restriction, that if she marries, she shall only be entitled to her thirds.

Item. It is my will and desire that my said wife shall be burthened with the payments of all my just debts.

Lastly, I nominate and appoint my loving wife Elizabeth Buckner my sole executrix of this my last Will and Testament in manner and form. In witness whereof I have hereunto set my hand and seal this 15th day of October, one thousand seven hundred and ninety-three.

(Signed) RICHARD BUCKNER.

Teste. Thomas Thompson.
      Richard Mothershead.
      (X) his mark.

Richard and Eliza Ariss Buckner had issue:

I. Ariss Buckner of "Auburn," Loudoun County, born Aug. 25, 1771, at "Albany;" died March 30, 1847; married April 21, 1793, Lucy, daughter of Bernard Hooe of "Hazel Plains," Prince William County. Lucy Hooe was born Feb. 11, 1775; died Feb. 6, 1885, at "Auburn." The ancestral home at Albany was burned by the British in the War of 1812, many valuable paintings, papers and other heirlooms being destroyed. Issue:

    1. Richard Bernard Buckner, born March 24, 1794, at Hazel Plains; died March 4, 1839, at St. Bernard, Fauquier County; married Feb. 28, 1828, at Washington, D. C., to Louisa Hipkins Berry-

MRS. WM. FITZHUGH THORNTON BUCKNER
PARIS, MO.

man, born May 1, 1807, at Port Royal, died July 16, 1886, at St. Bernard. Mrs. Buckner married (2d) Thos. H. Turner. Issue by first marriage:

  A. Ella Alice Buckner, born Dec. 23, 1830, at St. Bernard; married Oct. 23, 1848, at Washington, D. C., to Edward Jaquelin Smith, Attorney-at-Law, born April 4, 1818, at Winchester, Va.; died Oct. 28, 1887. Issue:
    aa. Philip Smith, born Feb. 3, 1850, of Tampico, Mexico.
    bb. Richard Bernard Smith, born Oct. 23, 1851, of Woolsey, Prince William County, Va.
    cc. Edward Warren Smith, born June 18, 1865; married Mary Carter, of Pike Station, New Hampshire.
    dd. Thomas Turner Smith, born June 18, 1865, of Washington, D. C.
    ee. Richard Buckner Smith, Dec. 21, 1866, of Wickliffe, Clarke County, Va.; married Annie Williams.

  B. Eliza Ariss Buckner, born Oct. 2, 1833; married B. Frank Gallaher, U. S. N.; both deceased. Issue:
    aa. Louisa Bernard Gallaher, U. S. National Museum, Washington, D. C.

  C. Richard Pratt Buckner, born Feb. 18, 1835 of Washington, D. C.; married Ella Berry of Maryland.

  D. Louisa Berryman Buckner, born May 7, 1839 of Delaplane, Fauquier County, Va.

2. Thomas Hooe Buckner of Washington County, Miss., son of Ariss and Lucy (Hooe) Buckner, was born in Loudoun County, Va.; died 1871; married (1st) Bettie Ann Thomas of Maryland, and had issue:

  A. Bettie Buckner, born Oct. 26, 1833; died Jan. 26, 1905; married Feb. 6, 1865, Lyman Godfrey Aldrich, born at Grafton, Mass., Jan. 31, 1839; died July 29, 1901, at Natchez, Miss. Issue:
    aa. Lyman D. Aldrich, born Dec. 27, 1868, Natchez, Miss.; married Grace D. Ballard.
    bb. Sarah Davenport Aldrich, born Dec. 23, 1873; married Oct. 30, 1895, to James Gordon Smith of Natchez, born May 21, 1870. Issue:
      aaa. Lyman Aldrich Smith, born Aug. 7, 1896.
      bbb. Frances Elizabeth Smith, born May 18, 1898.

Thomas Hooe Buckner by his second wife, Louisa Montgomery, born Jan. 17, 1824, whom he married at New Orleans in 1840, had issue:
  A. Davis M. Buckner, born 1841.
  B. Richard A. Buckner, born 1843; died.
  C. James H. Buckner, born 1845; died.
  D. Thomas H. Buckner, born 1847; died.
  E. Mattie Buckner, born Sept. 13, 1851, at Washington County, Miss.; married Jan. 19, 1871, Joseph H. Robb, born March 27, 1842, County Treasurer of Washington County. Issue:
    aa. Jessie Buckner Robb.
    bb. Anna Robb.
    cc. Helen Robb.
    dd. Florence Robb.

ee. Ida Robb.
ff. Joseph H. Robb.
F. Philip T. Buckner, born 1855; died.
G. Jessie Buckner, born 1875.
3. Bernard Hooe Buckner of Washington County, Miss., son of Ariss and Lucy (Hooe) Buckner, married in 1836, Fanny, daughter of David Higginbotham of Albemarle County, Va., and left issue.
4. Margaret Buckner, daughter of Ariss and Lucy (Hooe) Buckner, married (1st) George Washington Thornton of Rappahannock County, in 1825; he died September of the same year at Thornton Hill, leaving issue one daughter:
  A. Jane Augusta Washington Thornton, born Oct. 9, 1825; died March 7, 1887; married Feb. 3, 1848, at Louisville, Ky., James Burnie Beck, born Feb. 13, 1822, at Dumfrieshire, Scotland, lawyer, Member of Congress and U. S. Senator; died at Washington, May 3, 1890. Issue:
    aa. Margaret Buckner Beck, born June 29, 1849; died 1870; married James W. Corcoran, nephew of William W. Corcoran, the philanthropist.
    bb. Sophia Burnie Beck, born June 28, 1851; died.
    cc. Bettie Buckner Beck of Washington, D. C., born Nov. 27, 1853, Lexington, Ky; married April 17, 1877, Colonel Green Clay Goodloe, U. S. M. C., born Jan. 31, 1845. No issue.
    dd. George Thornton Beck of Cody, Wyoming, born June 28, 1856.
    ee. James Burnie Beck, born Aug. 26, 1858.
Margaret Buckner Thornton married (2d) Governor James Clark of Kentucky. She died at Winchester in 1836, leaving issue by this marriage:
    aa. Mary Clark.
    bb. Susan Clark, married —— Tompkins.
    cc. Richard Clark.
5. Mary Buckner, daughter of Ariss and Lucy (Hooe) Buckner, married Senator William Livingston Pratt of New Jersey, a descendant of the Livingston family of New York. He was a well-known writer and poet, author of "Memoirs of Cowper," etc.
6. Caroline Rebecca Buckner, daughter of Ariss and Lucy (Hooe) Buckner, married in 1836, Hon. Montgomery Blair of Maryland, Postmaster-General under President Lincoln. Issue:
  A. Bettie Blair, married General Cyrus B. Comstock.
7. Spencer Ariss Buckner of Auburn, Loudoun County, Va., son of Ariss and Lucy (Hooe) Buckner, married Helen Stuart Fitzhugh, daughter of Dr. Alexander Fitzhugh of "Boscobel," near Fredericksburg, Va. Issue:
  A. Spencer Ariss Buckner.
  B. John Fitzhugh Buckner.
  C. Lucy Clare Buckner.
  D. Mary Magruder Buckner.
II. Eliza Ariss Buckner, only daughter of Richard Buckner of "Albany," and his wife Eliza Ariss, was born previous to 1780; married Major

Wm. Fitzhugh, Jr.　　Frances　　Mary Elizabeth　　Chas. Madison, Jr.　　Virginia

CHILDREN OF CHARLES MADISON AND DAISY BUCKNER

Thomas Roy Miller. It is probable he is the Thomas Miller of Spottsylvania County whose commission as Lieutenant of Militia is dated Sept. 18, 1777. Issue:

1. Sarah Ataway Miller of Port Royal, Caroline County, married Samuel Lewis, son of Major George Lewis, and grandson of Col. Fielding Lewis and Elizabeth Washington. (For descendants of Sarah Ataway Miller see Washington and Lewis excursus).
2. Dr. Thomas Miller, a distinguished physician of Washington, D. C., married Virginia Collins, daughter of General Walter Jones of Washington, and granddaughter of Charles Lee, Attorney-General of the United States. Issue:

A. Mrs. Sterling Murray.
B. Mrs. Arthur Fendall.
C. Virginia Miller, Corresponding Secretary-General, National Society of D. A. R., Washington, D. C.
D. Lucy Miller, died unmarried.
E. Eliza Miller, died unmarried.
F. Maria Miller, died unmarried.
G. Harriet Miller, died unmarried.
H. William Miller.

George Buckner of Caroline County

GEORGE BUCKNER was one of the sons of William and Judith (Hawes) Buckner of "The Neck," Caroline County, and he is thought to have been born between the years 1725 and 1730. He is believed to have married either a Miss Hawes or an Aylett. He had issue, two sons and a daughter, and it is possible he may have had other children.

From data found in Spottsylvania County, it is evident that George Buckner owned at one time land in Fredericksburg. He is one of the witnesses to a deed in 1749, and previous to 1764 he had sold Lot 5, in that town. He was witness to another deed in April, 1791. His known issue was:

I. Richard Henry Buckner.
II. Capt. George Buckner.
III. Elizabeth Buckner.

The following records were copied from the Buckner and Hawes family bibles by Miss Mary Buckner. They are of great importance in definitely determining the dates of birth, etc., of the various members of these two families.

From the Buckner Bible

Washington Buckner, son of Richard and Charlotte Buckner, his wife, was born July 31, 1783; died July 22, 1801.

Caty, daughter of the above, was born Jan. 25, 1785.

Charlotte, daughter of the above, was born Feb. 13, 1787.

Elizabeth, daughter of the above, was born Jan. 25, 1789.

Bailey, son of the above, was born Oct. 11, 1789, and departed this life Jan. 15, 1832.

Ann Hawes, daughter of the above, was born Sept. 1, 1792.

Mary Hawes, daughter of the above, was born Aug. 3, 1794.

Caty and Richard Buckner were married by the Rev. A. Waugh, Dec. 23, 1801. Richard Buckner was born Dec. 7, 1775.

Richard Henry Washington Buckner, son of Caty and Richard Buckner, was born Dec. 9, 1810.

Charlotte Hawes, daughter of Samuel Hawes and Ann, his wife, was born Oct. 1, 1766, and departed this life Dec. 17, 1831.

RESIDENCE OF CHAS. M. BUCKNER
MARSHALL, MO.

The Buckners of Virginia

*Wm. Aylett Buckner was born Feb. 13, 1766, and departed this life Jan. 2, 1830.

Wm. Aylett Buckner and Charlotte Buckner were married Friday, June 23, 1797, by Rev. Abner Waugh.

Wm. Smith Bickley Buckner, son of Wm. Aylett Buckner and Charlotte, his wife, born April 16, 1798; departed this life Monday, March 21, 1836.

Unnamed daughter of Wm. Aylett Buckner and Charlotte, his wife, born Aug. 23, 1799; departed this life Sept. 8, 1799.

Lucy Ann Buckner, daughter of Wm. Aylett Buckner and Charlotte, his wife, born Nov. 13, 1800; died July 7, 1801.

Washington Buckner, son of Wm. Aylett Buckner and Charlotte, his wife, born Feb. 19, 1803; died July 24, 1803.

Emily Buckner, daughter of Wm. Aylett Buckner and Charlotte, his wife, born Oct. 27, 1804.

Ellen Buckner, daughter of Wm. Aylett Buckner and Charlotte, his wife, born March 17, 1807; died Sept. 15, 1807.

Ellen Buckner, second daughter of that name, born July 27, 1808. Name changed to Jane and christened by Rev. Saml. Low, May 3, 1810. Married Dr. Thomas Hawes, and secondly, Henry Anderson.

William S. B. Buckner and Mildred Hawes were married Oct. 7, 1817.

Mildred Charlotte Buckner, daughter of William S. B. and Mildred Buckner, was born Friday, Aug. 25, 1818, and died Oct. 20, 1836.

Ann Hawes Buckner, daughter of William S. B. Buckner and Mildred, his wife, was born March 17, 1820, in King William County.

William Aylett Buckner and Ann Hawes Buckner were married Tuesday, Oct. 17, 1837, at "The Neck," Caroline County, by Rev. Lawrence Battaile of the Baptist Church.

From the Hawes Bible

Samuel Hawes, born Feb. 1, 1727; married Ann Walker, June 20, 1751.

Ann Walker, born Aug. 23, 1731.

Elizabeth, daughter of Samuel and Ann Hawes, was born Nov. 20, 1759, and married Thomas Buckner, May 25, 1780.

Mary, daughter of Samuel and Ann Hawes, was born Feb. 2, 1764; married Robert Buckner, March 23, 1782.

Charlotte, daughter of Samuel and Ann Hawes, was born Oct. 1, 1766; married Richard H. Buckner, Sept. 26, 1782, and married secondly, to William Aylett Buckner.

Walker, son of Samuel and Ann Hawes, was born July 1, 1776; married to Polly Martin, Oct. 26, 1797; died May 18, 1828.

Polly Martin, daughter of Thomas and Mildred Martin, born Sept. 24, 1782.

Mildred, daughter of Walker and Polly Hawes, born Sept. 29, 1799; married Wm. S. B. Buckner, Oct. 7, 1817.

Ann Hawes, daughter of Walker and Polly Hawes, born Sept. 2, 1803; married Col. John Washington, March 7, 1820.

---

*Wm. Aylett Buckner was a son of William and Dollie (Roy) Buckner of "The Neck." His wife was the daughter of Samuel Hawes and widow of Richard Henry Buckner.

I. RICHARD HENRY BUCKNER, was born in Caroline County previous to 1760. He married Sept. 26, 1782, Charlotte, daughter of Samuel and Ann Hawes of King William County. Charlotte Hawes was born Oct. 1, 1766. Her second husband was William Aylett Buckner, to whom she was united June 23, 1797. He was a son of William and Dollie (Roy) Buckner of "The Neck," Caroline County, and cousin of her first husband. Richard Henry Buckner had issue:

1. Washington Buckner, born July 31, 1783; died July 22, 1801.
2. Catherine Buckner, born Jan. 25, 1785; married Dec. 23, 1801, to Richard Buckner of Caroline County, a son of William and Dollie (Roy) Buckner of "The Neck."
3. Charlotte Buckner, born Feb. 13, 1787; married David Stuart of King George County. Issue:
   A. Mary Stuart, married Madison Fitzhugh of Madison County, Va., and had issue, a son, Catlett, and others.
   B. Gibbons Stuart.
   C. Lucy Stuart, married Rev. —— Schuff, a Methodist minister.
4. Elizabeth Buckner, born Jan. 25, 1789; married Col. John Stuart of "Mount Stuart," King George County, and brother of David Stuart mentioned above. Issue:
   A. Harriet Stuart, married Edmund Pendleton Barbour of Culpeper County, who died in 1851. They had issue, three daughters, Philippa, Mary Conway, and Edmonia, who married Rene de Payen, who was a professor in the University of Chicago. The father of Edmund P. Barbour was Philip Pendleton Barbour, a brother of James Barbour who was Governor of Virginia in 1812. He was born May 25, 1783; died 1842. He was a member of the Virginia Assembly in 1812, and in 1814 was elected to Congress, and at the time of his death was a Justice of the Supreme Court of the United States.
5. Bailey Buckner, born Oct. 11, 1789; of whom presently.
6. Ann Hawes Buckner, born Sept. 1, 1792; married John Hooe of Prince William County, and had no issue.
7. Mary Hawes Buckner, born Aug. 3, 1794; married Thomas Conway of Caroline County. Issue:
   A. Charlotte Conway, married Edmund Taylor Thornton of "Hunter's Hill," Caroline County. After her death, Mr. Thornton married Mary Conway, his first wife's sister. Issue by Charlotte Conway:
      aa. Martha Thornton, died young.
      bb. Ella Thornton, died young.
      cc. Aylett Thornton, married and had issue. He removed to Colliersville, Tenn.
      dd. Annie Thornton, married Joseph Jesse.
      ee. Thomas Conway Thornton, married in Colliersville, Tenn., but died at "Hunter's Hill," leaving a widow and one child.

LIEUTENANT BAILEY BUCKNER
1812

Issue of Edmund Taylor Thornton and his second wife, Mary Conway:
- aa. Ella Thornton, married William Chewning of Caroline County, and had issue.
- B. Anne Conway, daughter of Mary Hawes Buckner and Thomas Conway, married Thomas Rowe. Issue:
  - aa. Henry Clay Rowe, married a Miss Conway and removed to Texas, where he now resides with a large family.
  - bb. George Aylett Rowe, died young.
- C. Sarah Conway, daughter of Mary Hawes Buckner and Thomas Conway, died unmarried.
- D. Mary Conway, daughter of Mary Hawes Buckner and Thomas Conway, married Edmund T. Thornton, as stated above.
- E. George Conway, son of Mary Hawes Buckner and Thomas Conway, married Miss Bettie Thornton; removed to Texas, where he died.
- F. Aylett Hawes Conway, son of Mary Hawes Buckner and Thomas Conway, married a cousin—Kate Fitzhugh of Caroline County.

BAILEY BUCKNER, second son and fifth child of Richard Henry and Charlotte (Hawes) Buckner, was born at "The Neck," Caroline County, Oct. 11, 1789. He removed to Culpeper County, where he met and married in 1814, Mildred, daughter of John and Helen (Piper) Strother of "Wadefield." (See Strother Family.)

Bailey Buckner was one of the most popular and prominent men of his time. Handsome in face, graceful in mien—he was considered the beau ideal of a Southern gentleman. Liberal and fond of entertaining his friends at his beautiful and hospitable home, "Wadefield," he was ably seconded by his accomplished wife, a woman of tireless energy, great vitality and strong personality. In those days of good house wives, she was known far and near for the excellent management of her household, the care and well-being of her servants, and for her well appointed and luxurious table. She took great pride in her husband's successful career, as well as in her boys at College, being a most devoted and tender mother, and it was her pardonable boast "that several of her sons could read Cæsar at the age of twelve." Upon the death of her husband she took entire charge of "Wadefield," which she managed so admirably as to rear and educate her large family of children in the manner their birth and position warranted.

Being a fluent and ready speaker, Baily Buckner naturally drifted into politics, and during his early manhood was appointed Deputy Sheriff of Rappahannock County, and was afterwards elected Sheriff. The old note book used by him in his official capacity, containing much interesting and valuable data relative to Rappahannock and Culpeper families of that period, is now in the possession of Henry C. Kirk, Jr., of Baltimore, Md., who is a direct descendant.

At the breaking out of the war with Great Britain in 1812, Bailey Buckner joined Captain Benjamin Cole's Company of the 5th Virginia Militia of Culpeper. He served as Serjeant at Camp Randolph and Camp Holly under Major William Armistead, and then as Lieutenant under Colonel John H. Cocke. He was promoted to the grade of Ensign, July 2, 1813, and Lieutenant, Dec. 7, 1813. After the war, he held a position of trust in the Treasury Department at Washington. The engraving of Bailey Buckner, depicts him in the uniform of a Lieutenant of the 5th Virginia Militia, and is a reproduction from the original painting on ivory.

Bailey Buckner died at "Wadefield," Rappahannock County, in 1832, aged 43 years, his early death cutting short the career of a most brilliant and popular man. His widow died at "Wadefield" in 1875, in the 80th year of her age. Issue:

   I. Elizabeth Buckner.
  II. Aylette Hawes Buckner.
 III. John Strother Buckner.
 IV. Sarah Catherine Buckner. Died young.
  V. Richard Henry Buckner.
 VI. George Walker Buckner.
VII. Samuel Wilson Buckner.
VIII. Lucy Pendleton Buckner.
 IX. Caldwell Calhoun Buckner.

I. ELIZABETH BUCKNER, daughter of Bailey and Mildred (Strother) Buckner, married Lawrence Hay Taliaferro, and had issue:
   A. Hay B. Taliaferro. Issue: Parke Benjamin and Wm. Mayo.
   B. Mildred Taliaferro.

II. AYLETTE HAWES BUCKNER, born at Fredericksburg, Dec. 14, 1816; died Feb. 5, 1894; married Sept. 16, 1841, in Lincoln County, Mo., Mrs. Eliza L. Minor, daughter of Major James Clark, formerly of Virginia, but at that time a citizen of Lincoln County. Mrs. Buckner was born Feb. 17, 1819.

Aylette Hawes Buckner received his finishing education at the University of Virginia, and while yet a mere boy was a teacher in the Washington Academy in Rappahannock County, He removed at the age of 21 years to Missouri and located in Pike County. In 1850 he moved to St. Louis and entered upon the practice of his profession,

MILDRED STROTHER BUCKNER

the law. He was chosen attorney for the Bank of the State of Missouri during the year following, and in 1854 was appointed commissioner of public works by Governor Sterling Price. He subsequently returned to Pike County and was elected Judge of the Circuit Court in 1857. In 1861 he was chosen by the State Legislature as a delegate to the peace congress. During the war he moved to St. Charles, but spent most of his time in St. Louis. He took an active part in politics and was a trusted adviser of the Democratic party during the reconstruction period. Although not permitted to vote, his counsel was sought by the anti-radical leaders of that period. He warmly advocated the coalition between the Liberal Republicans, led by Grattz Brown and Carl Shurz, in 1870, with the Democrats. which resulted in the election of Brown over McClurg, the election of the Democratic legislature which sent Frank P. Blair to the United States Senate, and the enfranchisement of thousands of ex-Confederates.

In 1872, Judge Buckner became a candidate for Congress in the district which then embraced Audrain, Callaway, Monroe, Lincoln, Montgomery, Pike, Ralls, St. Charles and Warren Counties. Judge A. J. King was serving his first term and he and Judge Buckner were residents of the same county, St. Charles. Judge Theodore Brace, now of the Supreme Court, was also a candidate and had the support of his home county, Monroe, and one of the three delegates from Warren. Judge King had St. Charles, and the remainder of the counties were for Judge Buckner. Judge Buckner was elected over Judge T. J. C. Fagg by a large majority. During the same campaign he was sent as a delegate to the National Democratic Convention, and refused to vote to make the nomination of Horace Greeley unanimous, and supported O'Conner for the Presidency. In 1874, 1876 and 1878 he was renominated and re-elected without opposition. In 1880, Hon. A. M. Alexander of Monroe, became a candidate and carried his home county and Lincoln, but Judge Buckner had an easy victory in the convention. In 1882 his only opponent in the nominating convention was the Hon. Champ Clark, who received the vote of his home county.

In the redistricting in 1881, Callaway and Monroe Counties were taken from the district, and Franklin was added. At the close of his sixth term Judge Buckner voluntarily retired from Congress. For a brief period he resided on his farm at Saline, but soon returned to Mexico, where he spent the remainder of his life.

Judge Buckner died Feb. 5, 1894, at nine o'clock in the morning, just three months, almost to the hour, from the time he was stricken with paralysis. The funeral was held at the Presbyterian Church at Mexico, Mo., the services being conducted by the pastor, the Rev. A. A. Wallace. The attendance was extremely large and evidences of sorrow were everywhere manifest. The Circuit Court adjourned during the funeral services out of respect to his memory.

Judge Buckner was a tender and trusting husband and father, an unfaltering friend, an unpretentious but sincere Christian, and a model citizen. Issue:

 A. James Clark Buckner, born July 25, 1844, of Mexico, Mo.; married Nannie H. Buckner.
 B. Mildred Ann Buckner, born July 12, 1847, of Mexico, Mo.; married W. F. Whitney.
 C. Margaret Anderson Buckner, born Jan. 12, 1856; married Oct. 7, 1880, to Rev. William Hoge Marquess, born Feb. 22, 1854; Prof. in the Presbyterian Theological Seminary at Louisville, Ky. Issue:
  aa. William Hoge Marquess, Jr., born at Fulton, Mo., Feb. 25, 1888.
  bb. Eliza Buckner Marquess, born at Crescent Hill, Ky., Oct. 24, 1896.
 D. Charles Aylett Buckner, born July 13, 1859, of Mexico, Mo.; married Emilie D. ——.
 E. Stonewall Jackson Buckner, banker, of Mexico, Mo., born April 12, 1863, in Pike County, Mo.; married Jan. 3, 1884, to Ella Nora Ruloff, born Sept 2, 1864. Issue:
  aa. Ralph Ruloff Buckner, born Oct. 14, 1884.
  bb. Aylette Hawes Buckner, born Oct. 2, 1890.

III. JOHN STROTHER BUCKNER, second son of Bailey and Mildred (Strother) Buckner, was born at Fredericksburg, Jan. 28, 1819; died Dec. 14, 1898. He was married at Culpeper in 1846, to Lucy Ellen Gibson, who was born Aug. 2, 1827. Issue:

 A. Mary Elizabeth Buckner, born Dec. 14, 1847, at Barlow, Rappahannock County; married Richard Parham Spiers, and resides in Washington, D. C. Issue:

HON. AYLETTE HAWES BUCKNER

The Buckners of Virginia

    aa. Winfield Buckner Spiers, born May 22, 1872; died Feb. 9, 1899.
    bb. Mary Dandridge Spiers, born Feb. 17, 1874.
    cc. Helen Strother Spiers, born Feb. 8, 187—.
  B. Aylett Hawes Buckner, married Anna Burt of Alabama. Resides at Barlow, Rappahannock County. Issue:
    aa. Burtie Buckner, an artist of considerable ability.
    bb. John Strother Buckner, banker, of Culpeper, Va.
    cc. Aylett Hawes Buckner.
    dd. Martha Ball Buckner.
  C. Anne Eustace Buckner. Resides in Culpeper, Va.
  D. Eugenia Buckner, born Dec. 14, 1856; died Nov. 17, 1900; married Jan. 14, 1875, at Barlow, Va., to William I. Winfield, born Jan. 10, 1850, at Stony Creek, Dinwiddie County. Issue:
    aa. John Buckner Winfield, M.D., of Johnstown, W. Va., born Oct. 21, 1876; married Oct. 9, 1902, to Fannie K. McKee.
    bb. Edith Spottswood Winfield, born Feb. 29, 1880; married April 25, 1906, George Albert McKay, Lieutenant in the Engineers of U. S. N. Resides at Lake Bluff, Chicago, Ill.
    cc. Courtland Scott Winfield, born Jan. 28, 1883.
    dd. Gladys Gibson Winfield, born July 13, 1887.
    ee. Richard Marshall Winfield, born Aug. 21, 1891.
    ff. William Meade Winfield, born June 16, 1898. The address of the last four named above, is Sperryville, Va.
  E. Blanche Buckner, married John Dove of Richmond, Va., and had issue:
    aa. Lucille Dove, who married Raleigh Travers Green, editor of the "*Culpeper Exponent*," Culpeper, Va., and has issue. Mr. Green is a direct descendant of Robert Green, son of William Green, an Englishman. Robert was born about 1695, and settled in King George County about 1710, afterwards removing to what is now Culpeper. He died in 1748, his will being recorded in Orange County.

IV. SARAH CATHERINE BUCKNER, daughter of Bailey and Mildred (Strother) Buckner, died young.

V. RICHARD HENRY BUCKNER, third son of Bailey and Mildred (Strother) Buckner, married Kate Ashby, a daughter of William and Lucy (Strother) Ashby of Culpeper. No issue.

VI. GEORGE WALKER BUCKNER, fourth son of Bailey and Mildred (Strother) Buckner. Died unmarried.

VII. SAMUEL WILSON BUCKNER, M.D., of Turpin, Mo., fifth son of Bailey and Mildred (Strother) Buckner, was born at "Wadefield," Rappahannock County, Oct. 31, 1824; married at Clarksville, Mo., June 8, 1854, to Fannie Robertson, who was born near Flemingsburg, Ky., March 27, 1834. Issue:
  A. Lucie Buckner, born March 17, 1855; died May, 1893; married Terry T. Wells, and left issue, two sons.

  B. Lizzie Buckner, born Nov. 20, 1857; married Dr. William Robertson. Issue:
    aa. Fannie Robertson, born May 23, 1886.
    bb. L. Buckner Robertson, born June 17, 1888.
  C. Bailey Barbour Buckner, born Nov. 4, 1859; unmarried.
  D. Thomas Robertson Buckner, born Jan. 8, 1861. Residence, Clarksville, Mo.
  E. Rev. George W. Buckner, Pastor of the First Christian Church of McComb, Ill., was born March 17, 1863; married (1st) Anna Griffith, who died at Macon City. Married (2d) at Augusta, Ill., to Mary Pickens. Issue by first wife:
    aa. Samuel Buckner.
    bb. Clark Buckner.
    cc. George Buckner.
  F. Julia Buckner, born Nov. 27, 1869, at Louisiana, Mo.; married in 1892, to John Cornish, a prominent merchant of Turpin, Mo., and has issue, two sons and three daughters.
  G. Lyda Buckner, born Oct. 18, 1871; married Homer Wells, who died Feb. 5, 1900. Issue:
    aa. Joseph Estes Wells, died March 30, 1905.
    bb. Thomas Cust Wells.
    cc. Samuel Wells.

VIII. LUCY PENDLETON BUCKNER, youngest daughter of Bailey and Mildred (Strother) Buckner, became the second wife of Henry Child Kirk of Baltimore, Md. She was married Nov. 20, 1860, and died Sept. 26, 1876. Mr. Kirk was born Feb. 9, 1826, and is the President of Samuel Kirk & Son Company, Baltimore, the oldest manufacturers of silverware in the United States. Henry Child Kirk married (1st) Virginia Hardesty, and after the death of Lucy Buckner, his second wife, he married Eliza Hollins.

  Mr. Kirk is descended from an old Quaker family who settled in Bucks County, Pa.

Issue of Henry Child Kirk and Virginia Hardesty.
  A. Olivia Hardesty Kirk, married W. H. Conkling of Davenport, Iowa.
  B. Alice Virginia Kirk, married M. L. Millspaugh of Baltimore, Md.
Issue of Henry Child Kirk and Lucy Buckner:
  C. Mildred Buckner Kirk, born March 7, 1863; married Oct. 19, 1885, to William T. W. McCay, born Sept. 8, 1863, a prominent grain broker of Baltimore. Issue:
    aa. Mildred Buckner McCay, born Jan. 27, 1893.
  D. Henry Child Kirk, Jr., of Baltimore and Mt. Washington, Md., born Dec. 16, 1868; married Oct. 22, 1891, to Edith Huntemüller, born March 26, 1872 Issue:
    aa. Edith Buckner Kirk, born Dec. 20, 1892.
    bb. Mary Huntemüller Kirk, born March 21, 1896.
    cc. Anne Strother Kirk, born Aug. 29, 1901.
Issue of Henry Child Kirk and Elizabeth Hollins:
  E. Lydia Hemsworth Kirk, born 1880.

MAJOR CALDWELL CALHOUN BUCKNER

MAJOR CALDWELL CALHOUN BUCKNER, youngest son of Bailey and Mildred (Strother) Buckner, was born at "Wadefield," Feb. 9, 1829; died May 22, 1898; married at "Chestnut Valley," Caroline County, Nov. 22, 1853, Louisa Fitzhugh Dickinson, daughter of William I. Dickinson, and his wife, Jane Richard Buckner, who was a daughter of Thomas Buckner of "Lake Farm," Caroline County.

William I. Dickinson was a large land and slave owner, and a most successful planter. When a young man, he was elected Sheriff of Caroline County. His daughter, Louisa Fitzhugh Dickinson was a woman of sterling qualities. Her disposition was modest and retiring, and her axiom through life was "peace at any price, save with the loss of honor." She demanded from others, the respect she gave to them. Generous to a fault, universally popular, beloved by rich and poor alike, she was composed, dignified and patient in every emergency, and exercised a gentle restraining influence upon the strenuous nature of her husband, Major Buckner. Mrs. Buckner died Jan. 9, 1902, at the residence of her daughter, Mrs. William G. Brown of Philadelphia, and is buried at West Laurel Cemetery in that city.

Major Buckner was educated at Rappahannock Academy, and afterwards entered into the mercantile business in Baltimore. Later on, he became a partner with Charles Bayne, the father of Howard R. Bayne of New York. Soon after his marriage, he removed to Spottsylvania County, and lived at "Marengo," where his second son, William Dickinson Buckner was born. In 1858 he purchased "Island View," in Orange County, and began raising thoroughbred stock, of which he was an excellent judge. He often joked with his neighbors by reminding them that "General Grant's men selected seventeen of his thoroughbreds, while they did not take any of theirs."

Although Major Buckner was a Southerner from head to foot, yet he did all in his power to oppose secession, but when war was declared, he felt that it was his duty to stand by his state, whereupon he joined General Rosser's Brigade of Cavalry, and was a member of the 7th Virginia Regiment. That he was gallant and courageous in the face of the enemy was but natural, considering the line of brave men from whom he was descended. The following letter addressed to him at the conclusion of the war by General Charles Henningson, is an attestation of his bravery under trying circumstances.

WASHINGTON, MARCH 3, 1877.

COL. C. C. BUCKNER,

Dear Sir:

In reply to yours, I have no copy of the document to which you refer, nor even the precise date of the order; though there is a channel through which I may perhaps obtain it. Of the substance I have a very distinct recollection. It warmly commended the gallantry of McCulloch's Rangers in a skirmish with the advanced guard of General Rosecranz, which descending the Big Sewell attempted vigorously to drive in our outposts, and reconnoitre or establish itself in our position of Camp Defiance.

Special notice was deservedly made of the conduct of Lieut. C. C. Buckner commanding the company on that occasion.

I the more readily remember this because it was the only order of the kind I was called on to issue during my connection with the Wise Legion, and because of other peculiar circumstances. More than a week previously, General Floyd with several thousand men retired precipitately late in the afternoon from the Big Sewell, which he had been occupying, and abandoning some stores, retreated many miles eastward into an absurd position, notifying verbally General Wise that Rosecranz was coming up the valley with sixteen thousand men, and ordering the former to prepare to follow him and protect his rear. This Wise could only do by remaining where he was, on ground which had extraordinary defensive capabilities, for any one capable of appreciating them. Here Wise determined to make a stand at all hazards and despite all orders to the contrary, and it was hence called Camp Defiance, with double reference to Floyd's command and Rosecranz's advance. As an impression prevailed that our force was less than it really was at this time, I ascertained by personal count that we numbered over seventeen hundred bayonets and artillerymen. You may remember that Wise addressed the troops, as I did briefly afterwards stating the fact. Wise also left it optional with any men or officer who chose, to retire eastward as escort for some quartermasters stores then about to be sent off. He said furthur that he did not believe that Rosecranz had the force alleged, but whether he had or not, he meant to fight there to the bitter end, and believed he could "stay till the cows came home." No man or officer went to the rear, the troops cheered and the command seemed tolerably confident. There were, however, a few officers who had seen war before who privately expressed to me their misgivings that troops so utterly raw could make a stand against such an obviously great disparity of force. I had some anxiety myself as to the result for the first half hour, in case we were at once attacked in more than one direction. That affair at the foot of the Big Sewell dispersed all apprehension. The enemy were not only vigorously repulsed, but the McCulloch rangers under your lead drove them to the top of the hill, which we might have temporarily occupied had it been our purpose to do so. You were recalled to where originally stationed, and here several weeks afterwards when General Rosecranz was camped on the Big Sewell with 10,000 and General Lee in Camp Defiance with a larger force was many days opposite to him, when Rosecranz finally retreated down the valley, your company was still at the front, exactly where it had at first been placed. This affair therefore had a significance which did not attach to subsequent skirmishes, or even sanguinary engagements. It was no small merit to have been able to command those Rangers and reduce them to discipline and obedience, as was done by Imboden, their gallant captain and yourself. They had literally "kicked out the worthless officers" they had first elected; they had set orders at defiance, plundered and were in a chronic state of mutiny. They

LOUISA FITZHUGH (DICKINSON) BUCKNER

would not have officers from their own ranks. They "wanted gentlemen over them," they said, but "gentlemen who were men." Imboden and you were selected and reluctantly undertook the arduous duty, which no one else could be found willing to attempt, and with the creditable success of rendering that company the most obedient and manageable in the whole force, I am, dear sir,
Very truly yours,
(Signed) CHAS. FREDERICK HENNINGSON.

At the end of the war, finding the day had gone against him, he accepted the inevitable with equanimity and resignation; bearing in his noble heart "malice to none." In after years, nothing gave him greater pleasure than to entertain as friends, those who had once been his enemies; and in this connection we quote from the "History of the 14th Connecticut Volunteers," who during the war had seen some severe fighting in the vicinity of the Buckner homestead, and who revisited their old battlefields in 1891.

" . . . . . From this place we went to the ford, driving across with the water deep to the wagon body. Going over the hill to the Morton House we turned to the left and stopped to make inquiries at a house prominent in view on the hill. A man of elderly appearance and stately mien approached the gate to speak to us. He was the proprietor of the place, and announced himself to us as Major Caldwell C. Buckner. He pressed us to enter his grounds and prolong our stay. He was cordial, affable, courteous and intelligent, awakening our interest in him at once. When introduced to each of us in turn and told who we were, he seemed to enjoy the surprise given him, and he said with a merry twinkle of his eyes 'I should know you were not Southern gentlemen, for if you were a bottle would have been in sight before this.' He told us that he was in the Confederate service during most of the war. He said 'that when he got through the service he was thankful that he got through alive, and felt that he had had enough of war' that he was 'like the man who made a bargain with the devil, that if he would leave him alone, he would let him alone,' and that he had 'not been to a military meeting or a monument unveiling since.'. He was surprised to learn from us how serious an engagement had taken place on his premises in February, 1864, having scarcely heard of it before. He regaled us with many witty stories and legends of the war days, and devoted himself assiduously to our entertainment, urging that we spend days with him. Failing to induce us to be his guests at table, he insisted on adding, on behalf of himself and his wife, sundry improvements to our lunch set out on his porch, such as conserves and relishes, and pitchers of milk and new cider, partaking with us somewhat for hospitality's sake. So, with such pleasurable sociability, resting on the grass in the shade, soldier fashion, looking over the battlefield and contrasting its appearance with that it bore on a certain chill and bloody day nearly twenty-eight years before, the halcyon hours of this unmatched day sped on until we saw that we must begone. Now our warm hearted host, loth to have us leave him, hunted up an excuse to detain us, and finding and bringing on some melons, we must, forsooth stay until these had been well discussed. When we in earnest started to leave, the Major accompanied us to his gate, showing signs of real regret at our departure."

This first meeting of the "Blue and the Grey,"—outside of battle—at the Buckner home, was followed by several others in the years to come, and that this chance meeting of "erstwhile" foes was cemented by a firm friendship is evinced by the following letters.

ISLAND VIEW, SEPT., 27, 1894.

REV. H. S. STEVENS, WASHINGTON, D. C.,

My Dear Friend:

Your valued letter of recent date is at hand, and I am gratified at the prospect of seeing the Fourteenth, and especially yourself and my other friends. It will afford me pleasure to turn my house, yard and farm over to them any day that you may come. I shall expect you, Col. Broach, Moore and eight or ten others of your own selection, to lunch with us on that day. . . . . Since I saw you, I have given one of my daughters to a genuine, Simon pure Yankee, and a Pennsylvania Yankee at that, and after this I think I can be received as a member of your regiment.

Very truly and sincerely your friend,

C. C. BUCKNER.

THANKSGIVING DAY, NOV. 29, 1904.

MAJOR CALHOUN C. BUCKNER,
 ISLAND VIEW, VIRGINIA.

Dear and Honored Sir:

Having at various times in very recent years enjoyed the hospitalities of your home and the courtesies of yourself and your family, we wish to indicate somewhat our appreciation of your kindness and our regard for you by sending you a clock—a Connecticut clock—right from the "Mint."

We hope our token will be acceptable to you, and that when at your fireside, enjoying your home with your dear ones, you gaze upon its face noting for you the halcyon moments as they pass, or when detained in your chamber by illness, or lying, mayhap, sometimes sleepless at the midnight hour, you hear its tone vibrating on the quiet air, you may be reminded that in

MARSHALL DULANY BUCKNER

distant homes men of Connecticut, who a few years ago were strangers to you have remembered you with feelings of the highest regard and the warmest and sincerest friendship.

(SIGNED BY 11 MEMBERS OF THE 14th CONN. VOLS.)

At the close of the war Major Buckner returned to his estate, "Island View." He found his home swept of everything. Servants, blooded stock, machinery, barns, stables and fences all destroyed—only the house remaining. Being possessed of indomitable pluck and energy, he set himself to repair the ravages of war. His old black war horse, "Josh," and a yoke of oxen served him for a ploughing team, and he soon had crops growing. There was no meat to be had, but game was plentiful, so he picked up the army bullets which had peppered his fields and moulded them into gun-shot; and being a good wing shot he could fill his game bag and replenish the larder as often as necessary.

He was not the kind of man to repine at the adversities of war, indeed, adversity was simply a spur to higher achievements, but he set himself the task of preparing for the education of his children. Often has he said to them, "Boys, I'll mortgage my land to send you to school and college as long as you will be studious and diligent, for this is all you can expect to get from me, for a good education is the best inheritance an industrious boy can have."

Major Buckner was a most delightful host, and "Island View" a most hospitable home. Widely read, polished and refined in bearing, a deep and original thinker, his friends took especial delight in his entertainments and instructive conversation.

Worthy son of a worthy "Sire," he passed to his eternal rest May 22, 1898, meeting the end calmly and with Christian resignation. Issue:

I. BAILEY BUCKNER, born Oct. 1, 1854; married Laura Pannill. Issue:
    1. Marshall Lee Buckner (girl), born Sept. 28, 1889.
II. WILLIAM DICKINSON BUCKNER, of whom presently.
III. LOUISA C. BUCKNER, born May 25, 1858.
IV. JOHN STROTHER BUCKNER, born June 22, 1860; died at West Point, N. Y., May 7, 1879.
V. AYLETT HAWES BUCKNER, born May 30, 1863; died April 25, 1899; married Jan. 3, 1894, to Eleanor Brune of Cartersville, Va. Issue:
    1. Mary Carter Buckner, born Dec. 28, 1894.
    2. James Scott Hawes Buckner, born April ——, 1898.
VI. MARSHALL DULANY BUCKNER, born June 1, 1866. He was educated at the Virginia Midland Academy, where he gained the orator's gold medal of the Piedmont Literary Society. He went to Los Angeles, Cal., where his brother, William Dickinson Buckner, was engaged in engineering, to enter into

mercantile pursuits. He was stricken with a fatal illness, and passed away at the threshold of a promising career, Feb. 11, 1889. He was an exemplary student, and the embodiment of manliness, truth and honesty.

VII. LUCY BUCKNER, born Feb. 20, 1869; married Sept. 11, 1894, to William G. Brown of Philadelphia, Pa., Secretary of Reading R. R. Co., and Secretary of Reading R. R. Coal and Iron Co. Issue:
1. Barclay Brown, born July 8, 1895; died June 15, 1897.
2. Louise Dickinson Brown, born Dec. 13, 1897.
3. Edith Hamilton Brown, born June 18, 1900.

WILLIAM DICKINSON BUCKNER, second son of Major Caldwell Calhoun and Louisa (Dickinson) Buckner, was born Aug. 4, 1856, at "Marengo," near Fredericksburg. His early education was derived at the Rappahannock Academy, he afterwards taking the scientific course at Randolph Macon College where he graduated in 1879. This course included Pure and Applied Mathematics, Chemistry, Geology, Physics, Philosophy, History, Astronomy, Political Science, and a special course in Engineering. He also took a three years' course in English, Latin and German. For two years after leaving college, he taught school and devoted his spare time to practical surveying. In 1881 he was assistant engineer on the extension of the Chesapeake & Ohio R. R. through eastern Kentucky. In Jan. 1882, was transitman-in-charge of a locating party and made the first surveys of the Kentucky Central R. R. between Paris and Winchester, Ky., and was later under Eppes Randolph, who was afterwards chief engineer of the Ohio River Bridge, Cincinnati and Western Division of the C. & O. R. R. He then became assistant engineer of construction on a Division of the Kentucky Central R. R.

In the Fall of 1883, Mr. Buckner went to Mexico as transitman on the Mexican and Western R. R., was advanced to be engineer in charge of location in 1884, and chief engineer of construction in 1885. While in Mexico, he became a fluent Spanish scholar. Being desirous of studying irrigation in California, he resigned his position in Mexico, and in 1886 was assistant to the city engineer of Los Angeles, Cal., and staked out the first electric railroad built in that city. He was chief engineer in 1888 of the Santa Ana & Pacific R. R., and had charge of the construction of the Southern Riverside Irrigation Canal, and various other large enterprises, while conducting a general engineering office in Los Angeles. In 1890, he went to Europe as assistant to the Vice-President of the Chino Land and Water Co., in establishing a plant and railroad connections for the Chino Sugar Beet Factory,

LOUISE DICKINSON BROWN

which received the first bounty paid by the United States on beet sugar. During his sojourn abroad he studied and perfected himself in the French language.

Soon after his return to this country, Mr. Buckner was appointed chief engineer and superintendent of construction to the Cartagena-Magdalena R. R., of Columbia, S. A. Being much enfeebled in health through tropical fevers, he occupied himself during the years 1894 to 1897, in the promotion of real estate investments in New York, but in 1897 he once more turned to engineering, accepting the appointment of assistant chief engineer of the Guayaquil & Quito R. R., in the Republic of Ecuador. Owing to the poor health of the chief engineer, Wm. Finley Shunk, the responsibilities of the position were practically assumed by Mr. Buckner. He had charge of the engineering parties occupied in finding a way to climb the precipitous Andes, and was also made general manager of that portion of the road which was being operated by the Government of Ecuador.

Mr. Buckner's varied engineering life at the frontier has given him many novel experiences, some of which we take from the *Worcester Telegram* (Mass.) of February 9, 1902.

"William D. Buckner, New England manager of the Bond Department of Wood, Harmon & Co., with an office in the State Mutual building, has some extremely positive ideas on the Isthmian canal, based on three or four years' residence in Mexico and Central and South America.

"Mr. Buckner thinks the Panama route is by all means the best, and believes that the United States will make a great mistake if it decides upon the Nicaraguan way. The Panama route, he says, is not only much shorter, but the engineering problems presented are not nearly as difficult, and the ultimate cost, even with a bonus to the French company, will be much less. The Nicaraguan route is full of quicksands and the way lies through swamps where bottom cannot be found.

"The proposed Panama canal is to be nearly parallel with the Panama railroad, and at each terminus is a magnificent harbor and a great city. Viewed not only from the standpoint of an engineer, but also as a commercial problem, Mr. Buckner thinks that every advantage is with the Panama route.

"He went to Ecuador in 1898 as assistant chief engineer of the Ecuador Development Co., in which New York capitalists were interested, including former Mayor Abram S. Hewitt. The company obtained with much difficulty a valuable concession from the government of Ecuador, and extended a railroad running from Guayaquil to Chimbo through to Quito. Mr. Buckner witnessed a South American revolution and the story of his stay in Ecuador reads like a chapter from Richard Harding Davis' 'Soldiers of Fortune.'

"The chief engineer of the company was William F. Shunk, one of the celebrated engineers of the country. Mr. Buckner was assistant chief and superintendent of the railroad that was in operation when the company arrived in Ecuador, besides having charge of a section of the road that was building.

"The party left New York Oct. 8, 1898, on the steamer Advance, bound for Colon. The only particular happening of the passage was the knocking in of Mr. Buckner's stateroom door by a big wave one night, resulting in a salt water bath. The steamer passed near the Cuban coast, between Cuba and Hayti. The coast was rugged and mountainous and appeared to be uninhabited.

"Colon was reached Sunday, Oct. 15, at 7 o'clock, and one hour later the party took the railroad for Panama. Colon is an extremely unpleasant city. Its location was doubtless selected because of the fine, deep harbor. The country around is low and flat, with pools of black, stagnant water on every hand, and a rank tropical growth of vegetation in every space. The distance from Colon to Panama is 47 miles.

"The country is level most of the way, dotted here and there with small, coneshaped mountains, pushed up by volcanic eruptions in some pre-historic time. The country is thickly settled with negroes and Chinese, and a mixture of the two races. The only signs of agriculture are occasional gardens or banana groves. There were no signs of agriculture as a means of support.

"Before reaching Panama the mountains close together, forming a ridge, the connecting link between the Andes and Rocky mountains. Panama is a city of 36,000 people, with buildings almost entirely of wood, the chief building material of all South American cities. Fires are said to be common and destructive. The streets are narrow and come to a common center, like the spokes of a wheel. At the center is a park, the Spanish plaza. The people are slow and deliberate, this being especially noticeable to one accustomed to the bustle of New York. Bars, billiard and roulet tables at the hotels were doing a good business, for open gambling in various forms is licensed by nearly all the South American republics and is a considerable source of revenue. Sunday is a day of amusement. In Panama there is a lottery drawing every Sunday at 1 o'clock, a bull fight at 4 and the theatre at 8, with gay music by a band on the plaza between times.

"Mr. Buckner and party waited five days in Panama for a steamer, the Imperial, which carried them to Guayaquil, the seaport of Ecuador, in four days. Guayaquil, Mr. Buckner describes as an uncleanly city of about 30,000 inhabitants. Refuse matter of all kinds is thrown and allowed to remain in the streets, to the utter disregard of all sanitary law. The city is considered the third most unhealthy in the world. The two that are worse are Rio de Janeiro and a place on the coast of Africa, the name of which Mr. Buckner could not recall. The uncleanliness is apparent not only in the crowded streets of the city, but also in the country homes of the well-to-do. There seems to be no doubt but this uncleanliness is the leading cause of the terrible epidemics of disease that sweep the country.

"On the morning of Oct. 26 the party took the Quayaquil & Quito railroad, the only railroad in the country, for Chimbo, then its terminus. For 30 miles the way was over a dead level country, sometimes called the alluvial plain and fever district. The land was cultivated for sugar cane or grazed by cattle. Several large sugar-making plants were passed and one where a sort of brandy was made from sugar cane, called pisco. That is the drink of the common people. The Spanish gentleman drinks wine.

"This plain is frequently entirely submerged during the rainy season and the houses are built upon piles, from five to seven feet above ground.

"Beyond is a gentle rolling country, with higher elevation and better natural drainage. Here the banana and coffee are the staple products. These two grow on the same land at the same time, the luxuriant shade of the banana tree furnishing the necessary shade for the protection of coffee. Next came the foot-

EDITH HAMILTON BROWN

hills of the Andes, where the railroad takes the left bank of the Chimbo river, and begins to climb in earnest. Here, too, the vegetable kingdom seems to defy the power of man to subdue it. Plants, weeds and flowers of every description grow up to the very rails on either side of the track, forming almost a canopy under which the trains pass, with the leaves and branches brushing the windows.

"Chimbo is a small village located among the foothills of the Andes, owing its importance to the fact that it was the end of the railroad. Pack trains of horses, mules, donkeys and a few llamas came to the town from the mountain towns and cities above, leaving their burdens to be shipped by rail to the coast, and carrying back freight brought by rail from Guayamas. The pack trains brought down coffee, hides, roots, herbs and potatoes, which do not grow well in the hot climate around Guayaquil. The foothills are called hills in contrast to the towering Andes, but in reality are high mountains. The scenery is grand. The Chimbo river at Chimbo is nothing but a series of rapids, and is the only thing in the country that seems to be in a hurry.

"The work before the party was to continue the 55 miles of railroad from Guayaquil to Puente de Chimbo, and to Quito, a distance of 231 miles. The principal engineering difficulties were met between Chimbo and the plateau on which is situated Quito and other cities. After this plain was reached the work was comparatively easy. The construction work was in three sections, of which Chief Engineer Shunk was in charge of one, and Mr. Buckner was in charge of another. Mr. Buckner was also manager of the 55 miles of railroad already in operation, which was turned over to the American company by the government, according to the terms of the concession.

"Mr. Shunk was then 65 years old, an agreeable and entertaining man, with a vast and varied fund of information. It was his genius largely that constructed the elevated railroads of New York and Brooklyn, regarded among the greatest examples of engineering skill in the world.

"The concession to the American company was pushed through the Ecuador congress with great difficulty, as it was strongly opposed by the church party. The measure was finally adopted by a majority of one vote. The concession included the payment to the American company of 17,000,000 of Ecuador's silver dollars, worth 47 cents each in American money; the free right of way, together with immense tracts of land on each side of the railroad and other valuable privileges.

"The American company owns the railroad for 75 years, when it reverts to the government of Ecuador.

"Quito is 231 miles east and north of Chimbo, the terminus of the road at the time the concession was granted. There are only seven towns of any size between Guayaquil and Chimbo. The two largest have sugar factories with capacities of 50 tons each. These towns have a population of 1,200 and 2,200. The road is a narrow guage. Before the railroad was built 70,000 mules and horses were used to bring freight from the mountains to Guayaquil. They traveled for the most part over a splendidly constructed national highway, with stone bridges over rivers and streams. After leaving Chimbo, going toward Quito, the grade rises rapidly, being 8,000 feet in 65 miles. The country in that direction is entirely mountainous and densely timbered with valuable hardwood, but without settlements of any consequence. From Sibambe the road runs across the center of the great plateau of central Ecuador to Quito, which is 9,350 feet above the sea level and has a delightful climate. It has a population of 65,000. The large towns of the plateau are Cajamba, 15,000; Riobamba, 60,000; Ambate, 30,000; Lacunja, 25,000; Manhache, 10,000. The plateau is 60 miles wide and 170 miles long, with an elevation of 9,500 feet, and is surrounded by snow-capped mountains. The snows feed the mountain streams, so there is an abundance of water all the year around.

"It is expected to equip the railroad with electricity some time soon and water will be relied on to furnish power. Along the line of the railroad are undeveloped coal fields and also traces of oil. Coal sells at from $10 to $18 a ton along the line of the railroad, and at Quito no fuel is used other than wood and charcoal.

"Mr. Buckner said yesterday that he couldn't begin to give an idea of the queer things he saw. One day, while ascending a steep mountain side, he met a rosy cheeked, buxom Indian lass driving three large black bulls loaded with cabbages. The road was extremely narrow, and he had to whoop and yell to keep the bulls from running into him and throwing him down the side of the cliff. The girl seemed to think she was having a bully time at his expense. She was about the color of a persimmon just turning. Nearly all the mountain people have a splendid ruddy color.

"Two nights of an engineering trip were passed in Indian huts or caverns made in the side of the mountains and thatched roofs thrown over them. 'The roads or trails I traveled over,' said Mr. Buckner, 'can never be described. Suppose you plant 500 deep churns closely on the side of a mountain cliff, fill them with oil, tar, mud and refuse two-thirds full, then try to ride over them as you come down the steep mountain side. It is not only exciting, but dangerous. Your mule must step into one of these churns each time, or else he will slip down the cliff. It was risky enough to undertake the descent of one of these slippery cliffs on a dark night, hoping to reach one of the engineering camps, and expecting that my mule would see, but she fell seven times in the first quarter of a mile, and I then tried it on foot, but fell down the side of the cliff and brought up in some jungle 30 feet below the path. I then slid the rest of the descent like Balaam going through Jerusalem, and reached the camp a sight to behold.

"'After reaching the valleys of the interior the aspect of everything changes and is entirely different from the coast district. There you will see an Indian woman driving a herd of graceful llamas, each laden with vegetables for the market at Riobamba. As she trudges along the road with a baby peeping over her shoulder, she works a primitive spinning wheel, so that by the time she is at the end of her journey she will have a good supply of yarn ready spun.

"'Riobamba is a city of more refined people and the prettiest girls in Ecuador. We got mixed up in a revolution, like Davis' characters in his book, the 'Soldiers of fortune.' We met Col. Alfaro, brother of the president, just as he was going out to battle with the revolutionists, and had to celebrate before his departure. Wines and champagne were in abundance and toasts were in order, of which Uncle Sam received the greater number. They went so far as to wish that Uncle Sam would come down and take charge of the whole of Ecuador and annex it to the United States. Whether this spirit was sincere or not I am not prepared to say, but it shows the way they talk in that country.

"'I was located in Duran most of the two years that I was in the country and had quarters on the upper floor of the terminal building of the railroad. We could stand on the front balcony and shoot alligators and pelicans in the Guayas river.

"'Just back of Duran was a lake 10 miles wide with an average depth of four feet. The lake teemed with wild duck. The railroad ran along the side of the lake, and we sometimes shot ducks from a flat car as they flew across the track.

"ISLAND VIEW"

It was great sport, as it required accurate shooting to hit a duck from a moving car. We took a canoe on the car and occasionally sent out an Indian to pick up the game.

"'One night we had President Alfaro, president of the republic of Ecuador, and his official staff, at dinner, my idea being that we should feast him with the wild ducks and other game from the lake. But the odor from the ducks we had in stock lifted the cover from the ice chest and let them escape. We had no time to shoot more, but managed to get together a good bill of fare, and our duck supper became a banquet instead. Everything passed off nicely, including a dozen bottles of wine. We were greatly pleased with the success and results of the banquet.'

"Mr. Buckner remained in Ecuador until he was stricken with the fever that is the scourge of the country. He was critically ill for some time, but finally recovered and is now none the worse for his hardships."

In October, 1901, Mr. Buckner accepted a position as New England manager of the Bond Department of Wood, Harmon & Co., of New York, and was afterwards made office manager of the Title Trust Co. of New York, of which Mr. William E. Harmon was managing director.

In 1904, Mr. Buckner was the organizer of the Prospect Park Bank of Brooklyn, N. Y., of which he is the first Vice-President and executive officer. The noteworthy success attending this venture has more than justified the wisdom and forethought that originally prompted the establishment of the institution. Under the management of its first Vice-President it has steadily grown and prospered, and is destined to become one of the strongest financial institutions of Greater New York.

In addition to his other achievements, Mr. Buckner has been a leading factor in many New York real estate transactions, which have proven both successful and profitable. He also finds time to conduct a large stock farm and shooting lodge at "Island View," the family seat in Orange County, of which he is the owner. It may also be remarked "en passant," that it is entirely due to Mr. Buckner's tenacity and zeal, that the history of "The Buckners of Virginia" has, after many discouragements, taken tangible form in the production of this volume.

II. CAPTAIN GEORGE BUCKNER of "Braynefield," Caroline County, son of George Buckner, was born 1760, and died Nov. 18, 1828. He is said to have served as an officer in the Revolutionary army. In 1789 he was a Justice of Caroline County, and was also member of the House of Delegates in the years 1798, 1799 and 1800. He was twice married, but left no issue by either wife. His second wife was Dorothea Brayne Benger, widow of Col. William McWilliams of Fredericksburg. She was a granddaughter of Elliott Benger who married Dorothea Brayne in Spottsylvania County Jan. 4, 1733. His estate was administered in the above named county in 1759. His son and heir, John Benger, married Elizabeth Johnston of Spottsylvania. He died in 1766, his will being probated Nov. 3, of that year. He left two daughters, Ann, who married William Thompson of Spottsylvania, Gent., and Dorothea, who married Capt. George Buckner. By this marriage the Buckners are allied with the Spottswood family, as Dorothea Brayne, who married Elliott Benger, was an aunt of John Spottswood who died in 1758, and who mentions in his will, "my part of the estate in England which will descend to me and my cousin, John Benger, after the death of my mother and her three sisters." Governor Alexander Spottswood married Butler Brayne who was one of the four daughters and co-heiresses of Richard Brayne of St. Margaret's Parish, City of Westminister, Gent., and his wife Anne Begnold, daughter and sole heir of James Begnold of Shierre, County of Surrey. The daughters, through their mother, were heirs to considerable landed estate in England, contained in the Manors of Greens Hall, Tower Hill and Grunshall Netty, in the County of Surrey, and the Manor of High Cheer in the County of Berkshire.

By his marriage to Dorothea (Brayne) McWilliams, Captain George Buckner became the owner of "Braynefield," Caroline County, which was one of the finest estates in that part of Virginia.

III. ELIZABETH BUCKNER, daughter of George Buckner of Caroline County, was probably the eldest child, as she was married in 1770 to John Washington who is believed to have been very closely connected with the family of President George Washington. Issue:

    1. John Washington, born Sept. 24, 1772; is believed to have been unmarried at the time of his death Oct. 2, 1802.
    2. George Washington, born July 8, 1775; died 1815; married Jan. 1, 1794, to Elizabeth, daughter of Dr. John Coates of Maryland. Issue:
        A. Catherine Washington, born June 27, 1796; married Oct. 10, 1811, to Robert Sutton. Issue:
            aa. Judith Ann Sutton, married —— Shepherd.

TOMB OF CAPT. GEORGE BUCKNER

"Inscription"

Here lies the body of
GEORGE BUCKNER
who departed this life on the 18th November, 1828
Aged 68 years 1 month.

He was an officer in the Army of the Revolution and lived to enjoy the blessings for which he had fought, and to fill with honor to himself and benefit to his country, in many important Civil offices under the government he had hazarded his all to establish. The grief of all who knew him is an emphatic testimonial of his public and private worth. His aged widow who has enjoyed with him many years of harmony and happiness, has caused this tribute of affection to be erected to his memory. When such friends part, 'tis the survivor dies.

       bb. Susan Maria Sutton.
       cc. Robert Sutton.
       dd. Henry Sutton.
       ee. Oscar Sutton.
B. George Washington, born Aug. 6, 1798; d. s. p. Feb., 1815.
C. Colonel John Washington, born Sept. 13, 1800; died Sept. 27, 1850; married Ann Hawes. Issue:
    aa. George Washington, married Mildred Chandler. Issue:
        1. Thomas Washington.
        2. John Washington.
        3. George Washington.
        4. Cora Washington.
        5. William Washington.
        6. Clement Washington.
        7. Henry Washington.
    bb. Dorothea Washington, became the first wife of George Burke and left one child, Thomas Henry Burke, a very promising lawyer. He married Miss Tevis, and removing to California, there died, leaving a widow and two children.
    cc. Walker Washington, M.D., married Mollie, daughter of Lawrence and Sarah T. Washington of Westmoreland County, sister of Robert Washington who married Walker Washington's cousin, Bettie Wirt. Issue:
        1. Augustine Washington, a civil engineer and married at Paducah, Ky.
        2. Walker Washington, M.D., married. Residence, Tottenville, Staten Island.
        3. Richard Washington., U. S. Gov. Dept., Washington, D. C.
    dd. John Washington of "Spring Hill," Caroline County, attorney-at-law, died Sept. 25, 1887. Married Byrd Boyd of Essex County. Issue:
        1. J. Boyd Washington of Caroline County.
        2. Mary Washington, died in childhood.
        3. Walker Hawes Washington of Richmond.
        4. Dollie Buckner Washington.
        5. Fannie Prior Washington.
        6. Eugene Washington.
        7. Roberta Boyd Washington.
D. Susan Elizabeth Knox Washington, born Oct. 7, 1802; married Dec. 5, 1821, to Thomas Henry Burke. Issue:
    aa. George Washington Burke.
    bb. Wm. Henry Burke.
    cc. Edward G. Burke.
    dd. Selina Burke.
E. Ann Washington, born Sept. 11, 1804; married Feb. 4, 1825, to Ezekiel D. Withers. Issue:
    aa. Rolla Montgomery Withers, married and resides in Missouri.
    bb. Ann Eliza Withers, died unmarried.
    cc. Edward Withers.
    dd. Evadne Withers, married Stephen Riggs of Ohio.

F. Selina Washington, born Oct. 15, 1806; married Daniel Payne, and had issue:
    a. Elizabeth Payne, married Dr. William Wirt of "Wirtland," son of the Westmoreland County famous William Wirt.* Issue:
        aa. Bettie Wirt, married Robert Washington, son of Lawrence and Sarah T. Washington, and had issue: Lena, Wirt, Taylor and other children.
        bb. Daniel Washington Wirt.
        cc. William Washington Wirt.
        dd. Agnes Washington Wirt.
    b. Selina Payne, born Nov. 9, 1829.
G. Dorothea Washington, born Nov. 11, 1808; died Nov. 4, 1844; married Norborne E. Sutton.
H. William Washington, born March 22, 1810; died Aug. 4, 1843; married Mrs. Vass of King William County.
I. Elizabeth Washington, born Feb. 8, 1812; married William Taliaferro.
J. Caroline Washington, born May 15, 1814; died Aug. 15, 1815.

---

*William Wirt was born in Bladensburg, Md., Nov. 8, 1772; was admitted to the bar in 1792, and in 1806 settled in Richmond, Va., where he became a prominent lawyer. He distinguished himself at the trial of Aaron Burr in 1807, as one of the counsel for the prosecution. He held many State offices, being Clerk of the House of Delegates, Chancellor of the Eastern Shore of Virginia, and member of the House of Delegates. He was United States District Attorney in 1816, and Attorney-General in 1817, holding the latter office till 1829, through three administrations. He was nominated for President in 1832 by the anti-Masonic party, and received the electrical vote of Vermont. He wrote "Letters of a British Spy" (1803); "The Rainbow," and other essays; "Sketches of the Life and Character of Patrick Henry" (1817), and various addresses. He died in Washington, D. C., Feb. 18, 1834.

"BRAYNEFIELD"
RESIDENCE OF CAPT. GEORGE BUCKNER

"You tell a pedigree of threescore."
—Henry VI.

Thomas Buckner of Gloucester County

THOMAS BUCKNER, one of the four sons of the first John Buckner of Virginia, resided in Gloucester County, and was one of the most prominent men in the Colony. He occupied several official positions of trust and emolument, being Coroner in 1702, Justice in 1705, Sheriff in 1712, and was a member of the House of Burgesses in 1718. He was also a member of the vestry of Petsworth Parish, and was one of the signers "versus Transubstantiation" in 1714.

He married previous to the year 1698, Sarah, a daughter of Captain Francis Morgan, who was a Justice for York County.

Thomas and Sarah Buckner had issue at least three children—Francis, Thomas and Ann. There is a tradition that they also had a son named Samuel, who eventually married the widow of Thomas Buckner, 2d. The identity of this Samuel Buckner is a moot point, as there must have been two Samuels living at the same period in Gloucester County. There was a Samuel Buckner who was Sheriff in 1732, Justice in 1739 and a member of the House of Burgesses in 1744, in which year he died. This Samuel could not have been the one who married Mary Timson, the second wife of Thomas Buckner, 2d, as Thomas Buckner did not die until 1755, while the Samuel above died in 1744.

One argument advanced against the possibility of Thomas and Samuel being brothers is, that the canons of the Church of England forbade the marriage of a man with his deceased brother's wife. But this is not a strong argument, as this Church law was frequently violated, especially in early Colonial days. One must bear in mind the exigencies of the times, and that the clergy of those days were extremely lax in upholding the rules of the church—as far as intermarriage was concerned.

If Samuel Buckner, who married the second Thomas Buckner's widow, was not the son of Thomas Buckner, 1st, then whose son was he?

Prof. William Carter Stubbs of New Orleans, has devoted much time to tracing the line of Samuel Buckner, and considerable weight must be given to his conclusions.

Prof. Stubbs is of the opinion, that the immigrants, John and Philip Buckner, had a brother Thomas who settled in Gloucester County, where he patented 1,000 acres of land in Petsworth parish in 1669, in conjunction with Thomas Royston, and that this Thomas may sometimes be confused with the Thomas Buckner who married Ann Morgan, and who was a son of the first John Buckner. Dr. Stubbs states that this Thomas Buckner lived near the "Dragon," and that he had issue, a son Samuel, a daughter Ann, and perhaps other children.

At the time of the Buckner search in the English records, the Editor had not received the data collated by Dr. Stubbs, and he was, therefore, in ignorance as to the latter's conclusions, neither had Dr. Stubbs any knowledge of what the English search might reveal, as it had not been finished at that time. A glance at the Buckner pedigree chart shows that John and Philip Buckner had an elder brother named Thomas, who was baptized in 1628, and it is quite possible that he also came to Virginia. This is strong evidence in favor of Thomas Buckner being a brother to John and Philip, but there is also no shadow of a doubt but that John Buckner had a son named Thomas. The descendants of Thomas Buckner of the "Dragon," will be enumerated later on.

Thomas and Sarah (Morgan) Buckner had issue:

I. FRANCIS BUCKNER, a member of the vestry of Petsworth parish in 1729. He died in 1730, and was succeeded by Samuel Buckner. If he left issue, nothing is known of them.

II. ANN BUCKNER, of whom presently.

III. THOMAS BUCKNER.

THOMAS BUCKNER was born about 1692. He was a Justice and Vestryman of Petsworth parish, Gloucester, and Sheriff of Caroline County in 1747. He is believed to have married twice, his first wife being a daughter of Philip Smith and granddaughter of Baldwin Mathews of York County. He married (2d) Mary Timson, daughter of Samuel and Sarah (Mathews) Timson. She was also a granddaughter of Baldwin Mathews and she married for her second husband Col. Samuel Buckner. Thomas Buckner died about 1756. His will is dated June 2, 1755, and was probated in 1756. He had issue by his first wife:

I. MARY BUCKNER, married in 1763, John Chisman, and had issue:
  1. Mary Chisman, born about 1765.
  2. John Buckner Chisman, born about 1768.

John Chisman married (2) Elizabeth, daughter of Major Miles Cary and Ann, his wife, and had:
  1. Miles Chisman, born 1781.
  2. George Chisman, born 1783.
  3. Charles Chisman.
  4. Mathew Chisman.
  5. Patty Chisman.

II. BALDWIN MATHEWS BUCKNER, son of Thomas and Mary (Timson) Buckner, died in 1778. He was married twice, his first wife being Dorothy (born 1730; died 1757), daughter of Col. Samuel Buckner.

Will of Baldwin Mathews Buckner

In the name of God, Amen. I, Baldwin Mathews Buckner of the Parish of Ware and County of Gloucester, being weak in body but of perfect and sound mind and memory do make and publish this my last will and testament in manner following (viz.) first, it is my will and desire that if my executors can't raise as much money from my estate as will purchase each of my younger sons a tract of land as they shall come of age, that then they either swap or sell my land and the land swapped for or bought with the money that they sell my land for be equally divided among my four sons, them and their heirs forever. Also it is my will and desire that after all are paid the remainder of my personal estate and slaves be equally divided among my sons as they shall come of age, also if my executors can provide a Tract of Land for each of my younger sons as they my executors think is sufficient. Item. I give my land wherein I live to my son Thomas Buckner to him and his heirs forever, also if my son Samuel shall choose to be a Ship Carpenter that then my executors choose five negro boys out of my estate and bind with him to such master as they shall think proper which said . . . . I give my son Samuel, he being accountable for the appraised value as they were appraised taken of the Inventory when he receives his proportion of my estate, also it is my will and desire that each of my sons pay Sarah Lemmon twenty-five shillings annually for her maintenance and that she be at liberty to live with which of my sons she chooses.

Lastly, I constitute and appoint my brother John and Mordecai Buckner, my friends John Cary and John Chisman, my sons Thomas, Samuel, Robert and John Buckner my executors of this my last will and testament, and that my brothers John and Mordecai be guardians to my sons and have full power to act for the benefit of my children in the same manner as if I myself was present, and that they give no security for their administration. In witness whereof I have hereunto set my hand and fixed my seal this 5th day of April, 1774.

BALDWIN M. BUCKNER [SEAL].

Witnesses: John Elliot.
John Tompkins.
Geo. Booth, Jr.
John Buckner.

At a court held for Gloucester County on Thursday the 5th day of Nov., 1778, this will was this day proved in open court by the oath of John Buckner a witness thereto, who also made oath that he saw John Tompkins and Geo. Booth, Jr., the other two witnesses who are dead, sign the said will as witnesses in the presence of the said Testator, and thereupon the same was by the court admitted to record and is recorded.

Teste. Thomas Nelson, Jr. [C.C.].

Baldwin Mathews Buckner had issue by his first wife, Dorothy Buckner:

1. Thomas Buckner, Captain during the Revolution, Commissioned 2d Lieutenant 7th Virginia Regiment, March 7, 1776; 1st Lieutenant, Nov. 13, 1776; Captain, July, 1777; transferred to 5th Virginia Regiment, Sept. 14, 1778; Captain, Oct. 3, 1778; taken prisoner at Charleston, May 12, 1780; exchanged July, 1781; transferred to 8th Virginia Regiment, Feb. 12, 1781; served to Jan., 1783. He was afterwards a member of the Order of the Cincinnati. He married in 1780, Elizabeth, daughter of John and Elizabeth (Cooke) Throckmorton, and they had issue:
   A. Elizabeth Buckner, married (1st) in 1808, John Cooke, born 1746; and (2d) Col. William Jones of "Concord."
   B. Ann Buckner, married Richard M. Thornton.
   C. Mary Buckner, married John Thruston.
2. Baldwin Mathews Buckner, son of Baldwin M. and Dorothy Buckner. Nothing is known of his descendants if he had any.
3. Samuel Buckner, son of Baldwin M. and Dorothy Buckner, married Elizabeth Tomkies, and had issue, a daughter Elizabeth. Her father died previous to 1798, and she had as guardian John S. Stubbs, the husband of her maternal Aunt Catherine Tomkies.

By his second wife—whose name is unknown—Baldwin Mathews Buckner had issue:

    4. Robert Buckner, who married Frances Walker and died in 1784. She had married previously a Debnam, and after the death of her second husband she married James Jones. By Robert Buckner she had issue:

      A. Charity Buckner, who married Col. William Jones of "Concord," as his third wife.

    5. John Buckner, born in 1763; married Elizabeth ———. After his death, his widow married in 1822, Robert Garrett. Issue:

      A. Ann Buckner, married Lewis Dunston.
      B. Rachel Buckner, married William Fletcher.
      C. Elizabeth Buckner, married James West.
      D. Peyton Buckner.
      E. Baldwin Buckner, married ———, and had issue:
          aa. Peyton Buckner.
          bb. Rachel Buckner.

III. JOHN BUCKNER, son of Thomas and Mary (Timson) Buckner, died in 1790. He was a lawyer and a member of Petsworth vestry, Gloucester County, in 1789. He married Nov. 24, 1785, Dorothy, daughter of James and Ann Scrosby of Christ Church Parish, Middlesex County. James Scrosby's will was probated March 23, 1772.

John and Dorothy Buckner had issue, a daughter, Ann Timson Buckner, who married the Rev. Servant Jones. She is a legatee under the will of her uncle, John Scrosby of Gloucester, Feb. 8, 1791; and also under the will of her uncle, James Scrosby of Mathews County, April, 1792. After the death of John Buckner, his widow married (2d) John Russell, and (3d) John Dunn.

IV. WILLIAM BUCKNER, son of Thomas and Mary (Timson) Buckner, removed to Mathews County where he was a Justice in 1792. He married in Kingston parish, Sept. 11, 1773, Elizabeth, daughter of Capt. Thomas Smith of the above named parish. Issue:

    1. Mary D. Buckner, born April 24, 1775.
    2. Lucy Seignora Buckner, married ——— Philpotts. She was administratrix of the will of her father, William Buckner, in 1823.

V. COLONEL MORDECAI BUCKNER, son of Thomas and Mary (Timson) Buckner, resided in Spottsylvania County. Living at a period when the Colony was continually at war with the French and Indians, his trend was towards a military career, in which capacity he gained an enviable notoriety.

The following notices of him are found in *Crozier's Virginia Colonial Militia:*

"Mordecai Buckner, Gent., Quarter-Master till properly discharged in 1755 in the forces raised for defence of this State."

"Mordecai Buckner, Captain in Col. Adam Stephen's regiment raised in 1758 by this State."

"Mordecai Buckner, Gent., Captain till properly discharged in a regiment raised for immediate defence of this State, under command of Col. Stephen, in 1762."

"Mordecai Buckner, entitled to 3,000 acres of land agreeable to the King's Proclamation of 1763."

Mordecai Buckner's military renown during the various Colonial Wars, brought him to the personal attention of General George Washington, under whom he had served in several campaigns. At the breaking out of the Revolution he was tendered the command of the Sixth Virginia Regiment, Feb. 13, 1776. The heirs of Colonel Mordecai Buckner have still a claim against the Government of the United States for services rendered by him in the Revolutionary War. The amount adjudged by Congress as due Colonel Buckner was $36,000 with extensive possessions in the Public Lands in Ohio. Under the system inaugurated in the Act of 1785, passed by the Continental Congress, the State of Virginia in her cession of territory, reserved 4,204,800 acres of land between the Scioto and Little Miami rivers, nearly one-sixth the area of the State, to satisfy the claims of the officers and soldiers in her Continental Line.

In 1742, Mordecai Buckner was a Justice of Spottsylvania County, and was also appointed in the same year Justice of Gloucester County. He was married in 1768 to Elizabeth Beverley, the widow of Beverley Stanard, whom she had married April 19, 1750. Beverley Stanard's will is dated Feb. 20, 1765, probated July 1 of same year. In it he mentions his wife Elizabeth, and his children, William, Larkin, Elizabeth, Mary, Sarah and "the child my wife now goes with." Elizabeth's parents were Larkin Chew and Mary Beverley of Spottslyvania County, their marriage license being dated Sept. 30, 1733. Mary

Beverley was a daughter of Captain Harry Beverley and Elizabeth, daughter and heiress of Robert Smith of "Brandon," Middlesex County. Harry Beverley was captain of a sloop which was captured by the Spaniards. He escaped, however, in 1717. His will was proved Feb. 2, 1730. Captain Beverley was a son of Major Robert Beverley who died 1687, and Mary, widow of George Keeble. His brother Robert was the celebrated historian of Virginia.

Larkins Chew's will is dated March 27, 1770, probated in Spottsylvania County Sept. 21 of same year. His son-in-law, Mordecai Buckner, being one of the executors. With other legatees, he mentions his daughter Elizabeth, wife of Mordecai Buckner, and to her children he leaves land in Orange County.

By his marriage with Elizabeth Beverley Stanard, Mordecai Buckner became allied to three of the most influential families in Virginia—Beverley, Chew and Stanard, besides bringing into the Buckner family the estate of "Roxbury" in Spottsylvania County. The tradition in the family is, that Colonel Buckner was an extremely wealthy man; but whatever wealth he may have had during his lifetime, it is evident that at the time of his death his estate was but moderate, for in the Guardians Bonds, under date of Feb. 5, 1788, we find that Beverley Stanard was guardian to John Buckner and Baldwin M. Buckner, orphans of Mordecai Buckner, with William Stanard as security, the bond being in the sum of £8,000, which according to law, was placed at double the value of the estate.

The exact date of Colonel Buckner's death is unknown, but it must have been previous to 1788, for on Jan. 1st of that year, William Stanard is administrator of the estate of Mordecai Buckner of Berkeley Parish, Spottsylvania County, in which mention is made of John and Baldwin Buckner, the sons. It is probable that Colonel Buckner died the latter part of 1787, for on June 7, 1787, his mother, Mary Buckner, makes her will, in which she names as executors her sons John, Mordecai and William. In this will she mentions "My first husband, Thomas Buckner, who by his will dated June 2, 1755, devised his estate to me, leaving it to my discretion to divide the same among his youngest children at my death, I divide the same among the following: Son John, son Mordecai, son William. And whereas, during the time of my intermarriage with Col. Samuel Buckner, and at the same time holding the estate of my first husband, Thomas Buckner, the estate of Samuel Buckner became indebted to the estate of the said Thomas to a considerable amount in moneys, be the amount what it will, the same is to be divided between my three sons above named."

Col. Mordecai Buckner and his wife, Elizabeth Beverley Stanard, had issue, two children, John Chew Buckner and Baldwin M. Buckner.

I. JOHN CHEW BUCKNER was born in 1770, and died without issue in 1820.

II. BALDWIN MATHEWS BUCKNER, born at "Roxbury," April 20, 1772; died at his residence, "Chestnut Hill," Orange County, Dec. 27, 1827; married Fanny, second daughter of Captain May Burton of the Revolutionary Army, born at her father's Manor "Burtonsville," Orange County, April 6, 1780; died at "Chestnut Hill," Dec. 5, 1872. Issue:

1. Elizabeth Beverley Buckner, born August 7, 1796; died in Richmond, May 1, 1864; married Dec. 14, 1824, a distant relative, Ansalem Brock, a son of Captain Joseph Brock who commanded the defences at Chimborazo Heights, Richmond, during the War of 1812; born at his father's residence, "Mount Airy," Madison County, Sept. 23, 1797; died suddenly during a temporary sojourn in Chesterfield County, Aug. 12, 1868. Issue:

A. Agnes Frances Brock, died in infancy.
B. Joseph Baldwin Brock, M.D., Surgeon-in-Chief under General Robert E. Lee during last two years of the Civil War, and lost his life in the disaster at the Capitol in Richmond, April 27, 1870; married Landonia Amelia, daughter of William Andrews of Spottsylvania County, who died in Warren County, Dec. 2, 1901, leaving issue:

aa. Alice Beverley Brock, married Edward Pugh Wilkins of Alexandria, residence, Warren County. Issue: Julian Brock Wilkins, born Aug. 8, 1884; died Nov. 30, 1892.
bb. Mary Maud Brock, unmarried.
cc. Joseph Baldwin Brock, married Fannie L. Coleman of Warren County, and had issue: (1) Helen Landonia Brock, born April 26, 1890; (2) Francis Joseph Brock, born Nov. 12, 1892.

C. Sarah Ann Brock, writer, author of "Richmond During the War," and other works, married Reverend Richard Fletcher Putnam, M.A., of the Protestant Episcopal Church, an accomplished and learned divine, literary critic and reviewer, a son of the late John Putnam, an early Boston publisher, distinguished as the founder of "*The Ladies' Magazine*," the first periodical for women, and "*The Juvenile Miscellany*," the first periodical for juvenile readers, ever brought out in America; and a lineal descendant of the family who settled at Danvers, Mass., in 1634, and from whom came Generals Israel and Rufus Putnam of the War of the Revolution. The Rev. and Mrs. Putnam have resided for several years in Brooklyn, N. Y. No issue.

D. Horace Edgar Brock, died in infancy.

E. Charles William Penn Brock, M.D., of Richmond, Medical Director of General James L. Kemper's Army Corps, C. S. A., Surgeon to the Richmond Police Department, 1865; since 1881, Chief Surgeon of the Chesapeake and Ohio R. R.; 6th President elect of the National Association of Railroad Surgeons, 1883; President of the Virginia Medical Association, 1898; Chairman of the Richmond Chapter of the Society of Alumni of University of Virginia; married Elizabeth, only daughter of the late John H. Tyler, Sr., of Richmond. Issue:

   aa. Elizabeth Tyler Brock, married Edwin Littleton Hewitt, a son of Thomas Marshall and Josephine (Allen) Hewitt of Charles City County, Va., and grandson of the late Joseph Allen of Richmond. No issue.

   bb. Virginia Allen Brock, married Floyd Hughes, lawyer of Norfolk, Va., younger son of the late Hon. Robert W. Hughes, Judge of the United States District Court of the Eastern District of Virginia, and Eliza M. Johnston, daughter of the Hon. Charles C. Johnston, and niece of General Joseph E. Johnston, C. S. A. Issue: Charles Brock Hughes, born Aug. 10, 1894; Virginia Floyd Hughes, born Aug. 29, 1896.

   cc. Charles Bolton Brock, M.D., of Richmond, unmarried.

   dd. Ausalem Tyler Brock, lawyer, of Richmond, unmarried.

F. Elizabeth Beverley Brock, married Joseph Reinhart of Shepherdstown, Jefferson County, West Va. Lieutenant in Company F., 1st Virginia Cavalry, C. S. A., General Fitzhugh Lee's command. Issue:

   aa. Brock Reinhart, civil engineer, married Willie Reed Carpenter, daughter of Dr. George Carpenter of "Cohongoronto," West Va., and had issue, George Brock Reinhart, born Oct. 11, 1896; died April 19, 1898.

   bb. Joseph Baldwin Reinhart of New York City, unmarried.

2. John May Buckner, second child of Baldwin Mathews and Fanny (Burton) Buckner, was born at Chestnut Hill, Orange (now Greene) County, Feb. 8, 1800; died in infancy.

3. Horace Buckner, third child of Baldwin Mathews and Fanny (Burton) Buckner, was born at Chestnut Hill, June 28, 1803; died at his residence in Madison County, Va., July 8, 1837. Married Mary Clarissa Walker, a daughter of Merry Walker of Madison, born Jan. 11, 1806; died May 3, 1889. Issue:

- A. Elizabeth Merry Buckner, born July 11, 1827; married Benjamin Wayland of Madison County, and had issue:
  - aa. Selina Wayland.
  - bb. Annie Wayland.
- B. Benjamin Franklin Buckner, born April 30, 1829; went in early manhood to Missouri, died in that State in 1882, his brother, Dr. Baldwin M. Buckner, having his remains brought back to Virginia and buried in the family plot, at his father's residence in Madison.
- C. Sarah Ann Amelia Buckner, born Feb. 20, 1831; died April 12, 1860; married Sept. 19, 1850, Jackson Thornton of Greene County, Va.; died July 12, 1858, leaving issue, one son, who survived him several years.
- D. Baldwin Mathews Buckner, Jr., M.D., of Madison County, born Jan. 4, 1833; married his first cousin, Amelia Frances Walker of Madison. Issue:
  - aa. Fannie Thornton Buckner, born Oct. 13, 1876; married Dec. 18, 1900, to Michael Howard Gaar of Madison.
- E. Addison Walker Buckner of Madison County, born June 22, 1835; married Bettie L. Garth of Madison, and had issue, nine children, of whom are now living:
  - aa. William Garth Buckner.
  - bb. Elizabeth Buckner.
  - cc. Benjamin Buckner.
  - dd. Edna Buckner.
  - ee. Mary Buckner.
  - ff. Horace Buckner.
  - gg. Jeb Stuart Buckner.
- F. Mary Horace Buckner, born March 3, 1838; married Abram W. Gaar of Madison, died Aug. 8, 1857. No issue.

4. Baldwin Mathews Buckner, M.D., fourth child of Baldwin Mathews and Fanny (Burton) Buckner, was born May 4, 1813; died at his residence, "Edgewood," Louisa County, Va., Sept. 8, 1886. Married three times. First wife, Sarah Catherine Foushee, a daughter of William Foushee of Madison Court House. She died April 18, 1843, aged twenty-five years, leaving issue:
   - A. William Mordecai Buckner, born Oct. 23, 1835, at Madison Court House. Served in Confederate Army throughout the war. Is now a merchant in Greene County, Va. Unmarried.
   - B. Fanny Buckner, born July 18, 1838, at Madison Court House; died Dec. 21, 1841.
   - C. Horace Buckner, born Dec. 6, 1841, at Madison Court House; died at his father's residence, "Edgewood."

Baldwin Mathews Buckner married (2d) Jan. 12, 1848, Mary Ann Wilkinson, daughter of the Rev. Robert Wilkinson of "Woodlawn," Louisa County. She died March 2, 1864, and had issue:
- A. Elizabeth Catherine Buckner, born March 28, 1849, at "Woodlawn;" died June 28, 1867, at "Plain View," Louisa County.
- B. Robert Arthur Buckner, President of City Council of Roanoke City, Va., born at "Woodlawn," Oct. 5, 1850; married Belle

The Buckners of Virginia

Overton Harris, daughter of Rev. William A. Harris, President of the Wesleyan Female College, Staunton, Va., and has issue: Dorothy Gordon Buckner, born March 11, 1895, at Roanoke City.

C. Linden Chapman Buckner of Roanoke City, born June 25, 1853; married Elizabeth Overton Jones of Guinette County, Georgia, and has issue:
    aa. Margaret Davis Buckner, born Sept. 8, 1895, at Roanoke City.
    bb. Mary Wilkinson Buckner, born April 18, 1898, at Roanoke City.

D. Baldwin Mathews Buckner (4th), born at "Plain View," Oct. 9, 1854; died Nov. 7, 1856.

E. Charles Montgomery Buckner, born at "Plain View," Oct. 10, 1857; died July 30, 1858.

F. Walter Buckner of Richmond, Va., born at "Plain View," Aug. 30, 1859; unmarried.

G. Leigh Buckner, M.D., of Roanoke City, Va., born Oct. 26, 1861; married Oct. 4, 1892, Kathryn Hulda Brickham of New Orleans, born Dec. 3, 1872. Issue:
    aa. Edna B. Buckner, born Sept. 11, 1893; died Feb. 3, 1894.
    bb. Elizabeth Wyatt Buckner, born Oct. 1, 1896.
    cc. Leigh Buckner, born Sept. 23, 1899.
    dd. Kathryn Alexander Buckner, born June 3, 1900.

H. Mary Blanche Buckner, born Aug. 23, 1862; married Hermann Christian Crueger of Roanoke City. Issue:
    aa. Linden Wyatt Crueger, born at Roanoke, Feb. 12; died March 6, 1887.
    bb. Hermann Christian Crueger, born at Roanoke, Oct. 19, 1891.
    cc. Baldwin Buckner Crueger, born at Roanoke, July 8, 1893.
    dd. Walter Frederick Crueger, born at Roanoke, Oct. 22, 1895.
    ee. Gustav Adolf Crueger, born at Roanoke, Aug. 4, 1897.
    ff. Mary Elizabeth Crueger, born at Roanoke, May 10, 1899.

Baldwin Mathews Buckner, married (3rd) Margaret Julian Scott, and had issue:

A. Caroline Howard Buckner, born at "Plain View," Oct. 10, 1867; married at "Edgewood," Rev. Charles L. Bane of the Methodist Episcopal Church; died April 29, 1900, at Charlottesville. Issue:
    aa. Baldwin Buckner Bane, born Aug. 2, 1891.
    bb. Robert Franklin Bane, born April 7, 1893.
    cc. Carrie Howard Bane, born Feb. 8, 1896.

B. Gertrude Baldwin Buckner, born at "Plain View," Feb. 24, 1870. Unmarried.

C. Katherine Foushee Buckner, born at "Plain View," Aug. 23, 1872. Unmarried.

Ann Buckner of Gloucester County

ANN BUCKNER, granddaughter of John Buckner, the immigrant, and daughter of Major Thomas Buckner, Sheriff and Burgess of Gloucester County, and his wife Sarah, daughter of Captain Francis Morgan, 2nd, of York County, was born March, 1698. She married Thomas Booth of Gloucester County, whose will, dated 1756, is recorded in Hanover County, to which place he afterwards moved. Ann Buckner was the second of the four wives of Thomas Booth, the last two being Susannah Thornton, and Lucy Cooke, widow (1737), of Gregory Smith.

Thomas Booth was a son of Thomas Booth (born 1663; died 1736), the immigrant, who came from Lancashire, England, and his wife Mary, a daughter of Mordecai Cooke of "*Mordecai's Mount*" 1650. Thomas and Mary (Cooke) Booth lie buried on Ware River, Gloucester County, at the old Booth House, now Jarvis' Farm. Upon the tomb are engraved the arms of Booth of Barton, County Lancaster, impaling Cooke of Whitefield, County Suffolk. The heraldic description of the arms being as follows:

Cooke Arms

Or, a fesse between two lions passant gules.
Crest: A wolf's head argent, ducally gorged gules.

Booth Arms

Argent, three boar's heads erect and erased sable.
Crest: A demi-St. Catherine ppr. couped at the knees, habited argent, crowned or, in the dexter hand a Catherine wheel, in the sinister a sword, the point downwards.

The tomb, which is even now in a good state of preservation, bears the following inscription:

(Arms)
"Underneath this loanly Tomb lieth ye
Body of Mary Booth the wife of

Mordecai Cooke.

> Thomas Booth Gent deceased
> Who lieth near her. She was daughter
> Of Mordecai Cooke Gent of Ware Parish
> Gloucester County in Virginia. Who departed
> this life January 21st, 1723.
> This Monument is erected by the
> Sons and Daughters of the said
> Thomas and Mary Booth in Memory
> Of our Dear and tender Mother."

George Booth of "Poropotank," Gloucester County, son of Thomas (born 1685; died 1756) and his wife Ann (Buckner) Booth, had a daughter Sarah, who married Thomas Baytop, born 1749; died 1812, in Gloucester County. He was Captain of Artillery during the Revolution, serving in Col. Charles Harrison's Regiment.

Rev. James Baytop, of "Springfield," Gloucester County, born 1792; died 1860; son of Captain Thomas Baytop, married Lucy Taliaferro Catlett of "Timberneck," the granddaughter of Charles Carter of "Cleve."

Anne Walker Carter Baytop, daughter of Rev. James Baytop, was born 1817; died 1894; married March 4, 1835, to Jefferson W. Stubbs, born "Valley Front," Gloucester County, March 30, 1811; died Jan. 22, 1897. He was presiding Justice of Gloucester County, President of Gloucester Charity School Fund, and Recording Steward of the M. E. Church South for fifty years. Issue:

I. Major James New Stubbs, C. S. A., born 1839. Lawyer and State Senator of Gloucester County; married Elizabeth Medlicott, and has issue:
   1. Jefferson D. Stubbs.
   2. William Carter Stubbs.
   3. Emma L. Stubbs.
   4. Samuel M. Stubbs.
   5. James Lucien Stubbs.

II. Thomas Jefferson Stubbs, C. S. A., born 1841. A.M., Ph.D., Professor in William and Mary College. Married Mary Mercer Cosnahan, daughter of Capt. Joseph B. and Louisa Mercer (Waller) Cosnahan of Williamsburg, and has issue:
   1. Ann W. C. Stubbs.
   2. Thomas J. Stubbs, Jr.
   3. Lucy Taliaferro Stubbs.
   4. Mary Mercer Stubbs.

III. William Carter Stubbs, Ph.D., of New Orleans, La., born Dec. 7, 1843, at "Valley Front," Gloucester County. Brigadier-General C. S. A. Student of William and Mary College, 1860; graduate of Randolph Macon College, 1862; graduate of University of Virginia, 1868. State chemist of

Alabama, 1878; Professor of chemistry in Alabama Agricultural and Mechanical College, 1869; Professor of Agriculture in University of Louisiana, and Director of Louisiana Agricultural Experiment Station, 1886; Member of Camp No. 7, New Orleans, C. S. A.

Dr. Stubbs married July 28, 1875, at "Rocky Hill," Lawrence County, Ala., Elizabeth Saunders Blair, daughter of Henry D. and Mary L. (Saunders) Blair, of Mobile, Ala., and has no issue.

    IV.   Lucy Ellen Stubbs, died 1877; unmarried.
    V.   Mary Ann Stubbs, died 1893; unmarried.
    VI.   Dr. John Catlett Stubbs of Baltimore, died 1874; d. s. p.
    VII.   Martha Maria Stubbs, unmarried, residing at "Valley Front."
    VIII.   Elizabeth Baytop Stubbs, unmarried, residing at "Valley Front."

"To draw forth your noble ancestry."
—Richard III.

Thomas Buckner of Gloucester County

THOMAS BUCKNER, who lived near the "Dragon" Gloucester County, is believed to have been a brother of John and Philip Buckner the immigrants. He is in all probability the Thomas who was baptized in 1628 in Oxford, England, and was the elder of the three brothers—John being baptized in 1631, and Philip in 1639.

He patented 1,000 acres of land in 1669, in Petsworth parish, on the "Cheesecake" branches, and 2,000 acres in 1670, both grants were taken out in conjunction with Thomas Royston. He is said to have been a member of the Petsworth vestry in 1695. It is not known whom he married, but he left a son Samuel.

I. Samuel Buckner lived near the "Dragon," and died in 1745. He was a member of the Petsworth vestry and a church-warden in 1730. Was Sheriff of Gloucester in 1732, and Burgess in 1744, vice Lewis Burwell, who became one of the Council. His wife's name is unknown, but he had issue, Ann and Samuel, and possibly others.

   1. Ann Buckner, married Major Miles Cary (his second wife). Her will was probated in York County in 1768. She left her estate as follows: "To Mr. John Cary, son of my consort, Major Miles Cary; to Mrs. Ann Tomkins, wife of Capt. Bennett Tomkins; to Mr. John Chisman, and to my nephew, Baldwin Mathews Buckner."
   2. Colonel Samuel Buckner of Gloucester County, was a Justice from 1748-59. His will is dated Nov. 5, 1763, and was probated in 1764. His first wife is thought to have been Ann Alexander.

In the York records under date of Sept. 26, 1698, there is an agreement suit brought by Thomas Buckner and Sarah his wife, and David Alexander and Anne his wife, the said Sarah and Anne being daughters and co-heirs of Captain Francis Morgan, son of Francis Morgan.

In Hening, Vol. V., p. 399, we find an act docking the entail of the above property which was the share of Ann Alexander. Amongst others, Samuel Buckner and David Alexander, gents., are named as trustees. This David is said to have been a brother of Ann Alexander who married Col. Samuel Buckner.

By his first wife, Ann Alexander, Samuel Buckner had issue:

A. Dorothy Buckner, born 1730; died Dec. 8, 1757; married Baldwin Mathews Buckner (first wife), son of Thomas and Mary (Timson) Buckner. She had issue:
    aa. Thomas Buckner.
    bb. Samuel Buckner.
For detailed pedigree see Baldwin Mathews Buckner.

B. Mary Buckner, born 1732; died 1765; married 1760, Rev. Charles Mynn Thruston of Gloucester County. (See Thruston excursus.)

C. Elizabeth Buckner, born 1735; married Col. William Finnie of York County. By the will of Mordecai Cooke, Jr., Ware Parish, Gloucester, July 25, 1769, probated April 5, 1776, he left a legacy of £500 to Ann Finnie, the daughter of William and Elizabeth (Buckner) Finnie.
    aa. Ann Finnie.

D. Ann Buckner, born 1739; died Oct. 30, 1757.

Colonel Samuel Buckner married secondly, Mary, daughter of Samuel Timson, and widow of Thomas Buckner. He does not seem to have had issue by this marriage. Mary Buckner's will is dated June 7, 1787, and probated in Spottsylvania County. In it she mentions "her second husband, Col. Samuel Buckner, whose estate was indebted to that of her first husband, Thomas Buckner."

At "Marlfield," in Gloucester County, is a tomb which reads: "Here Lyeth ye Body of Dorothy Buckner, the wife of Baldwin Mathews Buckner and daughter of Colonel Samuel and Ann * * * * who Departed this Life the 8th of December, 1757, Aetat 2 * * * . Also ye Body of her sister Ann Buckner, who departed this Life the 30th of October, 1757, Aetat 18."

"MARLFIELD"
ONE OF THE OLD BUCKNER HOMES IN GLOUCESTER CO., VA.

"Boast not these titles of your ancestors."
—BEN JONSON.

Philip Buckner of Stafford County

PHILIP BUCKNER was a younger brother of the first John Buckner, and he is believed to have been the Philip Buckner who was baptized at St. Mary's Church, Oxford, Eng., March 19, 1639. The name of his wife is uncertain, but it is possible she may have been Elizabeth Sadler, who we find married a Philip Buckner, July 15, 1667, at St. James, Clerkenwell.

In his will, Philip Buckner mentions but two sons—Robert and Andrew, and he expresses a desire that "they may have learning." This would indicate that they were quite young, or at least in their 'teens in 1700, and as their mother's name is not mentioned, she was evidently deceased at that time.

The existing county records reveal but little concerning Philip Buckner, and practically nothing in regard to his children. There was a Robert Buckner in Gloucester in 1722, and he may have been the son of Philip.

The earliest land warrant to Philip Buckner was for 517 acres in Gloucester County granted to Mr. John Vickers and Mr. John Buckner, in which Philip Buckner has a headright. Feb 19, 1669.

On Oct. 10, 1692, Philip Buckner patented 90 acres of land in Chotank Parish, Stafford County. There is also a Mr. Anthony Buckner who had a grant of 2,506 acres in Stafford County, Sept. 20, 1678, and who had previously in conjunction with Lawrence Smith, March 17, 1672, patented 716 acres of land in Rappahannock County. There seems to be no clue to the identity of Anthony Buckner, unless he was a brother of John and Philip. He may have been the ancestor of John Anthony Buckner, who was the founder of the West Virginia branch of the family.

Issue of Philip Buckner of Stafford:
  I. Robert Buckner, alive in 1722.
  II. Andrew Buckner.

Will of Philip Buckner

In the name of God, Amen. I, Philip Buckner, of the County of Stafford, being sick and weak in body, but of perfect and sound memory, blessed be God, do make this my last will and testament, as follows:

First:—I bequeath my soul to God that gave it; my body to the ground from whence it came. To be buried with decent Christian burial. First, I bequeath to Judy Baltrup the mare "Bonny" and her colt and one great feather bed in the loft, and an old gold ring to be kept in her god-father's hands while the day of marriage or comes of age; and two brass kettles, one great and one little one and a copper skillet, one pewter candlestick, the rest are at her brother's and all her mother's wearing clothes in general of what sort soever that shall be found in my custody.

Second:—I bequeath my two sons, Robert and Andrew, all my land to be equally divided between them, and all the rest of my estate, movable and unmovable, to be equally divided between my two sons aforesaid, Robert and Andrew.

Thirdly:—I appoint my cousin, William Buckner, at York, to be my Excr., but if he shall refuse, then my cousin, Thomas Buckner.

Fourthly:—My will is that they take my children down with them and to remove their estates with them if they see fit, but to be sure to take my sons down that they may have learning.

Fifthly:—My will is that Broard Mann shall live upon my plantation as long as he will.

Sixthly:—My will is that Edward Mann shall pay Sara Napp, her tobacco that is due to her out of my own house before any probate of this my last will and testament, and do give him, the said Edward Mann, full power to do the same if he shall have occasion. Furthermore my will is, that Sara Napp stay here as long as she pleases, if she doesn't go for England.

PHILIP BUCKNER. (Seal.)

Signed and sealed in the presence of us:—
    Joseph Walker,
    Sara (X) Napp,
    Edward (X) Mann.   Nov. 21, 1699.

The above will was proved by the oaths of Ralph Walker and Sara Napp in the Court of Stafford, April 10, 1700, and there recorded.

MILL HILL—FORMERLY OWNED BY THOMAS BUCKNER
NOW THE PROPERTY OF EDWARD SON OF JOHN THORNTON

Thomas Buckner of Caroline County

THOMAS BUCKNER, fourth son of Richard and Elizabeth (Cooke) Buckner of Essex County, was born in Caroline County, May 13, 1728. He was a man of considerable wealth and local prominence, and the owner of two large estates, "Mount Pleasant" and "Mill Hill," both situated in Caroline County. He was married twice, his first wife being Judith Thornton, born Nov. 13, 1731; died June 19, 1757, to whom he was united in 1749. She is buried at Port Royal. (See Thornton excursus). By her he had issue:

    I. SUSANNA BUCKNER, born Dec. 22, 1749; married Peter Dudley of Spottsylvania County. She was living in 1784, as she and her husband are parties to a deed dated Sept. 9th, of that year. She was dead in 1798, as a deed dated June 22d of that year, recites that Peter Dudley is about to intermarry with Anna, widow of Peter Rawlings, and that Peter Dudley has sundry sons and daughters by a former marriage. In the Order Book of Spottsylvania County we find that on Nov. 17, 1780, Peter Dudley was commissioned as Ensign in the County Militia. Of the issue of Peter and Susanna (Buckner) Dudley, nothing is known.

    II. MARY BUCKNER, born Oct. 30, 1751; married Oct. 17, 1771, Catesby Woodford.

    III. WILLIAM BUCKNER, of "Mill Hill," born Oct. 1, 1753; married Elizabeth Monroe. Issue:

        1. Elizabeth Buckner, married Norbonne Taliaferro.
        2. Thomas Buckner, died young.
        3. Judith Thornton Buckner, married Meredith Yeatman.
        4. Warren Buckner, died young.
        5. Catherine Buckner, married William W. Monroe. Their Marriage Bond was issued in Caroline County, April 23, 1805.
        6. Spence Monroe Buckner, married in 1807, to Lucy Catesby Woodford, and by her had William Spence Buckner, born April 4, 1810; married Oct. 18, 1831, to Caroline Matilda Buckner.
        7. Mary Monroe Buckner, married her cousin, William Thomas Buckner, son of Thomas and Elizabeth (Hawes) Buckner.

    IV. THOMAS BUCKNER, of whom presently.
    V. ELIZABETH BUCKNER, born May 21, 1757; married Stephen Farish.

On Nov. 17, 1757, Thomas Buckner married for his second wife Elizabeth Taliaferro. She is believed to have been a daughter of Francis Taliaferro of Spottsylvania County, who mentions her in his will, Feb. 23, 1756.

Issue of second marriage:

VI. ROBERT BUCKNER, born Oct. 24, 1758; married March 23, 1782, Mary Hawes, born Feb. 2, 1764, daughter of Samuel and Ann Walker Hawes, of King William County. Issue:
1. Henry Buckner.
2. Benjamin Buckner.
3. Samuel Buckner.
4. John Buckner.
5. Ann Buckner.
6. Eliza Walker Buckner.
7. Robert Buckner.
8. Thomas Buckner.

VII. JUDITH BUCKNER, born Jan. 14, 1760; died 1833.
VIII. CHARLOTTE BUCKNER, born Sept. 13, 1761; married John Stephens.
IX. GILES COOK BUCKNER, born Sept. 20, 1763; died in infancy.
X. ANN BUCKNER, born Dec. 24, 1764; married Thomas Gatewood.
XI. HARRY BUCKNER, of whom presently.
XII. LUCY BUCKNER, born Oct. 18, 1768; died young.

THOMAS BUCKNER, fourth child of Thomas and Judith (Thornton) Buckner, was born Aug. 31, 1755; died 1804. His residence was "Deep Spring," Caroline County. His wife Elizabeth, born Nov. 20, 1759; married May 25, 1780, was a daughter of Samuel and Ann Walker Hawes, and sister of Mary Hawes, who married Robert Buckner, half brother to Thomas. They had issue the following children, some of their names being given in a letter written by Walker Buckner to Richard Buckner, of Oakland, Caroline Co., Va., in 1852:

1. Walker Buckner, born March 7, 1781.
2. Benjamin Hawes Buckner, born Nov. 3, 1783.
3. Ann Walker Buckner, born 1784.
4. William Thomas Buckner, born 1786.
5. Samuel H. Buckner, born Nov. 18, 1787; died young.
6. Richard Buckner, born Jan. 20, 1789.
7. Mary Aylette Buckner, born Nov. 27, 1790.
8. Charlotte Buckner, born Aug. 18, 1792.
9. Francis Buckner, born Feb., 1794.
10. William Aylette Buckner, born July 14, 1798.
11. Elizabeth Giles Buckner, born 1799.
12. Samuel Buckner, born Nov. 18, 1801.
13. Ellen Buckner.

I. WALKER BUCKNER, the eldest child of Thomas and Elizabeth (Hawes) Buckner, was born at "Deep Spring," Caroline Co., March 7, 1781. When quite young, he emigrated with four of his brothers to Bourbon Co., Ky., and died at Cane

Ridge in 1855. He married his cousin, Elizabeth Walker Buckner, and had issue one son.

 1. William Aylette Buckner, married Sally Taliaferro Woodford, daughter of William and Maria (Archer) Woodford. Issue:
  A. Walker Buckner, married ———— Clay.
  B. William Buckner, married Rosa Lindsay.
  C. Son ————.
  D. Elizabeth Buckner, married Brice Steel.

COPY OF A LETTER FROM WALKER BUCKNER, ADDRESSED TO RICHARD BUCKNER, OAKLAND, CAROLINE COUNTY, VIRGINIA:

CANE RIDGE, BOURBON COUNTY.

DEAR SIR:

I have received yours of April 6th, 1852, which gave me great pleasure, particularly as I heard from Mr. Thomas Woodford and William Buckner that you and my cousin Catherine had been dead five or six years. It has been so long since I have heard from you that I would not readily have known from whom the letter came, if you had not named our relations, from whom I was greatly pleased to hear. I hope you will give me information in regard to them several times in each year as long as we may live, and you may depend on me to do so as long as I exist.

I now comply with your request to give you an account of each member of my father's family. Ben failed in business and about twelve years ago removed to Missouri, where he now lives, well provided for by Billy, Aylett and myself. Sam was not so much embarrassed, but the three of us above named paid his debts. Aylett gave him more than one thousand acres of fine land in Mo., and about three thousand dollars. Billy and myself gave him at least eight thousand dollars in money and property. He left us one year after Ben. He is now doing well. Aylett has a large fortune. Billy died two years ago last August, and left at least eighteen thousand to his four children. Nancy lives about twelve miles from me. She and her family have plenty to live on. Ellen has been dead many years and she left a large family; all of them are doing well. Now, to myself, I never had but one child, who married Sally Woodford, the daughter of William Woodford, who married Maria Archer, who is dead. William has been married about three and a half years and has three sons. I have just sold one hundred mules for nine thousand dollars and one hundred and ninety beeves for nearly seven thousand dollars. I have seventeen head of beef cattle left on hand on the 20th of March, 1852, and twenty-three large steers now preparing for market. Within a month I have bought a hundred and ninety-three mules, some of them are colts, and ninety-one steers and twelve other yearling steers and eight other mules left over from last year's foaling and raised at home worth nine hundred and ten dollars. I have thirteen hundred and eighty-five acres of land where I live, with twenty thousand dollars worth of brick and stone buildings upon it, which I suppose would sell for nearly or quite one hundred thousand dollars, three hundred and twenty-six acres of good land in Davis County, Kentucky, and in Texas a claim for thirteen hundred acres of as good land as I ever saw. I was in Texas five years ago to see it, and I do not suppose the earth affords better land. It is within twelve miles of the sea. I have lately freed five negroes, and have four left, and plenty of debts to pay, but I shall not be long about it. Mr. Thomas C. Woodford, who married my sister Molly, died about the middle of January last. He left a good tract of land of two hundred and forty acres, worth fifty dollars per acre, and seventeen negroes, all of which he left free at his death. And now sir, at the age of seventy-one years, I take leave of you for the present, and wish you a long life and prosperity to your children and your grandchildren, with the greatest esteem and regard

I subscribe myself your relation,

WALKER BUCKNER.

II. BENJAMIN HAWES BUCKNER, second son of Thomas and Elizabeth (Hawes) Buckner, of Caroline Co., was born Nov. 3, 1783; died Dec. 6, 1854. He married Elizabeth Gatewood, born Sept. 8, 1790; died March 6, 1848. He located first in Kentucky, but afterwards removed to "Buckner Hill," now near the town of Buckner in Jackson Co., Missouri. He had issue:

1. William Thomas Buckner, born Aug. 5, 1807.
2. Aylette Hawes, of whom presently.
3. Elizabeth Walker Buckner, born Dec. 5, 1812; died Sept. 25, 1848; married April 1, 1829, Dr. A. N. Mills, born Feb. 9, 1807; died Nov. 13, 1849.
4. Joseph Warren Buckner, born Nov. 20, 1815; died Oct. 8, 1816.
5. Ann Warren Buckner, born Sept. 24, 1817; married Oct. 21, 1847, T. M. Adams, died without issue.
6. Benjamin Walker Buckner, born Feb. 7, 1820; died without issue.

JUDGE BENJ. F. BUCKNER

7. Richard Bolivar Buckner, born March 27, 1822; married Dec. 16, 1855, Louisa McCabe. Removed to San José, Cal.
8. Robert Henry Buckner, born May 17, 1824; married Dec. 24, 1853, Arabella A. Williams, born June 1, 1831. No issue.
9. Mary Ellen Buckner, born Dec. 5, 1826; died without issue.
10. Samuel Hawes Buckner, born June 24, 1829; died July 28, 1847.
11. Edward Everett Buckner, born Sept. 1, 1834; died Aug. 10, 1861.
12. Bernard G. Buckner, born Oct. 20, 1838; died March 16, 1848.

AYLETTE HAWES BUCKNER, son of Benjamin H. and Elizabeth (Gatewood) Buckner, was born in Henderson County, Ky., Sept. 16, 1809. He was a brilliant lawyer, and attained considerable eminence in his profession. He married at Jacksonville, Ill., Oct. 29, 1833, Charlotte Forsythe, who was born in Bourbon County, Ky., Nov. 23, 1815, and died Jan. 12, 1884. Aylette H. Buckner died Sept. 1, 1867, at Winchester. Issue:

A. Benjamin Forsythe Buckner, of whom presently.
B. Susan C. Buckner, born Sept. 16, 1839; died unmarried in 1859.
C. Daniel Turney Buckner, born May 24, 1843; Captain of 20th Kentucky Infantry, Union Army; died in 1889 at Winchester. Married Carrie Garner. Issue:
    aa. Susan D. Buckner, unmarried.
    bb. William Aylette Buckner, Attorney-at-Law; graduate of Kentucky Wesleyan College and student of law at the University of Michigan.
D. Garrett Davis Buckner, M.D., born at Paris, Ky., Nov. 2, 1847; died May 1, 1887; married in 1881 to Mary Betty Buckner, born Jan. 31, 1845. Issue:
    aa. Charlotte Forsythe Buckner, born Aug. 8, 1882.
    bb. Garrett Davis Buckner, born May 16, 1885.
    cc. Ella Simpson Buckner, born March 17, 1887.

Hon. Benjamin Forsythe Buckner, was born in Jacksonville, Ill., Aug. 19, 1836. His boyhood and early manhood was passed in Winchester, Ky. Like his father, he turned his attention to the profession of law, being admitted to the Bar in 1857. At the breaking out of the Civil War he entered the Federal army, serving under Buell, as Major of the 20th Kentucky Infantry. After the war he returned to the practice of his profession, and in 1870 removed to Lexington, when he entered into partnership with the Hon. W. C. P. Breckenridge. One of his legal associates has said of him: "Trained in the law from his early boyhood, educated liberally therein in his young manhood, he brought to the profession when he entered it in 1857, a strong and vigorous intellect, a temperament sanguine and aggressive, an energy and industry that never flagged, all supplemented and adorned with the highest learning of the schools."

He was elected Judge of the Common Pleas Court and later of the Circuit Court. On the Bench he acquired an enviable reputation for his judicial ability, his wide knowledge of the law, his promptness and decision in the disposition of cases, in the determination of legal questions, and the fair and impartial conduct of the business of his Court.

He resigned from the Bench in 1883, and removed to Louisville, where he practiced law until 1896, when he returned to Winchester where he remained until his lamented death May 6, 1901.

He was married March 5, 1863, to Helen B. Martin, who was born June 12, 1838, by whom he had issue:

    aa. Elizabeth Martin Buckner, born Feb. 17, 1866; married Dec. 12, 1894, Strander Douglas Goff, Winchester.
    bb. Sara Martin Buckner, born Dec. 1, 1867, Winchester.
    cc. Benjamin Forsythe Buckner, born Sept. 17, 1872, Winchester.

III. ANN WALKER BUCKNER, third child and eldest daughter of Thomas and Elizabeth (Hawes) Buckner, was born in Caroline Co. in 1784. She married in Kentucky, Dr. Charles Thornton, and her daughter married Dr. David Owen Tully.

IV. WILLIAM THOMAS BUCKNER, fourth child of Thomas and Elizabeth (Hawes) Buckner, was born in Caroline Co., in 1786. He removed to Kentucky with his brothers, and died near North Middletown in 1850. He was twice married, his first wife to whom he was united, Nov. 24, 1807, was his cousin, Mary Monroe Buckner, daughter of William and Elizabeth (Monroe) Buckner, of "Mill Hill," Caroline Co. She was born in 1792, and died in Kentucky, June 23, 1817. Issue by (1) wife:

1. Eleanor Buckner, died in infancy.
2. William Thomas Buckner, born 1812, Caroline County, Va.; died 1888, Paris, Ky.; married, 1821, Lucy Archer Woodford, and had issue:
    A. William Thomas Buckner, Jr., born Bourbon County, Ky., March 19, 1848; married at Winchester, 1875, to Clay Wornall, born 1856, and has issue:
        aa. James W. Buckner, born Sept. 18, 1876; died Sept. 28, 1876.
        bb. Benjamin Walker Buckner, born March 19, 1878; died March 9, 1881.
        cc. Thomas Moore Buckner, born Sept. 16, 1881.
        dd. James Monroe Buckner, born Feb. 22, 1883.

"MYSTIE"
SARAH MARTIN BUCKNER

The Buckners of Virginia

  ee. Lucy Wood Buckner, born Oct. 18, 1886.
  ff. John Woodford Buckner, born Aug. 6; died Sept. 7, 1890.

William Thomas Buckner, Sr., married (2nd) Sallie Clay, and by her had issue:

1. Elizabeth Hawes Buckner, married in Bourbon County, Ky., Feb. 15, 1840, to John Thornton Woodford, born Aug. 26, 1812, in Culpeper County, Va.; died March 20, 1892, by whom he had issue:
   A. Sallie Woodford Spear, born March 24, 1841, Paris, Ky.
   B. Mary Woodford Clay, born May 3, 1843; dead.
   C. Buckner Woodford, born Jan. 5, 1845, Paris, Ky.; married Nannie Brooks, born Dec. 20, 1846, and has issue:
      aa. John Woodford.
      bb. Elizabeth M. Woodford, married Thomas Clay, of Paris.
      cc. Samuel B. Woodford.
      dd. Buckner Woodford.
   1. John T. Woodford, born Aug. 12, 1847, Mt. Sterling, Ky.
   2. Catesby Woodford, born Aug. 12, 1849, Paris, Ky.
   3. Elizabeth Hawes Woodford, born May 9, 1852; dead.
   4. Henry M. Woodford, born Sept., 1854, Mt. Sterling, Ky.
   5. Benjamin Woodford, born Oct., 1856, Paris, Ky.
   6. Maria A. Woodford, born Oct. 12, 1858, Paris, Ky.
2. Henry C. Buckner, son of Wm. Thomas and Sallie (Clay) Buckner, married Susan Holt. Issue, a daughter Nellie.
3. Benjamin Buckner, son of Wm. Thomas and Sallie (Clay) Buckner, married Mary Spears. Issue, several children living in Paris.

Copy of Letter from William Thomas Buckner to Edward Pollard, of Ayletts, King William County, Va.:

Near N. Middletown, Ky., Feb. 15, 1843.

Dear Sir:

I am almost worn out with age and long protracted disease, and have a particular desire to hear once more at least from my old and valued friends in King William. I do not know which of them are still in the land of the living, but I hope to hear that many of them are still in the enjoyment of their former health and happiness.

Taking it for granted that my old friends take as much interest in my welfare as I do in their's, I will proceed to give some account of the manner in which I have spent the last twenty years, for I believe it has been nearly that long since I held any correspondence with you; during that time I have changed my residence several times, but not beyond the limits of Bourbon County, where I first located myself. As time has rolled on there has been a large addition to my property, and notwithstanding the loss of fifteen thousand dollars within the last two years, I have still more than my full share of the goods and chattels of this world. I wish that I could say that my happiness had kept pace with the increase of my fortune, but unfortunately for me and for my family, recent dispensations of Providence have rendered me perfectly and entirely miserable. I had been confined at home for several years with a disease of the kidneys, by which I had several times been brought to the verge of eternity, but all that I bore patiently, although I had been repeatedly warned by the best physicians of our State that I could not be cured, but the loss of two children, the last on the 24th of April last, a daughter sixteen years of age, who was a thousand times dearer to me than life itself, has left me with a broken heart as well as a shattered constitution. I have now four children left. My son William, a native of King William, and a daughter and two sons, children of my present wife. My daughter is married and has one child. One of my sons is 14 and the other 7 years old. My son William was unfortunately injured by some accident during my residence in Va., from which he has never recovered. He enjoys good health, however, and is an industrious good manager. He has a valuable farm containing 550 acres equal to any land in the Union, and everything else to make him comfortable. I should not have spoken thus in detail of his situation had I not been sure that you would be gratified to hear of him. When the weather is good I am sometimes able to walk out of doors. This is seldom the case in the winter, when for weeks together I am confined entirely to the house, and for years past, I have been half my time in bed. I am greatly reduced and have the appearance of a person 65 or 70 years of age.

The people of no state in the Union have suffered more severely by what is generally termed hard times than the citizens of Ky. They engage more eagerly in speculation and adventure than any I ever saw, and the consequence has been, that a great many have been totally ruined. There are probably more than fifty persons in this county, mostly farmers, many of them once considered rich, who are now entirely ruined, indeed destitute of everything. The sudden revolution in the price of our produce has ruined all who were in debt to any extent. The price of pork here in December last was about $1.25 per cwt; beef, $2. Hemp, the staple of our country, is now worth about $2 when less than

SAMUEL BUCKNER

fine, would not compensate those who raise it. Corn is worth from 37 to 50 cents per barrel. Low as all descriptions of produce is selling, it cannot be sold for cash. Land that sold readily for $80 per acre 3 years ago would not sell for $30 now. Great sacrifices of property have taken place, under executions in some instances not one-fiftieth part of the price of 4 years ago has been obtained, and it is thought by many that we have not experienced the worst yet, but I hope this prediction will not be verified. The only remedy for this state of things in the opinion of four-fifths of the people, is the establishment of another United States Bank. They have been led into this foolish error by their oracle, Henry Clay, who is the most selfish and reckless man in existence. He was long a pensioner of the former bank which scattered corruption and ruin throughout the United States, and which I hope has sunk never to rise again.

My principal object in addressing this letter to you, as I before stated, is to hear once more from my old friends in your part of the country. Give me the information sought in detail. I desire to know which of them are still living and which not. Some of them for whom I entertained the highest respect, indeed to whom I was devotedly attached, I know are gone, and I fear that others are to be added. I beg to be particularly informed in regard to the family of my deceased and much respected uncle, Mr. W. Hawes. Is his widow still living? Is his son, Walker, living and where? Let me hear whether the country round Ayletts has undergone any favourable changes; whether the old system of farming still prevails; whether Ayletts and Dunkirk have improved any or gone still further to decay. Whether, as in days of yore, you get a good supply of fish and oysters. While I am writing my mind falls back to the occurrences of 1812 and 15, and produces a state of feeling that I cannot describe. Do not delay more than a few days your answer. It is not often that I am able to write, and fear or rather apprehend that my time in this world will be but short. You and all my other friends in Va. have my prayers for your welfare and happiness.

If Mr. Richard Hill is living please state where he is. Should anything prevent Mr. Pollard's writing to me, that is if he is not living, or if living, removed from Ayletts, some other friend please write to me. Yours truly,

WILLIAM THOMAS BUCKNER.

V. SAMUEL H. BUCKNER, fifth child of Thomas and Elizabeth (Hawes) Buckner, was born in Caroline Co., Nov. 18, 1787, and died in infancy.

VI. RICHARD BUCKNER, sixth child of Thomas and Elizabeth (Hawes) Buckner, was born in Caroline Co., Jan. 20, 1789.

VII. MARY AYLETTE BUCKNER, seventh child of Thomas and Elizabeth (Hawes) Buckner, was born in Caroline Co., Nov. 27, 1790; married Thomas Catesby Woodford and died in Bourbon Co., Ky.

VIII. CHARLOTTE BUCKNER, eighth child of Thomas and Elizabeth (Hawes) Buckner, was born in Caroline Co., Aug. 18, 1792.

IX. FRANCIS BUCKNER, ninth child of Thomas and Elizabeth (Hawes) Buckner, was born in Caroline Co., Feb. 1794.

X. WILLIAM AYLETTE BUCKNER, tenth child of Thomas and Elizabeth (Hawes) Buckner, was born in Caroline Co., July 14, 1798. When he lost his father he removed with his mother and family to Kentucky, where he was educated and graduated in the profession of the law. With the spirit of adventure strong within him, he turned with the tide of emigration which had set in towards the South, and settled at Washington, Mississippi. It was while nursing his devoted friend, the only brother of Charlotte Ferguson, that he met and loved her. After their marriage he removed to Natchez, where he rose rapidly in his profession, until he stood among the foremost at a Bar, noted in that day for its brilliant members.

After practicing his profession for a number of years, he retired, his tastes and inclinations leading him toward a domestic life. He invested the considerable fortune he had acquired, in real estate, and this, he managed so carefully and successfully, that at the breaking out of the Civil War, he possessed estates which ranked him among the wealthiest cotton planters of the South. At the conclusion of the war, these estates, so far from being remunerative, became a burden, involving him in debt and leaving him with thousands of acres of land which for the time being were practically useless. This burden he shouldered manfully, refusing to avail himself of the universal custom of compromise, for he said, "I accepted the obligations in good

LOUISA MELVILLE BUCKNER

faith, and shall endeavour to discharge them dollar for dollar." To this task, he successfully devoted the remaining years of his life, leaving his children with worldly wealth diminished, but rich in the legacy of an honorable record.

William Aylette Buckner died Aug. 11, 1886, at Natchez, Miss., and was married to Charlotte Ferguson in 1827, at Washington, Miss. She was born Jan. 4, 1807, and died April 19, 1880. Issue:

1. George Ferguson Buckner, born 1827; died in infancy.
2. Jane Ferguson Buckner, of whom presently.
3. Elizabeth Buckner, born 1831.
4. David Ferguson Buckner, born Aug. 17, 1833; died Oct. 27, 1869.
5. William Buckner, born Oct., 1834; died Jan., 1898.
6. Anna Buckner, born 1836; died 1853.
7. John Buckner, born 1838; died 1851.
8. Mary Buckner, born Oct., 1840.
9. Edward Buckner, born Oct., 1842; killed at Shiloh, April 6, 1862.
10. Louis Buckner, born Sept. 11, 1844, of Newellton, La.
11. Margaret Ferguson Buckner, of whom presently.
12. Walker Buckner, born Dec. 12, 1848; died June 19, 1870.

JANE FERGUSON BUCKNER, second child of William Aylett and Charlotte (Ferguson) Buckner, was born Oct. 23, 1829; died March 25, 1865; married Jan. 17, 1860, Dr. Walter Monteith Stewart, born at Johnstown, N. Y.; died Aug. 29, 1863, at Natchez, Miss. Issue:

   A. Walter Monteith Stewart.
   B. Mary Buckner Stewart, died in infancy.
   C. Charlotte Pauline Stewart, born Nov. 15, 1863; married Oct. 22, 1884, to Ayres Phillips Merrill of Natchez, and has issue:
      aa. Ayres P. Merrill.
      bb. Pauline Stewart Merrill.
      cc. Mary Buckner Merrill.
      dd. Margaret Merrill.
      ee. Walter Stewart Merrill.
      ff. Violet Merrill.

MARGARET FERGUSON BUCKNER, eleventh child of William Aylett and Charlotte (Ferguson) Buckner, was born Dec. 9, 1846, and married Jan. 16, 1868, Richard Ellis Conner of Natchez, born Feb. 26, 1841. Issue:

   A. Charlotte Buckner Conner, born Oct. 28, 1868; married Sept. 24 1890, Abram Morrell Feltus.
   B. Jane Gustine Conner, born Feb. 9, 1870; married Jan. 22, 1890, John Aldridge Limerick.
   C. Richard Ellis Conner, born Oct. 2, 1871.
   D. Mary Conner, born Nov. 15, 1874; married June 26, 1895, Lewis Edward Murrell.
   E. Aylett Buckner Conner (daughter), born Nov. 17, 1884.

XI. ELIZABETH GILES BUCKNER, eleventh child of Thomas and Elizabeth (Hawes) Buckner, was born in Caroline Co., in 1799. She married Benjamin F. Bedford, of Bourbon Co., Ky., and left descendants who still reside there.

XII. SAMUEL BUCKNER, twelfth child of Thomas and Elizabeth (Hawes) Buckner, was born in Caroline Co., Nov. 18, 1801; died at Independence, Mo., in 1877; married April 5, 1821, at Winchester, Ky., to Louisa Malvina Dodge, who died Dec. 25, 1880, at Independence, Mo. Issue:

1. Arabella Buckner, died unmarried.
2. Mary Ellen Buckner, deceased, married Dr. John S. Wood. Issue: S. B. Wood, Kansas City.
3. Sarah Ann Buckner, deceased, married D. S. Hardin. Issue: Dr. Charles B. Hardin, Kansas City; Henry Hardin died without issue; Louisa Hardin, and Lena Hardin.
4. Elizabeth Buckner, deceased, married —— Flood. Issue: Maurice B. Flood, Kansas City.
5. Edwin H. Buckner, born 1829, of Kansas City.
6. Walker Buckner, son of Samuel and Louisa M. (Dodge) Buckner, was born Oct. 11, 1838, at North Middletown, Ky.; died Aug. 12, 1901, at Evanston, Ill.; married Sept. 2, 1858, at Pleasant Hill, Mo., to Margaret Ann Tully, daughter of Dr. D. O. Tully, born March 18, 1837; died July 12, 1885. Mr. Buckner had for many years been closely identified with Life Insurance, and at the time of his death was manager of several states for the New York Life Insurance Company. Issue:

    A. Katharine Louisa Buckner, born Dec. 16, 1860, unmarried, Milwaukee, Wis.
    B. Samuel Owen Buckner, born April 30, 1862, at Wellington, Mo.; married Nov. 21, 1894, at Milwaukee, Wis., to Zaidee Eddy Withington, born July 1, 1876. Mr. Buckner is the Agency Director of the Wisconsin Branch of New York Life Insurance Company. Issue:
        aa. Margaret Tully Buckner, born Sept. 23, 1895, at Milwaukee.
    C. Thomas Aylette Buckner, son of Walker and Louisa M. (Dodge) Buckner, was born at Bloomington, Ill., Jan. 18, 1865; married at Ottumwa, Ia., June 4, 1889, to Myrtie Lewis, born Dec. 11, 1867.

    Mr. Buckner was educated at a private academy, of which his uncle, William Aylette Buckner, was president. He began his business career in the Milwaukee office of the New York Life Insurance Company, April 7, 1880, when he was fifteen years of age, as an office boy, and rapidly advanced through all the intermediate grades of service. Previous to his promotion to the position of Inspector of Agencies, Feb., 15, 1892, he worked in the field as agent, and was subsequently Cashier of the Kansas Branch office, then Agency Director of the same. On Dec. 12, 1900, he was elected Fourth Vice-President, and on May 13, 1903, Vice-President. He has also been a Trustee of the Company since April 10, 1901. Endowed with a mind quick to grasp every opportunity, a remarkable reader of

THOMAS AYLETTE BUCKNER

character, and a business acumen second to none, it has been through his own unaided efforts that he, while still a young man, has risen to the high position he occupies in the Insurance world.

Mr. Buckner has issue one son:
 aa. Thomas Aylette Buckner, Jr., born Jan. 17, 1893, at Chicago, Ill., and one adopted daughter, Mary O. Buckner, born Aug. 15th, 1895.
D. Tully Scott Buckner, born Sep. 22, 1866; died Dec. 2, 1866.
E. Walker Buckner, Jr., born March 16, 1871, at Independence, Mo., married Dec. 11, 1894, at Milwaukee, to Eva May Orton, born June 26, 1870. Mr. Buckner is Superintendent of Agencies for the New York Life Insurance Company, with residence at Paris, France. Issue:
 aa. Tully Orton Buckner, born Aug. 17, 1895.
 bb. Walker Thornton Buckner, born March 19, 1899.
 cc. John Jay Buckner ⎫
 dd. Lewis Probasco Buckner ⎬ twins, born Mch. 16, 1902.

7. William Aylett Buckner, son of Samuel and Louisa M. (Dodge) Buckner, was born Oct 8, 1836, at North Middletown, Ky.; died Nov., 1886, at Independence, Mo.; married Charlotte Tully, daughter of Dr. D. O. Tully. She was born Oct. 11, 1848; died July, 1882. Issue:
A. John Tully Buckner, born 1872; resides unmarried at Sumter, S. C.
B. William Probasco Buckner, born July 10, 1878, at Independence, Mo., and is now one of the Agency Directors of the New York Life Insurance Co., with residence in New York City.

XIII. ELLEN BUCKNER, daughter of Thomas and Elizabeth (Hawes) Buckner. From the letter of her brother, Walker Buckner, in 1852, it is evident she was then deceased and had left a large family.

HENRY BUCKNER, sixth child of Thomas and Elizabeth (Taliaferro) Buckner of Mt. Pleasant and Mill Hill, Caroline County, was born Dec. 16, 1766; died in 1822 at Fayette County, Ky.; married Nov. 1, 1789, Elizabeth Catlett, born April 24, 1766. Issue:

1. John Catlett Buckner, born Aug. 17, 1790; died July 3, 1824, at Lexington, Ky.; married Mary Gano, April 23, 1813. Issue:
A. William Henry Buckner, of Erlanger, Ky., born 1816; died 1863; married in 1844, Catharine Ann Graves, born in 1826. Issue:
 aa. John Willis Buckner, born Dec. 29, 1841; died at Minneapolis, Minn., Dec. 18, 1904; married Mary Eliza Gano, born 1848; died 1876; a daughter of John Allen Gano, a distinguished preacher of the Christian Church. Issue:
  aaa. Katherine Gano Buckner, born March 15, 1867, married H. L. Clamp of Austin, Texas.

  bbb. Frances Buckner, born Oct. 1, 1869; married 1891, at Taylor, Texas, to L. D. Tobin, who died Oct. 10, 1899.
  ccc. Rev. Montgomery Gano Buckner, Harrodsburg, Ky., born at Centerville, Ky., Feb. 7, 1871; married at Mt. Sterling, April 5, 1899, to Mary Elsie Cassidy, born Dec. 23, 1879, and has issue: Allen Marion Buckner, born Oct. 10, 1900.
 bb. William Henry Buckner, born June 3, 1847; married Sept. 4, 1895, to Mildred Washington Wise.
 cc. Sophia M. Buckner, born 1852; married Aug. 1878, Thomas J. Turpin.
B. Margaret Buckner, daughter of John Catlett and Mary (Gano) Buckner, was born in 1818, unmarried.
C. Richard Buckner, son of John Catlett and Mary (Gano) Buckner, was born 1820; married in 1850, Belle Sanford. He died in 1864.
D. Elizabeth Buckner, daughter of John Catlett and Mary (Gano) Buckner, was born in 1822; died in 1887; married Morris J. Dudley.
2. George Buckner, son of Henry and Elizabeth (Catlett) Buckner, born Nov. 17, 1791; died in Missouri; married Aug. 16, 1818, Elizabeth Mansell.
3. Thomas Buckner, son of Henry and Elizabeth (Catlett) Buckner, born Feb. 20, 1793; died June 19, 1844; married (1) June 29, 1820, to Caroline Perry; married (2) Mildred Berry, April 22, 1823. She was born in Campbell Co., Ky., July 18, 1795, and had issue:
A. Henry Washington Buckner, born Sept. 4, 1824; died Jan. 2, 1827.
B. Hubbard Taylor Buckner, born Feb. 18, 1827; died Jan. 1, 1903; married Nov. 7, 1848, Lucy M. Sandford, born in Kenton Co., Ky., June 28, 1829. Issue.
 aa. Alexander Buckner, of whom presently.
 bb. Mildred Thomas Buckner, born March 1, 1852; died Oct. 2, 1852.
 cc. William Henry Buckner, born Dec. 22, 1853; died March 2, 1858.
 dd. George Hubbard Buckner, of whom presently.
 ee. Mary Lucy Buckner, born May 27, 1859.
 ff. Alice Elizabeth Buckner, born Feb. 18, 1862.
 gg. Sophia Belle Buckner, born July 2, 1869.

Alexander Buckner, son of Hubbard Taylor Buckner and Lucy M. Sandford, was born Feb. 3, 1850, and was married Sept. 1, 1884, to Lida Phillipps. Issue:
 1. George Phillipps Buckner, born June 13, 1885.
 2. Alexander Buckner, born Sept. 17, 1886.
 3. Hubbard Thomas Buckner, born Aug. 17, 1888.
 4. Almar Washington Buckner, born July 4, 1891.
 5. Mary Helen Buckner, born Dec. 25, 1894.
 6. Leida Buckner, born March 8, 1902.

George Hubbard Buckner, (usually known as Hubbard G.) son of Hubbard Taylor Buckner and Lucy M. Sandford, was born Sept. 22, 1856; married June 25, 1890, Ethaline Conn Buckner, daughter of Col. John A. Buckner, of Erlanger, Ky. Issue:

AYLETTE BUCKNER, JR.

The Buckners of Virginia

1. Mildred Louise Buckner, born Nov. 7, 1891.
2. Alice Elizabeth Buckner, born Dec. 16, 1893.
3. Susan Covington Buckner, born May 8, 1897.
4. Lucy Sandford Buckner, born April 19, 1896; lived only a few days.
5. Lucy Mary Buckner, born Oct. 21, 1899.
6. Sophia Belle Buckner, born Dec. 17, 1903.
7. George Hubbard Buckner, Jr., born Oct. 13, 1905.

C. Alice Elizabeth Buckner, daughter of Thomas and Mildred (Berry) Buckner, was born Sept. 6, 1829; died Sept. 2, 1892.
D. Sophia Buckner, daughter of Thomas and Mildred (Berry) Buckner, was born Oct. 24, 1832; died May 10, 1893; married Frederick Wise.
E. Thomas Berry Buckner, born April 10, 1835; died unmarried Jan. 25, 1868.

4. Henry M. Buckner, son of Henry and Elizabeth (Catlett) Buckner, of whom presently.
5. Elizabeth T. Buckner, daughter of Henry and Elizabeth (Catlett) Buckner, born May 17, 1798; died Aug. 9, 1879; married, 1830, Dudley Shipp.
6. William Buckner, son of Henry and Elizabeth (Catlett) Buckner, was born Nov. 15, 1801; died May 2, 1876; unmarried.
7. David P. Buckner, son of Henry and Elizabeth (Catlett) Buckner, was born Oct. 17, 1803; died Nov. 27, 1829; unmarried.
8. Lucy A. T. Buckner, daughter of Henry and Elizabeth (Catlett) Buckner, born Oct. 14, 1808; died July 18, 1849; married Feb. 5, 1829, Jesse D. Winn at Fayette County, Ky. He died in 1878, aged 67. Issue:

A. David Winn, deceased.
B. Mary E. Winn, deceased.
C. Catherine Winn, deceased.
D. Benjamin S. Winn, deceased—son, George Winn.
E. William H. Winn, born Fayette County, Ky., Jan. 20, 1836; married, 1861, Sarah E. Grubbs, born 1838. Issue:

    aa. John G. Winn, born April 10, 1862, Mt. Sterling, Ky.
    bb. Mary (Winn) Lockridge, born July 3, 1864, Mt. Sterling, Ky.
    cc. Jessie (Winn) Deering, born May 9, 1866, Cleveland, O.
    dd. Pierce Winn, born Nov. 15, 1868, Mt. Sterling, Ky.
    ee. Robert H. Winn, born Feb. 23, 1871; married June 1, 1904, Elizabeth M. Turney, born Dec. 10, 1880, Mt. Sterling, Ky.
    ff. Nellie (Winn) Lipscomb, born Jan. 20, 1878, Nashville, Tenn.

HENRY M. BUCKNER, fourth child of Henry and Elizabeth Catlett Buckner, was born April 15, 1796, in Caroline County, Va.; died June 30, 1876; married Sept. 18, 1828, Ethaline E., daughter of Captain Jack Conn, Centreville, Ky. The latter participated in the Battle of the Thames, Oct. 5, 1813, as a member of a company of sharpshooters. Henry M. Buckner removed to

Burlington, Ky., where he entered into a mercantile life, retiring in 1847 to his estate at "Edgewood," Erlanger, Ky. Issue:

1. Ellenora E. Buckner, born June 23, 1830; died Sept. 23, 1878, married Nov. 29, 1849, Benjamin E. Hall.
2. Col. John Alexander Buckner of Illawara, La., born Boone County, Ky., Aug. 15, 1832; died Oct. 22, 1903; married (1st) in 1859, Nellie Mason Kellam, died 1863, and by her had issue:
    A. John A. Buckner, born May, 1860; died 1863.
    B. Loulie Buckner, born July, 1861; died 1883.

Col. John A. Buckner, married (2nd) May 6, 1866, Susan Covington, born 1840; died 1880, and by her had issue:

    C. John A. Buckner, born July, 1867; died 1868.
    D. Ethaline Conn Buckner, born Jan. 13, 1872; married June 25, 1890; Hubbard G. Buckner. For issue see above.
    E. Henry M. Buckner, born Sept., 1876; died 1877.

Col. John Alexander Buckner attended the schools of Covington and Cincinnati, and Center College, Danville, Ky., graduating in 1852; after which, having determined to enter the ministry, he was sent to the Theological College at Princeton, N. J. He also attended a course of medical lectures in New York in order to prepare himself for the missionary field. In this work he went to Rio de Janeiro, remaining until the fall of 1856, when he returned to his home in Kentucky. He later purchased a cotton plantation in Louisiana and became a successful planter.

In September, 1863, he enlisted in the Confederate army at Hopkinsville, Ky., and was made Captain of Company A, 8th Kentucky Regiment, commanded by Col. Henry C. Burnett, afterwards Confederate States Senator from Kentucky. At the battle of Fort Donelson the regiment was commanded by Col. H. B. Lyon and Maj. P. W. Henry. Upon learning that surrender had been determined upon, Capt. Buckner disbanded his company, telling them he would not surrender, and with Lieut. Pressley Davis he crossed the Cumberland River and made his way back to Nashville and to Murfreesboro, where he joined Gen. A. S. Johnston's army, and was in the battle of Shiloh as volunteer aid to Gen. Charles Clark. In his official report of that battle, Gen. Clark complimented Capt. Buckner for his promptness, intelligence, and courage in the execution of his orders.

In July, 1864, Capt. Buckner was selected by Gen. John C. Breckinridge to succeed Maj. J. T. Pickett as assistant adjutant general upon his staff. When Col. Hunt was shot down at the battle of Baton Rouge, La., Capt. Buckner was, by unanimous consent, placed in command of the Second Brigade, in which posi-

WALKER BUCKNER

tion he displayed a high degree of skill and courage; and when Gen. Clark was thought to be mortally wounded, and the troops began to fall back in confusion, Capt. Buckner, with the assistance of Maj. Wickliffe, of the Nineteenth Kentucky Regiment, faced the brigade about and resumed the attack. Following the report of this action, by Gen. Breckinridge, he was promoted to rank of major, and subsequently brevetted lieutenant-colonel for gallantry in battle. He was also in the battle of Stone's River, and in his mention of the officers of his division who had distinguished themselves in the three days' bloody conflict Gen. Breckinridge says: "It gives me pleasure to name Lieut.-Col. Buckner, Assistant Adjutant General, who was absent on leave and returned on the first rumor of battle."

During 1864 Col. Buckner was in the Trans-Mississippi Department, and subsequently was on Gen. S. B. Buckner's staff, and placed in charge of the Cotton Bureau, discharging the delicate and difficult duties of the office with entire satisfaction to the government.

After the close of the war, Col. Buckner returned to his plantation home in the East Carroll Parish, La. Like all brave soldiers of the Confederacy, he counseled the acceptance of the inevitable, and set a good example by turning his attention to the raising of cotton and rebuilding the broken levees of the Mississippi River. He served for many years upon the Levee Board without compensation, and to his good judgment and industry, assisted by equally enthusiastic members of the Board, the planters from Greenville to Vicksburg are much indebted for their fine levee system.

Col. Buckner was a man of unyielding perseverance, and was eminently successful in business life.

 3. David Pendleton Buckner, son of Henry M. and Ethaline (Conn) Buckner, born Sept. 13, 1834; died Sept. 23, 1867; married Lucy Buckner, Oct. 17, 1864. Issue:
 A. David Pendleton Buckner, born 1867.
 4. James Henry Buckner, of whom presently.
 5. Sarah Ann Buckner, daughter of Henry M. and Ethaline (Conn) Buckner, born June 29, 1839; died Apl. 20, 1905; married Feb. 24, 1858, Stephen Henry. Issue:
 A. Annie E. Henry, born June 15, 1859; married Thomas S. Potts.
 B. John C. Henry, born July 18, 1861; died 1893.
 6. Mary Catherine Buckner, daughter of Henry M. and Ethaline (Conn) Buckner, born June 18, 1842; died Nov. 17, 1890.

7. Maria Louise Buckner, daughter of Henry M. and Ethaline (Conn) Buckner, born May 12, 1845; died Feb. 3, 1893.
8. Elizabeth Ethaline Buckner, daughter of Henry M. and Ethaline (Conn) Buckner, born Dec. 23, 1849; died April 9, 1900; married April 20, 1869, Garrett S. Wall. Issue:
   A. Garrett Buckner Wall of Richmond, Va., born April 6, 1870; married Louise ———. Issue:
      aa. Martha Buckner Wall, born 1899.
      bb. Garrett Buckner Wall, born 1903.
   B. Elizabeth Ethaline Wall of Des Moines, Ia., born Aug. 25, 1874 in Kenton Co., Ky.; married Dec. 18, 1901 to James Harvey Phillips; born 1869.
   C. Henry Buckner Wall, born Oct. 7, 1876.

JAMES HENRY BUCKNER, M.D., of Cincinnati, Ohio, fourth child of Henry M. and Ethaline E. (Conn) Buckner, was born Nov. 25, 1836, at Burlington, Ky.

At the age of two years he was sent to Covington, Ky., where he attended private schools. At the early age of nine years he entered the Preparatory Department of Cincinnati College, and afterwards was placed under the tutorship of Prof. De Soto, of Centre College, Danville, Ky. He subsequently went to the Academies at Exeter, N. H. and Groton, Mass., matriculating the following year at Dartmouth College. He returned home in the spring of 1857, and began the study of medicine with Dr. Evans, a prominent surgeon of Covington, Ky; soon afterwards removing to Cincinnati, and continuing his studies with Drs. Taliaferro and L. M. Lawson. In 1858 he entered the Ohio Medical College, where he took three courses of lectures, graduating in the spring of 1861. He then formed a partnership with his preceptor, Dr. Taliaferro. On Oct. 17th, 1861, Dr. Buckner married Miss Jane Olivia Ramsey, step-daughter of his preceptor and partner. Two sons were the result of this union, William Thornton, born April 19, 1863 and Henry Alexander, born Aug. 24, 1866. His estimable wife died May 3rd, 1892. In Sept., 1861, he was appointed Examining Surgeon of the United States for Naval recruits at Cincinnati, where he was associated with Captain, afterwards Commodore Winslow, who, as Commander of the "Kearsarge," participated in the famous fight with the "Alabama." Dr. Buckner was afterward assigned to duty as surgeon of the gunboat "Cairo," which, after the fall of Fort Donelson, was the first of the fleet to reach Nashville.

In the summer of 1862, Dr. Buckner resigned from the service

COLONEL JOHN A. BUCKNER

and resumed his private practice at Cincinnati. In 1862-3 he was demonstrator of Anatomy in the Ohio Medical College; from 1866 to 1871 Professor of Physiology in the Cincinnati College of Medicine and Surgery. In the latter year he was elected to fill the chair of Ophthalmology and Otology, made vacant by the death of Dr. Taliaferro. He was at the same time on the staff of the Good Samaritan Hospital, where he delivered clinical lectures on diseases of the eye and ear. He resigned his several positions in the fall of 1872, in order to take a foreign tour, during which, he visited the principal capitals of Europe, and took a special course of studies on the eye and ear at Vienna. After traveling through Italy he returned via England and Ireland to America. He then resumed his place in the Hospital and was subsequently elected to the staff of St. Mary's Hospital, in special charge of Ocular and Aural diseases, which position he held for fourteen years, resigning in the spring of 1890. In 1878 he was elected President of the Academy of Medicine of Cincinnati, and in the summer of 1882 he was elected Professor in the Toledo Medical College, delivering a course of lectures on the eye and ear. Was elected President of the Walnut Hills Medical Society in January 1887, and in 1894 he was elected Vice-President of the Ohio State Medical Society, and is a permanent member of the American Medical Association and the State Medical Society. He has contributed to the literature of his profession a number of valuable articles on diseases of the eye, ear, throat and surgery, and on chloroform.

Dr. James H. and Jane Olivia (Ramsey) Buckner had issue:
1. William Thornton Taliaferro Buckner, born April 19, 1863; married Oct. 3, 1893 at Murfreesboro, Tenn.; Elizabeth Irwin Harrison, born May 25, 1874, a niece of the late President Benj. Harrison. Residence, Cincinnati, O. Issue:
    A. Sophie Harrison Buckner, born Aug. 7, 1894.
    B. Elizabeth Harrison Buckner, born April 18, 1902.
2. Harry Alexander Buckner, born Aug. 23, 1866. Residence, Cincinnati, O.

"Look back into your mighty ancestors."
—Julius Cæsar.

The Buckners of West Virginia

ABOUT the year 1720 George Byrn, a man of some wealth and good family, left Ireland, and located in Prince William Co., Va. The name in all early records was spelled with only four letters, the addition of the final e, being added by his descendants.

It is very probable that George Byrn was a brother of Edmund Byrne, of Spottsylvania Co., whose will dated 17 Aug., 1744, probated 4 September, 1744, recites that he was from the county of Kilkenny, Ireland. He mentions as legatees his two brothers, George and Thomas Byrne.

In 1729 Thomas Byrn was one of the securities on an administration bond (Spotts. Records). On Dec. 17, 1728, a deed is recorded of a lease of two adjoining plantations in the fork of the Rappahannock River in St. George's Parish, to Thomas Byrn and Martha, his wife (Spotts. Records, Deed Book A.). After July 6, 1731, at which time Thomas Byrn is witness to a deed, the name disappears entirely from the records of Spottsylvania Co.

From the Prince William records we find that George Byrn was the General Surveyor for the county. Many of the drawings and maps made by his pen are still on file in the clerk's office.

In 1744, George Byrne and Lydia, his wife, gave bond, with Cuthbert Harrison as security, in the sum of £500 as guardians of William Brown, an orphan son of William Brown, late of Prince William county.

In 1766 Lydia conveyed her right of dower away in a tract of land called "Spiller's Neck" on Occoquan waters, to her son Samuel Byrne.

George and Lydia Byrne had three children:
    Elizabeth Byrne.
    Mary Byrne.
    Samuel Byrne.

I. ELIZABETH BYRNE married first a Buckner. Tradition states his name was Bolivar. The use of Bolivar as a Christian name in the Buckner family seems hardly probable at this early date, as Bolivar, the Great Liberator, was born in 1783, and was unknown to fame at the time the above Buckner must have

DR. JAMES H. BUCKNER

been born. Elizabeth's husband is said to have been descended from the Buckners of the "Neck," Caroline Co. The issue of this marriage was three children:
1. John Anthony Buckner.
2. Ann Buckner.
3. Clarissa Buckner.

About 1756 Elizabeth, widow of Bolivar (?) Buckner, wedded William, orphan son of William Brown of Prince William Co., born 1722; died in 1806. He was Captain under General Green in the Revolution. Issue:
1. John Brown, clerk of Prince William Co., 1805 to 1838; married, —— Thorpe and had issue: William, John, Jr.; Mark.
2. Thomas Brown, born Sept., 1760; died 1844 in Preston Co.; married Nancy Ash, Oct. 20, 1785, and had issue, Elizabeth, John Buckner, George, Lydia, Samuel Byrne, William, Mary Ann, Thomas F.
3. Lydia Brown, married Uriah Burns; died in Fauquier Co.
4. Mary Ann Brown, married Moses Tibbs; removed to Indiana.

II. MARY BYRNE, second daughter of George and Lydia Byrne; married George Ash of Prince William Co., and left issue.

III. SAMUEL BYRNE, son of George and Lydia Byrne; married his niece, daughter of Elizabeth and Bolivar (?) Buckner, and by her had seven children:
1. Peyton Byrne, married Barbara Linn, migrated to the mouth of Salt Lick, on Little Kanawha River, and there died May 11, 1824. Col. Benjamin W. Byrne, who was a State Superintendent of Free Schools for West Virginia, was a grandson. One of Peyton's sons was named Peyton Buckner.
2. Charles Byrne, Major of Militia; died 1843.
3. Thomas Byrne, physician; married Rebecca Dorsey of Morgantown, was a Member of the Legislature from Monongalia; went to Missouri in 1820, and there died.
4. John Byrne, went to Missouri, and there died.
5. Sarah Byrne, married (1st) Thomas Bland, and had issue: John, Samuel, Thomas. Married (2nd) Jacob Zinn, and by him had: Major William B., Charles, Clara, Pamelia, Peyton.
6. Mary Byrne about 1760 married Colonel John Fairfax, from whom descended General Buckner Fairfax of Terra Alta, Preston Co., West Va., who died in 1880.
7. Elizabeth Byrne, married Archibald Anderson of Little Kanawha, and had issue three daughters and a son, Samuel.

Elizabeth Brown, formerly Widow Buckner, *née* Byrne, Dec. 29, 1783, made her will with these words: "Item. I give and bequeath unto my son Anthony Buckner, one negro girl named Esther, with all her increase to him and his heirs."

"Item. I give and bequeath unto my daughter, Ann Cornwell, one negro woman named Juda."

"Item. I give and bequeath unto my daughter Clara Byrn, one negro named Hagar." This Clara Byrn married her uncle Samuel Byrne, and later became the wife of Col. David Scott, of Monongalia.

Anthony, or John Anthony, as many called him, married —— Seal. With his two daughters, Clara and Mary, he moved west of the Allegheny slopes. He was then immediately from Hardy, and prior to that from Prince William Co., where he was born July 15, 1748. He made his home near the banks of the Little Kanawha river, within the territory of Wood county. He is often mentioned in the county records, aiding in some internal improvement, or serving his neighbors in a confidential or public capacity.

In 1799, he is given as one of the purchasers at a public sale. July, 1801, he was appointed Road Surveyor, and in 1806 he was overseer to succeed Samuel Allen.

In 1807 he was one of three to allot and value the estate of Robert Thornton. In this year he was summoned as one of the twelve jurors from Wood county, in the famous Burr-Blennerhassett treason trial at Richmond, before Chief Justice Marshall of the U. S. Court. Anthony Buckner had been open in his denunciation of Burr. Upon being interrogated in court as to any expression of guilt or innocence in the pending case, he promptly and energetically replied that, "He had frequently declared the opinion that any man who did as it was said the prisoner had acted, should be hung." He was further asked, "Did you not say that you would give five pounds for Colonel Burr's head?"

Looking keenly at the prisoner, he said: "Yes, by G—d, and I'll do it yet."

As he poured out these emphatic words his piercing brown eyes seemed to look through one, and even the marbleized face of the distinguished defendant was seen to flush.

Of course, at the instance of the accused, who was his own counsel, Buckner was rejected from the panel.

About the year 1809 he married as his second wife, Catherine, widow of John Gibbens, and resided on a farm where Davisville now stands. Soon after, he purchased a tract of uncleared land four miles above, on the north side of Little Kanawha river, where he built a log cabin.

By his first marriage we have record of only two daughters, and by his last alliance of eight children, three of whom are living at this date (1905). Issue of the first marriage:

I. MARY BUCKNER, born about 1777, who married Abner Saunders, of Caroline county. She died April 8, 1862. Abner Saunders, on his mother's side, was of Welsh ancestry. On the paternal, he claimed descent from the celebrated

Indian Chief, Powhattan, whose blood coursed through the veins of the historic Pocahontas. He was born in 1771, and died April 3, 1838. His residence was at Newark, his farm being known as "Cool Spring." Issue:

1. Gustavus Buckner Saunders, married Dec. 23, 1824, Mary, daughter of James Foley. She died without issue, and Feb. 19, 1835, he wedded Elizabeth Crook, daughter of Allen Davis. By her he had one child, who died an infant in 1838. He died in 1875, and his widow moved to Lafayette, Mo.

2. Parmelia A. Jane Saunders became the second wife of Col. John Buckner Creel, April 5, 1827. He died Jan., 1838, and his wife April, 1864. Issue:

A. Battelle W. Creel, born 1828; married first Harriet West; second, Abigail Pennybacker. No issue. Residence, Elizabeth, West Va.

B. Laura M. Creel, born Oct. 13, 1829; died Aug. 12, 1894; married April 16, 1851, Charles B. Rockhold, and had issue:

    aa. Mark M. Rockhold, married Maria C. Talkington, and by her had seven children, viz.: Pearl, Myrtle, Mabel, Georgiana, Lewis Cleveland, Ruby, Robert Camden.

    bb. Charles B. Rockhold, Jr., born Dec. 25, 1852; died March 11, 1890; married Nov. 4, 1878, Laura A., daughter of Charles P. Creel, and had issue. Otho Guy, born May 12, 1880; Glenna Stainaker, born June 20, 1883.

    cc. Lilly Rockhold, married Sparks Young, and had issue: Virgie; Charles; Everett; Homer; Minnie.

    dd. William L. J. Rockhold, married first Lina Masters and by her had one child, Henry. Married, second, Lottie, daughter of L. F. Stone of Belpre, Ohio, and had issue by her: Lena; Frank S.

    ee. Mary Rockhold, married D. M. Harris of Springfield, O., and had issue: Brooksie; Ethel.

    ff. Anna Brown Rockhold, born Nov. 7, 1867; married Sept. 24, 1883, William Pool, of Spencer, West Va., and had issue: Robert Brown, born Aug. 1, 1884; died Sept. 13, 1885; Woodyard W., born Nov. 6, 1886; Mary Gertrude, born Jan. 13, 1891; Ophelia Pauline, born Jan. 27, 1893; Edward C., born Jan. 15, 1895.

C. Charles Pulaski Creel, born Aug. 15, 1830; married Nov. 29, 1853, to Mary H. Forbes, and had issue:

    aa. Martha Creel, born Nov. 15, 1854: died May 18, 1860.

    bb. Laura A. Creel, born, Jan. 7, 1857; married Nov. 4, 1878, Charles B. Rockhold, Jr., her cousin.

    cc. Florence Creel, born Oct. 27, 1860; died April 4, 1863.

    dd. John W. Creel, born March 6, 1863; married L. V. Fought, and had issue one child, Cleveland, born Aug. 19, 1885.

    ee. Anna P. Creel, born Sept. 13, 1865; married William Nailey of Newark, West Va. No issue.

    ff. Blanche P. Creel, born April 30, 1867; married Elijah Hennen. Issue, Rhea, born March 22, 1893; Nellie.

    gg. Minnie A. Creel, born Aug. 2, 1872; married March 28, 1895, Dr. F. B. Livermore. Residence, Cleveland, Ohio.

  hh. Fannie H. Creel, born Jan. 12, 1875.
  ii. Benjamin F. Creel, born June 27, 1877.
 D. John Anthony Buckner Creel, married Nancy Frazier, by whom he had issue seven children.
  aa. Edwin Creel, married Alice Elizabeth Stephens, and had issue: Lucy, Samuel, Elsie.
  bb. Edward Creel, married Mary Snider, and had issue: Lucy, Benjamin, Lewis, John.
  cc. Dora Creel.
  dd. Mollie, married John Webb and had issue: Nellie, Noah, Everett.
  ee. James Creel, of Elizabeth, West Va.
  ff. Florence Creel, married Nige Maurier. No issue.
  gg. Robert Creel.
3. Charles Robinson Saunders, third child of Abner and Mary (Buckner) Saunders, married April 9, 1837, Fannie M., daughter of Charles Price, and had issue seven children. She was born Nov. 7, 1818; died April 15, 1865; Charles R. Saunders died Oct. 15, 1875. Issue:
A. John Franklin Saunders, born 1839, married Mary Melrose. Residence, Buffington, West Va. Issue: Martha J., David, Walter, Annie.
B. Charles Abner Saunders, born 1842. Served in C. S. A. and was killed in action.
C. Mary Lauretta Saunders, born 1842; married Samuel Bumgarner. Residence, Harris, Sullivan Co., Mo. Issue: Dora, William, John, Calvin, Linnie, who married John Harris, Judson, Mo.
D. William Isaiah Saunders, born Oct. 26, 1844. Served in the Confederate Army. Married in 1877, Jennie Summerville. Residence, Reedy, Roane Co., West Va. Issue: Walter S., born Oct. 26, 1878; Lulu Grace, born Aug. 27, 1881; Charles Abner, born June 8, 1883.
E. George Buckner Saunders, born April 29, 1847; married April 16, 1874, Margaret E. Mooney; born May 4, 1848. Residence Odaville, Jackson county, West Va. Issue: Orpha J., born April 27, 1876; Lillie M., born Nov. 23, 1878; Sarah E., born Oct. 23, 1880; Frances E., born March 1, 1884; died Jan. 27, 1890; Georgia A., born Jan. 2, 1886; Martha J., born Feb. 7, 1888; a son, stillborn, March 26, 1891.
F. Lucy Elizabeth Saunders, born 1849; married Oct. 27, 1894, Alexander James Macnar. No issue. Residence, Salmon, Idaho.
G. Anthony Saunders, died an infant.
H. Margaret Saunders, died aged 12 years.
I. Britannia J. Saunders, born April 27, 1858; married May 4, 1891, Edward J. Chenveront of Mineral Springs, West Va. No issue.
J. James Emmett Saunders, born April 23, 1861. Residence, Seattle, Washington.
4. Peyton Buckner Saunders, fourth child of Abner and Mary (Buckner) Saunders, born March 10, 1805; died Jan. 28, 1854;

married Nov. 21, 1839, Hannah, daughter of John Foster of Newark, West Va. She died Dec. 15, 1885. Issue:

A. Lermine Louise, born July 29, 1844; married Dec. 25, 1872, to John G. Besse. Residence, Ridge Farm, Ill. Issue: Charles Cleveland, born April 7, 1875; died Jan. 14, 1889; Amy Foster, born Jan. 1, 1880; Clara Saunders, born Aug. 16, 1882.

B. Ophelia Boulware Saunders, born Sept. 10, 1846.

C. Alfred Pulaski Saunders, born April 7, 1850; married April 26, 1876, Ada Lewis. Issue: Thomas Earle, born May 11, 1881.

D. John Peyton Saunders, born Aug. 22, 1853; married March 30, 1880, Carrie Miller. No issue.

E. Anthony Saunders.

F. Lucy Saunders, died in infancy.

5. Britannia Jane Saunders, fifth child of Abner and Mary (Buckner) Saunders, married Dec. 6, 1841, William D. Timms, and had issue:

A. Nancy E. Timms, born 1842; married Leonard Bidwell of Newark. Issue: Emmeline B., John A., Rose.

B. Mary F. Timms, born June 21, 1843; married April 7, 1861, Orville C. Fought, and had issue 12 children. Residence, Stella, West-Virginia. Issue:

    aa. William A. Fought, born Dec. 4, 1861; married Carrie Chalfman. Issue: Roy W., Ula, Everett.

    bb. Hannah B. Fought, born March 31, 1863; married Alonzo Park. Issue: Peter, Josie.

    cc. Martha J. Fought, born Nov. 14, 1865; married John Hindman. Issue: Cora, Emma.

    dd. Henry J. Fought, born Feb. 5, 1868; married Mary Woods. Issue: Roger.

    ee. Mollie E. Fought, born May 27, 1870; married Phillip Meredith. Issue: Eber, Icy.

    ff. Orville C. Fought, born Sept. 23, 1872.

    gg. Lucy E. Fought, born March 12, 1875.

    hh. John M. Fought, born April 2, 1877; died July 8, 1884.

    ii. Ora May Fought, born Oct. 30, 1879.

    jj. Roxanna, born Jan. 25, 1882.

    kk. Cora F. Fought, died in infancy.

    ll. Edward Fought, born April 5, 1886.

C. Margaret Jane Timms, born Sept. 17, 1844; married, 1865, Alexander Barnes, of Vienna, West Virginia.

    aa. James Franklin, born July 29, 1866; died March 23, 1867.

    bb. Affie Viletta, born March 31, 1868; married Sylvester Dye, and has issue: Herbert H., Curtis A.

    cc. Susan Burns, born Jan. 17, 1870; married Vinton Dye.

    dd. Otis Alexander, born March 12, 1875; died Jan. 29, 1877.

    ee. Eura Abigail, born Jan. 17, 1878.

    ff. Hosea Alexander, born April 20, 1880.

    gg. Evalina Frances, born May 25, 1885.

D. John Abner Timms, born 1847; married April 12, 1882, America A. Pennybacker. Residence, Stella, West Virginia. Issue: William Harry, James W.

E. Clarissa Pulaski Timms, married Jacob C. Reese. Issue: Bertha, Abner, Georgie, Ada, Lyman.

6. Anthony George Washington Saunders, sixth child of Abner and Mary (Buckner) Saunders, born Jan. 1, 1812; died April 13, 1888; married Jan. 4, 1842, Mrs. Rebecca I. H. (Lewis) Ball, died Jan. 15, 1875. Married second, Elizabeth, daughter of Henry Steed. By last wife no issue. Issue by first marriage:

A. Lamont L. Saunders, born April 12, 1844; married May 21, 1868, Maggie A. Eckels, born Jan. 17, 1852. Residence, Charleston, West Virginia. Issue:
    aa. Violetta B., born March 6, 1869; married Fred Fisher, and has issue: Herman F., born July 26, 1894.
    bb. Frank, born March 9, 1871.
    cc. Harvey, born April 30, 1887; died June 7, 1888.
    dd. Alice Bard, born June 5, 1889.

II. CLARA BUCKNER, second daughter of the first marriage of John Anthony Buckner, was born Jan. 8, 1779. She married in 1798 George Creel, Jr., son of George, Sr., and grandson of David Creel. He was born Dec. 21, 1778, and died May, 1807. Clara Buckner died March 9, 1858, and is buried in the old Creel graveyard near Davisville, beside her second husband, Jeptha Kincheloe. Issue by George Creel, Jr.:

1. John Buckner Creel, called Colonel, born 1799; married first, Ann W., daughter of Daniel Kincheloe, Sr., Jan. 20, 1823, who died Feb. 26, 1824. From this union a son, George, was born, who died in early manhood. Married second, April 5, 1827, his cousin, Permelia A. Jane, daughter of Abner Saunders. John B. Creel died in 1838, and his second wife in 1864. Issue:

A. Battle W. Creel, married first, Harriet West; second, Abigail Pennybaker.
B. Laura M. Creel, married April 18, 1861, Charles B. Rockhold.
C. Charles P. Creel, married Nov. 29, 1853, Mary H. Forbes.
D. John Anthony Buckner Creel, married Nancy Frazier.

2. Bushrod Washington Creel, born 1804, died 1875; married first, May 3, 1832, Alcinda R., daughter of Robert Kincheloe, and by her had ten children. He married second, in 1859, Rebecca Thomas, issue, two children. Issue by first wife:

A. George R. Creel, born July 9, 1833; married March 21, 1879, to Catherine Harris, who died July 16, 1895. Residence, Davisville, West Virginia. Issue:
    aa. Richard Lee, born March 21, 1880; died June 17, 1886.
    bb. George R., Jr., born Oct. 2, 1881.
    cc. Samuel Tilden, born April 28, 1883.
    dd. Andrew Jackson, born April 10, 1885; died June 24, 1886.
    ee. Lewis Kincheloe, born Oct. 14, 1886.
    ff. Raymond, born Sept. 5, 1889.

B. Lucy F. Creel, born Oct. 16, 1835; married July 21, 1853, to Marcellus Clark. He was born Sept. 1, 1829; was in the Mexican War, member of Capt. Danl. Drake Henry's company of the Maryland Regt., under Col. Hughes, in Gen. Scott's Army. Served in Co. A., 36th Va. Regt., C. S. A., under Gen. Early. Residence, Parkersburg, West. Va. Issue:

- aa. Emma Elizabeth, born April 13, 1855; married Sept. 16, 1879, Lewis R. Whitney. No issue.
- bb. Robert Bushrod, born Aug. 26, 1856; died March 17, 1857.
- cc. George Washington, born Feb. 22, 1858; died March 28, 1859.
- dd. Marcellus, Jr., born April 1, 1860; died Sept. 19, 1880.
- ee. Marsolena, born April 2, 1866; married Oct. 18, 1885, to Frank Smith, of Parkersburg. Issue: Lucy Emma, born May 4, 1888; Juliette, born Jan. 22, 1891.
- ff. Paul Cook, born Nov. 5, 1867; died Jan. 10, 1868.
- gg. Lena, born Feb. 17, died May, 1872.

C. Mary Elizabeth Creel, born 1838; married Oct. 26, 1865, Dr. Erwin D. J. Bond. He was State Senator, 1885-1887. Member of House of Delegates, 1882-1883. Surgeon of 11th W. Va. Vol. Infantry; U. S. Pension Examiner in 1888. He was born 1834. Issue: Laura Alcinda, born Nov. 16, 1872.

D. John B. Creel, born April 25, 1839; died July 25, 1842.

E. Clara Kincheloe Creel, born June 22, 1841; married Nov. 23, 1881, to Ezra C. Phelps, son of George W., son of John. Residence, Hartford City, West Va. Issue:
- aa. Victor Ezra, born June 27, 1882.
- bb. Clara, born and died July 23, 1885.

F. John Alexander Creel, born May 10, 1843; married Dec. 13, 1872, Isabella Fouty, born Jan. 7, 1854. Residence, Davisville, West Va. Issue:
- aa. Beulah Alcinda, born June 14, 1873; married July 15, 1892, to James Thomas Roberts. No issue.
- bb. Alice Belle, born 1875; died March 5, 1893.
- cc. Edna Elizabeth, born April 4, 1877; died Dec. 24, 1888.
- dd. Bushrod Washington, born Feb. 4, 1879.
- ee. Fannie Victoria, born April 23, 1881.
- ff. Mary Ivy, born May 1, 1883.
- gg. Ruby Ethel, born May 25, 1885.
- hh. Lucy Mabel, born June 24, 1887.
- ii. Spencer Kennedy, born April 27, 1890.
- jj. Julia Agnes, born March 20, 1893.

G. Eleanor Sophia Creel, born July 18, 1846; married Jan. 9, 1879, W. J. Zimmerman. Residence, Charleston, West Va. No issue.

H. Hannah Jane Creel, born Sept. 13, 1848; married May 14, 1878, James W. Ross. Residence, Charleston, West Va. Issue:
- aa. Eugenia, born Jan. 6, 1880; died in infancy.
- bb. Shirley J., born August 31, 1883.

I. Bushrod Washington, born Sept. 17, 1850. Removed to Texas in 1861, and is supposed to have been killed there by Indians.

J. Elias Wickliffe Creel, born Sept. 17, 1850; married Aug. 29, 1883, Ella Sanford Triplett; born July 5, 1860. Residence, Davisville, West Va. Issue:
- aa. Lucy Mabel Virginia, born July 15, 1884.
- bb. Frank Bushrod, born June 21, 1886.
- cc. Ella Elizabeth, born Jan. 24, 1888.
- dd. Emma Dee, born Sept. 26, 1889.
- ee. Donna Jane, born May 25, 1893.

  K. Henry A. Wise Creel, born March 12, 1856; married Oct. 4, 1882, to Alma Lovista Smith; born Oct. 6, 1863. Residence, Davisville, West Va. Issue:
    aa. Edith Rathbone, born Sept. 17, 1883.
    bb. Eric Dering, born Nov. 21, 1886.
    cc. Eleanor Elizabeth, born March 18, 1895.
  L. Monroe T. Creel, born Dec. 3, 1860.
  M. William H. Creel, born Aug., 1863.

  By his second marriage, Jan. 6, 1809, to the Widow Catherine Gibbens, Anthony, or as he was sometimes called, John Anthony Buckner, had issue eight children, viz.:|

  I. JOHN PEYTON BUCKNER, born Sept. 15, 1809; died 1821, and was buried by a beech tree, beside his father, close to the original primitive log cabin, on land now owned by Gordon B. Gibbens.

  II. ANTHONY LEACH BUCKNER, born July 2, 1811; died in infancy.

  III. WILLIAM BUCKNER, born Aug. 14, 1814; died Nov. 17, 1898; married June 2, 1836, to Emily Martin, of Malden, West Va. She died June 7, 1884, and is buried on the Buckner farm. Issue:

   1. James Henry, born May 5, 1837; died 1839.
   2. Eleanor, born Jan., 1839; died in 1848.
   3. Mary, born 1841; died in 1849.
   4. Virginia, born Nov. 30, 1842; married Feb. 27, 1888, to Robert Freeman; born June 5, 1828. Residence, Goss, Mo. No issue.
   5. Martha F., born Oct. 20, 1844; married Sept. 11, 1865, to David M. Robinson; born July 24, 1843. Residence, Cicerone, Roane County, West Va. Issue:
    A. Annie F., born Nov. 22, 1866; married Nov. 3, 1889, to James P. Jones, born Feb. 2, 1867. Issue: Charles, born August 19, 1890. Clarence, born March 21, 1892. Mayford, born May 14, 1894.
    B. Charles W., born Aug. 15, 1868; died May 27, 1889.
    C. James A., born Dec. 29, 1869.
    D. Edmund D., born April 18, 1871; died Nov. 15, 1872.
    E. Dora B., born Nov. 24, 1873; died Oct. 6, 1879.
    F. Isaiah W., born Aug. 15, 1875; died Sept. 16, 1879.
    G. John O., born Sept. 19, 1878.
    H. Ernest E., born Aug. 5, 1881.
    I. Emily L., born July 11, 1884.
   6. Emily Jane Buckner, born Feb. 7, 1847; unmarried.
   7. Melissa Buckner, born May 5, 1852; married Nov. 7, 1870, to T. J. Nutter; born July 12, 1840. Residence, Cisko, Ritchie County, West Va. Issue:
    A. Edward, born March 9, 1871.
    B. Josie, born April 13, 1874.
    C. John, born April 13, 1877; died April 20, 1892.
    D. Nioma, born March 21, 1884; died March 21, 1886.
    E. Ella, born March 28, 1889.
    F. Lloyd, born May 4, 1892.
    G. Ida, born June 30, 1893.
    H. William Anthony Buckner, born Dec. 14, 1853; died Oct. 25, 1859.
    I. Nancy Ellen Buckner, born April 30, 1856; married August 13, 1870, to George Augustine; born July 31, 1854. Residence,

Parkersburg, West Va. Issue: Grace, born Aug. 6, 1877; Norman, born Sept. 14, 1880; Albert, born April 1, 1887; Birdie, born Feb. 17, 1894.

J. John Peyton Buckner, born April 30, 1858; married Jan. 31, 1878, to Emma A., daughter of John Hickman. Issue: Ivy Blanche, born Dec. 7, 1880; Lina, born Jan. 25, 1885; Roy, born Jan. 1, 1887; Icy, born Sept. 9, 1890; Clark, born May 22, 1895; Effie, born March 11, 1894.

IV. ELEANOR BUCKNER, born March 26, 1816; died about 1826, after her father's demise.

V. ALEXANDER BUCKNER, born Jan. 14, 1818; died unmarried, April 17, 1883.

VI. DAVID BUCKNER, born March 3, 1820; died 1825.

VII. ROBERT BUCKNER, born Oct. 29, 1823; married Jan. 20, 1850, Louisa Clementine, M. S., daughter of William and Mary (Barnett) Leach; born Dec. 19, 1831. Issue:

1. James Monroe, born Oct. 1, 1851; died May 30, 1866.
2. Nancy Elizabeth, born July 28, 1854; married August 22, 1875, to James S. Hickman; born April 8, 1852. Issue: Sylva, born July 13, 1876; died May 21, 1888. Sampson Lathrop, born August 21, 1878.
3. Robert Clayton, born March 12, 1860; married Dec. 31, 1890, to Dora Deem.
4. Noah Walker, born June 17, 1868; married Dec. 26, 1890, to Flora Harper. Issue: Ruby Agnes, born March 4, 1892.

VIII. BUSHROD BUCKNER, born Nov. 6, 1825; married first, Sept. 16, 1847, Rhoda, daughter of George and Sebrah Barnett, who died 1854. Issue:

1. Jefferson Monroe, born July 24, 1849; married August, 1876, to Jeanette M. Golden; born August 21, 1855. Issue: Alice Lillian, born Feb. 4, 1878; died Feb. 19, 1893. Mary, born May 2, 1880. Oscar, born April 30, 1883. Charles, born Jan. 21, 1886. Nellie, born June 5, 1889. French Vernon, born Feb. 1; died Feb. 14, 1893. Son, died day of birth, Feb. 5, 1894. Blondel Marie, born May 5, 1895.
2. George A., born May 10, 1851; married Oct. 16, 1873, Alma Sophronia, daughter of Jeptha and Eleanor (Butcher) Bibbee; born Dec. 6, 1853. Mr. Buckner was Postmaster of Leachtown, his residence, for twenty-one years. Issue: Thomas Willard, born Sept. 21, 1874; Clarence Merton, born July 4, 1876; died July 12, 1878; Ella Leach, born May 15, 1878; Nettie Blanche, born Nov. 8, 1886.
3. Benjamin Franklin, born March 14, 1853; married first, March 14, 1878, to Lucy Ellen Prince; died without issue, April 5, 1881. Married second, August 15, 1886, May Melissa Tippens; born March 11, 1868. Issue: Clarence Carl, born Feb. 21, 1888; Cora Belle, born Nov. 24, 1889; Myrtle, born Nov. 6, 1893.

BUSHROD BUCKNER, by his second wife, Nancy J. Baker, of Beaver County, Penna., whom he married in 1856, had issue:

1. Mary E., born May 2, 1858; married April 20, 1880, to Charles W. Evans, of Athens, Ga. Issue: Guy Oliver, born May 1, 1881; Clarence Clyde, born April 30, 1883; Merton Budd, born Oct. 21, 1890.

2. Oscar, born Jan. 21, 1860; married July 24, 1881, to Maggie C. Evans; born Aug. 17, 1861. Issue: Norman Carroll, born Dec. 19, 1882; Arthur Newton, born Feb. 27, 1885; Barnett Monroe, born Nov. 10, 1893.
3. James B., born Jan. 20, 1857; died Jan. 13, 1860.
4. Arthur, born Aug. 25, 1865; died Sept. 25, 1888; married Dec. 27, 1886, to Cora E. Fairfax; born Jan. 19, 1866. Issue: Arva, born and died in 1888.
5. Dennis Walter, born July 5, 1873; married Dec. 25, 1894, to Myra J. McDonald.

"Thy name and honourable family."
—Titus Andronicus.

Lewis and Washington Families

Washington Arms. Argent, two bars, and in chief three mullets gules.

IN 1653 John Lewis patented land in Gloucester County on a branch of Poropotank Creek, which branch was then called Lewis' Creek. The names of those on account of whose importation he was entitled to the land (*i. e.*, 50 acres for each person) were, John Lewis (probably himself), Lydia Lewis (probably his wife), William Lewis, Edward Lewis and John Lewis, Jr., probably his sons.

Edward Lewis patented lands on the Rappahannock, and John Lewis, Jr., patented April 22, 1668, 100 acres in New Kent, and in 1677, 2,600 acres in New Kent and Gloucester, "next below the plantation of said John Lewis," 600 acres of which were granted said John Lewis by patent dated Nov. 23, 1663. His residence in 1676 was near Major Thomas Pate's, where Bacon the rebel encamped, and he suffered severely from the depredations of Bacon's troops. In 1680 he was a Captain of horse in the militia of New Kent, and one of its Justices. In 1675 he was termed Major of foot, and with Lt.-Col. John Smith, Captain Philip Lightfoot, Mr. Thomas Royston and Mr. John Buckner, patented 10,000 acres of land in New Kent.

    I. JOHN LEWIS, married Isabella ———. Some writers state that her name was Warner, but no conclusive evidence as to its correctness is forthcoming. It is probable that John Lewis was the son of John and Lydia Lewis, above mentioned.

    II. JOHN LEWIS, son of John and Isabella Lewis, was the founder of Warner Hall. He was born Nov. 30, 1669; died Nov. 14, 1725. He married Elizabeth Warner, daughter of Col. Augustine Warner, and Mildred Read, his wife, daughter of Col. George Read and Elizabeth Martian. She was born Nov. 24, 1672, and died at Warner Hall Feb. 5, 1719-20.

    In 1715 Colonel Lewis became a member of the Council. It is probable that Warner Hall came to the family through his wife. At the Hall are the tombstones of Augustine Warner, the elder, and of Mary, his wife. Augustine was member of the Council 1659-1667. He had a daughter Sarah, married Lawrence Townley, and a son, Augustine Warner, Speaker of the House of Burgesses. The latter married Mildred, daughter of Col. George Read, and had issue:—

1. George Warner, baptized in 1677.
2. Robert Warner.
3. Elizabeth, married John Lewis.
4. Mildred, married Lawrence Washington.
5. Mary, married John Smith of Purton.

In the York County Records is this entry: "John Smith of Purton, in the County of Gloucester, in Va., Gentleman, for Thirty pounds current money, sells to William Buckner of York, in Va., Gentleman, twenty-nine acres, which is my share of a parcel of land my grandmother, Madam Mildred Warner, bought of Mr. Thomas Read, according to the division made between Mr. John Lewis, Mr. John Washington and myself, coheirs to my uncle, Mr. Robert Warner, deceased, to whom the said land was given by the said Madam Mildred Warner." Recorded Feb. 24, 1708.

John and Elizabeth Warner Lewis had fourteen children, but the names of the following are the only ones to be ascertained. It is probable that some of those lacking died in infancy.

1. Catherine Lewis, baptized Nov., 1702.
2. Elizabeth Lewis, baptized Nov. 26, 1702.
3. John Lewis, born March 22, 1702.
4. Charles Lewis.
5. Robert Lewis, baptized May 4, 1704.
6. Elizabeth Lewis, baptized May 7, 1706.
7. Isabella Lewis, baptized Dec. 18, 1707, married Dr. Thomas Clayton July 14, 1720, had one child, Juliana; died in infancy.
8. Anne Lewis, baptized Feb. 14, 1712.

III. JOHN LEWIS, married Frances, daughter of Henry Fielding of King and Queen County. He was Major in 1731, Colonel in 1734, and Member of the Council in 1751 and during other years. Frances, the wife of Major John Lewis, died Oct. 27, 1731. He married (2nd) Priscilla Churchill, widow of Robert Carter of Nominy, and daughter of Col. William Churchill. He died Jan. 17, 1754. Issue:

1. Warner Lewis, born Oct. 10, 1720.
2. Fielding Lewis, born July 7, 1725.
3. Mildred Lewis, born Dec. 12, 1726; died July 5, 1729.
4. John Lewis, born Nov. 20, 1728.
5. Charles Lewis, born Feb. 25, 1729.
6. Frances Lewis.

IV. COL. FIELDING LEWIS, resided in Spottsylvania County, where his home "Kenmore" in Fredericksburg still stands. He married twice; first on Oct. 18, 1746, to Catherine, aunt to Genl. Geo. Washington and daughter of Major John Washington of "Highgate," Gloucester County. She died in 1749-50 and left issue:

1. John Lewis, born June 22, 1747.
2. Francis Lewis, born Nov. 23, 1748; died without issue.
3. Warner Lewis, born Nov. 29, 1749; died in infancy.

Colonel Fielding Lewis, married May 2, 1750, Betty, only sister of General George Washington, and had issue:

1. Fielding Lewis, born Feb. 14, 1751.
2. Augustine Lewis, born Jan. 22, 1752; died young.
3. Warner Lewis, born June 24, 1755; died young.

4. George Washington Lewis, born March 14, 1757.
5. Mary Lewis, born April 22, 1759; died Dec. following.
6. Charles Lewis, born Oct. 3, 1760.
7. Samuel Lewis, born May 14, 1763; died Sept. 3, 1764.
8. Bettie Lewis, born Feb. 23, 1765.
9. Lawrence Lewis, born April 4, 1767.
10. Robert Lewis, born June 25, 1769.
11. Howell Lewis, born Dec. 12, 1771.

Will of Fielding Lewis

Will of Fielding Lewis of St. George's Parish, Spottsylvania County. Dated Oct. 19, 1781; probated Jan. 17, 1782. Witnesses: George Noble, Benj. Ledwick, John Butler, Gerard Alexander, Will Booth, William Carpenter.

Executors: Wife and my sons, John, Fielding and George. Legatees: Wife, Betty Lewis, during life, the use of all my lands in Spottsylvania County, except that part rented to my son John; son John, after the death of his mother, all my lands in Spottsylvania County and in Fredericksburg; son Fielding, 1,000 acres of my Frederick County lands on which he lives; son George, remainder of Frederick County lands bought of Robert Carter Nicholas, except 1,000 acres to my son Lawrence; son-in-law Charles Carter, Esq., son Lawrence, 1,000 acres of land in Frederick County; son Robert, one-half of ten thousand acres of land located for me in the County of Kentucky, by Mr. Hancock Lee, and one-half of 20,000 acres located or to have been located for me by Nathaniel Randolph, in the County of Kentucky; son Howell, remaining half of above lands in Kentucky. All my lands purchased at the Land Office, except what is already disposed of to my sons Robert and Howell equally; my share in the Dismal Swamp Company, my lands bought of Marmaduke Naughflett in partnership with General Washington; my lands bought of Dr. Wright and Jones, in Nansemond County, in partnership with General Washington and Dr. Thomas Walker, and the 320 acres of land in Frederick County, bought of George Mercer's estate, also my share in the Chatham Rope Walk, at Richmond, to be sold by my executors, and the money arising to be paid to my six sons before mentioned, in equal portions.

Codicil, dated Dec. 10, 1781. To son Robert Lewis, a tract of land purchased of Francis Willis, Jr., adjoining the tract of 320 acres of land in Frederick County, also the said tract of 320 acres to son Howell Lewis, and the whole tract of 10,000 acres in Kentucky to son John."

It will be readily seen from the above will, that Fielding Lewis was a very wealthy man. He was County-Lieutenant in 1758, and in 1761 was Commander-in-Chief of the Militia, his commission being dated Nov. 12th of that year.

V. MAJOR GEORGE WASHINGTON LEWIS of "Marmion," King George County, was Major in Baylor's Regiment, and commanded the Washington Life Guards during the Revolution. He married Oct. 15, 1779, Catherine, daughter of William Daingerfield, of Spottsylvania County. He died in 1821. Issue:

1. Samuel Lewis, born Nov. 11, 1780.
2. Mary Willis Lewis, born June 22, 1782; married Major Byrd Charles Willis.
3. Daingerfield Lewis, born July 14, 1785; married Lucy, born 1785, daughter of Thomas Pratt and Jane Brockenbrough.

VI. SAMUEL LEWIS, married Sarah Attaway Miller Sept. 15, 1803, daughter of Major Thomas Roy Miller, and his wife Eliza Ariss Buckner of Port Royal, Caroline County. Issue:

1. George Washington Lewis, born Nov. 12, 1804; married his cousin Jane Brockenbrough Lewis of Marmion, King George County, Feb. 29, 1829.
2. Thomas Lewis, born June 15, 1806; died unmarried in 1833.
3. Eliza Lewis, born Feb. 20, 1808; married James W. Finney of Kentucky; died 1833.
4. John Bankhead Lewis, born Feb. 22, 1810; married Elizabeth Briggs; died June 17, 1878, at Shellfield, Westmoreland County.
5. Mary Willis Lewis, born Jan. 30, 1812; married John Casey of Morganfield, Ky.; died April 3, 1886.
6. Sarah Attaway Lewis, born Dec. 13, 1814; married John Putnam of Tallahassee, Fla., Oct. 1833; died 1872.
7. Henry Howell Lewis, born Feb. 7, 1817; married Ann Ogle Tayloe November 30, 1841; died in Baltimore March 17, 1893.
8. Catherine Daingerfield Lewis, born Oct. 15, 1820; married her cousin Fielding Lewis of Marmion, King George County; died July, 1849.

BUCKNER DESCENT FROM WASHINGTON FAMILY.

I. John Washington of Whitfield, Lancaster County.
II. Robert Washington of Warton, Lancaster County. Gent.
III. John Washington of Warton, Lancaster County.
IV. Lawrence Washington of Northampton, Mayor of Northampton 1538; died 1583.
V. Robert Washington of Sulgrave, æt. 40, in 1583.
VI. Lawrence Washington of Sulgrave and Brengton; died Dec. 13, 1616.
VII. Lawrence Washington, Rector of Purleigh, Essex; died 1654-5.
VIII. John Washington, born in England, 1633. Emigrated to Virginia.
IX. Lawrence Washington, died in Virginia, 1697.
X. Augustine Washington, born 1694; died 1743.
XI. George Washington, born Feb. 22, 1732; died Dec. 14, 1799; first President of United States.

XII. Elizabeth Washington, sister of above, married Fielding Lewis.
XIII. Major George Washington Lewis, Captain of Washington's Life Guard, married Catherine Daingerfield and had with other issue:
XIV. Samuel Lewis, born Nov. 11, 1780, married Sarah Attaway Miller, daughter of Thomas Roy Miller and Eliza Ariss Buckner, and granddaughter of Richard and Eliza (Ariss) Buckner of "Albany," Westmoreland County, Virginia.

> "*Think of your ancestors and your posterity.*"
> —Tacitus.

Stith Family

ARMS.—Argent, a chevron engrailed between three fleur-de-lis sable.

HE first of this family of whom anything is known was Colonel John Stith of Charles City County, who patented land there in 1663. In 1676 the House of Burgesses, which met under Bacon's auspices, accused him of having been one of the chief causes of the existing troubles, and disfranchised him. He was a practising lawyer in 1680; Sheriff of Charles City County in 1691, and Burgess in 1685, 1692 and 1693. The name of his wife is unknown, but he had issue, a son, Colonel Drury Stith, who had a patent for 680 acres of land in Charles City in 1703; Sheriff in 1719-20, and 1724-5. He removed to Brunswick County about 1725 and was the first clerk of the county in 1732, holding the office until 1740. He married Susannah, daughter of Launcelot Bathhurst, who emigrated from England to Virginia in the latter part of the seventeenth century, and who was the second son of Sir Edward Bathhurst, knighted in 1643 by King Charles I. Drury Stith is mentioned by Colonel William Byrd in "A Journey to the Land of Eden" (Westover MSS.), in the paragraph wherein the author, under date of September 13, 1733, says: "By the way, I sent a runner half a mile out of the road to Colonel Drury Stith's, who was so good as to come to us. We cheered our hearts with three bottles of pretty good Madeira, which made Drury talk pretty hopefully of his copper mine. We easily prevailed with him to let us have his company, upon condition we would take the mine in our way."

Of the descendants of Colonel Drury Stith, at least eight became county clerks, certainly the following: Griffin Stith, one of the early clerks of the County Court of Northampton; Drury Stith, Charles Turnbull, Edward Randolph Turnbull, Robert Turnbull, respectively the ninth, fourteenth, fifteenth and sixteenth clerks of the County Court of Brunswick; Edward Randolph Turnbull, Jr., the first clerk of the Circuit Court of Brunswick after the separation of the offices ; David Meade Bernard, the second clerk of the Corporation Court of Petersburg, and John Randolph Stith, one of the clerks of the County Court of Northumberland.

Colonel Drury Stith and Susannah (Bathhurst) Stith had issue, Drury Stith of Brunswick County, Burgess 1744-53 ; vestryman of St. Andrews, 1755 ; married about 1718 Elizabeth Buckner, his first wife, daughter of William and granddaughter of the first John Buckner.

    1. Captain Buckner Stith, son of Drury and Elizabeth (Buckner) Stith, was of Rock Spring, Brunswick County, and the author of an elaborate treatise on the culture of tobacco. He married Ann —— and died about 1791, leaving issue :
        A. Colonel John Stith of Brunswick, who married a daughter of Lawrence Washington of King George Co.
        B. Colonel Robert Stith of Windsor, King George Co., who married another daughter of Lawrence Washington. One of his daughters, Fanny Townsend Stith, being the mother of David Mead Bernard.
        C. Richard Stith of Brunswick.
        D. Buckner Stith of Brunswick, whose daughter was the grandmother of Judge Needham S. Turnbull and the Hon. Robert Turnbull of the Brunswick family of that name.
        E. Ann Stith married William Eaton, of Warren, N. C.
        F. Susannah Stith married Andrew Mead.
        G. Catherine Stith was the second wife of Robert Bolling, of Centre Hill.
        H. Griffin Stith married (1st) the widow of Samuel Washington (2d) Mary Dent Alexander, (3d) —— Gwatkin. Issue :
            aa. Griffin Stith, clerk of Northampton Co. 1781, and held that office until his death in July, 1789.

I. The Rev. William Stith, born 1689, nephew of Col. Drury Stith, was a son of John Stith and Mary, a daughter of Col. William Randolph of Turkey Island. On the death of her husband, Mrs. Stith, at the instance of her brother, Sir John Randolph, removed to Williamsburg and placed her son William in the grammar school attached to the College of William and Mary, where he pursued his academic studies, and graduated. His theological studies were completed in England, where he was ordained a minister of the Episcopal Church. On his return to Virginia in the year 1731 he was elected Master of the Grammar School in the College, and Chaplain to the House of Burgesses. On July 16, 1736, he was installed as Rector of Henrico Parish, and resided at Varina, where he wrote his "History of Virginia." In 1752 he was elected

President of William and Mary College, to which he removed and over which he presided until his death in 1755. The Rev. William Stith married his cousin, Judith Randolph, daughter of Thomas Randolph of Tuckahoe. Issue:

1. Elizabeth Stith,
2. Judith Stith,
3. Mary Stith,

II. Captain John Stith, son of John and Mary (Randolph) Stith, married Elizabeth, daughter of the Rev. Charles Anderson of Westover, and Frances, his wife, had issue: Anderson Stith, who married Joanna, daughter of William Bassett and his wife, Elizabeth Churchill. Issue:

1. Bassett Stith, born 1765, married July 8, 1790, Mary, daughter of Col. Nicholas Long of Halifax, N. C. Issue:
   A. Maria Stith, married Judge Joseph J. Daniel of the Supreme Court of N. C. Issue:
      aa. William A. Daniel, Married Miss Joyner and had issue: Sally, d. s. p.; William A., Jr., d. s. p.; and John Daniel of Halifax, N. C.
      bb. Mary Long Daniel, married George Loyall Gordon, son of General William F. Gordon of Albemarle Co. Issue:
         aaa. Armistead Churchill Gordon of Staunton, who married Maria Breckenridge Catlett and had issue: Margaret Douglas, Mary Daniel, James Lindsay, Jr., and Armistead Churchill Gordon, Jr.
         bbb. Lavinia Bassett Daniel, married Turner W. Battle of North Carolina and had issue: (1) Judge Jacob Battle, married first, Iva Steele, and had issue: Jacob, Jr., married second, Nellie Gripton. (2) Joseph Daniel Battle, d. s. p. (3) Harriet W. Battle, married Bennett Bunn, and had: Turner, Joseph Daniel and William Bunn. (4) Turner W. Battle, Jr. (5) George Gordon Battle, married Martha Dabney Burwell Bagby, daughter of Dr. George W. Bagby. (6) Rev. Gaston Battle, married first, Turner, daughter of Judge John Manning of North Carolina, and had John Manning; married, second, Nannie Speight; married, third, Bettie Plummer Wright of Petersburg, Va.
      cc. Frances Daniel Gordon, d. s. p.
      dd. Lavinia Battle Gordon, d. s. p.
      ee. James Lindsay Gordon, some time Assistant District Attorney of New York City.
      ff. Mary Long Gordon, married Dr. Richard H. Lewis of Raleigh, N. C.
   B. Maria Long Stith, married Edmund Freeman. Issue:
      aa. Emily Freeman, married Hampden Sidney Smith of Raleigh, N. C., and had issue: Edmund Freeman, George and Hampden Freeman.
      bb. George Freeman, d. s. p.

- C. Virginia P. Stith, married Nathaniel Macon Eaton of North Carolina. Issue:
  - aa. Senora Stith, married Franklin Lockhart and had issue: Franklin, Sally, Nathaniel, James Daniel, Joseph, Senora and Virginia S. Lockhart.
- D. Nicholas Long Stith, married Anna Austin Hill and had issue:
  - aa. Frederick Hill Stith, married Elizabeth Carter and had issue: Mary Long Stith.
  - bb. Mary Long Stith, d. s. p.
  - cc. Alberta Bassett Stith, married —— Jones.
  - dd. Marshall Stith, d. s. p.
  - ee. Bassett Stith, d. s. p.
  - ff. Anna Hill Stith.
- E. Albert Stith, d. s. p.
- F. William Stith, d. s. p.
- G. Martha Stith, married General John R. J. Daniel of North Carolina. Issue:
  - aa. William Augustus Daniel, d. s. p.
  - bb. John Napoleon Daniel, d. s. p.
  - cc. General Junius Daniel, C. S. A., killed at the Battle of the Wilderness, May, 1864; married Ellen Long.
  - dd. Virginia Frances Daniel, d. s. p.
- H. Lavinia Stith, married Robert Newson of Norfork, Va. Issue:
  - aa. Mary Bassett Newson, married —— Winborne of Tenn.
1. Frances W. Stith, second wife of General J. R. J. Daniel, d. s. p.
2. Major John Stith, son of Anderson and Joanna (Bassett) Stith, settled in Georgia.
3. Elizabeth Stith, resided in Halifax, N. C., with her brother, Col. Bassett Stith and d. s. p.

" Signior, is all your family within?"
—Othello.

Thruston Family

HERE is in the possession of the Thruston family, an ancient vellum bound, metal-clasped book, containing on its time-stained yellow leaves a combination of recipe, prescription and family memorandum. From this repository we are enabled to give some authentic data relative to the early history of the family.

The first entry upon its pages runs thus: "John Thruston, ye son of Malachias Thruston of Wellington in Somerset was baptised in ye parish church of Wellington, ye 8th day of June 1606, being Whitsonday." This John Thruston, whose hand, it is supposed, made the first entry in the book, was Chamberlain of the City of Bristol, England, for eleven years and eleven months. His son Edward was twice married, and was the father of twenty-four children, only a small proportion of whom arrived at maturity.

The name in England is spelled both Thruston and Thurston, and the arms used by them are very similar. The Thurstons of Anderton, County of Lancaster, use "Sable, three buglehorns argent, stringed or" (See Glover's Ordinary; Cotton MS. Tiberius, D.10; Harleian MSS. 1392 and 1459).

The Thrustons of Talgarth, County Merioneth, and the Thrustons of Market-Weston Hall, Suffolk, formerly of Hoxne Abbey, Suffolk, use "Sable three buglehorns, stringed or garnished azure," which coincides with the blazon used by the American family of Thrustons.

Malachias Thruston, of Wellington, County Somerset, was born previous to 1600. His wife died Feb., 1651, and is buried in the Parish Church of Buckland. John Thruston, their son, was baptized in the Parish Church of Wellington, June 8, 1606. He was Chamberlain of the City of Bristol for nearly twelve years. His first wife was Thomasine Rich, daughter of the Rev. Peter Rich, who was some time "Preacher of God's Word," in the town of Heytesbury, County of Wiltshire. Thomasine Rich was baptized in the Parish Church of Heytesbury, Aug. 24, 1604; died Nov. 30, 1647, and is buried in St. Thomas' Churchyard, Bristol.

John Thruston married a second time, Jan. 12, 1648, according to his own entry in the little account book. He does not, however, mention his wife's name. Of his children two, viz.: Malachias and Edward, settled in Virginia. John Thruston died April 8, 1675, and is buried on the south side of St. Thomas' Church, Bristol, by the side of his first wife.

ISSUE OF JOHN AND THOMASINE THRUSTON:

I. Robert Thruston, born March 15, 1629; died May 22, 1641.
II. John Thruston, born Feb. 1, 1630; died Feb. 3, 1630.
III. John Thruston, born February 11, 1631; died July 13, 1644.
IV. Thomasine Thruston, born February 6, 1632; married September 11, 1653, to John Hunt.
V. Justian Thruston, born September 11, 1634; died May 27, 1645.
VI. Alice Thruston, born September 26, 1635; died January 14, 1661.
VII. Ann Thruston, born December 23, 1636.
VIII. Malachy Thruston, born January 19, 1637; emigrated to Virginia and was a lawyer in the Colony from 1670 to 1683 in Norfolk County.
IX. Edward Thruston, of whom presently.
X. A son, still born, April 14, 1640.
XI. Robert Thruston, born May 26, 1641; died 1650.
XII. Grace Thruston, born August 11, 1642; buried August 2, 1644.
XIII. Thomas Thruston, born November 8, 1643; buried March 16, 1644.
XIV. Milecious Thruston, born December 22, 1644; died December 28, 1658.
XV. Simon Thruston, born November 28, 1645; died January 24, 1646.
XVI. Justian Thruston, born November 17, 1647.

ISSUE OF JOHN THRUSTON BY HIS SECOND WIFE:

I. Mary Thruston, born May 11, 1650; died December 11, 1652.
II. Martha Thruston, born May 11, 1650; died September 6, 1650.
III. Grace Thruston, born June 2, 1651.
IV. Rachael Thruston, born May 6, 1652.
V. Mary Thruston, born September 16, 1653; died April 28, 1668.
VI. John Thruston, born January 24, 1654; died May 26, 1656.
VII. James Thruston, born January 25, 1654.
VIII. Sara Thruston, born June 1, 1656.

Edward Thruston, son of John and Thomasine Thruston, was born at Bristol January 30, 1638. He was in Virginia at least as early as 1666, as it was in that colony he married his first wife. He returned to Bristol and married a second time, and again came back to the colonies. An entry in the account book, made by his son Edward reads "1717. My father Mr. Edward Thruston came from Boston to live with me Edward Thruston, junior, and I having Book of him thought fitt to keepe ye births and marriages of my ffamily as follows."

This Edward Thruston, Jr., settled in Norfolk County, Va., and his original will, with a wax seal bearing the Thruston arms is still preserved in the clerk's office.

Edward Thruston the elder was married in Virginia October 28, 1666, to Ann Loveing, daughter of Thomas Loveing, merchant, of Martin's Hundred, Va. She died at Bristol December 17, 1670. He married secondly in Bristol August 2, 1671, Susanna Perry, daughter of Nicholas Perry, lawyer, of Great Marlow. From 1680 to 1683 Edward Thruston resided at Ashton, England, at which place his second wife died August 2, 1683. He removed to Virginia to live June 13, 1717.

ISSUE BY FIRST WIFE, ANN LOVEING:

I. John Thruston, born December 2, 1668, at Martin's Hundred, Va. Married September 23, 1690, to Ellinor, widow of John Cary of Chew, and had issue Justian Thruston, born August 26, 1691; married John James and went to Virginia in 1713 to receive her estate at Martin's Hundred, James City County.

II. Thomasine Thruston, born November 28, 1670, at Bristol, England; buried December 5, 1670, in St. Thomas' Churchyard.

ISSUE BY SECOND WIFE, SUSANNA PERRY:

I. Thomasine Thruston, born July 6, 1672; died February 18, 1673.
II. Elizabeth Thruston, born May 26, 1675; married September 10, 1701, to Rev. John Astley, Vicar of Willcott. Had a daughter Jane, born April 30, 1703.
III. Mary Thruston, born December 13, 1677.
IV. Edward Thruston, born February 5, 1679, at Ashton; settled in Virginia prior to 1713. Married August 31, 1706, Elizabeth, daughter of Rev. Thomas Housden, minister of the Upper Parish of Nansemond, Va. Issue:
 A. Mary Thruston, born December 9, 1707.
 B. John Thruston, of whom presently.
 C. Elizabeth Thruston, born April 8, 1712; died January 18, 1782; married May 5, 1772, to Cornelius Calvert.
 D. Frances Thruston, born January 7, 1714; died August 21, 1749; married —— Smith.
 E. Edmund Thruston, born July 14, 1717.
 F. Susanna Thruston, born July 30, 1719; died October 27, 1748; married William Robertson and left issue a son, Moses, born 1742, and a daughter, Frances, born 1744.
 G. Perry Thruston, born August 30, 1721.
 H. Thomas Thruston, born Dec. 4, 1725; died February 15, 1738.

Col. John Thruston, son of Edward Thruston, the younger, was born Oct. 24, 1709; died Feb. 20, 1766. He made his home in Gloucester County, where the quaint homestead of "Landsdowne"

is still standing, and has for its inmates two of his last descendants—Thruston sisters. He married Dec. 6, 1737, Sarah Mynn, born 1717; died May 12, 1786, whose first husband was a Mr. Hanes. Issue:

1. Reverend and Col. Charles Mynn Thruston, of whom presently.
2. Elizabeth Thruston, born April 27, 1740; died 1766; married Col. Thomas Whitney of Gloucester County.
3. Sarah Thruston, born April 27, 1743; married Col. John Thornton of Hanover County.
4. Mary Thruston, born May 17, 1746; died March, 1766; married Hugh Walter of Gloucester County.
5. John Thruston, born May 20, 1750; died Feb. 16, 1782; married Aug. 6, 1771, to Sarah Stevenson.
6. Frances Thruston, born March 20, 1752; died 1780; married Dr. and Col. William Hubbard of Charlotte County.
7. Edward Thruston, born July 12, 1753; died June 24, 1754.
8. Jemima Thruston, born Dec. 18, 1755; died July 4, 1756.
9. Mildred Thruston, born Oct. 2, 1756; died Sept. 3, 1758.
10. Robert Thruston, born Jan. 14, 1759; was living in 1802; had a daughter married to Prof. Bracken of Batterton School, which was allied to William and Mary College.

The Rev. and Colonel Charles Mynn Thruston, known as "The Fighting Parson," was born Nov. 6, 1738. He was one of the most celebrated men of a celebrated period. Nothing shows more clearly the enterprising spirit of Virginians, and more thoroughly explains how the old families of the State became scattered and interwoven with those of the South and West, than the history of Charles Mynn Thruston of "Mount Zion," near White Post, Frederick (now Clarke) County, Va.

Mr. Thruston was educated at William and Mary College. When twenty years of age he acted as Lieutenant of Provincials, under the command of Washington, in the campaign which resulted in the evacuation of Fort Duquesne. He afterwards studied for the ministry, was ordained by the Bishop of London, and chosen rector of a parish in his native county. In 1769 he removed to Frederick County, Va., where he continued in his calling until the commencement of hostilities with the mother country. He had been among the most prominent in repelling the attempt to introduce the Stamp Act into Virginia, and he now embarked in the common cause with unconquerable zeal. He exerted himself to produce arms and ammunition, and addressed the people at public gatherings by the most spirit-stirring and eloquent harangues. Not content with this, Parson Thruston threw aside the gown, and, seizing the sword, raised a volunteer company composed of the élite of the young men of the county, he being chosen Captain, and marched to join Washington in New Jersey. He had his arm shattered in making a bold and vigorous attack on a strong Hessian redoubt near Amboy, and upon being carried from the field was attended by the surgeon of General Washington. He was afterwards promoted to the rank of Colonel.

He never resumed his pastoral relations, but held various public offices, among which were those of Presiding Judge of the Court of Frederick County, and member of the Legislature.

In 1809, consulting the interest of a numerous family, which, besides his own children, embraced a number of grandchildren, he removed to Louisiana, and purchased the plantation upon which was afterwards fought the Battle of New Orleans. The descendants of the invaders whom he had encountered in 1776 in 1815 perished over his grave. He died in 1812, and was buried at the spot where the battle which afterwards occurred raged fiercest.

A number of interesting anecdotes might be told of Col. Thruston, but one, which has been already published, will suffice to illustrate his character. A party of four soldiers was reported to be at his mill in the act of removing his flour, which, they claimed, they had been ordered to do by Col. Nelson. He immediately armed himself and ejected them from the premises. The next day a Lieut. Graves with fifteen troopers appeared at the mill, and threatened, without proper authority, to remove the flour. Col. Thruston, who, in the meantime had learned of their approach, stationed himself at the door of the mill, with loaded musket, determined to sacrifice his life rather than submit to an oppression which he considered to be as iniquitous as the Stamp Act, which he had so vigorously opposed. The Lieutenant, after placing his men in various threatening attitudes, without avail, and observed that force on his part meant bloodshed, took the advice of bystanders, who warned him that the Colonel meant what he said, and would certainly shoot if he, the Lieutenant, persisted; so he relinquished his purpose. Afterward Col. Thruston, learning that the men were in need of food, gave the officer all the flour wanted, and invited him to dine with him. Several of the neighbors had offered to assist Col. Thruston in defending his mill, but he declined, saying that no one but himself should die in defense of his property.

Gen'l Charles Lee, lame from a wound, was staying at Col. Thruston's at the time, and learning of the trouble, hobbled down to the mill and re-inforced the Colonel with language clothed in very vigorous English, for which the Lieutenant threatened to throw him into the mill-dam. He changed his mind, however, upon learning who he was addressing.

Col. Thruston married twice. His first wife was Mary Buckner of Gloucester County, in 1760; she was the daughter of Col. Samuel Buckner, and died after bearing him three sons. Her cousin, Ann Alexander, daughter of Col. Alexander of Gloucester County, Va., took charge of the children, and shortly after became his second wife, 1766. She bore him nine children.

ISSUE BY FIRST WIFE, MARY BUCKNER:

1. John Thruston, born Oct. 15, 1761; died Feb. 15, 1802; married Oct. 13, 1782, to his first cousin, Elizabeth J. Whiting, daughter of Col. Thomas Whiting. He was an officer in the Revolutionary War, and settled at Louisville, Ky., where he became one of the most prominent citizens. Issue:
    A. Charles Mynn Thruston, a distinguished lawyer of Louisville.
    B. Alfred Thruston of Louisville.
    C. Algernon Thruston.
    D. Elizabeth Thruston, married Woodson Pope, Clerk of Jefferson County, Ky.
2. Buckner Thruston, born Feb. 9, 1764; married 1798 to Janette January, daughter of Peter January of Kentucky. He was a distinguished lawyer, and in 1804 was elected United States Senator from Kentucky. He served in this capacity for several years, when he was prevailed upon by President Madison to accept a vacancy which occurred upon the bench of the Supreme Court of the District of Columbia, which position he held until his death in 1845. He had a highly cultivated mind, and Gen'l Charles Lee of the Revolution—an Englishman, who came to this country, and was remarkable for his great intellectual culture, as well as for his blunt eccentricities—left him his valuable library, remarking in his famous will that he bequeathed it "to the only man he had met in America who was capable of appreciating it."

    The Thruston family of Cumberland, Ind., are the descendants of his oldest son Charles, who was for twenty years a prominent officer in the U. S. Army. He had other sons who became distinguished and useful citizens, and two daughters, who married prominent men.
3. Charles Mynn Thruston, born Aug. 3, 1765; died Dec. 11, 1800; married Jan. 20, 1796, to Frances Clark, daughter of John Clark, and widow of Dr. James O'Fallon, of Louisville, Ky. She was a sister of Gen'l George Rogers Clark and of Governor William Clark of Missouri.

ISSUE BY SECOND WIFE, ANN ALEXANDER:

1. Sarah Alexander Thruston, born Dec. 15, 1766; married Dec. 17, 1784, to George Flowarden Norton, of Winchester, Va., and had issue:
A. John Norton, U. S. Marshal, for Mississippi; died unmarried.
B. Charles Norton, an officer in U. S. Navy.
2. Frederick Thruston, born March 15, 1770; died before 1848, in Louisiana. Unmarried.
3. Mary Buckner Thruston, born July 31, 1772, living in 1848; married May 28, 1792, to Col. Charles Magill, of Winchester, Va., a distinguished officer in the Revolutionary Army, and a leading lawyer of Winchester. Issue:
A. Charles Magill.
B. Archibald Magill.
C. John Magill.
D. Alfred Magill.
E. Henry Magill.
F. Augustine Magill.
G. Buckner Magill.
H. Elizabeth Magill.
I. Anne Magill.
J. Mary Magill.
K. Frances Magill.
4. Frances Thruston, born Feb. 3, 1774; died 1813; married April 25, 1793, Frederick Conrad of Winchester, Va. They removed to Louisiana, where they raised a large family. Three of their sons, Frederick, Charles and Frank, became lawyers, and Alfred a prosperous merchant. Charles Conrad was a member of both Houses of Congress, and also Secretary of War under President Fillmore. He was a member of the Confederate Congress, and married a daughter of Lawrence Lewis, grandniece of Gen'l George Washington.
5. Elizabeth Mynn Thruston, born April 6, 1775; married Aug. 10, 1794, to Henry Daingerfield of Winchester, Va.
6. Alfred Thruston, born May 14, 1778; married but had no issue.
7. Louisa Thruston, born March 23, 1782; married 1797, to Captain Edmund H. Taylor, a prominent and wealthy citizen of Louisville, Ky., and had issue.
8. Sydney Ann Thruston, born May 2, 1783; died Sept. 12, 1803; married Hon. Alfred Powell of Winchester, Va., a distinguished lawyer, who represented that district in Congress. Admiral Levin M. Powell, U. S. N., was the only child of the marriage.
9. Edmund Taylor Thruston, born Oct. 24, 1785; died previous to 1848. Was for a time in the U. S. Navy. Married and lived in Mississippi, and had one daughter.

Some four or five descents since.
—Alls Well that Ends Well.

Dickinson Family

ALTHOUGH little has hitherto appeared in print regarding the Virginia family of Dickinson, yet, an examination of the early records of the colony reveals the fact that the name is to be found amongst those of the first settlers. The present members of the family claim descent from John Dickinson, or Dickenson, as it was sometimes written, who was in Virginia as early as 1654. He is believed to have been one of three brothers, the others afterwards settling in Maryland and Pennsylvania. There were two John Dickinsons who were in Virginia in 1635, and there was a Benjamin Dickinson in Boston, New England, in 1627.

In this excursus of the family no attempt has been made to trace the name to its original source, but sufficient data is given to show the antiquity of the name in the Colony of Virginia.

From Hotten's List of Emigrants

1620. Jeremiah Dickinson, aged 26, came in the "Margaret and John" in 1620.

Elizabeth Dickinson, aged 38, came in the "Margaret and John" in 1623. (Muster Rolls taken in 1624.)

Feb. 16, 1623. Jane Dickinson, living at James City.

Feb. 16, 1623. Jeremiah Dickinson, living at Bass's Choice.

1624. Peter Dickinson. (In list of burials in Elizabeth City.)

June 6, 1635. John Dickenson, aged 22; George Dickenson, aged 19, came in the "Thomas and John."

Aug. 21, 1635. William Dickenson, aged 21, came in the "George."

Nov. 20, 1635. John Dickenson, aged 24, came in ship "Expedition."

Register of St. Peter's, New Kent County

1754. Susanna, daughter of Griffith and Ann Dickinson, born March 14, baptized April 7.

Register of Bruton Church, Williamsburg
Births

1742. Judith, daughter of Thomas and Elizabeth Dickinson, was born.

1745. Thomas, son of Thomas and Elizabeth Dickinson, was born.

1746. Mary, daughter of Thomas and Elizabeth Dickinson, was born.
1750. Agnes Rutton, daughter of Thomas and Elizabeth Dickinson, was born.
1753. Elizabeth, daughter of Thomas and Elizabeth Dickinson, was born.

Deaths

1675. John Dickinson.

Persons who had Slaves Baptized

1750. Thomas Dickenson, one slave.
1765. Arthur Dickinson, one slave
1766. John Dickenson, one slave.

Spottsylvania County Records

1775. Will of Nathaniel Dickenson, Spottsylvania County, dated Oct. 21, 1775; probated May 16, 1776.

Witnesses: Andrew Manning, John Coleman, Hannah Coleman. Executors: Wife Elizabeth, and sons William and Nathaniel Dickenson.

To wife Elizabeth all the estate, real and personal, during her life, then to be divided between sons Nathaniel, Richard and Elijah Dickenson, and Betty Pulliam and Fanny Garton; but if said Fanny Garton should marry, she may enjoy her part during her life, and at her death it is to return to Elijah Garton's* children; son William Dickenson.

Sept. 16, 1779. Elijah Dickinson, witness to a deed.

1782. Nathaniel and William Dickenson, Serjeants, to whom Richard Dickenson is heir (Order Book 1782-86).

---

*Elijah Garton was a son of Uriah Garton of St. George's Parish, Spottsylvania County, and his wife Winifred. Uriah's will is dated March 5, 1752; probated Aug. 5, 1755, in which he leaves to his son Elijah, "the plantation whereon Ephraim Knight now liveth."

ORMESBY—FORMERLY OWNED BY MRS. ROYSTON
DAUGHTER OF JOHN THORNTON

"Come they of noble family?"
—Henry V.

Strother Family

THE name Strother is an ancient one, and is believed to be of Scandinavian origin. Whatever may have been its derivation, it has existed in its present form in the County of Northumberland, England, from the eleventh century, and by intermarriage many of the descendants of the name have become allied with the most prominent families of the Borders.

Alan del Strother, by his marriage in 1350 with Constance, daughter of William de Lyam, obtained three messuages in Alnwick, as well as the Manor of Lyam. This Alan was the son of William del Strother, living in 1318, and who, according to the Calverly MSS. (British Museum), became of Kirknewton by his marriage with Joanna, daughter of Walter Corbet, grandson of Patrick, 5th Earl of Dunbar, by his wife Ada, natural daughter of William the Lion of Scotland (1165-1214).

The above William had a son, Henry del Strother, who received a grant for his services at the Battle of Durham, and succeeded to the estates at Kirknewton; and two other sons, designated Alan, Sr., and Alan, Jr. The former was the Constable of Roxburgh Castle, and lived until 1408. The younger Alan married Constance de Lyam and became the progenitor of the Strothers of Wallington. He died about 1381. There were two other sons, John and William. The latter was Mayor of Newcastle on several occasions, from 1354. He married Matilda, daughter of Peter Draper, Member of Parliament for Newcastle in 1348, by Agnes, daughter of Richard de Emeldon, Mayor of Newcastle in 1306. Joan—the only daughter apparently—married first—William, second son of William, Sire de Courcy, and secondly—the famous John de Coupland. Alan Strother, Jr., had a son, Alan, who married Margaret Jadys, and died during the lifetime of his father. In 1440 William del Strother, a grandson of William of Lyam, married a daughter of Robert Wallington, and lived at Castle Strother in Glendale.

Coming to a later date, we find the following entries in Northumberland records.

ENROLMENT OF APPRENTICES AND FREEMEN:

WILLIAM STROTHER, apprenticed to Thomas Classon, merchant, date of indenture, 1544-5; enrolment as freeman, 1546.

WILLIAM STROTHER, son of William Strother of Kirknewton, Northumberland, Gent; apprenticed to Robert Corneforthe, boothman, Aug. 18, 1656; enrolment Dec. 3, 1656; admission to the Eastland Company of Merchant Adventurers, Sept. 24, 1664.

The Virginia Strothers

William Strother, the first of the name and founder of the family, is said to have emigrated from Northumberland, England. It is possible he might have been the William Strother of Kirknewton who was a member of the Company of Merchant Adventurers in 1664. He settled in Cittenborne parish on the Rappahannock River, near the present Port Conway. The first appearance of his name is on July 12, 1673, *when he came to the court of old Rappahannock to designate the mark of his cattle. This county was formed in 1655 from Lancaster, but abolished in 1692, when Richmond and Essex were formed from it. Among William Strother's neighbors were Captain Anthony Savage, and the latter's son-in-law, Francis Thornton (son of William Thornton), who were the Virginia progenitors of these two well known families.

The will of William Strother is dated Dec. 30, 1700, and was probated in Richmond County, Nov. 4, 1702. In it he names wife Dorothy; devises one-half the land he lives on with "mansion" to his eldest son William, after death of testator's wife. The other half to son James; rest of his lands to sons Robert and Benjamin, after providing for the education of his son Joseph; special bequest to grandson "Will" Strother; all the rest and residue of personal estate, with crops of corn, tobacco and servants, to wife Dorothy Strother, during the time of her widowhood, but if she should marry again, son James to order an account to be taken of the personal estate, that it may be equally divided between her and sons James, Jeremy, Robert, Benjamin and Joseph.

Executors: Wife and son James.

Witnesses: James Phillips, Edward Langdree, William Smith.

---

*In the Land Office, Richmond, there is a patent for 500 acres of land entered in 1658 to William Strowder. This is probably intended to be "William Strother," and as the land is in Rappahannock Co., next to where William Strother lived in 1673, it would make him to be in Virginia 15 years before he had his cattle mark registered.

Visitation of Northumberland, A.D. 1615.

William Strother—dau. of Edm. Horsley of Milborne, Esq of Newton, Esq.

　William Strother—Jane, dau. of John Selby of Twysell, Esq. of Newton, Esq.

　　Lancelot Strother of Langton—Elinor, dau. of John Coigniers of Sockburne, Esq. and Newton, Esq.

| Lancelot | John of Langton and Newton. Living 1615. | Anne | Elizabeth | Jane | Elinor | Catherine | Mary |

William

Seal of John Strother of Newton, 1615—"A man on horseback, armed."

Strother Arms—Gules on a bend argent. three eagles displayed azure.　Crest—A greyhound sejant or.

ISSUE OF WILLIAM AND DOROTHY STROTHER:

I. William Strother.
II. James Strother.
III. Jeremiah Strother.
IV. Robert Strother.
V. Benjamin Strother.
VI. Joseph Strother.

WILLIAM STROTHER, eldest son and second of the name, was born probably before 1655. He was a planter, and lived at the family seat of his father, now King George County. In the Spottsylvania Records under date of Oct. 1, 1725, we find the following:

"WILLIAM STROTHER of King George Co., planter, to George Proctor of Spotts. Co., planter, £100 ster., 1500 acres in Spotts. Co., on ye Branches of ye Hasell Run—it being the fourth part of a grant to William Cocke, Esq., Chickley Corbin Thacker, Francis Thornton, Jnr., and William Strother, party to these presents, in joynt partnership, by patent dated 20 Dec. 1718, joining the lands of Majr. Augustine Smith, Buckner and Rashton, and Mann Page, Esq."

WILLIAM STROTHER was a vestryman of Hanover parish; and Sheriff of King George County. His wife Margaret, born April 2, 1678, was a daughter of Francis Thornton (son of the first William Thornton of Gloucester County) and his wife Alice, daughter of Captain Anthony Savage, Justice and High Sheriff of Gloucester County. In 1722 he gave to his son, "Will" Strother, Jr., the land devised him by his father, except what had been sold to John Strother. On July 26, 1726, William Strother's will was admitted to probate, and his widow qualified as executrix. The contents of the will are unknown, as the Will Book (1720–44) of King George County containing it was lost during the Civil War.

On Aug. 1, 1727, Margaret Strother, widow, conveyed to her son William 300 acres of land given by her grandfather, Anthony Savage, to her father, Francis Thornton, and wife, Alice, on the Rappahannock River; except one-half acre for burying ground, including the graves therein.

On the same day she deeded to her son, Francis, of Hanover County, certain slaves, with reversion to her grandson, William Strother.

ISSUE OF WILLIAM STROTHER (II.) AND MARGARET THORNTON:

I. William Strother.
II. Francis Strother.
III. Anthony Strother.
IV. Benjamin Strother.

William Strother (III.) was born about 1700. After the destruction of the old mansion house of his grandfather, the first William Strother, he sold his estate near Port Conway, and purchased one on the river, opposite Fredericksburg, in 1727. The latter place was sold by his widow and executrix, Nov. 3, 1738, to Augustine Washington, father of General George Washington. On May 26, 1727, he received a grant for 266 acres in King George County, and Sept. 12, 1731, as "Captain" William Strother, 372 acres in Prince William County. He was Sheriff and Justice of King George County, and vestryman of the parish. He married Margaret Watts, who, on his death, married (2nd) John Grant. In March, 1737, she asked for a reapportionment of the estate of her late husband, and Hancock Lee, Abram Kenyon and John Grant were appointed to make it and to set aside to her one-seventh of the estate. On Nov. 3, 1738, Anthony Strother (brother of William) qualified as "guardian to Elizabeth, Agatha, Margaret, Ann and Jane, five of the children of William Strother, deceased," and gave bond to pay five-sevenths of the debts of said William. He died in 1732, and in his will directs sale of his lands in King George and Prince William Counties, and names his wife as executrix. Issue:

1. Elizabeth Strother, married Nov. 9, 1738, John Frogg of Prince William County, who subsequently moved to the Valley of Virginia, and lived near the family of his wife's sister. A son, John Frogg, Jr., married Agatha Lewis, his first cousin, and was killed at the Battle of Point Pleasant.

2. Agatha Strother, married John Madison (a near relative of President Madison), first clerk of Augusta County, 1745; member of the Vestry, also of House of Burgesses and the House of Delegates. He died in Botetourt County, March, 1784. Issue:

A. William Strother Madison of Botetourt, married Elizabeth Preston.
B. George Thomas Madison, a lawyer of Botetourt, married Susanna, sister of Hon. Patrick Henry.
C. Roland Madison, married Anne, daughter of General Andrew Lewis, and removed to Kentucky.
D. James Madison, born Aug. 27, 1749, near Port Republic, then in Augusta, now in Rockingham County, was an ardent patriot in the Revolutionary War, and first resident-Bishop (1785) of the Episcopal church in Virginia; married, 1779, Sarah Tate of Williamsburg, and had issue:
    a. James Catesby Madison.
    b. Susan Madison, married R. G. Scott of Richmond, Va.
E. George Madison, married Jane, daughter of Major Francis Smith.

F. Margaret Madison, married Judge William, son of Judge Samuel McDowell of Kentucky, and had among other children, Agatha, who married Hon. James G. Birney, first Abolition candidate for President.

MARGARET STROTHER, daughter of William Strother. (III.), born in King George County, Sept. 3, 1726; married (1st), April 26, 1744, George Morton, who died in a short time; (2nd), Oct. 16, 1749, Gabriel Jones, born May 17, 1724, in Frederick County. He was the son of John Jones of Montgomery County, Wales, and his wife, Elizabeth, who emigrated to Virginia about 1720. John Jones died about 1727, and his widow and children returned to England. In April, 1732, Gabriel Jones was admitted as a scholar of the Blue-Coat School, Christ's Hospital, London, where he remained until 1739. Under the date of April 12, 1739, appears the following entry on the records of the school:

"Gabriel Jones is this day taken and discharged from the charges of this hospital forever, by Elizabeth Jones, his mother, and by Mr. John Houghton, of Lyon's Inn, in the County of Middlesex, solicitor in the High Court of Chancery, with whom he is to serve six years."

Elizabeth Jones, mother of Gabriel, was born in 1689, and died Jan. 1, 1745. At the age of twenty-one years Gabriel was admitted to the Bar, having served out his term of apprenticeship. The Jones family were of "gentle blood," but reduced circumstances. The arms on the book-plate of Gabriel Jones, viz.: "Argent a lion rampant vert, vulned in the breast gules. *Crest*. "The sun in splendour or," are identical with that used by Sir William Jones, the noted Oriental scholar (1746-94), and tend to show some degree of kinship with that celebrated man.

Gabriel Jones returned to America about 1746, and located in Frederick County, taking up a tract of land near Kernstown. In the same year he was appointed King's attorney for Augusta County. On Oct. 16, 1749, he was married by the Rev. James Keith to Mrs. Margaret Strother Morton, daughter of William Strother of King George. Gabriel Jones was a vestryman of Rockingham parish in 1752. He was for a long time so prominent at the Bar of the Valley of Virginia that he was called "The Lawyer." In 1757-58 and 1771 he represented Augusta in the House of Burgesses. When Rockingham County was constituted in 1777 he became a citizen there, and was immediately appointed prosecuting attorney.

He was a member of the State Convention in 1788. Gabriel Jones was a man of great ability and integrity, his only fault, so tradition says, was an extremely irritable temper, which, when aroused, expressed itself in the strongest terms he could command, mingled with very pronounced profanity.

An anecdote is related of him which shows the estimation in which he was held by the Court. On one occasion, during the trial of a cause before the county justices of Rockingham he had Alexander Hugh Holmes, afterwards Judge, as his adversary. Mr. Holmes was mischievous and witty, and irritated Mr. Jones to such an extent that he became angry and profane. The Court abstained from interfering as long as possible. To think of punishing Lawyer Jones was out of the question; so the Presiding Judge gave it as the decision of the Court "That if Mr. Holmes did not quit worrying Mr. Jones, and making him curse and swear so, Lawyer Holmes should be sent to jail."

Mr. Jones was a very intimate friend of Gen. George Washington, as well as being a close friend of Lord Fairfax, and at the latter's death he became one of his executors. Gabriel Jones remained in active practice up to the time of his death in 1806 at the age of 82 years. His wife, Margaret Strother Jones, died in 1822, in her 97th year. Issue:

- A. Margaret Jones, married Colonel John Harvie, lawyer of Albemarle; member of Congress, and for many years Register of the Land Office of Virginia. Their descendants are very numerous, many of them being highly distinguished.
- B. Elizabeth Jones was (3d) wife of John Lewis of Fredericksburg, son of Colonel Fielding Lewis, who married a sister of General Washington. Issue:
    - aa. Warner Lewis, died young.
    - bb. Fielding Lewis.
    - cc. Gabriel Jones Lewis, born Sept. 10, 1775; died Feb. 7, 1864; married Nov. 24, 1807, Mary Bibb, and had issue, Elizabeth, born Nov. 11, 1813, who married Colonel James McDowell Storting.
- C. ——— Jones, married John Hawkins of Kentucky.
- D. William Strother Jones, born March 21, 1756. He was a student of William and Mary College in 1767; Captain in the Continental Army during the Revolution, and subsequently a Colonel of Militia. He married Frances Thornton Buckner, widow of Dr. Horace Buckner of Culpeper, and daughter of Francis Thornton of "Fall Hill," Spottsylvania County, who married in 1759, Ann, daughter of the Rev. John Thompson, by his wife, Butler Brayne, widow of Governor Spottswood. Issue:

MARY WADE STROTHER
WIFE OF COL. WILLIAM MENEFEE

  aa. William Strother Jones, Jr., of Vaucleuse, Frederick
County; born Oct. 7, 1783. He married (1st) Ann Maria
Marshall, a niece of Chief Justice Marshall; (2d) Ann
Cory Randolph. William S. Jones died July 13, 1845. Issue:
    aaa. Frances Jones, born Oct. 15, 1808; married Dec.
18, 1828, David Walker Barton.
    bbb. William Strother Jones of New York.
    ccc. Captain James F. Jones, died 1866.
    ddd. Lt.-Col. Francis B. Jones, 2d Va. Regt., C. S. A.,
killed at Malvern Hill.
    eee. R. B. Jones.
 4. Anne Strother, married, May 27, 1744, Francis Tyler; resided
in Culpeper, and later in Augusta County.
 5. Jane Strother, married Jan. 26, 1749, Thomas Lewis, born in
Donegal, Ireland, April 27, 1718, the eldest of the distinguished
sons of Colonel John Lewis and his wife, Margaret Lynn. The
latter was the sister of the celebrated William Lynn, Doctor of
Physic, of Fredericksburg, who died there in 1758. Thomas
and Jane Strother Lewis have many descendants living in the
South and West.

FRANCIS STROTHER, second son of William and Margaret Thornton Strother, was born probably in Richmond, now King George County. On Aug. 1, 1727, Margaret Strother gave by deed to her son Francis of Hanover County, certain slaves with reversion to her grandson William Strother. On Jan. 22, 1745, William Coleman conveyed to Francis Strother of St. Martin's Parish, Hanover County, 583 1-3 acres in St. Mark's Parish, Orange County, near the county seat of the present Rappahannock County. Here he removed and settled close by his son John, until his death in 1752. His will, dated April 17, 1751, is probated April 16, 1752, in Culpeper County. In it he mentions his wife Susannah; sons John, George, Anthony, Robert and Francis, and daughters Mary, Behethland, Elizabeth and Susannah. He married Susannah Dabney of the Hanover family of that name. It has been erroneously supposed that she was the daughter of Cornelius Dabney and his wife, Sarah Jennings, and much has been written and said as to the claim of her descendants to a share in a great "Jennings estate" in England. The absurdity of the claim will be apparent when it is understood that her son, John Dabney Strother, was born in 1721, the same year Sarah Jennings was married. The latter fact is proven by the following entry in the first minute book of Hanover County: "Ordered, that it be recorded that on —— day of April, 1721, Cornelius Dabney, late of England, intermarried with Sarah Jennings." The Dabney family was in Virginia as early as 1664, as appears from Land Grants. In the Register of Saint Peter's Parish, New Kent County, are the following entries: "Nelthan, daughter of James Dabney, baptized ye 8 Jan. 1698–9. Elizabeth, daughter of George Dabney, baptized ye 11th of Nov. 1698. John, son to Cornelius Dabenie, deceased ye 7th of April, 1688. Elizabeth, daughter to Cornelius Dabenie, deceased ye 4th of April, 1688."

1. John Dabney Strother, born 1721, in Hanover County; died April, 1795. He married Mary Willis Wade, and removed shortly after his marriage to "Wadefield," Culpeper County. He was a Captain in the Culpeper Militia in 1756. His will is dated March 29, 1795, and is probated in Culpeper April 20, 1795. Issue:

   A. Joseph Strother, married Ann Stuart, the daughter of Robert Stuart of Culpeper County, whose will was probated Sept. 21, 1789. In his will, which was dated May 14, 1770, he mentions his wife Mary, and his daughters, Lucy, who had married a Pulliam, Nancy Strother, and his son Robert. Joseph Strother was Deputy Sheriff of Culpeper in 1784 and 1795. In the "Va. Calendar of State Papers" we find that he petitioned the Legislature to require or permit the Land Register to issue to him a warrant for 900 acres of land, when he removed to Jefferson County, Ky., in 1800, as stated in the foregoing petition. His three daughters, Sarah, Mary Wade and Lucy, had married prior to his leaving Virginia. The children of Joseph Strother and Ann Stuart were as follows:

   aa. Mary Wade Strother, born April 20, 1771; married William Menefee, Dec. 14, 1790. She was accounted a great beauty in her day, and an old water color portrait of her is now the prized possession of Mrs. Nannie Carter Rice, a daughter of Mrs. Virginia Ashby Carter. Her husband, commonly referred to as Colonel Menefee, was the son of John Menefee, born 1739-40; died June 2, 1832; and Mildred Johnston, died Dec. 27, 1792. Colonel Menefee was born Dec. 20, 1762, and died Dec. 22, 1841. He lived in Rappahannock County. His portrait in oil is also in the possession of Mrs. Rice. Issue of Mary Wade Strother and William Menefee:

   1. Ann Stuart Menefee, born Sept. 19, 1791; married Oct. 20, 1808, to Thomson Ashby of Fauquier County, born March 31, 1785.
   2. Mildred Johnston Menefee, born Nov. 5, 1792; died, Dec. 27, 1792.
   3. Mildred Johnston Menefee (2d), born May 25, 1794; died Jan. 21, 1816; married March 31, 1812, to Gabriel Tutt. Issue:
      aaa. William Tutt, born Oct. 8, 1814.
      bbb. Philip Tutt, born Jan. 14, 1817.
      ccc. Betsy Tutt, born ———; died April 28, 1830.

COL. WILLIAM MENEFEE

4. Sarah Strother Menefee, born Dec. 18, 1795; d. s. p. at the home of her niece, Mrs. Virginia Ashby Carter, in Warren County, Va.
5. Benjamin Strother Menefee, born Oct. 12, 1797, married Oct. 16, 1834, to Elizabeth McCrane of North Carolina.

bb. Sarah Strother, born Oct. 28, 1776; died Jan. 22, 1813; married Oct. 18, 1794, to Edward Pendleton, who was born Aug. 12, 1770, and died Feb. 13, 1803. The record in the family Bible mentions only one child, Ann Stuart Pendleton, born Aug. 15, 1795; married to Thomas Shivers on April 21, 1812; died Nov. 3, 1827. His wife died May 7, 1832.

cc. Lucy Strother, daughter of Joseph and Ann Stuart Strother, married Francis Wyatt Green.

dd. Benjamin Strother, d. s. p.

ee. William Strother, married Mildred Medby.

B. Susannah Strother, married John Lawler.

C. Mary Strother, married Charles Browning of Culpeper, son of Francis and grandson of Francis Browning, who settled at Gaines Cross Roads, now Rappahannock, in 1735. Issue:
aa. Willis Browning, married Elizabeth White. Issue:
aaa. John A. Browning, married Mary Lewis Willis of Rapidan, Va. Issue:
1. Charles Browning, deceased. Luray.
2. Belle Browning, married Dangerfield Lewis of Cleve, King George County, and had issue, a son.
3. Elizabeth Browning, married —— Wood.
4. Fannie Lewis Browning, d. s. p.
5. John A. Browning of Rappahannock.
6. George Lewis Browning, attorney-at-law, Madison, Va.
7. Willis Browning of Browning & Co., New York.

D. Sarah Strother, married William Hughes.

E. Lucy Strother, married Francis Covington.

F. Mildred Strother, married William Covington.

G. Anne Strother, married John F. Strother. (For record see Jeremiah, son of Jeremiah Strother of Orange County.)

H. Elizabeth Strother, married Capt. John Browning of the Continental Line, son of Frank Browning.

I. John Strother, inherited the family seat of "Wadefield." He married Helen Piper, and had issue:
aa. Nancy Strother, born Nov. 20, 1784; married June, 1799, William Pendleton, and had issue: John, James, Albert, William and French Pendleton, nearly all of whom left issue.
bb. Polly Strother, married Col. Ward, and had issue.
cc. French Strother, married his cousin Mary Ann Browning.
dd. Lucy Strother, married William Ashby. (For record see Ashby Family.)

ee. Sallie Strother, died.

ff. Kate Strother, died.

gg. Elizabeth Strother, married William Thompson. He was a grandson of the Rev. John Thompson, who was born near Belfast, Ireland, and became minister of St. Mark's, Culpeper, in 1740. In 1742 he married the widow of Governor Spotswood, by whom he had two children, viz.: Ann, born 1744; died 1815; married Francis Thornton of the "Falls." William Thompson, the son, married Sarah, daughter of Charles Carter of "Cleve."

hh. John Strother, died.

ii. Mildred Strother, married Bailey Buckner of Culpeper. (For record see Buckner Family.)

jj. Sarah Catherine Strother, married Dr. Thomas Barbour, a descendant of James Barbour, who came from Scotland and settled in Virginia during the latter part of the 17th century. He married a Miss Taliaferro, and his only son, James, settled in Culpeper, where he was a vestryman of St. Mark's in 1731, and Presiding Justice in 1764. He died in 1775. His son James, third of that name, married Frances Throckmorton of Gloucester. He was a member of the House of Burgesses from Culpeper in 1764, County Lieutenant of the Militia in 1775, an officer in the Continental Army, and Judge of the first Court ever held in Kentucky. His son, Thomas Barbour, married Mary Pendleton Thomas of Orange. He was a member of the House of Burgesses from Orange, and was also a member of the State Legislature. Philip Pendleton Barbour, son of the above-named Thomas, married Frances Todd Johnson. He was born May 25, 1783, and died in 1842. He was a member of the Virginia Assembly in 1812; elected to Congress in 1814, continued therein until 1825, and was chosen Speaker of the House in 1821. He was a lawyer of great distinction, and held office as Judge of the General Court of Virginia. In 1829 he, together with ex-President Madison, represented Orange County in the Constitutional Convention of that year, and on the death of ex-President Monroe, succeeded him as President of that distinguished body. In 1830 he was appointed United States District Judge for the Eastern District of Virginia, and in 1836 was Justice of the Supreme Court of the United States, holding that position until his death. The arms used by the Virginia Barbours are identical with those ascribed to the Barbour family of Staffordshire, England, viz.: "Gules three mullets argent, within a bordure ermine, a canton or. *Crest:* A passion Cross on three grieces gules. *Motto:* Nihilo nisi cruce." Dr. Thomas Barbour died in St. Louis in 1849, of cholera, incurred in the course of his profession. Issue: Philip P., Thomas of Missouri, John of Missouri, Fannie, who married a Todd, of Louisville, Ky., Adele, Chalmers, Mildred.

"WADEFIELD"

WILLIAM STROTHER, son of Francis and Susannah (Dabney) Strother, was born probably in Hanover County about 1725. From the failure of Francis Strother of St. Mark's to mention him by name in his will, doubt has been expressed as to his being a son. But apart from this failure, the cause of which does not appear, there can hardly be a reasonable doubt on the point. On Aug. 1, 1727, Margaret (Thornton) Strother gave by deed to her son Francis Strother of Hanover County, certain slaves with reversion to her grandson William Strother. The connection here would clearly indicate that William was the son of Francis, rather than of anyone else, a conclusion further strengthened by the fact that none of the other sons, so far as can be ascertained from records and other sources, had a son named William of his age. In 1749, there was a grant of 400 acres in Orange County, adjoining Francis and John Strother, to William Strother, son of Francis, which grant was subsequently sold by William to John Strother. The Rev. George Strother of Trimble County, Ky., born in Culpeper County, Va. (son of John H. Strother and Anne, daughter of Capt. John Strother), was, consequently, a great-nephew of this William, and living in the same region, must have known him. The former has left a record in which he places William as a son of Francis of St. Mark's, and brother of his grandfather John, who, he says, was born in Hanover County. As will be seen below, the names of the children all show evidence of descent from a Dabney intermarriage—such as "Susannah," name of the wife of Francis of St. Mark's, and also of his daughter and William "Dabney" Strother.

He was a large landed proprietor in Culpeper and Orange. He married (1st) prior to Feb. 20, 1752, Mrs. Sarah (Bayly) Pannill, the widow of William Pannill. She was originally of Urbana, in Middlesex County. On Oct. 25, 1759, he as " of the County of Orange, Planter, and Sarah his wife, late widow and relict of William Pannill, late of the County of Culpeper," conveyed to her sons William and David Pannill, 400 acres in Orange. His wife died in 1774, and her will, dated Aug. 23, 1774, was probated Dec. 22, 1774, in Orange County. She leaves legacies to grandson William, son of David Pannill, to grandson Gerard Banks, son of her daughter Frances Banks, to granddaughter Sarah Bailie Hawkins, to Sarah Runnolds, daughter of Tabitha Runnolds, to first child that may be born to son Joseph Pannill; and balance of estate to be divided between son William Dabney Strother, and daughters Frances Banks, Susanna Hawkins and Sarah Strother. He married (2d) June 9, 1775, Anne Kavanah. Late in life he removed to Woodford County, Ky., where he died in 1808. Issue:

   A. Susannah Strother, married Capt. Moses Hawkins of the 14th Va. Regt., who was killed Oct. 14, 1777, in the Revolutionary War. His children received a land warrant for his services. They lived in Woodford County, Ky., and were:
      aa. Sarah Baily Hawkins.
      bb. William Strother Hawkins, married Katherine Keith.
      cc. Moses Hawkins, married ———— Castleman.

   B. William Dabney Strother, thought to have been killed at the Battle of Guilford Court House in the War of the Revolution.

   C. Sarah Strother, born Dec. 11, 1760; married Richard Taylor, son of Zachary Taylor and Elizabeth Lee, son of James Taylor (2d) and Martha Thompson, son of James Taylor, the immigrant, of Carlisle, England, and his first wife ————. He was a Lieut.-Col. in the 2d Va. Regt. in the Revolution. Issue:
      aa. Hancock Taylor, married (1st) Elizabeth Hord; (2d) Anna Lewis.
      bb. Zachary Taylor, born Nov. 24, 1784; married Margaret Smith; was 12th President of the United States.
      cc. George Taylor.
      dd. William Dabney Taylor.
      ee. Richard Taylor.
      ff. Joseph Pannill Taylor, married Evaline McLean.
      gg. Elizabeth Lee, married John Gibson Taylor.
      hh. Sarah Taylor, married French Strother Gray, son of Col. George Gray and Mary, daughter of James Strother.
      ii. Emily Taylor, married John S. Allison.

ELIZABETH STROTHER, daughter of Francis and Susannah (Dabney) Strother, married James Gaines, son of Henry Gaines and his wife, Isabella Pendleton, in Culpeper County, probably between the years 1766–1775. James Gaines was born in Culpeper in 1742, and after his marriage removed to North Carolina. His mother, Isabella Pendleton, was the daughter of Henry Pendleton, born 1683; died 1721, and his wife, Mary Taylor. He was the grandson of Henry Pendleton of Norwich, England, whose son Philip, born

"WADEFIELD"

WILLIS BROWNING

1650, emigrated to Virginia in 1674 and died in New Kent County in 1721. Capt. James Gaines was an officer of the Revolutionary War, during a part of which he served with distinction at the head of a company of volunteers. He was the nephew of Edmund Pendleton, who was for many years Presiding Judge of the Virginia Court of Appeals. James Gaines was a man of great intellect and talent. He was a member of the North Carolina Convention which ratified the Constitution of the United States. Some time after this he removed to Tennessee, and died at Kingsport in 1830. Issue, order conjectural:

A. Edmund Pendleton Gaines, born in Culpeper County March 20, 1777; died in New Orleans June 6, 1849; married (1st) Frances Toulmin, daughter of Judge Harry Toulmin, first Territorial Judge in the Alabama portion of the Mississippi Territory; (2d) Barbara Blount, daughter of Gov. William Blount of Tennessee, a son of E. P. Gaines, Jr., now resides in Washington; (3d) Mrs. Myra (Clark) Whitney, daughter of Daniel Clark. He entered the United States Army as an Ensign Jan. 10, 1799, becoming successively Brigadier and Major-General, remaining continuously in the army until his death.

B. George Strother Gaines, born in Stokes County, N. C., 1784; died in Alabama 1873; married Ann Gaines; was an early and influential settler in Alabama, then Mississippi Territory.

C. Frances Gaines, married Charles Lynn.

D. James Gaines, married Fannie Rodgers.

E. Agnes Gaines, married Joseph Everett. A daughter, Susan Dabney Everett, married James O'Brien, and had a daughter, Eliza Ann O'Brien, born Sept. 25, 1819; married Sept. 11, 1835, Governor William G. Brownlow. They had seven children, one of whom, Col. John Bell Brownlow, married Mary Fouche, and resides in Washington, D. C.

F. Patsy Gaines, married —— Everett.

G. Nancy Gaines, married —— Asher.

H. Lucy Gaines, married David Childress.

I. Elizabeth Gaines, married Samuel Moore.

J. Susanna Gaines, died unmarried.

K. Sarah Gaines, died unmarried.

L. Behethland Gaines, married James Lyon, of Stokes, N. C. Issue:
    aa. James Gaines Lyon, married Rosanna Fisher, daughter of Col. George Fisher, of South Alabama; removed to Alabama; one daughter, Sarah B. Lyon, married Charles K. Foote of Mobile, and had among other children Nellie G., wife of ex-Representative R. H. Clarke, a distinguished lawyer of Mobile.
    bb. Francis Strother Lyon, born 1800 in Stokes, N. C., removed to Alabama, resided at Demopolis, was a distinguished lawyer; married Sarah Serena Glover, daughter of

Allen Glover, and had among other children, Mary A. Lyon, who married William Henry Ross, a prominent citizen of Mobile, son of John Ferrill Ross (first Treasurer of Ala.) and Anne Amelia Fisher.
 cc. William Lyon.
 dd. Kittie Lyon.
 ee. Elizabeth Lyon, married —— Martin,
 ff. Sallie Lyon, married —— Flippin.
 gg. Nancy Lyon.
4. Mary Strother.
5. Behethland Strother, married Oliver Wallis.
6. Susannah Strother, married Thomas Gaines, son of Henry and Isabella (Pendleton) Gaines. Issue:
A. Philip Gaines, married —— McGavock.
B. James Strother Gaines, married Judith Easley, and had among other children, John Strother Gaines, who married Letitia Dalton Moore, and had Amanda M. Gaines, who married Charles A. Rice, and who were the parents of Susan L. Rice, who married John B. Clotworthy of Hillman, Ga.
C. Richard Thomas Gaines.
D. Elizabeth Strother Gaines.
E. Susan Gaines.
F. Henry Pendleton Gaines.
G. Francis Gaines, married —— Cardwell.
H. George W. Gaines, married —— Joyce of North Carolina.
I. Francis Thornton Gaines.
7. Anthony Strother, married Frances Eastham; removed from Culpeper to Hardy County. Issue:
A. Robert Strother.
B. John Strother.
C. Francis Strother.
D. Benjamin Strother.
E. Rev. Philip Strother, a Methodist minister. Descendants are in Carter County, Ky.
8. George Strother of Culpeper County, married Mary Kennerly. Will dated June 20, 1767, probated Aug. 20, 1767. Issue:
A. John Strother, who was in the Creek War.
B George Strother, was in the Army 1794-99. Went to Tenn.
C. Margaret Strother, married Col. George Hancock of Botetourt County, Va., was Member of Congress 1793-97. A daughter, Caroline Hancock, married Major William Preston of Ky., and their daughter, Henrietta Preston, married Gen. Albert Sidney Johnston, the parents of Col. Wm. Preston Johnston of New Orleans, La.
9. Francis Strother, Jr., married Anne Graves, lived in Culpeper County, where he died. He was Lieutenant of Militia in that County in 1756. His will, dated Aug. 2, was admitted to probate Oct. 20, 1777. Issue:
A. Francis Strother, removed to Georgia with his uncle, Col. John Graves; his son, Charles R. Strother, was a lawyer and in the Georgia Secession Convention, 1861.

Strother.

  B. John Strother, a seaman, died in England.
  C. Samuel Strother, died young.
  D. George Strother, died young.
 10. Robert Strother, married Elizabeth ———. In 1771 he executed a deed to Charles Browning for land in Culpeper.

ANTHONY STROTHER, son of William and Margaret Thornton Strother, was born Aug. 1, 1710, and died Dec. 10, 1765. He was named after his ancestor Captain Anthony Savage. He was a prominent merchant of Fredericksburg, Spottsylvania County, and lived across the river from the town. In 1751 Gov. Dinwiddie, who had appointed James Patton, Joshua Fry, and Lunsford Lomax Commissioners to treat with the Indians, wrote Col. Patton to proceed immediately to Fredericksburg, "and there receive from Anthony Strother the goods sent as a present by His Majesty to the Indians." On Jan. 27, 1734, he received a grant for 600 acres in Spottsylvania County, on "Goard Vine Fork." On May 17, same year, he purchased for £40, 387 acres in St. Mark's Parish from Benjamin Rush of King George County. In 1750 he purchased of Hancock Lee of King George for £175, Lots 35 and 36 in the town of Fredericksburg. On Nov. 3, 1760, Anthony Strother of King George County, Gent., and Mary, his wife, sold to William Lewis of Fredericksburg the above lots for £300, thereby making a profit of £125 on the original purchase. Feb. 2, 1764, he sold to Hon. John Tayloe of Richmond, 322 acres in Fauquier County, for £827. In 1739 William Thornton conveyed to Anthony Strother and Behethland his wife 250 acres below the falls of the Rappahannock in King George County.

His will, probated Oct., 1766, directs his property to be kept together as a whole for ten years, and then sold, and the proceeds equally divided between his widow and children. He married (1st) Aug. 25, 1753, Behethland Starke, born Dec. 27, 1716, who died Dec., 1753; and (2d) in 1754, Mary James, born Dec. 28, 1736. His widow, Mary, married (2d) Col. Henry Smith (brother of Daniel Smith, U. S. Senator from Tenn.) and removed to Russell County, Va. The names of the children, with dates below, are from the family Bible. Children by his first wife:

  A. William Strother, born Aug. 29, 1734; died March 18, 1743.
  B. Anthony Strother, born May 10, 1736, married Frances Kenyon, daughter of Abram Kenyon. He was High Sheriff of King George in 1762 and 1763, and also a Justice; and lived at the old home of his father. Issue:

  aa. George Strother, who inherited the family seat.
  bb. Anthony Strother, married Elizabeth Newton.
  cc. John Strother, married ―――― Price.
C. Elizabeth Strother, born Sept. 22, 1738; died Aug. 3, 1745.
D. Margaret Strother, born Sept. 23, 1740; died Feb. 4, 1740-1.
E. John Strother, born Feb. 11, 1741-2.
F. Francis Strother, born Nov. 23, 1743; died Aug. 15, 1745.
G. Alice Strother, born Jan. 18, 1744-5; died March 18, 1744-5.
H. William Strother, born April 30, 1746.
I. Betty Strother, born Aug. 8, 1747; died Sept. 10, 1748.
J. Benjamin Strother, born June 25, 1750; died 1807. He entered the Virginia Navy in 1776 and served three years on the ship "Tempest," under Captain Saunders. He afterwards went into the land service and there remained until the close of the Revolution. He settled in Berkeley, now Jefferson Co., and built "Park Forest," near Charlestown. He married Kittie Price, and left five children.
  aa. Elizabeth Strother, married Benjamin Pendleton.
  bb. Catherine Strother, married Joseph Minor Crane.
  cc. Mary Strother, married Richard Duffield.
  dd. Margaret Strother, married Cato Moore.
  ee. John Strother, born Nov. 18, 1782; died Jan. 16, 1862; married Sept. 7, 1815, Elizabeth Pendleton Hunter. He held a commission in the U. S. Army dated March 13, 1813, and served in the War of 1812. At the close of the war he became Clerk of the Court for Berkeley County, which office he retained for a number of years. Issue:
    aaa. Emily Strother, married James L. Randolph.
    bbb. David Hunter Strother, born Sept. 26, 1816; died March 8, 1888. He was for a time a pupil of Prof. Samuel B. Morse. In 1841 he went abroad to study art in France and Italy. In 1851 he began the literary work which made him famous under the *nom de plume* of "Porte Crayon." In 1861 he entered the service of the United States as Captain in the Topographical Corps and was promoted to be Colonel of the 3d West Va. Cavalry, and at the close of the war was brevetted Brigadier-General. In 1866 he was Adjutant-General of the State of Virginia, from which position he resigned to resume his literary labors. In 1879 he was appointed Consul-General of the United States at the City of Mexico. He married (1st) Ann D. Wolff, May 15, 1849, by whom he had one daughter, Emily, who married J. Brisben Walker of New York City. He married (2d) Mary Elliot Hunter, May 6, 1861, at Charlestown, West Va.
K. Starke Strother, born April 12, 1752.
L. Behethland Strother, born Dec. 2, 1753.

    ISSUE BY SECOND WIFE:

M. James Strother, born Nov. 19, 1755, was in the Revolutionary War. He married Elizabeth B. Morton and lived in Fauquier

JOHN STROTHER
SON OF CAPT. JOHN DABNEY STROTHER

but about 1807 removed to Russell County, Va., leaving descendants.
N. Mary Strother, born June 2, 1757, married Benjamin Ficklin of Fauquier.
O. George Strother, born Sept. 1, 1760, died Dec. 6, 1769.
P. Betty Strother, born July 20, 1763.

BENJAMIN STROTHER of Stafford, son of William and Margaret Thornton Strother, married Mary Mason, the widow of George Fitzhugh. She was a sister of George Mason of "Gunston Hall," and daughter of Col. George Mason and his wife, Mary Fowke. The latter, a member of the King George and Stafford family of that name. Col. Gerard Fowke was the first of his name who came to this country. He was Colonel in the English army, and Gentleman of the Privy Chamber of King Charles I. He came to Virginia about the time that his unfortunate monarch was beheaded. He had three sons—Gerard and Richard of Virginia, and Chandler, who settled in Maryland. *Arms*, "Vert, a fleur-de-lis argent. *Crest*, An Indian goat's head erased argent."

On Jan. 8, 1723-4, "Margaret Strother, wife of William Strother, Jnr.," gave a power of attorney to "loving brother" Benjamin Strother to convey dower. This was Margaret Watts, wife of William, and the power of attorney fixes definitely the fact that Benjamin was a son of William Strother. On July 14, 1741, he received a grant of 419 acres of land in Stafford County. In 1756 Thomas Hurt executes a conveyance to him; and in 1760 he makes a deed of certain slaves to his daughter Anne. He was a vestryman of old Acquia Church in 1756. In 1790 John James, his administrator, asked for commissioners to settle his account. Issue:

    A. Mary Strother, married Col. William Bronaugh of London.
    B. Alice Strother, married Dec. 16, 1756, Robert Washington, born June 25, 1729, son of Townsend and Elizabeth (Lund) Washington, who were married in King George County Dec. 22, 1726. A son, Lund Washington, born Sept. 25, 1767, was the father of Col. Peter G. and Col. L. Q. Washington.
    C. ———, married Henry Tyler, who was clerk of Stafford County, 1764. His son, Thomas G. Strother Tyler, succeeded him.
    D. Anne Strother, married John James, and had a large family. The third son, Hon. Benjamin James of Stafford, married Jean Stobo of Charleston, S. C., and had Susan, born May 9, 1804, who married John Garlington of Laurens, S. C.

II. JAMES STROTHER, son of William Strother (the founder of the family), and his wife, Dorothy, died in 1716—without issue, in which year his will was probated in Richmond

County. He devised his property to his brother Joseph, his mother being one of the witnesses to the will.

III. JEREMIAH STROTHER, son of William and Dorothy Strother, was a freeholder in Westmoreland County, as early as 1703, as appears by a purchase from J. W. Smith; and subsequently a planter in King George County, but removed to Orange (now Culpeper) about 1736, where he died in 1741. As he was 86 years old at the time of his death it is evident he must have been born in 1655. As the first appearance of his father's name in the records of the colony is in 1673, there is a probability that he and his brothers were born in England. The will of Jeremiah Strother is dated June 7, 1740, and was probated March 26, 1741, in Orange County. He devised all his property to his wife, "Elener," for life or widowhood, and after her marriage or death to son Christopher; special legacies to sons James, William, Francis, Jeremiah and Lawrence; and daughters Catharine and Elizabeth. It is probable that the widow was either very much younger than her husband, or was his second wife, as it seems hardly feasible that she "should marry again" if she was anywhere near the age of her husband, Jeremiah, who was 86 years old at his death. Issue:

I. JAMES STROTHER lived in King George County. In 1733 he was Deputy Sheriff under Benjamin Strother; in 1741 was Sheriff and Justice; in 1742 Collector, and in 1747 Inspector at Falmouth. He afterwards removed to Culpeper, where he died intestate in 1761, leaving a large personal estate, which was divided between his children, his real property passing to his eldest son, Francis.

He married Margaret, daughter of Daniel French, of King George County, and Margaret, his wife, who was a daughter of John Pratt, and Margaret, his wife, of King George. Daniel French was descended from the family of that name who originated in the County of Roscommon, Ireland. Issue:

 A. French Strother, born in King George County about 1730. He lived on a handsome estate of 1500 acres, lying on Mountain Run, on the Fredericksburg Road, between Culpeper and Stevensburg. He was a vestryman and warden of St. Mark's Parish. He represented Culpeper County for over a quarter of a century in the General Assembly; before, during and after the Revolution, was a member of the Virginia Conventions of 1776 and 1788, opposing in the latter, with Patrick Henry, George Mason and others, the adoption of the Constitution of the United States. He was County Lieutenant, and also Presiding Justice of the County Court of Culpeper.

 For his boldness and aggressiveness during the Revolutionary struggle he has been denominated by Grigsby as "The

Fearless." He died intestate in Aug., 1800, and is buried at Fredericksburg. His wife was Lucy, daughter of Robert Coleman (died 1793), formerly of Caroline County. Issue:

    aa. Margaret French Strother, married Capt. Philip Slaughter; born 1758; died 1849; and had many distinguished descendants.

    bb. Gilley Strother, married Col. John Evans. Commander French Chadwick of the U. S. N. is a grandson.

    cc. Lucy Strother, died unmarried.

    dd. Elizabeth Strother, married Nimrod Evans, and d. s. p.

    ee. Mary Strother, married Daniel Gray, her first cousin.

    ff. Daniel French Strother, married Fannie, daughter of Judge John Thompson of Louisville, Ky., son of the Rev. John Thompson and his wife, the widow of Governor Spottswood.

    gg. George French Strother, born in Culpeper. He was a lawyer, and represented his district in Congress 1817-20, when he resigned to become Receiver of Public Moneys at St. Louis, where he died in 1840. He married (1st) Sarah Green Williams, daughter of Gen. James Williams, of "Soldier's Rest," Orange County, and wife, Eleanor, daughter of Moses Green, youngest son of Robert Green, the immigrant. He married (2d) Theodosia, daughter of John Hunt of Lexington, Ky., by whom he had issue two children, Sallie and John. By his first wife he had only one child, James French Strother, born at Culpeper Court House, Sept. 4, 1811; died Sept. 20, 1860; married Nov. 2, 1832, Elizabeth, daughter of John Roberts of Culpeper, who was commissioned Major in the Revolutionary War, March 5, 1779. He was a lawyer and a member of the Virginia Assembly; member of the Constitutional Convention of 1850, and in Congress 1851-53. He had issue:

        aaa. George F. Strother, d. s. p.

        bbb. John Roberts Strother, married —— Payne.

        ccc. James French Strother, married —— Botts.

        ddd. William Strother, d. s. p.

        eee. Judge Philip W. Strother, a distinguished lawyer of Pearisburg, Va., who married Nannie S., daughter of Col. A. G. Pendleton.

        fff. Sallie Williams Strother.

        ggg. John Hunt Strother, deceased.

        hhh. W. Johnson Strother, M. D., married —— Shackleford.

        iii. Col. Lewis Harvie Strother, U. S. A.

        jjj. Charles Strother, d. s. p.

B. James Strother, son of James and Margaret (French) Strother, died unmarried in 1764. His will, probated in Stafford County, gives property to his brother, French, and sister, Mary Gray,

C. Mary Strother, daughter of James and Margaret (French) Strother, lived in Stafford County, married George Gray. Issue:

    aa. George Gray, married Mildred, daughter of the Rev.

John Thompson, and in 1800 removed to Louisville, Ky. He was an active participant in the Revolutionary War. Issue:

  aaa. George Gray, Jr.
  bbb. James Strother Gray.
  ccc. French Strother Gray.
  ddd. Minor Gray.
  eee. Anderson Gray.
  fff. Henry Weedon Gray.

 bb. Daniel Gray, married Mary, daughter of French Strother; she was his first cousin.

2. William Strother, son of Jeremiah and Eleanor Strother, married Mildred, daughter of Charles Taliaferro, in Spottsylvania County, in 1729, and died in Westmoreland in 1749. In his will he mentions son William, who married Winifred ———.

Charles Strother, who died at Charleston, S. C., in 1773, and was buried in St. Michael's churchyard, leaving sons George and William, is thought to be a son of William. George Strother was a Lieutenant in Marion's Brigade, 1781. Both he and William settled in the old Cheraw District, Chesterfield County, S. C.

3. Thomas Strother.
4. Catharine Strother.
5. Elizabeth Strother.
6. Lawrence Strother, married Elizabeth ———. Living in Orange County in 1742.
7. Jeremiah Strother, married Catharine Kennerly; lived in Culpeper County, removed to South Carolina, and settled on the Saluda River. One son, John F. Strother, returned to Virginia, and married Anne, daughter of Capt. John Strother, and had a son, George Strother, who removed to Trimble County, Ky., and was long a minister.
8. Christopher Strother, married Ann ———. In 1746, as of Caroline County, he executed a conveyance of 350 acres in Culpeper; and Oct., 1749, as of Fairfax County, he conveyed to Capt. Benjamin Strother "the lands in King George in Hanover Parish, given him by his father, Jeremiah Strother." About 1750 he removed to Edgecombe County, N. C., but on the formation of Franklin was thrown in that county. One daughter, Ann Strother, married Garrett Goodloe, son of the Rev. Henry Goodloe, of Caroline County, Va., and had a son, James Kemp Goodloe, who married Mary Reaves Jones, daughter of Daniel Jones, son of the first Edward, early prominent in Granville County, N. C., and had Col. Daniel R. Goodloe of Washington, D. C.

IV. ROBERT STROTHER, son of William and Dorothy Strother, was of King George County, where he died in 1735, his will being probated Nov. 7 of that year; his wife, Elizabeth, is named as executrix. His wife was Elizabeth Berry, the daughter of a clergyman. Issue:

1. Elizabeth Strother, married twice, but died childless.
2. Enoch Strother, married Mary Key, and died prior to June 4, 1772, when she administered his estate; after his death, in consequence of the annoyance of the British, she removed to Clarke, and thence to Fauquier County, where descendants now reside.
3. John Strother.
4. Robert Strother.

V. BENJAMIN STROTHER, son of William and Dorothy Strother, married Mary, daughter of Adam Woffendall; lived in King George County, where he died in 1752, his will being probated May 5. He was a Justice of Richmond and continued as such in King George, in which county he was a Sheriff and large landed proprietor. Issue:

1. Richard Strother, d. s. p. in 1761; will dated Nov. 22, and probated Dec., 1761.
2. George Strother, married Mrs. Tabitha (Payne), widow of William Woffendall; lived in King George; will dated Nov. 13 and probated Dec. 13, 1761. Issue:
   A. John Strother.
   B. George Strother.
3. Benjamin Strother, married Anne ———. In 1754 Mary Strother gave to her son Benjamin, of Hanover Parish, the land given by her father. In July, 1758, Benjamin Strother and Anne, his wife, of same Parish, executed a deed. In 1759 he was fined for not keeping a road in order to Port Royal.
4. John Strother.
5. Samuel Strother.
6. Francis Strother.

VI. JOSEPH STROTHER, son of William and Dorothy Strother, was a Justice in Richmond, and continued as such in King George, where he was also Sheriff and Vestryman. He owned and lived on a part of his father's old home near Port Conway. He married Margaret, daughter of Grace and ——— Berry. His will was probated Aug. 7, 1766. Issue:

1. Mary Strother, married William Wren.
2. Margaret Strother, married ——— Clannahan.
3. Dorothy Strother, married ——— Walker.
4. Thomas Strother of Stafford County.
5. Nicholas Strother, died 1779.
6. Joseph Strother, married ——— Berry; died in King George 1762. As "Capt. Joseph Strother," he was granted, May 28, 1748 lands lying partly in King George and partly in Westmoreland County. In his will he names wife, and brother-in-law Benjamin Berry, as executors; an only daughter, Elizabeth Nicholas Strother, who died unmarried, and he left legacies to his nephews, Nicholas Wren, William Clannahan and Joseph Walker.

Fauquier County Records

Appraisement of Estate of James Strother, Sr., deceased. Recorded Nov. 23, 1778.

Appraisement of Estate of Reuben Strother, Jr., deceased, as shown by Reuben Strother, Sr. Recorded June 26, 1815.

Inventory and appraisement of Estate of Jeremiah Strother, deceased. Recorded June 28, 1825.

Estate of Jeremiah Strother, deceased, in account with Susannah Strother, administratrix. Recorded Aug. 30, 1827.

Will of James Strother of Leeds Parish, Fauquier County. Dated Dec. 17, 1821; probated Jan. 28, 1828.

Daughter, Margaret Utterback; wife, Mary; sons, Lewis Strother, Jeremiah Strother, John Strother; daughters, Molly Kemp and Nancy Jackson, to have certain property at the death of their step-mother.

Executors, sons Lewis, Jeremiah and James Strother.

Appraisement of Estate of Benjamin Strother, deceased. Recorded Jan. 26, 1836.

Will of Reuben Strother of Fauquier County. Dated Jan. 30, 1832; codicil, Jan. 22, 1836; probated Feb. 27, 1837.

Son-in-law William Rawlings; son Thomas Strother; daughter, Ann Pearle, wife of William Pearle; daughter Susannah Glascock; daughter Charlotte Elliott; son French Strother; son John Strother; son-in-law George Sryhock, who married my daughter Mary; son William Strother; son-in-law William Rawlings, who married my daughter Lucinda; daughter Patsy Strother; children of my daughter, Sarah Newlin, deceased.

Executors, Wm. Rawlings and friend Geo. Love.

Codicil. Revokes trusts to Wm. Rawlings, and wills to Thomas Strother, Ann Pearle, Susannah Glascock and French Strother their parts respectively.

Division of Estate of Jeremiah Strother, deceased. Recorded Oct. 24, 1837. Heirs, widow, Susannah Strother; Alexander Strother, Olivia Richards, Hedgman Strother, Sarah Ann Strother, Enoch Strother.

Appraisement of Estate of Enoch Strother, deceased. John Strother, administrator. Recorded Aug. 27, 1845.

Will of Lewis Strother of Leeds Parish, Fauquier County. Dated Feb. 14, 1833, probated May 23, 1842.

Daughters, Mary Sisson, Sarah Jane Harrel, Susan Jackson, Catharine Ann Holmes, Margaret George Holmes; son Jackson Farrow Strother; daughters Elizabeth Strother, Juliet Ann Strother, Lucy Cornelia Strother. Mentions a plantation sold to John Sisson, called Chadwell Place. Wife Nancy Strother.

Executors, son Jackson Farrow Strother, and John Sisson.

Will of Mary Strother of Fauquier County. Dated Sept. 9, 1836. Probated May 25, 1847.

Niece, Lucy Gutridge, now Lucy Rector, and her sister, Harriet Rush; niece Courtney Ann Vowles; niece Mary Maria Pilcher; niece Louisa Pilcher; niece Mary Fishback, daughter of Philip Fishback. Revokes deed of trust made by her to Daniel Vowles, dated July 6, 1833.

Executor, friend Andrew Turner.

Capt. Thomas Ashby in Va. 1700, died 1752.

- Capt. John, born 1707, died 1797, m. (1) Jane Combs, m. (2) Cath. Hufman
- Capt. Robert, born 1710, Will Prob. 1792, m. 1783 Cath. Combs (2d wife)
- Stephen
- Thomas
- Henry
- Benj.
- Eliz. m. —— Harden
- Sarah
- Rose
- Ann

Children of Capt. Robert:
- Capt. Nimrod, died 1764, m. 1759 Frances Wright
- Benj.
  - William
- Enoch m. Sarah Henley, had issue
  - Robert
  - Alex
- Ann m. Geo. Farrow
- Winifred m. 1764 James Peters
- Molly m. —— Athol
- Capt. John — Mary Turner, born 1740, born 1750, died 1815, died 1826

Children of Capt. Nimrod:
- Martin
- Thomas Bryan
- Nathaniel, born 1748, died 1811, m. 1777 Margaret Mauzey and had issue

Children of Capt. John and Mary Turner:
- Lewis — Leannah Buckner, died 1806, and had issue
- Edward
- Eliza m. Col. John Peters and had issue
- Jennie m. Joseph Dorrell and had issue
- Charlotte m. (1) Mann Satterwhite (2) Wilson Parker

- John

" By the glorious worth of my descent."
—Richard II.

Ashby Family

THE name of Ashby is found in the early records of the colony of Virginia, but the direct pedigree of the family in this country has been traced only from the beginning of the eighteenth century. John Asbie was one of the first settlers at Jamestown, August 6, 1607 (Brown's Gen. of U. S., p. 167). Edward Ashby is amongst the list of tithables for Northampton County, in 1666, but whether he was one of the forbears of the Ashbys of Fauquier is not definitely known.

Mr. John Ashby is mentioned as one of the corporators of the Royal African Company, 1673. (Va. Hist. Coll. vol. vi. p. 41).

The family is distinctly English in origin, the name being a derivation of the Saxon word "ash," and the Danish "bye"—meaning town. The ancient castle of Ashby in Leicestershire is first mentioned in the time of Edward the Confessor. At the time of the Norman Conquest, it was held by Hugh, under the Countess Judith, to whom it had been presented by her uncle, William the Conqueror. The ruined castle was rebuilt in 1480, by Sir William Hastings, and crowns a height to the south of the town of Ashby-de-la-Zouch. It was immortalized by Sir Walter Scott in his "Ivanhoe," and it was in this castle that Mary, Queen of Scots, passed several months in captivity.

The immediate ancestor of our Virginia branch of the Ashby family, was Captain Thomas Ashby, who located about 1700, in what is now Fauquier County, and removed later into the Shenandoah Valley. He died in 1752, his will being probated in Frederick County. His landed estate was quite large and was divided amongst the following children:

  I. John Ashby.
 II. Robert Ashby, of whom presently.
III. Stephen Ashby.
 IV. Thomas Ashby.
  V. Henry Ashby.
 VI. Benjamin Ashby.

VII. Elizabeth Ashby, married ——— Harden.
VIII. Sarah Ashby.
IX. Rose Ashby.
X. Ann Ashby.

Will of Capt. Thomas Ashby

In the name of God, Amen. I, Thomas Ashby of Frederick County, in the Colony of Virginia, being very sick and weak of body but of perfect mind and memory, thanks be to Almighty God, and calling to mind the uncertainty of this life, do make here my last will and testament in the following manner and form, revoking all former and other wills heretofore by me made, and this only to be taken for my last will and testament. Imprimis I resign my soul into the hands of the Almighty and most merciful God, trusting in and by the merits of his son my ever blessed Saviour, Jesus Christ, that it shall together with my body be raised, remitted and glorified, and as to my body I desire it may have a christian burial, and for such temporal estate wherewith it hath pleased my good God to bless me with I give and dispose of in the following manner, viz.: Item: I give unto my son Thomas Ashby one shilling sterling to have no other part of my estate whatsoever. Secondly, I give and bequeath unto my son Benjamin Ashby all that tract or parcel of land as Goose creek whereon Enoch Berry now lives, to him my said son and his heirs forever. Thirdly, I give and bequeath unto my son Henry Ashby all that tract or parcel of land whereon he now lives which was laid off and apart by James Guin, deceased, from my other land unto my said son and his heirs forever, but if the said son should die without issue the said land to fall to my son Stephen and his heirs forever. Fourthly, I give and bequeath unto my son Stephen Ashby after his mother's death all this tract or part of land whereon I now live and which was also laid off and divided by the said Guin as aforesaid, to him my said son and his heirs forever, but if my said son Stephen should die without issue that then the said lot or tract of land is to fall to my son Henry Ashby and his heirs forever. Fifthly, I give unto my daughter, Elizabeth Harden, one shilling sterling, and that she have no other part of my estate. Sixthly, I give unto my daughter Sarah Ashby one shilling sterling. Seventhly, I give unto my daughter Rose Ashby one shilling sterling. Eighthly, I give unto my daughter Ann Ashby one shilling sterling. Ninthly, I give and bequeath unto my cousin Ruben Berry one cow and calf to be delivered to him at the age of twenty-one. Tenthly, I give unto my cousin Ann Berry one cow and calf to be delivered to her at the age of eighteen or on the day of marriage. Eleventhly, It is my desire that if the land whereon John Hardin now lives and for which I have a mortgage on now if the —— should be projected that one of my executors, namely, my son Robert Ashby, shall sell the same and pay unto my daughters Sarah and Rose five pounds to each of them and the remainder to be equally divided between my loving wife, Rose Ashby, my son Stephen and my daughter Ann Ashby, and in case the money be paid according to the tenor thereof that then my son Robert shall divide and pay the same as I gave that in case the land was sold. Twelfthly, I give and bequeath to my loving wife, Rose Ashby, my horse I bought of John Ashby, also two mares and colt to be at her own disposal and as for the rest of my movable estate to have the same during her widowhood, but if she should marry that then she is to have no more than a third part of such movable estate and then the remainder to be equally divided by my executors between my son Stephen and my daughter Ann Ashby. Lastly, I nominate and appoint my dutiful and loving sons Robt., John and Henry Executors of this my last will and testament. And in testimony that this is my last will and testament I have hereunto set my hand and seal this 10th day of April, one thousand seven hundred and fifty-two—1752.

THOMAS ^{His}_{mark} ASHBY. { SEAL. }

Signed, sealed and acknowledged before and in the presence of us.

JAMES CATLETT.

FRANCIS ^{His}_{mark.} HOWELL.

PETER WOLF.

Captain John Ashby, son of Thomas Ashby, was born in 1707, in the present Fauquier County. At an early age he developed a love for adventure, and crossing the Blue Ridge Mountains, through Ashby's Gap, which was named for him, located on the Shenandoah River, near Millwood, Clark County. He was a Captain in the 2d Virginia Rangers, and from 1752 to 1754, commanded Fort Ashby, at the junction of Patterson Creek and the Potomac. At this period, Colonel George Washington was in command of the Colonial Militia, and in his diary and letters to the Governor of Virginia, frequent references are made in regard to the military services of Captain John Ashby.

Captain Ashby died in 1797, at the advanced age of 90 years, and was buried at Winchester. He was well fitted physically for the life of a frontiersman, being tall, erect, with eagle eyes and wonderful powers of endurance. It is said of him, that he knew not the sensation of fear nor pain.

He was a staunch Episcopalian, and for years was a vestryman in the "Old Chapel," the first Episcopal Church founded in the Valley of Virginia, one of his fellow vestrymen being Thomas, Lord Fairfax.

Captain John Ashby was twice married, first to Jane Combs of Maryland, May 11, 1740, and had issue by her six children. He was married secondly, at the age of 83, to Catherine Hufman of Fauquier County (Marriage Bond, Oct. 27, 1783), and by her had one daughter, Charlotte, who married first Mann Satterwhite, and secondly Wilson Parker of Maryland.

Issue by first marriage:

1. John Ashby.
2. Lewis Ashby.
3. Nathaniel Ashby.
4. Edward Ashby.
5. Elizabeth Ashby.
6. Jennie Ashby.
7. Charlotte Ashby.

II. LEWIS ASHBY, second son of Captain John Ashby and Jane Combs, died in 1806. Married Leannah Buckner. Issue:

A. Alfred Ashby, died unmarried.
B. Mildred Ashby, married Lewis A. Smith.
C. James Ashby.
D. John Ashby.
E. Buckner Ashby, born 1790, died 1860, married Miss Baker. Issue:
    aa. Lewis Ashby, C. S. A., killed in battle.
    bb. William Ashby, C. S. A., 12th Cavalry, killed by last shot fired at Appomatox Court House, April 9, 1865.
    cc. Buckner E. Ashby, married Miss Johnson.
    dd. Sidney Lewis Ashby, married Ambrose Catlett.
    ee. Kate Ashby, married Joel Morehead. Issue:
        aaa. Amanda Morehead, married Joseph Wallingford at Mt. Gilead, Mason Co., Ky. Issue:

The Buckners of Virginia

1. Buckner Ashby Wallingford, born April 15, 1834, married in 1859. to Rebecca Wurts, died Feb. 12, 1888. Issue:
A. Annie Wallingford, married Feb. 16, 1881, to Davis C. Anderson of Cincinnati, son of Larz Anderson, born April 9, 1803, near Louisville, Ky., died 1878, married Oct. 22, 1834, to Catharine Longworth of Cincinnati, and grandson of Richard Clough Anderson, born in Hanover County, Va., in 1750, died in 1824 at "Soldiers' Retreat," Louisville, Ky. Issue:
    aa. Buckner Wallingford Anderson, born in Cincinnati, April 12, 1883.
    bb. Rebecca Anderson, born in Cincinnati, April 29, 1886.
B. Buckner Ashby Wallingford, Jr., of Cincinnati, born Maysville. Ky., July 16, 1867, married June 3, 1902, to Annie Rives Longworth, born 1870. Issue:
    aa. Buckner Ashby Wallingford, 3d, born Jan. 23, 1904.
2. John Wallingford, deceased, son of Joseph and Amanda (Morehead) Wallingford.
3. Joel Wallingford, son of Joseph and Amanda (Morehead) Wallingford.
4. Kate Wallingford, married Nathan Cochran of Lexington. Issue: Ashby Cochran, deceased.

F. Jennie Ashby, daughter of Lewis and Leannah Ashby.

III. NATHANIEL ASHBY, third son of Captain John Ashby and Jane Combs, was born in Virginia, in 1748, in what is now Clarke County, and died in Woodford County, Ky., in 1811. He married December 3, 1777, Margaret, daughter of Colonel John and Hester (Foote) Mauzey of Fauquier. He married, secondly, Ann Ashby, who died in 1819. Nathaniel Ashby was commissioned as Ensign in the 3d Virginia Regiment March 11, 1776, and at the close of the Revolution he was Captain of a company which for several years was stationed on the frontiers. He removed to Kentucky about 1790, and locating near Lexington, became a man of wealth and influence. His first wife, Margaret Mauzey, was the granddaughter of Colonel Henry Mauzey, who fled from France in 1695 and settled in Fauquier County. They had issue:

1. Dr. Mauzey Q. Ashby, born 1787, died in 1874. Graduated in medicine in 1809 in Philadelphia. He practiced his profession with distinguished success for many years, and was possessed of large landed estates in Kentucky and Missouri. He married Miss Logan of Kentucky and had issue:
A. Margaret Ashby, married Judge Samuel H. Woodson of Missouri.
B. Ellen Ashby, married Hon. George Hamilton of Ball County, Ky.
C. Mary Ashby, married Dr. Samuel McKee of Danville, Ky., a brother of Colonel McKee, who was killed in the Mexican War.
D. Logan Ashby.
E. Joseph Ashby.
2. William Richardson Ashby, born 1790, died 1844. He was in early manhood a soldier under General Harrison in the Indian Wars, and was present at the Battle of Tippecanoe. He married Rebecca, daughter of Captain Thomas Buck of Warren County. Issue:

    A. Thomas M. Ashby, born May 12, 1819; died 1878; married Elizabeth Almond. Issue:
        aa. Dr. T. A. Ashby.
        bb. William Richardson Ashby of Baltimore, Md.
    B. Elizabeth Ann Ashby, born Sept. 25, 1820; died 1904; married William M. Buck of Va. Issue:
        aa. M. D. Buck.
        bb. Col. J. A. Buck.
        cc. Lucy R. Buck.
        dd. Laura V. Buck.
        ee. Dr. R. C. Buck.
        ff. Anne N. Buck.
        gg. Wm. R. Buck.
        hh. Edward A. Buck.
        ii. Frank L. Buck.
3. John R. Ashby, died in 1837; unmarried.
4. Elizabeth Ashby, married Judge January of Kentucky. No issue.
5. Sallie Ashby, married Judge L. L. Todd of Indiana. Issue:
    A. Dr. Robert Todd of Indianapolis.
    B. Dr. L. L. Todd of Indianapolis.
    C. Elizabeth Todd, married ——— Taylor of Alabama.
6. Margaret Ashby, married Major Taylor of Kentucky.
7. Anne Ashby, married Judge Thomas Marshall Duke of Kentucky, grandson of Col. Thomas Marshall of Va., and nephew of Chief Justice John Marshall.

IV. EDWARD ASHBY, fourth son of Captain John Ashby and Jane Combs.

V. ELIZA ASHBY, daughter of Captain John Ashby and Jane Combs, born in Clarke County, Va., married Col. John Peters of Fauquier County; died 1782. Their son, William Peters, married Frances Woodruff, daughter of Owen Woodruff of Fauquier, and were the parents of Judge B. J. Peters of Kentucky, born 1805, died 1900.

VI. JENNIE ASHBY, daughter of Captain John Ashby and Jane Combs, married Joseph Dornel of Kentucky and left descendants living in that State.

VII. CHARLOTTE ASHBY, daughter of Captain John Ashby, by his second wife, Catherine Hufman, whom he married Oct. 27, 1783, married (1st) Mann Satterwhite, of Fayette Co., Ky.; (2d) Wilson Parker of Maryland. Charlotte Ashby had issue by her first husband as follows:
    1. Eliza Satterwhite, married Edward A. Turpin of Powhatan Co., Va.
    2. Henrietta Satterwhite, married William Henry Turpin, brother of Edward.
    3. Ann Satterwhite.
    4. Ellen Satterwhite.
    5. John Satterwhite.
    6. Theodore Brooke Satterwhite, married Eliza Jane, daughter of Stark Taylor of Fayette Co., Ky. Issue:
        A. Victoria Virginia Satterwhite, married John Foster Anderson of Louisville, Ky. Issue:
            aa. Pauline Howard Anderson, married Henry Tinsley of Jefferson Co., Ky., and had issue: William Daniel Tinsley; Virginia Tinsley married Walter Werner; Orville Anderson Tinsley; Henry Tinsley; Cora Keith Tinsley married Ira Clifford Money.

  bb. Orville Martin Anderson, d. s. p.
  cc. Julia Keith Anderson, d. s. p.
  dd. Cora Anderson married Herbert Sanford Carpenter, and had a daughter Cora, who married George Albert Legg.
  ee. Lillian Satterwhite Anderson.
 B. Florence Satterwhite.
 C. Mann William Satterwhite, married Lizzie, daughter of George Gray of Louisville, Ky.
 D. Maurice Langhorne Satterwhite, married Ella Graham.

Charlotte Ashby by her second husband, Major Wilson H. Parker, had issue:

 1. Warren O. Parker, born 1821; married Rebecca E. L. McConnell in 1844. Issue:
 A. John W. Parker, died in infancy.
 B. William Moore Parker, C. S. A., with "Morgan's Cavalry," died from wounds in battle at age of sixteen.
 C. Ann Eliza Parker, married Grant Cooke and had issue:
 D. Ashby Parker, died in infancy.
 E. Howard S. Parker, Attorney-at-Law, removed to Lincoln Co., Mo., and served two terms in the Legislature before he attained the age of 25 years. Was Prosecuting Attorney at time of his death in 1885.
 F. Sarah Moore Parker, married Thomas Scudder of St. Louis, now residing at Columbia, Mo., has one daughter, Mary Hord Scudder.
 G. Mary B. Parker, married Charles Wickliffe Robinson. Issue:
  aa. Douglas Ashby Robinson.
  bb. Charles Wickliffe Robinson.
  cc. Katherine Howard Robinson.
  dd. Mary Taylor Robinson.
 H. Elizabeth Clarkson Parker, married Dr. George A. Bradford; resides at Columbia, Mo.
 I. Warren Ashby Parker of Brooklyn, N. Y.
 2. Montgomery H. Parker, second son of Charlotte Ashby and Wilson H. Parker, married (1) Nannie Hunt of Lexington, Ky., and had three children: Montgomery H. Parker, Jr., Mrs. Graves and Mrs. Lulie Gregg. By his second marriage to Annie May Cooper he had Cooper, Lila and Mary Parker.
 3. Belviard Parker, third son of Charlotte Ashby and Wilson H. Parker, married Sarah Sprake of Fayette Co., Ky. Issue:
 A. William Parker.
 B. Orpheus Parker.
 C. Belviard Parker.
 D. Wilson Parker.
 E. Marion Parker.
 F. Smith Parker.
 4. Howard S. Parker, fourth son of Charlotte Ashby and Wilson H. Parker, married (1) Lucy Ellis and had a daughter Nannie. Married (2) Mary Barton and had by her William B., and Edmund Lee Parker.

Captain Robert Ashby of Fauquier County, second son of Captain Thomas Ashby, was a Captain in the Fauquier County Militia, his name being mentioned twice on the Order Books, viz.: Sept. 27, 1759, and June 26, 1761. His second wife was Catherine Combs, to whom he was married in 1783. His will is dated June 2, 1790, and was probated Feb. 27, 1792. Perhaps he was a widower at the time of his death, as no mention is made of his wife. He was guardian to his two grandsons, Martin and Thomas Bryan, orphans of his eldest son Captain Nimrod Ashby. Issue of Robert Ashby:

1. Captain Nimrod Ashby of Fauquier, died June 29, 1764; married Nov. 30, 1759, to Frances Wright. He was a Captain in the Fauquier County Militia, his commission being dated Sept. 24, 1761. He left issue two sons:
   A. Martin Ashby.
   B. Thomas Bryan Ashby.
2. Benjamin Ashby had known issue one son:
   A. William Ashby.
3. Enoch Ashby, of whom presently.
4. Ann Ashby, married George Farrow. Issue:
   A. Benjamin Farrow, Jr.
5. Winifred Ashby, married Jan. 17, 1764, to James Peters.
6. Molly Ashby, married ———— Athel.
7. Captain John Ashby, youngest son, who has been frequently confused with his uncle, John Ashby, the brother of Captain Robert Ashby.

Enoch Ashby, son of Captain Robert Ashby, married Sarah Henley, daughter of Capt. Charles Henley of King William County. Issue:
   A. Robert Ashby, married Ann Walters, Feb. 26, 1793.
   B. Alexander Ashby, married Ann, daughter of Capt. Charles Browning and Mary Strother. Capt. Browning was a grandson of Francis Browning who settled near Gaines Cross Roads in 1735. He is believed to have come from Caroline County. Issue:
      aa. Charles Henley Ashby, married Maria Woolfolk.
      bb. Frederick Ashby.
      cc. Mary Ann Ashby.
      dd. Robert Francis Ashby.
      ee. Lloyd Browning Ashby.
      ff. Benjamin Ashby
      gg. Cassandra Ashby.
      hh. Dorothy Ashby.
      ii. America Henley Ashby.
      jj. Sarah Ashby, married John Carlisle of Kentucky, and had a son—Buford Carlisle.

Ann Ashby, daughter of Capt. Robert Ashby, married Capt. George Farrow, who died Dec. 27, 1804. Anne Farrow died Oct. 6, 1807. Issue:
   A. Benjamin Farrow, born Dec. 4, 1773, in Fauquier; died Oct. 18,

1845, in Prince William County; married Lucy Smith, born 1776, a daughter of Col. John Smith of Orlean, Fauquier County. Issue:
  aa. Nimrod, Franklin and Joseph died in infancy.
  bb. Margaret Ann Farrow, born Feb. 10, 1800; married James Barton, ancestor of Judge John Barton Payne of Chicago, Ill.
  cc. Sarah Smith Farrow, born July 4, 1803; married William Winston Browning, born Dec. 25, 1794, at Culpeper, Va. Issue:
    1. Sarah Louise Browning, married William James Knox, M.D., born in Kentucky, and had an only daughter, Virginia, who married Cabell Maddox, and has issue, a son.
  dd. Lucy Mildred Farrow, born Aug. 6, 1804; married Camm Temple Page.
  ee. Mary Louise Farrow, married William Payne.
  ff. Amanda Farrow, married James Howison.
  gg. John F. Farrow, born Dec. 28, 1808; married his first cousin, Susan Margaret Smith, daughter of Col. John Smith, Jr., of Orlean.
  hh. George Ashby Farrow, born April 12, 1811; married Amanda Hansborough.
  ii. Thomas Farrow, married Emily Hansborough.

Sketch of Captain John Ashby of Belmont

John Ashby, son of Robert Ashby, was born April 1st, 1740, in Fauquier County, and lived near Delaplane Station. Robert Ashby's house is still standing and is owned and occupied by one of his descendants, George Chancellor, Esq. It is a quaint old structure and has been often visited by persons interested in old homesteads. Robert Ashby left a considerable estate and was a man of rugged force, though of limited education. Brought up, as he seems to have been, on the confines of the settlements of Virginia, his childhood was spent amid the hardships and dangers of frontier life. When he was but twenty years of age, the Valley of Virginia was yet a tractless forest with a few settlers here and there without schools and churches. His son John was born not long after the time when attention began to be attracted toward the Valley, and grew up with the spirit of adventure that marked the period. John was precocious in the qualities that distinguished men in those times. He was early trained to the use of arms and horses. Constant contact with the Indians instructed him in all the arts of the woodsman, and as the frontiers were in these times subject to hostile incursions and sudden attacks, he early acquired the experience of the soldier. His abilities naturally ran to leadership. And we find him, when he was just a little beyond his majority, in command of a company of men, and well on in the possession of a reputation for courage, horsemanship and skill as a leader of men, that grew with his years to the end.

His name and career have been confused with those of an uncle who had the same name and who was likewise distinguished for courage and leadership in his day. In the historical accounts we have of these two men, little effort is made to distinguish between them, and one is at times at a loss to know which of the two men is referred to. They were for some years contemporaries and had much the same traits and the same devotion to their country. They had, too, the same military title. They lived, however, on different sides of the Blue Ridge, in different counties, and this circumstance sometimes serves to distinguish them. The ease with which they may be confounded may be seen from the account of the Ashby Family given in Hayden's Virginia Genealogies, p. 450, where not only most of the exploits and honors of the younger John Ashby, but even his father's wives, are bestowed upon the elder.

The following record gathered from the family papers, public records and historical accounts, has been prepared by one of his descendants, Howard R. Bayne, Esq., of New York.

In these times forts were established at certain points along the frontier which were manned by an apparently irregular body of troops in the service of the State of Virginia, and commanded by men who held their commission from the State. They were known as rangers and were selected to stand between the homes and settlements of their fellow countrymen and the hostile tribes of Indians in the wilderness beyond the frontiers. One of these forts was called Ashby's Fort and was commanded by a Captain John Ashby. It was situated on Patterson's Creek and had a garrison of sixty men in 1756. This Captain Ashby is frequently mentioned by Washington in his correspondence with Governor Dinwiddie. See Spark's life of Washington, Vol. 2, p. 107 (Ed. 1834), also p. 145. See also Memorial Edition of Writings of Washington published by Putnams, Vol. 1, letters to Governor Dinwiddie, dated May 22nd, 1756, and August 4th, 1756. See also Kercheval's History of the Valley, p. 85 (2nd Ed.). This Captain John Ashby, I have little doubt, was the uncle of the subject of my sketch, and seems to have held the title of Colonel at a later day. I have not been able to verify the family tradition that Captain Ashby, the elder, was actually in the engagement at which Braddock met his death. During all this period, however, he was in actual military service at one point or another, in one expedition or another. In the return of the 2nd Company of Rangers, commanded by him, dated October 21st, 1757, the earliest enlistment reported is that of Leonard Harper, August 18th, 1755. The next is that of Daniel Morgan, August 30th, 1755, the Daniel Morgan afterwards so celebrated in the Revolutionary War. These returns of course showed the constituency of the command at the date of the return. This particular return may be found in the Virginia Magazine of History and Biography, Vol. 2, p. 152. As the subject of my sketch was at the date of this return but 17 years of age, I conclude it was not he but the elder Ashby who is described in the return as the Captain of the Rangers. According to family traditions and the authorities below cited, it so happened that the younger Ashby was at Fort Loudon when the news of Braddock's defeat was yet fresh. Whether he himself bore the dispatches, or was detailed at that point is uncertain. Family tradition has it that he was one of the Virginia Contingent that under Washington's command did such good service in retrieving the disasters of that ill-fated expedition. I have not been able to find that any officer by the name of Ashby was present at the battle. But it is extremely probable that if not actually enlisted, the younger Ashby was hovering around the expeditions. (See Va. Hist. Coll. vol. xi. pp. 208, 216.) Though still young at this time, he was experienced and trustworthy, and his daring courage and splendid horsemanship, both perhaps well known to Washington, would have justified entrusting him with dispatches to Governor Dinwiddie or the nearest military station in the line of governmental communication, Fort Loudon. It was no light mission to bear such dispatches alone through many miles of uninhabited country, infested with hostile bands lying in wait for the remains of a defeated, disorganized army.

But by whomever the dispatches were brought to Fort Loudon, now Winchester, it is quite certain they were carried from that point to Williamsburg, the seat of Government, and returns made by John Ashby, the younger, with such expedition as to render his ride a marvel in that day and a historical exploit often mentioned since. Indeed, so remarkable was it, that on his return the commander of the fort was about to upbraid him for his delay when he was amazed at Ashby's presenting him with the answers to the dispatches. The service to the public was so highly prized that the fact was certified upon the records of the Frederick County Court. See Pollard's 2nd Year of the War, p. 46 (Ed. 1863, Richardson, N. Y.); Ashby and His Compeers, by Rev. James B. Avirett, p. 240-41 (Ed. 1867, Smith & Dulany, Baltimore); Force's Arch. 1, 373.

The materials to form a connected account of Captain John Ashby are slight and unsatisfactory. So, prior to the expedition ordered by Lord Dunmore, Governor of the Colony, against the Indians under Cornstalk, there is little recorded worthy of mention beyond what I have recited. From this time, however, his record though not full of details, is reasonably clear.

It will be recalled that the murder of the family of the famous Indian Chief Logan in the spring of 1774, caused an uprising against the whites on the part of the Indians on the Western Border that justly excited the apprehension of the entire Colony. Dunmore ordered two divisions to assemble for the purpose of crushing the hostiles. That in the lower Shenandoah Valley he himself commanded, while that in the upper Shenandoah was commanded by Andrew Lewis.

These two columns were to converge at the mouth of the Kanawha, Point Pleasant. Starting with the two regiments, numbering about 1,100 men, from the vicinity of what is now the beautiful Village of Lewisburg in West Virginia, in September, 1774, General Lewis began his arduous march to Point Pleasant on the Ohio. The hardships of such an expedition cannot be appreciated, can hardly be imagined in our day. The forests were trackless, and the difficulties of overcoming the barriers of nature were increased by the need of constant watchfulness against predatory bands of revengeful savages.

Arrived at the rendezvous, Lewis and his troops could learn nothing of Dunmore or the wing under him. While preparing to cross the Ohio, Lewis was attacked by Cornstalk and thus the Battle of Point Pleasant was fought. It was desperately contested ending in the defeat of the Indians, but with heavy loss to the Virginians. It was a memorable struggle and the last in the horrible series of the Savage assaults upon the Virginia frontier. The Indians largely outnumbering the whites, consisted of the best fighting men of the Delawares, Mingoes, Cayugas and Wyandots. It is often stated that John Ashby commanded a company under Lewis in this expedition and distinguished himself at the Battle of Point Pleasant. In the official accounts of the battle, he is not mentioned as an officer actually engaged. He may have been with the divison under Lord Dunmore. There seems to be no doubt that he was actually in the expedition. He was reported to have been killed (Force's Arch. 1, p. 373), but this rumor doubtless arose from the fact that upon the cessation of hostilities, Ashby did not immediately return home. With some other companions, he took this occasion to pass over into Kentucky (October 10th, 1774) where he probably at the time had extensive tracts of land, taken up by patents under royal grants for public services. This excursion over, Captain Ashby and his comrades found the return home more difficult than they had imagined. The country was if anything wilder and more dangerous than when marching westward under Lewis. So Ashby and his friends kept to the river in a perrogue. But once trusting to the stream, they seemed to find no safe landing, for the banks swarmed with hostiles, from whom the wanderers had many narrow escapes. They passed on down the Ohio and once so far from home they found it more easy to go on with the current than turn back and attempt an unknown route through a strange land. So they glided on having more than one adventure, from the Ohio into the Mississippi, and upon her broad bosom they floated to the far South, landing at New Orleans, whence they returned home by way of Pensacola and Charleston. (Western Journal XII., 116, Collins, Ky., 1, 18). It was claimed of him, as the result of this trip, that he was the first white man who ever went from the Kanawha to New Orleans all the way by water.

When the minute men began to organize in those stirring days preceding the Revolution, Ashby came again to the front. He was in 1775 appointed Captain in the Culpeper Minute Battalion and in September marched from Culpeper Court House in response to the call of the Committee of Safety to join in the attack upon Lord Dunmore's forces at Norfolk.

(Certificate of John Marshall in my possession—copy in Archive's New York Sons of Revolution).

The flag of his Company bore the coiled rattlesnake with the legend "Don't tread on me." One of his lieutenants was a young man who afterwards far outstripped his Commander in fame—John Marshall. The Company participated in the engagement at Great Bridge near Norfolk, under Colonel William Woodford, December 9th, 1775, resulting in the overthrow of Dunmore's forces. See Cook's Virginia, 486 (Ed., 1892).

The troops wore "strong brown linen bunting shirts dyed with leaves, and the words 'Liberty or Death' worked in large white letters on the breast, bucktails in each hat, and a leather belt about the shoulders with tomahawk and scalping knife." Most of them had fowling pieces and squirrel-guns. Slaughter's History St. Mark's Parish, p. 107 (Ed., 1877).

The minute men were soon made a party of the regular troops of the Colony, and after the Battle of Great Bridge, Captain Ashby's company doubtless became a part of the Third Virginia Regiment. In February, 1776, he was commissioned a Captain in the Regiment in which he served through the Campaigns of 1776 and 1777 in the War of the Revolution. (Certificate of John Marshall, Joseph Blackwell, John Blackwell, V. Peers, Thomas Marshall, in my possession, copies in Archives New York Sons of Revolution).

A touching incident occurred when these now regularly enlisted borderers, having marched from the Shenandoah Valley under Morgan, were reviewed by Washington at Boston. As he was riding along the lines, Morgan saluted him and reported: "From the right bank of the Potomac, General." "Washington dismounted," says John Esten Cook in his History of Virginia, p. 450, "and with tears in his eyes went along the ranks, shaking hands in turn with each of the men." And well he might. For he doubtless knew most of them personally, since the days of Braddock, and how true and brave they were going to be to the cause he had so much at heart, no one knew better than Washington himself.

I do not know what were the movements of Captain Ashby's Regiment just preceding the Battle of Harlem Heights, but there is no doubt that the successful issue of that engagement was due in great part to the coolness and fighting quality of these Virginia troops under the command of Col. Leitch. When all the field officers fell, Captains Ashby, West and Thornton, acting in splendid concert, so managed their Virginia troops as to extricate the movement from defeat, and bring for the first time in many a day victory to the American arms.

The moral effect of this engagement was out of all proportion to the number of troops employed or the harm done the enemy. It revived the spirits of the American people to a point they had not hitherto reached, and showed that in spite of the disastrous Long Island campaign the British soldiers were not invincible, at least when confronted by Virginians well officered.

The letter of Lieut.-Col. Gustavus P. Wallace, 25th Virginia Regiment, dated September 18th, 1776, published for the first time in Hayden's Virginia Genealogies, p. 703, describing this battle, is so quaint and interesting that I cannot forbear reproducing it in full. It is as follows:

CAMP ON MORRISES HEIGHTS, SEPT. 18, 1776.
(10 miles above N. Y.)

Dear Brother:

On Sunday last one large ship and two small ones passed our battery on Powles Hook and came up North River about 3 miles—four others went up East River and at the same time five ships of the line drew up before the town and then ensued a very heavy cannonading from the shipping and our batterys. On the town being cannonaded our people were obliged to evacuate it but before they got out of the town a large party landed from the ships in East River and beat back a New England Brigade that was posted there to prevent their landing. Though our regiment had been out of camp under arms for two nights before, we were ordered to cover the retreat of the cowardly Yankeymen but before we could get up we were countermanded by General Green who' commanded us. The enemy marched then to York and took some few that were in the town but a great many reached us; that night our regiment was kept under arms the whole night and in the evening about 9 o'clock we heard our picquet guard that belonged to a New England Brigade attacked by the enemy, on which our Regt. was drawn up in a small field that we had been in all night and about five or six minutes after we saw the picquet guard running like the devil, on which we were ordered to advance from seven companies over half a mile which we did and then formed in the woods on the side of a hill just above a meadow that was 50 yards wide. We then came in sight of our enemy who were posted on the opposite side of the meadow on a woody hill on which Capt. West, Capt. Thornton, Capt. Ashby and a rifle company from Maryland was ordered under the command of Col. Leitch to cross the swamp above the meadow and flank the enemy. After our seven companys of musketry were drawn up on the side of the hill the enemy fired upon our right-wing which brought on a pretty hot engagement across the meadow—the distance was so great that there was little execution done on either side until a Connecticut Brigade got betwixt us and the enemy in a thicket that lay on one side of the meadow from which they killed a few. This drew the enemy's attention to us & those that were in the thicket, on which Major Leitch was ordered to surround them and in attempting it he and his party fell in with about 1500 of the enemy who like to have taken Leitch and his party, but they made a manful stand and exchanged three rounds, when our poor Major received three balls through his side on which his party were obliged to retire, but did great execution. We had in that part of our Regt. 3 killed and 8 wounded—we had in the main part of the Regt. (where I was) 3 wounded, one thought to be mortally. The Major is thought to be in a good way. Thos. Hungerford got slightly wounded in the foot. Col. Weedon got part of the hilt of his sword taken off by a ball.

All of our officers and soldiers behaved with the greatest bravery, and the troops that were engaged got Gen'l Washington's thanks yesterday in public orders. I forgot to tell you that the enemy retreated from the field of battle and we took possession of it on which we found nearly fifty dead where Leitch engaged them, and a great deal of blood and two dead bodies on the place where we fired. They were seen to carry away their dead from the part where we fought them, by a deserter who came in last night we were told that they had lost in killed and wounded and missing 150 in all. We have about 40 killed, wounded and taken; in a little time we expect a general engagement, where there certainly will be on both sides a great number fall. When Leitch attacked them they retreated from us and we took the ground they occupied. The wood they lay in was cut to pieces by our balls. Though I say it that should not say it the Virginia Regiment has got great honor in this engagement 4 & 5 Virginia Regts. we pray for more Virginia troops & think success.

I have sent half my clothes to King's Bridge about five miles above this for fear of losing our camp. My compliments to the two Mr. Taliaferros & their Ladys, Vas Jones & his Lady & all my good friends in Virginia. You will please show this letter to the above gentlemen though they will be puzzled to read it. I am Dr Sir with many compliments to your Lady & family.

Your effect. Brother,

GUST B. WALLACE.

The high record of the 3rd Virginia was maintained throughout the trying New Jersey campaign. It was soon Washington's 10th Legion.

At Brandywine (September 11th, 1777) the 3rd Virginia behaved with great gallantry, remaining firm after both its flanks were turned (Cooke's Va., 1892, p. 450). According to family tradition, Captain Ashby was the first to succour Lafayette on being wounded in that battle. This incident was told to my uncle Turner Wade Ashby by Lafayette himself, at a reception given to the latter at Warrenton, Va., in 1825. Ashby was subsequently himself wounded in the same engagement. He, however, participated in the Battle of Germantown (October 4th, 1777). According to the certificates of his comrades in arms above referred to, he withdrew from active service in the winter of 1778, very much afflicted by severe rheumatic complaints contracted in the army.

According to Heitman-Historical Register, Officers of the Continental Army (1893), Captain Ashby resigned Oct. 30th,

1777. If this be the correct date of his resignation, he may have nevertheless continued in active service pending acceptance, or have withdrawn it, or requested action be postponed upon it. Certainly on that day he settled his accounts with the pay-master of the Regiment at Camp Whitpen. Certif. V. Peers; Va., Dec. 31.

Upon his retirement from the army to his death in 1815, there is little to record. The country during this period had entered upon an era of prosperity which was checked, and that but temporarily only, by the second war with England in 1812, which the gallant old veteran lived to see terminate successfully and honorably in favor of his country. Too old to take part himself, but true to his brave and patriotic instincts, he gave to his country's service in that memorable struggle, at least four sons, John, Samuel, Nimrod and Thomson (Pollard's 2nd Year of the War, p. 46 (1863), and it is stated a fifth, Turner, the father of General Turner Ashby, C. S. A. (Avirett's Ashby and His Compeers (1867), p. 16. Thomson was a lieutenant in Captain Benjamin Cole's Company.

The others, I believe, were all officers of higher rank.

So far as I am now informed Captain Ashby never sought civil or political honors of any kind. After a long and honorable military service, he retired to the easy, independent life of a country gentleman of good estate. He had inherited considerable wealth from his father to which in spite of the generous living to which he and all of the name were given, he had added a comfortable amount by judicious investments especially in the State of Kentucky, where his brother *Benjamin, after serving actively throughout the War of the Revolution, and others of the family had settled.

Captain Ashby lived at "Belmont," not far from Delaplane Station, in Fauquier, in the simplicity and contentment of the time. According to the fashion of his people he entertained all comers with simple but gracious hospitality.

Illustrative of this ingenuous and social life is a sweet little story which I have often heard from the past generation of the family and which I think ought to be preserved.

*Heitman—(Historical Register, Washington, D. C., 1893), gives the following as the record of Benjamin Ashby: Ensign 11th Regiment (Va.) November 30th, 1776; Regimental Quartermaster, January 1st, 1777; 2nd Lieutenant, June 1st, 1777; Regiment designated 7th Va., September 14th, 1778; 1st Lieutenant, March 13th, 1779; retired January 1st, 1782. See also Calender Virginia State Papers, I, 410).

Sitting upon his portico one hot summer day and looking far across the green sloping meadow to the County Road that skirted his lands, the old soldier descried a weary traveller wending his way slowly along. Calling up one of the negro boys, of whom there were a number always in immediate attendance for general service about the house, the Captain told him to go out at once to the traveler and invite him in Captain Ashby's name, to come to the house for rest and refreshment for himself and his horse. The invitation was as graciously accepted as given, and the stranger, turning aside from the public road, entered the long lane that led to Captain Ashby's home, the darkey preceding him and opening the gates, with as much interest and pleasure in the occasion as if he were the master himself. The Captain was at this time a great sufferer from rheumatism as well as wounds received years before, in the service, but never quite healed. The traveller was gracefully and cordially received by the disabled soldier, who went as far as to greet him as his bodily infirmities would admit of. He was pressed to dine, and after dinner, he was pressed to spend the night. Next day he was pressed to abide yet longer that the civilities of the neighbors might be extended to him. The traveller yielded to the warm hospitality of his host and bided several days with him, receiving every attention that Captain Ashby and his friends could command. The stranger proved to be an English surgeon traveling in quest of health and information, a gentleman of great intelligence and professional skill. Becoming interested in Captain Ashby's ailments the kind gentleman volunteered his services to bring him relief from his suffering, and such was his application, that ere long the patient was greatly eased of his rheumatism and quite cured of his wounds. It was thus that the Captain entertained an angel unawares, but angel or not, he would have entertained him much the same. And so the traveller took up his journey, without leaving for us of this day any other record whatever of himself.

The following letter from Benjamin Ashby to Captain John Ashby is in my possession.

Dear Brother:

If Mr. Smith should bring my Horse out, you will oblige me in a particular manner if you would spare me a Bell, and endeavour to procure by some means a Saddle and Bridle of any sort for me and send them with the Horse, for it is impossible for me to get such a thing in this Country and you know there will be no doing without; I also should be glad of a pr. of Shoes and Stockings by the same opportunity, these articles perhaps you may get at my Fathers. Pray Don't Neglect getting the Land Warrants to the amount of two thousand Acres if you can spare the money as I think I can lay them upon good Land. You had also better by all means send them as soon as possible as the sooner I get them the better.

Pray let me hear from you by the first opportunity and write me how everything goes, my Comps. to Molly and all my other friends.

Yr. Brother,
BENJ'N ASHBY.

27th June, 1780.
Captain John Ashby, Jun.

John Ashby of Bellemont, was born April 1, 1740; died April 4, 1815. Captain Ashby married Mary Turner of Maryland; born May 23, 1750; died 1826. Issue:

I. MARTHA ANN (PATSIE) ASHBY, born Jan. 5, 1770; married March 28, 1786, to William Withers of Culpeper. Issue:
    A. Eliza Withers, married John Griffin. Issue:
        aa. Marthr Griffin.
        bb. ———, married ——— Roberts.
        cc. Mary Turner Griffin.
        dd. John Samuel Griffin.
        ee. Blackford Griffin.
    B. Mary Withers, married Lewis Connor of Woodville, Culpeper.
    C. Samuel Withers, M.D.
    D. Martha (Patsie) Withers, married Charles Yancey of Tenn.

II. DOROTHEA ASHBY, born January 25, 1772; married June 23, 1789, Robert Jones of Culpeper, and afterwards removed to Illinois. Issue:
    A. Gabriel Jones.
    B. Robert Jones.
    C. John Ashby Jones.
    D. Rev. Slaughter Jones.
    E. Harriet Jones, married Charles Adams. Issue:
        aa. James Robert Adams.
        bb. Dorothea Adams, married ——— Leachman.
        cc. William Adams, married Eliza Haynes.
        dd. Edwin Thomson Adams, killed at Gettysburg.
        ee. Browning Adams.

III. SAMUEL ASHBY, born August 17, 1773, held a commission as Major in the War of 1812. He married Martha, daughter of Colonel Clarkson. Major Ashby inherited land in Kentucky, left to him by his father. He died in 1816. Issue:
    A. Maria Ashby, married Samuel Chancellor. Issue:
        aa. William Chancellor, died aged 30 years.
        bb. Fitzgerald Chancellor, died aged 13 years.
        cc. Ashby Chancellor, married Mildred Wallace, and had issue: Rush Chancellor, married Lilly Elzey of Loudoun, and had issue: Mildred and Ashby Chancellor.
        dd. John Chancellor.
        ee. Robert Chancellor.
        ff. Virginia Chancellor, married Col. George W. Hans-

brough, and had issue: Marion, Livingston and Maria Hansbrough.

gg. George Chancellor, married Josie Briggs, and had issue: Archer and Samuel Chancellor.

hh. James Chancellor.

ii. Dr. Livingston Chancellor, died unmarried, aged 23 years.

B. John Henry Ashby, married Dec. 23, 1829, Alcinda Grigsby. Issue:

    aa. Martha Ashby.

    bb. Natila Ashby, married Granville Page, and had issue: Infant, died young, and Rena Page, who married and settled in Independence, Mo.

C. John Jamieson Ashby, married Oct. 19, 1831, to Sarah Adams. Issue:

    aa. Samuel Ashby, died young.

    bb. Martha Clarkson Ashby.

    cc. Caroline Elizabeth Ashby, married John T. Ogilvie. No issue.

    dd. Luther Rice Ashby, d. s. p.

    ee. Capt. John Turner Ashby, C. S. A., married Louisa Herndon. Issue:

        1. Alice Ashby, married Thomas Leachman and had issue, one daughter—Louise.

        2. Sallie Ashby.

        3. John Turner Ashby.

        4. Julian Ashby.

    ff. James Samuel Ashby, C. S. A., killed at Gettysburg.

    gg. Henry Stribling Ashby, C. S. A., married Mary W. Delaplane. Issue:

        1. George Ashby, died young.

        2. Emma Ashby, married Delaney F. D. Butts, and has issue: Harry, Mary, Delaney, Hunter, Heath and Daniel Butts.

    hh. Virginia Ashby, married Dr. Thruston Wolfe. Issue:

        1. Scott Wolfe.

        2. Salena Wolfe.

        3. Thruston Wolfe.

    ii. Scott Ashby, married Lucy Belle Almond. Issue:

        1. Jamieson Ashby, married Mary Webb, and have issue, Webb Ashby.

        2. George Ashby.

        3. Webb Ashby.

        4. Mollie Ashby.

D. Mary Ashby, married Taliaferro P. Grantham of Missouri. Issue:

    aa. Samuel Grantham of St. Louis.

    bb. Maria Grantham.

E. Catherine Ashby, married Philip Tutt of Missouri. Issue:

    aa. James Tutt, married a Fristoe of Cooper Co., Mo.

    bb. Edward Tutt of California.

F. Clarkson Ashby, married Sarah E. Cocke, Dec., 1832.

G. Martha Ashby, married Rev. Chas. M. Schroffe, who died Aug., 1876.

The Buckners of Virginia

H. Caroline Ashby, married Gilbert Moxley Bastable. Issue:
    aa. Mattie Bastable, married Dr. Henry R. Noel. Both deceased. Issue:
        1. Mattie Noel, deceased.
    bb. Lucy Bastable, married —— Platar of Maryland. Both d. s. p.
    cc. Mollie Bastable, married A. T. Forbes.
    dd. Maria Bastable, d. s. p.
    ee. Elizabeth Bastable, married Alfred Forbes. Issue:
        1. Gilbert B. Forbes, deceased.
        2. Alfred T. Forbes.
    ff. Laura Bastable, d. s. p.
    gg. Annie Bastable, d. s. p.
    hh. Gilberta Bastable, d. s. p.
    ii. Virginia Bastable, married W. C. Bevan. Issue:
        1. Franklin C. Bevan, married —— Morrisi.
        2. Reginald Bevan, deceased.
        3. Lawrence Bevan, deceased.
    jj. Gilbert M. Bastable, of Calverton, Va., married (1st) Mary A. Semmes, by whom he had Virginia and Mary, both of whom are dead. He married (2d) Mrs. Elizabeth Powell. Issue:
        1. Caroline Bastable.
        2. Elizabeth Bastable.

IV. JOHN ASHBY, Jr., born Sept. 9, 1775, was a Captain in the War of 1812. His will is probated in Fauquier County, April 25, 1831. Captain Ashby was married twice, his first wife being Sallie Smith, and his second, Mrs. Mary Pickett, *née* McNish, of Warrenton. Issue by first wife:

    A. William Ashby, married Aug., 1827, Hebe Carter of Ridgeville. Issue:
        aa. Wirt M. Ashby.
        bb. Shirley Ashby.
    B. Eliza M. Ashby, married, Oct. 5, 1826, Richard H. Neal.
    C. Lucy S. Ashby, married Robert S. Ashby.
    D. Mary Turner Ashby.
    E. Susan Ashby.
    F. Richard Ashby.

ISSUE OF CAPT. JOHN ASHBY, JR., BY SECOND MARRIAGE:

    A. Belle Ashby, married Andrew Chunn, Delaplane, Fauquier County. Issue:
        aa. Mary Meta Chunn, born Nov. 25, 1850; married Jan. 15, 1870, to Major D. C. Hatcher. Issue:
            1. Harry Ashby Hatcher, born Dec. 3, 1870.
            2. James Morris Hatcher, born Sept. 26, 1872; married Lucy Menor Rust, and has issue: Maisie Hatcher, born 1902; Gertrude Ashby Hatcher, born 1904; James Morris Hatcher, born 1906.
            3. Edwin Chunn Hatcher, born July 28, 1874.
            4. Mary Meta Hatcher, born June 25, 1882.
        bb. Roberta McNish Chunn, born Sept. 26, 1860; married Oct. 19, 1882, Loyd O. Gold, who died Feb. 19, 1899. Issue:

1. Isabel Ashby Gold, born Sept. 29, 1883; married April 6, 1904, Robert Follansbee.
2. Roberta Chunn Gold, born July 3, 1887.
3. Loyd O. Gold, born Jan. 14, 1897.

cc. Ada Belle Chunn, born Feb. 19, 1864; married June 27, 1883, Edmund S. Edmonds. Issue:
1. Mary Evelyn Edmonds, born May 17, 1884.
2. Edmund Chunn Edmonds, born May 30, 1886.
3. Isabella McNish Edmonds, born Feb. 24, 1888.
4. Ashby Carter Edmonds, born June 19, 1890.

dd. Taylor D. L. Chunn, born Jan. 29, 1874; died in Butte, Montana, Aug. 8, 1906; married Jan. 28, 1900, Alice McAbee. Issue:
1. Ruth McAbee Chunn, born Dec. 6, 1900; died Feb. 2, 1904.
2. Isabel McNish Chunn, born March 28, 1902.

B. Roberta Ashby, married Erasmus Taylor. Issue:

aa. Mary Edwina Taylor, born in Fauquier County, Dec. 11, 1852; married Nov. 18, 1885, George Alvin Smith of Richmond. Issue:
1. Roberta Ashby Smith, born Aug. 31, 1886.
2. Benj. H. Smith, born Oct. 11, 1887.
3. Mary Eleanor Smith, born Jan. 27, 1889; died May 28, 1891.

bb. Edmund Pendleton Taylor, born at Meadow Farm, Orange County, Sept. 27, 1854; married Aug. 17, 1892, Virginia Gildersleeve of Abingdon. Issue:
1. Mary Ashby Taylor, born June 22, 1893.

cc. John Ashby Taylor, born at Meadow Farm, April 20, 1856; married Jan. 24, 1885, Isabel Clayton King of Augusta, Ga. Issue:
1. Louise Montfort Taylor, born Dec. 6, 1885.
2. Marion Ashby Taylor, born Oct. 26, 1888; died April 14, 1890.
3. Charlotte Nalle Taylor, born May 9, 1890.
4. Elizabeth Clayton Taylor, born July 31, 1892.
5. Roberta Ashby Taylor, born July 1, 1894.
6. Jaquelin Plummer Taylor, born Oct. 3, 1897.

dd. Jaquelin Plummer Taylor, born at Meadow Farm, Nov. 25, 1857; died Feb. 22, 1858.

ee. Isabel McNish Taylor, born at Meadow Farm, March 5, 1859; died Jan. 7, 1861.

ff. Jaquelin Plummer Taylor, born at Meadow Farm, March 2, 1861; married June 12, 1895 Katharine Wall of Buck Lodge, Ind. Issue:
1. Mary Katharine Taylor, born Dec. 5, 1899.
2. Jaquelin Erasmus Taylor, born Sept. —, 1904.

gg. James Longstreet Taylor, born at Meadow Farm, March 17, 1864; died Jan. 16, 1867.

hh. Anna Welsh Lapsley Taylor, born at Meadow Farm, June 16, 1866; married Jan. 30, 1900, W. W. Burgess of Orange. Issue:

The Buckners of Virginia 263

        1. Rose Clagett Burgess, born Jan. 30, 1901.
        2. Wm. Wallace Burgess, born Sept. 1, 1903.
    ii. Bessie Revely Taylor, born at Meadow Farm, Aug. 6, 1868; married Jan. 26, 1892, A. Boyd Cayce of Richmond. Issue:
        1. Ashby Jeffires Cayce, born Oct. 10, 1894.
    jj. Lucy Allen Taylor, born at Meadow Farm, June 10, 1871; married Dec. 12, 1900, Paulus A. Irving of Richmond. Issue:
        1. Paulus A. Irving, born Nov. 16, 1901.
        2. Lucy Taylor Irving, born Feb. 4, 1903.
    kk. Sara Patton Taylor, born at Meadow Farm, March 4, 1873; married April 5, 1902, George R. Pope of Roselle, New Jersey. Issue:
        1. Sara Bainbridge Pope, born Jan. 24, 1903.

V. NIMROD ASHBY, born Oct. 7, 1778, died in Fauquier County, 1830. Captain in the War of 1812. Married Elizabeth Thomas Adams. Issue:
    A. Mortimer Williamson Ashby, died in infancy.
    B. Rebecca Wood Ashby, married Charles C. Smith, of Preston Co. West Va. No issue.
    C. Wilson Ashby, died aged 12 years.
    D. Edwin T. Ashby, died unmarried.
    E. Albert Adams Ashby.
    F. Nimrod Thomson Ashby, married April 7, 1838, Adelia Smith. Issue:
        aa. Nimrod T. Ashby, married Virginia Olinger.
        bb. Richard Henry Ashby, married Bettie Morehead.
        cc. Louisa Ashby, married John Olinger.
        dd. Elizabeth Thomas Ashby, married Daniel Moffett.
        ee. Charles Ashby, married Mildred Morehead.
        ff. John Marshall Ashby.
        gg. Joseph Ashby.
        hh. Rebecca Wood Ashby, married James Olinger.
        ii. Mary Arthur Ashby, married La Viga Moffett.
        jj. Lesbia Turner Ashby.
    G. Mary Elizabeth Ashby, married Nov. 5, 1835, Hugh R. Green. Issue:
        aa. Alberta Green, died young.
        bb. Robert Green, 17th Va. Infantry, C. S. A., died at Charlottesville, July 19, 1862, after Battle of Williamsburg.
        cc. Hugh Rust Green, M.D., married Kate Settle. Issue: Mary, Betsy, Robert and Jane Green.
    H. Ann Amanda Ashby.
    I. Jane Wilson Ashby, married Richard H. Rust. Issue:
        aa. William Rust of 7th Va. Cavalry, C. S. A., killed near Berryville, August, 1864.
        bb. Nimrod Ashby Rust, married Blanche Jordan and had issue: Frank, William and Genevieve Rust.
        cc. Clarence Rust, died in infancy.
    J. Samuel Turner Ashby, born in Fauquier County, Feb. 11, 1820; died at Culpeper, June 5, 1882; married Feb. 20, 1845, Martha Turner Chunn, born in Fauquier, June 8, 1824; died Jan. 29,

1881. She was a daughter of Capt. Andrew Chunn, by his second wife, Sarah Davis. Issue:

    aa. Alice Ashby, born in Washington, D. C., Nov. 13, 1846; married Dec. 17, 1867, Robert McGill Mackall of Georgetown, D. C. Now living in Culpeper, Va. Issue:

        1. Bessie Belt Mackall, born June 24, 1875.

    bb. Blanche Ashby, born in Fauquier, June 1, 1849; married Dec. 11, 1873, to Maurice Washington Lambert of Loudoun County, Va. Issue:

        1. May Ashby Lambert, born Oct. 1, 1874.

        2. Maurice Ashby Lambert, born July 17, 1876. Now a lawyer in Raleigh, N. C.

    cc. Frank Ashby, born in Fauquier, March 30, 1851; died in Culpeper, Sept. 8, 1876.

    dd. Hunter Ashby, born in Fauquier, Jan. 7, 1853; died in Culpeper, April 15, 1884.

    ee. Rebecca Ashby, born in Fauquier, May 25, 1854; died Sept. 20, 1857.

    ff. Bernard Ashby, born in Fauquier, Dec. 21, 1855; married April 26, 1900, to Caroline Thomas Butler, daughter of ex-Judge William Butler of the United States District Court of Pennsylvania.

    gg. Estelle Ashby, born in Fauquier, July 29, 1859; married Jan. 3, 1883, to Isaac L. Johnson of Pennsylvania. Issue:

        1. Helen Johnson, born Aug. 24, 1884.

        2. Hunter Ashby Johnson, born Oct. 9, 1886.

        3. Mary Alice Johnson, born Oct. 17, 1888.

        4. Mattie Gray Johnson, born March 19, 1890; died Aug. 21, 1890.

        5. Charles Edgar Boyle Johnson, born Nov. 2, 1892; died Feb. 20, 1894.

        6. Estelle Virginia Johnson, born Dec. 9, 1897.

    hh. Norman Ashby, born in Fauquier, Sept. 21, 1860; married Oct. 28, 1885, to Mary Stallard of Culpeper. Issue:

        1. Norma Ashby, born Oct. 8, 1886.

        2. Bernard Ashby, born Jan. 14, 1890.

        3. Hunter Ashby, born March 21, 1893.

    ii. Grace Ashby, born in Fauquier, July 27, 1861; married Ernst F. Hauch of Tacoma, Wash., Oct. 18, 1893. He died March 25, 1905. Issue:

        1. Martha Ashby Hauch, born May 28, 1896.

    jj. Samuel Turner Ashby, born in Fauquier, Nov. 21, 1863.

    kk. Mattie Chunn Ashby, born in Fauquier, June 9, 1865; married Nov. 14, 1891, to General William Birney. Residence, Washington, D. C.

K. Adeline T. Ashby.

L. John Robert Ashby, died Sept. 5, 1875; married Oct. 4, 1848, to Ellen Gilliss Todd, died Feb. 12, 1865. Issue:

    aa. Annie Gilliss Ashby, born Sept. 26, 1849; married June 8, 1872, Henry James Anderson. Issue:

The Buckners of Virginia

1. Eleanor Ashby Anderson, born Nov. 21, 1876; married Oct. 18, 1904, Auguste Zerega Huntington.

bb. Irving Gilliss Ashby, born May 30, 1851; married Nov. 27, 1879, Kate Upperman. Issue:
1. Ethel Irving Ashby, born Nov. 3, 1882; married Dec. 23, 1904, Sidney Breese Stevens.

cc. Elizabeth Todd Ashby, born July 3, 1853; married Oct. 17, 1876, Frederick R. Wallace. Issue:
1. Frederick Ashby Wallace, born June 21, 1881.

dd. William Todd Ashby, born Oct. 6, 1856; married April 18, 1883, Nina McKnew. Issue:
1. Eleanor Ashby, born June 21, 1884.
2. Lellig Wallace Ashby, born Feb. 23, 1886; died Jan. 24, 1893.
3. William Todd Ashby, born Feb. 26, 1894.

ee. Edwin Ashby, born Nov. 28, 1857; died Sept. 11, 1858.

ff. Jay Taylor Ashby, born April 29, 1861; married Oct. 26, 1892, Eleanor Elizabeth Baker.

gg. Maria Terese Ashby, born Dec. 23, 1864; died Jan. 25, 1865.

hh. Mary Sweetser Ashby, born Dec. 23, 1864 (twin sister of above); died Dec. 8, 1892; married April 9, 1890, Charles Francis Bacon. Issue:
1. Mary Ashby Bacon, born Dec. 8, 1892.

VI. WILLIAM ASHBY, born December 19, 1780; died 1841; married 1805, Lucy Strother of Culpeper. Issue:
   A. Helen Mary Ashby.
   B. John Ashby, married Emily Buckner, born 1804, daughter of William Aylett and Charlotte (Hawes) Buckner. Issue:
      aa. Bailey Ashby.
      bb. William Aylett Ashby of Culpeper, born 1837, married 1870, to Nellie Alcocke, and had issue: Charles Aylett Ashby, born July 19, 1874; and Julian Warrington Ashby, born 1876.
      cc. Charlotte Hawes Ashby, born July 3, 1834; married July 3, 1855, Capt. Joseph Richard Manson of Brunswick County. Issue:
         1. Ashby Manson, born Oct. 10, 1856; married Nov. 2, 1880, Bettie Cunningham. Issue: Nannie, Richard, Charlotte, Ashby, Tally, Edwin, Andy and Thomas Manson.
         2. Matilda F. Manson, born May 13, 1859; married the Rev. Charles D. Crawley. Issue: Charlotte Crawley.
         3. Thomas J. Manson, born Feb. 3, 1861; married Nov. 14, 1882, Etta Barron. Issue: Lucy, Floyd, Florence, Claiborne, Kate and Millie Manson.
         4. Lucy Strother Manson, born April 28, 1862; married Thomas G. Wynne. Issue: Willie, Maude and Annie Wynne.
         5. J. Richard Manson, born Oct. 15, 1867.
         6. Harry Manson, born Dec. 23, 1869; married 1893, May Burton. Issue: May, Harry and Lura Manson.
         7. William Buckner Manson, born May 22, 1871.

8. Charlotte Manson, born Nov. 20, 1872; married William E. Smith. Issue: Clinton, Lucile, Emma and Maclin Smith.
9. John E. Manson, born Nov. 17, 1876.
10. Sidney Lynn Manson, born Oct. 4, 1878; married Oct. 31, 1905, Rosa Campbell.

dd. Lucy Ashby, married Robert Randolph Henry of Tazewell, Dec. 16, 1869. Issue: John Randolph, Charlotte L., William B., Lucy Ashby, C. S. Ashby, Robert E., and Aylette Buckner.

C. Ann Ashby, married Francis William Jones. Issue:
 aa. Helen Mary Jones, married George J. Sumner.
 bb. John William Jones, married Page Helm.
 cc. Lucy Marshall Jones, married Charles Hunter of Staunton.
 dd. Pendleton Jones.
 ee. Edloe Jones.
 ff. Robert Meade Jones.
 gg. James Lawrence Jones.
 hh. Mattie Bernard Jones, married Rev. R. T. Hanks.
 ii. French Jones.
 jj. Clarence Jones.
 kk. Willie Page Jones (girl).

D. Elizabeth Mildred Ashby, born Jan. 19, 1814; died Oct. 6, 1837; married Nov. 8, 1836, to David Meade Bernard of Petersburg. Issue:
 aa. George S. Bernard, lawyer, of Petersburg, born Aug. 27, 1837; married June 23, 1870, Fanny Rutherford, daughter of Samuel J. Rutherford of Richmond. Issue:
  1. Fanny R. Bernard, born April 28, 1871; married John C. Cocke of Roanoke.
  2. Kate E. Bernard, born Feb. 19, 1873; married Theophilus A. Feild, Jr., of Petersburg.
  3. Janet M. Bernard, born March 14, 1875.
  4. Ella A. Bernard, born July 19, 1877; married Edmund Cary Nalle of Washington, D. C.
  5. George S. Bernard, Jr., born Oct. 17, 1881; married Mary C. Gilliam.

E. Martha Turner Ashby, died Dec. 11, 1848; married Nov. 3, 1842, Capt. Robert E. Meade of Brunswick County, died Jan. 21, 1888. Issue:
 aa. Robert Turner Meade, married Jan. 25, 1871, Hattie Mertens Johnson of Petersburg.
 bb. Lucy Ashby Meade, born Sept. 30, 1843; died July 24, 1882; married May 6, 1863, Capt. C. Tacitus Allen of Brunswick, Va. Issue:
  1. Robert Meade Allen, d. s. p.
  2. Ellen Taylor Allen, born April 18, 1866; married in 1888, Hugh Mayes of Princeton, Ky. Issue: Virginia B. Mayes, born April 15, 1892; Annie Mead Mayes, born May 11, 1896; Dorothy Allen Mayes, born Oct. 13, 1904.

The Buckners of Virginia

3. Stuart Ashby Allen, born Jan. 18, 1868.
4. Annie Meade Allen, d. s. p.
5. Herbert Percy Allen, d. s. p.
6. Hattie Carr Allen, died Oct. 21, 1889.

F. Dr. Charles William Ashby, born Aug. 11, 1811; married Sarah Elizabeth Dickinson, daughter of William I. Dickinson of Caroline County, April 26, 1854. Issue:

    aa. Lucy Dickinson Ashby, born March 27, 1856; married Charles Carter Carmichael. Issue:
        1. Mary Spottswood Carmichael.
        2. Charles Ashby Carmichael.
        3. Lucy Dickinson Carmichael.
    bb. Jane Pollock Ashby, born Oct. 6, 1857; married Henry Burns Coghill. Issue:
        1. Wm. I. Dickinson Coghill.
    cc. Mary Louisa Ashby, born July 18, 1859; married William Henry Camp. Issue:
        1. Mary Jeffery Camp, born Nov. 15, 1882.
        2. Ashby Pendleton Camp, born Oct. 5, 1885.
        3. William H. Camp, born Sept. 14, 1889.
        4. Charles Ashby Camp, born Jan. 12, 1894.
        5. Harriotte Pelletier Camp, born July 13, 1897.
    dd. Alice Royal Ashby, born July 1, 1861; married Lawrence L. Coghill. Issue:
        1. Elizabeth Ashby Coghill.

G. French Ashby, died unmarried.
H. Strother Ashby, died unmarried.
I. Kate Ashby, married Richard Henry Buckner, son of Bailey and Mildred (Strother) Buckner.
J. Mary Wade Ashby, born Feb. 28, 1830, at Culpeper, Va.; married Oct. 19, 1862, to Rev. William Warden; born at Staunton, June 26, 1823; died at Rappahannock County, Va., March 2, 1894. Issue:

    aa. Charles William Warden of Bristol, Va.; born Aug. 29, 1863; married at Staunton Oct. 19, 1887, to Mary Taliaferro Arthur; born June 13, 1869. Issue:
        aaa. Arthur Hills Warden, born July 21, 1888.
        bbb. Mary Ashby Warden, born May 25, 1895.
    bb. Herbert P. Warden of Mexico, Mo., born March 19, 1865.
    cc. Turner Ashby Warden, born Dec. 25, 1866.
    dd. Arthur Lee Warden, born May 31, 1868.
    ee. Eugene French Warden, born Oct. 19, 1870.
    ff. Mary Pauline Warden, born Aug. 28, 1873.

K. Philip Ashby, d. s. p.
L. George Strother Ashby, d. s. p.

VII. ELIZABETH ASHBY, born Sept. 10, 1782; married Col. John Tutt of Culpeper, son of John Tutt of same place, whose will was proved in 1812. Issue:

A. Mary Ann Tutt, married Isaac Lionberger. Issue:
    aa. John R. Lionberger, married Margaret Clarkson of Missouri. Issue:
        1. Isaac H. Lionberger, lawyer, of St. Louis, Mo., has issue: Margaret, John, Louise, Anne, Ruth, David.

2. Marion Lionberger, married —— Davis, and has one son, John L. Davis.
3. Margaret Lionberger, married —— Potter and has issue: Clarkson and Harry C. Potter; the latter has a son, Clarkson Potter.
- bb. Elizabeth Lionberger, married Judge John C. Richardson. Issue:
    1. John C. Richardson, who died and left a daughter, Mrs. Alice C. Fitzgerald.
    2. Mollie Richardson, married —— Campbell.
- cc. DeWitt Lionberger, had four children, Harry (deceased), Anne, Jane and Mary.
- dd. Isabel Lionberger, married George L. Leyburn.
- ee. Frank Lionberger, has issue, Frank, and two daughters, Elizabeth and "Chat."
- ff. David Lionberger, d. s. p.
- gg. Sarah Lionberger, married Ferdinand Rogers.
- hh. Frances Lionberger, married —— Howard, and has issue, a daughter Mary.

B. Martha Tutt, married —— Hutcheson of Missouri.
C. Robert Tutt, died unmarried.
D. John Tutt, went to San Francisco and married.
E. Dorothea Tutt, married —— Rhodes of Texas. Issue:
- aa. Mary Rhodes, married William Yager.
- bb. Edward Rhodes.
- cc. John Rhodes.

F. Virginia Tutt, married —— Colston.
G. Samuel Tutt, died unmarried.
H. Julia Tutt, died unmarried.

VIII. THOMSON ASHBY, born March 31, 1785, was a Lieutenant in the 5th Va. Regiment, Capt. Benj. Cole's Company, from Culpeper, in the War of 1812, serving in that capacity three months and twenty-two days. He died July 14, 1850. Married Oct. 20, 1808, Ann Stuart Menefee; born Sept. 19, 1791, in Culpeper. Issue:

A. Robert Stuart Ashby, born Sept. 18, 1809 of Alexandria, Va., Captain in C. S. A.; married Lucy Ashby, daughter of John Ashby, Jr., of Fauquier, who died in 1831. Issue:
- aa. Gertrude Ashby, unmarried, living in 1906, at Washington, D. C.
- bb. Bertrand Ashby, died unmarried.
- cc. Genevieve Ashby, married Frank Yager; died without issue.
- dd. Vernon Ashby, married Mrs. Jones.
    1. Lucy Stuart Ashby, born Dec. 17, 1887.
    2. Bertrand Wilbur Ashby, born Feb. 6, 1890.
    3. Robert Turner Ashby, born June 30, 1892.
- ee. Mae Ashby, married Dr. John Bayne of Washington, and has issue:
    1. Lucy Ashby Bayne, born Sept. 13, 1874; died Oct. 3, 1905; married Nov. 23, 1898, Elisha S. Theall.
    2. John Henry Bayne, born Dec. 5, 1875; died June 10, 1876.

3. Robert Ashby Bayne, born Sept. 18, 1877; died May —, 1879.
4. Mae Ashby Bayne, born April 6, 1879; married Nov. 22, 1899, David B. Tennant, and has issue, John Bayne Tennant, born Feb. 11, 1902, and Annie Buffington Tennant, born Aug. 9, 1903.
5. Joseph Breckenridge Bayne, born June 28, 1880.
6. Gertrude Ashby Bayne, born Oct. 21, 1883.
7. Harriet Addison Bayne, born Nov. 2, 1885.
8. Genevieve Bayne, born Nov. 4, 1887; died Dec. 7, 1887.
9. Louise Dudley Bayne, born Aug. 29, 1891.

ff. Stuart Ashby, died unmarried.

gg. Lulie Ashby, married Llewellyn Cooke, and has issue: Hortense Cooke.

B. Turner Wade Ashby, born Aug. 18, 1811, Lieut. in the U. S. A. in Mexican War; Postmaster at Alexandria, Va., prior to 1861. Died April 20, 1893; married Lizzie Gregory. Issue:

aa. Edith Turner Ashby, married Hubert Snowden. Issue: Edgar Snowden, born April 2, 1880; Elizabeth G. Snowden, born Jan. 5, 1882; Edith Ashby Snowden, born May 21, 1889.

bb. Gregory Ashby, M. D.

cc. Janet Ashby, married Rev. Charles Edward Woodson, a minister of the Protestant Episcopal Church. Issue: Edith Ashby Woodson, born Jan. 26, 1892; Elizabeth G. Woodson, born Jan. 24, 1896.

C. Meriwether Ashby, born Oct. 20, 1813; died unmarried.

D. Frances Virginia Ashby, born June 9, 1816; died June 2, 1895; married May 15, 1835, Westwood M. Carter; died August 6, 1896. Issue:

aa. Meriwether Thomson Carter of Pueblo, Col., born in Virginia, July 18, 1842; married Clara B. Churchill of Barry, Ill., Dec. 6, 1892.

bb. Turner Carter, d. s. p.

cc. Jennie Carter.

dd. Joseph M. Carter of Pueblo, Col., born in Virginia, July 21, 1846; married Mary Brown, April 8, 1880. Issue:
1. Bettie Scott Carter, born May 25, 1882.
2. Thomson Ashby Carter, born Sept. 4, 1884.
3. Oscar Francis Carter, born Sept. 16, 1886; died June 9, 1887.

Joseph M. Carter, married (2d) Feb. 27, 1890, Clara Olinger. Issue:
1. Josephine Hitchins Carter, born Dec. 5, 1890.

ee. Nannie Strother Carter, born in Virginia, April 14, 1855; married James W. Rice of Fauquier, Co., Dec. 27, 1882. Issue:
1. Virginia Ashby Rice, born in Virginia, Oct. 24, 1883.
2. Robert E. Lee Rice, born in Colorado, Aug. 21, 1885.
3. James Westwood Rice, born in Colorado, May 15, 1888; died Nov. 24, 1888.
4. Mary Gertrude Rice, born in Colorado, June 30, 1890.

        ff. Gertrude Miller Carter, born in Virginia, Feb. 11, 1860; died in Colorado, Nov. 19, 1893; married Douglas Mitchell in Pueblo, Dec. 29, 1886. Issue:
          1. Florence Ashby Mitchell, born July 2, 1889.
        gg. Oscar F. Carter of Alexandria, Va., married Ellen S. Lloyd. Issue: Gardiner Lloyd Carter, born March 1, 1890; Emma Virginia Carter, born Aug. 28, 1894.
   E. William Samuel Ashby, died March 10, 1818.
   F. Francis Westwood Ashby, born May 25, 1819; died July 17, 1870; married Margaret Gregory. Issue:
        aa. Carroll Westwood Ashby of Alexandria, Va., married Harriet Lumley. Issue: Carroll W. Ashby, born June 5, 1897.
        bb. Nellie B. Ashby, married Dr. William R. Purvis of Alexandria, Va.
        cc. Margaret Ashby, unmarried.
   G. Thomson Ashby, born and died Oct. 7, 1821.
   H. John William Ashby, born May 12, 1823; died unmarried Dec. 30, 1856.
   I. Mary Ellen Ashby, born June 14, 1826; died Oct. 2, 1869; married Charles Bayne, born Nov. 5, 1818, near Baynesville, Westmoreland County; died Oct. 18, 1885, near Fincastle, Va. Issue:
        aa. Son, died in infancy.
        bb. Nannie Thomson Bayne, born Jan. 13, 1849; died Sept. 10, 1896; married Dr. David Branch Clark of Richmond, Va., now of New York City. No issue.

HOWARD R. BAYNE, son of Mary Ellen Ashby and Charles Bayne, was born at Winchester, Va., on May 11th, 1851. His father, Charles Bayne, was the son of Richard Bayne and Susan Pope of Westmoreland County, Va.

At the beginning of the Civil War, Mr. Bayne's parents were living in Baltimore, Maryland, where his father was engaged in the tobacco business. The sympathies of Mr. Charles Bayne being entirely with the Southern cause, his residence in Baltimore became uncomfortable, if not perilous to his liberty. He left Baltimore early in the War with his family and became one of that numerous class, known as refugees, which flocked to Virginia from all parts of the country. As the war progressed Mr. Bayne and his family constantly had to change their residence in order to keep within the Southern lines and finally, about 1863, he took up his residence in Richmond, where he remained until 1870. He entered his son Howard in the Preparatory School at Richmond College, from which, after taking the full college course, he graduated in 1872, receiving the academic degree of M. A.

Among the honors that Howard R. Bayne received at college was that of Salutatorian, Final Orator and Best Debater's medallist. After graduating, he taught two years at the University

HOWARD RANDOLPH BAYNE

School in Richmond, and for the next three years he was principal of the Pampatike Academy at the home of Col. Thomas H. Carter, in King William County, Va. He took the summer Law course under Prof. John B. Minor, at the University of Virginia, in 1878, and graduated in law at Richmond College in 1879, receiving the professional degree of B.L. He was admitted to the Richmond Bar in July, 1879, and shortly afterwards formed a partnership with James Alston Cabell, under the firm name of Bayne & Cabell, which continued until July, 1882, when Mr. Bayne left Richmond to take up his residence in New York City. He was admitted to the New York Bar in July, 1882, and has practiced at that Bar continuously ever since.

On April 27, 1886, he married Lizzie S. Moore, daughter of Dr. Samuel Preston Moore of Richmond, Virginia, Surgeon-General of the Confederate States Army. Dr. Moore had been Surgeon in the Old Army from which he resigned when his native State, South Carolina, left the Union. Mrs. Moore was the daughter of Major Jacob Brown, U. S. A., who was killed in the Mexican War at the attack upon the troops he commanded at Fort Brown, now Brownsville, Texas, named in his honor.

Mr. Bayne resided in New York City from 1882 to 1890, when he removed to New Brighton, Staten Island, where he has resided ever since. He is a member of the New York City Bar Association, Sons of the Revolution, the Society of Colonial Wars, Richmond County Country Club, Virginia Historical Society, Trustee of the Staten Island Academy, Vestryman of Christ Church, New Brighton, and President of the Staten Island Association of Arts and Sciences. He has been for a number of years one of the trustees of the New York Southern Society, of which he was one of the organizers, also of the Council of "The Virginians," in New York, of which Society he is at present Governor.

He was in 1905, appointed by Governor Higgins, a member of the Probation Commission of the State of New York.

While at the Virginia Bar he edited Converse's Indexes (Virginia and West Virginia Law).

In 1879 he and Rev. Dr. Peyton Harrison Hoge, now of Louisville, Ky., took a tramp of over 800 miles through the State of Virginia, writing letters in the course of their long walk, to the *Richmond Dispatch* under the assumed names respectively of "Ego and Alter." These letters attracted much attention at the time, and were afterwards published in book form, Mr. Hoge, being Ego, and Mr. Bayne, Alter. Mr. Bayne is also the author of Monographs "The Year 1619 in the Colony of Virginia," and "A Rebellion in the Colony of Virginia," published by the New York Society of Colonial Wars. He has also contributed numerous articles on legal subjects to the *Railroad Gazette* and other papers.

Mr. Bayne has taken a prominent part in numerous movements for the betterment of social and civic conditions in his community. His greatest activity in politics was in opposition to the famous "Snap Convention of 1892" which sought to shelve Grover Cleveland in the interests of David B. Hill, as candidate for the presidency. This movement caused a revolution in the Democratic party in New York State and brought forth the celebrated "Anti-Snap Convention" of May, 1892, to which Mr. Bayne was a delegate. He was then elected a member of the State Committee and was also sent as one of the contesting delegation to the Chicago Convention to voice the sentiment of New York for Mr. Cleveland. This movement was completely successful, securing not only the nomination, but also the election of Mr. Cleveland to the presidency. Issue:

1. Samuel Preston Moore Bayne, born Oct. 7, 1887; died April 12, 1888.
2. Mary Ashby Moore Bayne, born Sept. 18, 1889.
3. Lloyd Moore Bayne, born Aug. 17, 1892.

dd. Estelle St. Pierre Bayne, born June 30, 1853; married Fletcher Platt Jones of Bedford County, Va. Issue: May Ellen, born Nov. 8, 1876; married Charles J. Osborn of New York; Charles Ashby, born June 14, 1878; Bettie Miller, born Nov. 22, 1880; married Richard H. Bateson of New York, a great nephew of Jefferson Davis.

ee. Frances Scott Bayne, born April 24, 1856; died Dec. 20, 1893, unmarried.

ff. Charles Ashby Bayne, died in infancy.

gg. Hunter W. Bayne, born April 7, 1860; died Feb. 11, 1887, unmarried.

J. Edwin Thomson Ashby, born Dec. 10, 1828.

K. Bettie Scott Ashby, born June 8, 1831; died Oct. 7, 1882; married Elisha J. Miller of Alexandria. Issue:
  aa. Ashby Miller, married Nellie English of Alexandria.
  bb. Gertrude Miller.
  cc. Julian Miller, M. D.

L. Benjamin Thornton Ashby, born Sept. 8, 1833; died unmarried.

IX. TURNER ASHBY of Rosebank, born Aug. 30, 1789; died 1837; married Dorothea Green of Culpeper, in 1820. Issue:

A. James Ashby, married Fannie Moncure. Issue:
  aa. John Moncure Ashby, married Minnie Duval. Issue:
    1. Charles Green Ashby, d. s. p.

GEN. TURNER ASHBY

      bb. James Ashby, married Mary Buchanan Moncure. Issue:
          1. Fannie Moncure Ashby.
          2. Richard Moncure Ashby.
          3. Virginia Buchanan Ashby.
          4. Mary Wallace Ashby.
          5. Nannie Hull Ashby.
          6. Dorothea Green Ashby.
          7. James Ashby.
          8. J. Moncure Ashby.
   B. Bettie Ashby, married George Mason Green. Issue:
        aa. Dora Green, married Dr. G. M. Wallace, and had Emily, Mary and Gus Wallace.
        bb. John Cook Green.

C. TURNER ASHBY, Jr., General in C. S. A., was born in Oct., 1828, near Markham, Fauquier County. He commanded a cavalry company made up of young men of his neighborhood, and when Virginia seceded in 1861, Captain Turner Ashby with his company were among the first to reach Harper's Ferry to volunteer their services.

He was assigned to the 7th Va. Cavalry, and by his bravery and dash at once attracted the attention of General Stonewall Jackson, who promoted him to the command of the 7th Cavalry. His younger brother, Richard Ashby, was a Lieutenant in his company, and was advanced to a Captaincy when Turner was promoted to a higher grade. Captain Richard Ashby who was a brave and brilliant officer, was killed in 1861, in an engagement on the Baltimore & Ohio Railroad, near Hancock, Md. His death had a saddening effect upon his brother, between whom there were strong ties of affection. Arousing all the fire and fervor in his nature, he threw all the energy and passion of a wounded heart into the cause in which he enlisted. His reckless daring, contempt for danger and chivalric spirit were aroused to the highest degree of enthusiasm and activity, so that he soon became one of the most distinguished cavalry leaders in the Confederacy. In 1862 he was made Brigadier-General and had command of the cavalry under Stonewall Jackson in the Valley Campaign.

Superbly mounted, and conceded to be one of the best riders in the South, he virtually lived in the saddle, and undertook and performed almost incredible feats. He had many narrow escapes, and seemed to bear almost a charmed life, but he was instantly killed while leading the 58th Va. Regiment into battle on the afternoon of June 6, 1862, near Harrisonburg, Va.

The tribute paid to his memory by Stonewall Jackson, who never gave undeserved praise, is the best monument to his character and memory:

"As a partisan officer I never knew his superior; his daring was proverbial; his powers of endurance almost incredible; his tone of character heroic, and his sagacity almost intuitive in divining the purposes and movement of the enemy."

General Turner Ashby and his brother, Captain Richard Ashby, lie side by side in the Confederate Cemetery at Winchester, Va.

D. Richard Ashby, Captain 7th Va. Cavalry, C. S. A., killed at Hancock, Md., in 1861.

E. Mary Ashby, married George V. Moncure, and had issue fourteen children, six of whom died in infancy. The others are as follows:

 aa. Turner Ashby Moncure, married Catherine Jewett of Bakersville, Cal. Issue:
  1. Jewett Moncure.
  2. Parker Moncure.
  3. George V. Moncure.
  4. Turner A. Moncure.
  5. Solomon J. Moncure.
 bb. John Moncure.
 cc. George V. Moncure, married Elizabeth Ford. Issue:
  1. George V. Moncure.
  2. Margaret W. Moncure.
  3. Nannie W. Moncure.
  4. Turner A. Moncure.
  5. Mary A. Moncure.
 dd. Robert S. Moncure, married Elizabeth Dexter of Washington, D. C. Issue:
  1. Catherine A. Moncure.
  2. Robert C. Moncure.
 ee. James A. Moncure, of Richmond, Va., married Maria Gray. Issue:
  1. James A. Moncure, Jr.
  2. Julia Gray Moncure.
  3. Maria A. Moncure.
 ff. Bettie Ashby Moncure, married M. W. Moncure. Issue:
  1. Elizabeth A. Moncure.
  2. Virginia B. Moncure.
  3. Michael Wallace Moncure.

F. Dora Ashby, married Powhatan Moncure of Oakenwold, Stafford County. Issue:

The Buckners of Virginia

    aa. Powhatan Moncure, M.D., of Bealton, Va., married in 1889, Lelia Carter of Fauquier County. Issue:
        1. Mildred Washington Moncure, born 1890.
        2. Dorothea Ashby Moncure, born 1892.
        3. Powhatan Moncure, born 1895.
        4. Jack Moncure, born 1901.
    bb. Fannie Moncure, married Samuel Taylor of Berryville.
    cc. Ashby Moncure, married Miss Stump of California.
    dd. Henry Moncure, d. s. p.
    ee. Frank Moncure.
    ff. Dora Ashby Moncure, married Rev. William J. Morton, Rector of Christ Church, Alexandria, Va., son of Dr. Charles Bruce Morton, and has issue:
        1. Charles Bruce Morton.
        2. William Jackson Morton.
        3. Powhatan Moncure Morton.
        4. Dorothy Ashby Morton.
    gg. Alice Belle Moncure, married H. H. Wallace.

X. MARSHALL ASHBY, born Nov. 8, 1798, married Jan. 3, 1826, Lucinda Cooke of Fauquier County. Issue:
  A. Maria Louisa Ashby, married John Brooke. Issue:
    aa. John Robert Brooke.
    bb. Lucy Brooke, married ———— Davies of Gloucester.
    cc. Bessie Brooke, married Tazewell Taylor of Norfolk.
    dd. Warner Brooke.
    ee. Agnes Brooke, married Capt. Wise, U. S. N. of Norfolk.
    ff. Ashby Brooke.
    gg. Lewis Brooke.
    hh. Daniel Brooke.
  B. Dr. John Washington Ashby, married Agnes Taylor. Issue:
    aa. John Taylor Ashby.
  C. Sarah Kate Ashby, married William Ellis Cocke. Issue:
    aa. Henry Cocke.
    bb. Marshall Cocke.
    cc. Ashby Cocke.
  D. Mary Elizabeth Ashby, married a son of General Wilkinson of Louisiana.
  E. Helen Ashby, married Thomas Hayden Gibbs. Issue:
    aa. Andrew Coyle Gibbs.
    bb. Randolph Howard Gibbs.
    cc. Annie Lucretia Gibbs.
    dd. Helen Hayden Gibbs.
    ee. Edwin Hayden Gibbs, married Georgie Lamb. Issue:
        1. Marshall Ashby Gibbs.
        2. Francis B. Gibbs.
  F. Henry Ashby, General in C. S. A., killed at Knoxville, by E. C. Camp (a Northerner), July 11, 1868.
  G. Fannie Ashby, married Colonel Harris of New York.
  H. Laura Ashby, married Daniel G. Purse of Savannah. Issue:
    aa. Ashby Purse.
    bb. Daniel Purse.

I. Lucy Ashby, married ———— Wilkinson.
J. Eugenie Ashby, married Dr. Burroughs of Savannah.

Fauquier County Records

In the Marriage Bonds of the above named county, the following entries are to be found:

Nov. 30, 1759, Nimrod Ashby and Frances Wright.
Jan. 17, 1764, Winifred Ashby and James Peters.
April 7, 1766, Nimrod T. Ashby and Adelia Smith.
April 24, 1766, William Ashby and Mary Tibbs.
Dec. 3, 1777, Nathaniel Ashby and Peggy Mauzey.
Aug. 2, 1781, Benjamin Ashby and Jane Ash.
April 18, 1782, Ann Ashby and William Smith.
April 28, 1783, Robert Ashby and Jane Combs.
Oct. 27, 1783, John Ashby and Catherine Huffman.
March 28, 1786, Patty Ashby and William Withers.
June 23, 1789, Dolly Ashby and Robert Jones.
Feb. 26, 1793, Robert Ashby and Ann Walters.
Oct. 18, 1796, Anna Ashby and Thomas Walters.
Dec. 27, 1803, George Ashby and Rebecca Davis.
Aug. 26, 1816, Maria Ashby and Samuel Chancellor.
Jan. 3, 1826, Marshall Ashby and Lucinda Cocke.
Oct. 5, 1826, Eliza. M. Ashby and P. H. Neal.
Aug. —, 1827, William Ashby and Hebe Carter.
Dec. 23, 1829, John H. Ashby and Alcinda Grigsby.
Oct. 19, 1831, John J. Ashby and Sarah Adams.
Dec. —, 1832, William C. Ashby and Sarah E. Cocke.
May 17, 1835, Frances V. Ashby and Westwood M. Carter.
Nov. 5, 1835, Mary E. Ashby and Hugh G. Green.
April 24, 1838, Milly Ashby and John Foley.

NOTE.—From 1840 to 1854 no marriages were recorded.

Will Books

Inventory of Capt. Nimrod Ashby, deceased, in Fauquier County, June 29, 1764.

July 4, 1764, Administrator's account of Nimrod Ashby in Frederick, Stafford and King George Counties.

June Court, 1764. Robert Ashby, guardian to Martin and Thomas Bryan Ashby, orphans of Nimrod Ashby, deceased.

Will of John Ashby of Fauquier County, Va. To son Samuel Ashby half of tract of land on Horner's Fork containing by patent 800 acres; also whole tract of land containing 200 acres adjoining a tract of 500 acres entered in the name of John Marshall, near the Kentucky river, both these tracts being in Kentucky; also lot of land in the Manor of Leeds which I purchased of Daniel Routt. To son John Ashby half tract of land lying on waters of Horner's Fork of Licking in Kentucky; also lot of land in Manor of Leeds purchased of John Adams. To daughter Martha Ann Withers, negro, and after her mother's death £60. To daughter Dolly Jones, negro, also loan of 2 negroes during her life, and afterwards to her children. To daughter Elizabeth Tutt, negroes. To three daughters above mentioned a tract of 1,000 acres on north fork of Licking in Kentucky, to be equally divided. To son Nimrod, negroes. To son William, negroes, also a lot of land in Manor of Leeds adjoining the land of Nimrod

Farrow. To son Thomson Ashby, lot of land in Manor of Leeds known by name of my mountain plantation; also negroes. To son Turner, lot of land on Goose creek, adjoining the land of Thomas Adams; also negroes. To son Marshall Ashby, negroes, etc. To sons Turner and Marshall, after their mother's death, the land I live on; the land I purchased of John Hickman, and land purchased of John Adams. To three sons, Nimrod, William and Thomson, half of 1,000 acres on north fork of Licking in Kentucky; also 1,450 acres on main branch of Licking. To beloved wife Mary Ashby, negroes, etc. Wife to be executrix, and sons Samuel and Nimrod executors. Dated Jan. 18, 1812; probated Aug. 28, 1815.

Will of Samuel Ashby of Fauquier County, Va. To wife Martha, all estate during life or widowhood, afterwards to be equally divided among our children, viz.: Maria, Henry, Jameson, Mary, Catherine, Clarkson, Martha and Caroline. Land and mill purchased of Mrs. Martha Chunn to be sold. Executors, wife Martha, my brothers Nimrod, Thomson and Turner, and Peter Adams. Dated Jan. 13, 1816; probated Feb. 26, 1816.

Oct. 12, 1815. Settlement of accounts of the guardian of Sarah Ashby, in the presence of Willoughby Ashby, her guardian appointed by County Court of Shelby in Kentucky. Recorded in Fauquier County, Feb. 26, 1816. Signed by Nimrod Ashby, Turner Ashby, Peter Adams.

Appraisement of estate of Major Samuel Ashby in Fauquier County, deceased. Dec. 23, 1816.

Will of Nimrod Ashby of Fauquier County, Va. To wife Elizabeth T. Ashby all estate during her life or widowhood, then to my ten children, viz.: Edwin T., Albert A., Nimrod T., Mary Elizabeth, Ann Amanda, Jane H., Samuel T., Adeline E. and John Robert Ashby. Executrix, wife Elizabeth T. Ashby. Dated Jan. 27, 1829; probated March 24, 1830.

Will of John Ashby of Fauquier County, Va. All estate after payment of just debts, to be equally divided among my six daughters, viz.: Eliza Neale, Mary Turner Ashby, Lucy S. Ashby, Susan Ashby, Belle Ashby and Roberta Ashby. Mentions his son William having received his portion of the estate. Mentions wife Mary Ashby, and if he should have another heir, to share with the daughters. Executor, John P. Phillips. Dated March 27, 1831; probated April 25, 1831.

Will of John H. Ashby of Fauquier County, Va. Directs sale of land on Crooked Run, also all the undivided interest which he has in the land belonging to the estates of Samuel Ashby, deceased, and Martha Ashby, deceased. To wife Alcinda, all rest of estate for life or widowhood, and after her death to be applied to education and maintenance of my daughter Martha C. Ashby and of such child or children as may hereafter be born to live to the age of 21 years, then estate to be sold and out of the proceeds wife to receive ⅓ part; balance to be divided between brothers and sisters. Mentions sister Mary D. Grantham and brother John J. Ashby as her trustee. Executors, Josiah Tidball, Thomas P. Knox. Dated April 19, 1834; probated June 28, 1834.

Sept. 23, 1837. Heirs of Turner Ashby, deceased, in account with Dorothea F. Ashby as guardian. Heirs—Elizabeth T. Ashby, James G. Ashby, Mary Ashby, Richard Ashby, Francis M. Ashby, Dorothea F. Ashby.

Jan. 27, 1846. Mary Ashby, guardian of Isabella McNish Ashby, Roberta Ashby.

Feb. 15, 1847. Martha Ashby, allotted Div. No. 4, of estate of Andrew Chunn, deceased.

In the name of God Amen, I, Mary Ashby, of the County of Fauquier and State of Virginia, being weak in body but of sound and perfect memory, do make and publish this my last will and testament, in manner and form as follows (that is to say): First, I give and bequeath unto my son Marshall, thirty dollars also all claim that I may have to negro man Simon, that was purchased from James Adams by my said son, as he was purchased for him and the bill of sale made to him. Secondly, I give and bequeath unto my son Nimrod, for the use of his son Edwin Thomson Ashby, one hundred and fifty dollars, which legacies or sums of money, I will and order shall be paid to the said respective legatees. Thirdly, I give and bequeath unto the children of my daughter Dolly Jones, deceased, one sixth part of my estate, after paying out the aforesaid legacies. Fourthly, I give and bequeath unto my five children, Martha Withers, Nimrod Ashby, William Ashby, Elizabeth Tutts and Thompson Ashby, the residue and remainder of my estate of what kind and nature whatever, to be equally divided among them, but it is my will and desire that the legacy which I have given to my daughter Martha Withers may not be under the controul, or subject to the payment of the debts, forfeitures or engagements of my daughter Martha Withers' husband, William Withers. Therefore, it is my will and desire that the legacie I have given to my said daughter Martha Withers, I give to her in trust nevertheless she being authorized to dispose of the legacy hereby given her as she may think proper, amongst her four children, to witt: Eliza, Mary, Samuel and Martha, at such times and in such portions as she may think proper, and I do hereby appoint my son Marshall Ashby, Trustee in order that the said deed of trust may be carried into effect, and in case said trustee shall refuse to act or die it is my desire that my Executors hereafter named may choose another trustee in order that said deed may be carried into effect. Lastly, I do appoint my three sons, Nimrod, William and Thomson my sole Executors of this my last will and testament, hereby revoking all former will by me made. In witness whereof I have hereunto set my hand and seal this twenty-fourth day of February in the year of our Lord one thousand eight hundred and twenty-six.

MARY ASHBY. {SEAL.}

Signed and acknowledged in the presence of Joseph Chilton, Josiah Tiddball, April 14, 1826; Robt. M. Stribling, April 24, 1826, at a Court held for Fauquier County on the 23d day of May, 1826.

This last will and testament of Mary Ashby, deceased, was proved by the oath of Joseph Chilton, a witness thereto, and ordered to be recorded. And the Executors named in said will having, by their note in writing addressed to the Court, refused to take upon themselves the burden of the execution hereof. On the motion of John Tutt, who made oath thereto, and together with William Ashby and John Ashby his Securities, entered into and acknowledged a bond in the penalty of five thousand dollars, conditioned as the law directs. Certificate is granted the said John Tutt for obtaining letters of administration on the said decedent's estate, with her will aforesaid annexed in due form.

Teste, JNO. A. W. SMITH, Clk.

A copy teste,
A. R. BARTENSTEIN, Clerk.

Order Books

Sept. 27, 1759. Captain Robert Ashby.
June 26, 1761. Captain Robert Ashby.
Sept. 24, 1761. Captain Nimrod Ashby.
Oct. 22, 1770. Captain John Ashby, Jr.

Thornton.

Overwharton Parish Register

The following entries in the name of Ashby are found in the Parish Register of Overwharton, Stafford County:

Elias Ashby married Winifred Million, Sept 4, 1745.
Frances, daughter of Elias and Winifred Ashby, born March 15, 1749.
Thomas Ashby, son of Robert and Mary Ashby, born March 5, 1749.
Jess, son of Margaret Ashby, born May 20, 1750.
Elisha, son of Charles and Winifred Ashby, born Dec. 26, 1751.
Millie, daughter of Robert and Mary Ashby, born Sept. 11, 1751.
Wilmoth, daughter of Robert Ashby, Jr., born Oct. 28, 1753.
John Ashby married Sarah Macoullough, Feb. 26, 1756.
Catherine Ashby married Isaac Murphy, Jan. 1, 1750.
John, son of John Ashby, born June 6, 1756.
William, son of Robert Ashby, baptized July 25, 1756.
Hankisson, son of Thomas and Mary Ashby, born Feb. 6, 1757.
Bailey Ashby, son of John and Sarah Ashby, born Nov. 22, 1758.

Thornton Family

THIS family, one of the oldest and most prominent in Virginia, originally settled in Gloucester County. The first of the line in this country was William Thornton, who is thought to have been a native of Yorkshire, England.

About the earliest mention of him was on May 11, 1646, when "William Thornton" obliged himself by a paper recorded in York County (including Gloucester), to care for the cattle of a certain John Liptrot until the latter came of age. On Feb. 16, 1665-6, William Thornton received a grant of 164 acres of land in Petsworth parish, Gloucester. He was a vestryman of the above named parish in 1677.

In the Essex County records there is a power of attorney dated September, 1673, from William Thornton of Gloucester, to James Kay of Rappahannock, on the north side of the river adjoining the lands of Anthony Buckner, Col. William Ball and Mr. Richard Whitehead. There is also recorded in Essex in 1708, a deed dated July 16, 1675, from "William Thornton of Gloucester, gent.," to Francis and Rowland, "two of his sons." William Thornton resided in Stafford County in 1708. The name of his wife is not known, but he had issue: William, Francis and Rowland.

I. WILLIAM THORNTON, JR., of Gloucester, who was born March 27, 1649; died Feb. 15, 1727. He was married three times, but the names of his wives is unknown. Like his father, he was a vestryman of Petsworth parish. Issue by first wife:

1. Elizabeth Thornton, born Aug. 26, 1672.
2. Margaret Thornton, born Aug. 14, 1674.
3. Mary Thornton, born May 11, 1676.
4. Esther Thornton, born Jan. 6, 1677.
5. Sarah Thornton, born Aug. 17, 1679.
6. Jane Thornton, born Aug. 10, 1681.
7. Judith Thornton, born Oct. 22, 1683.

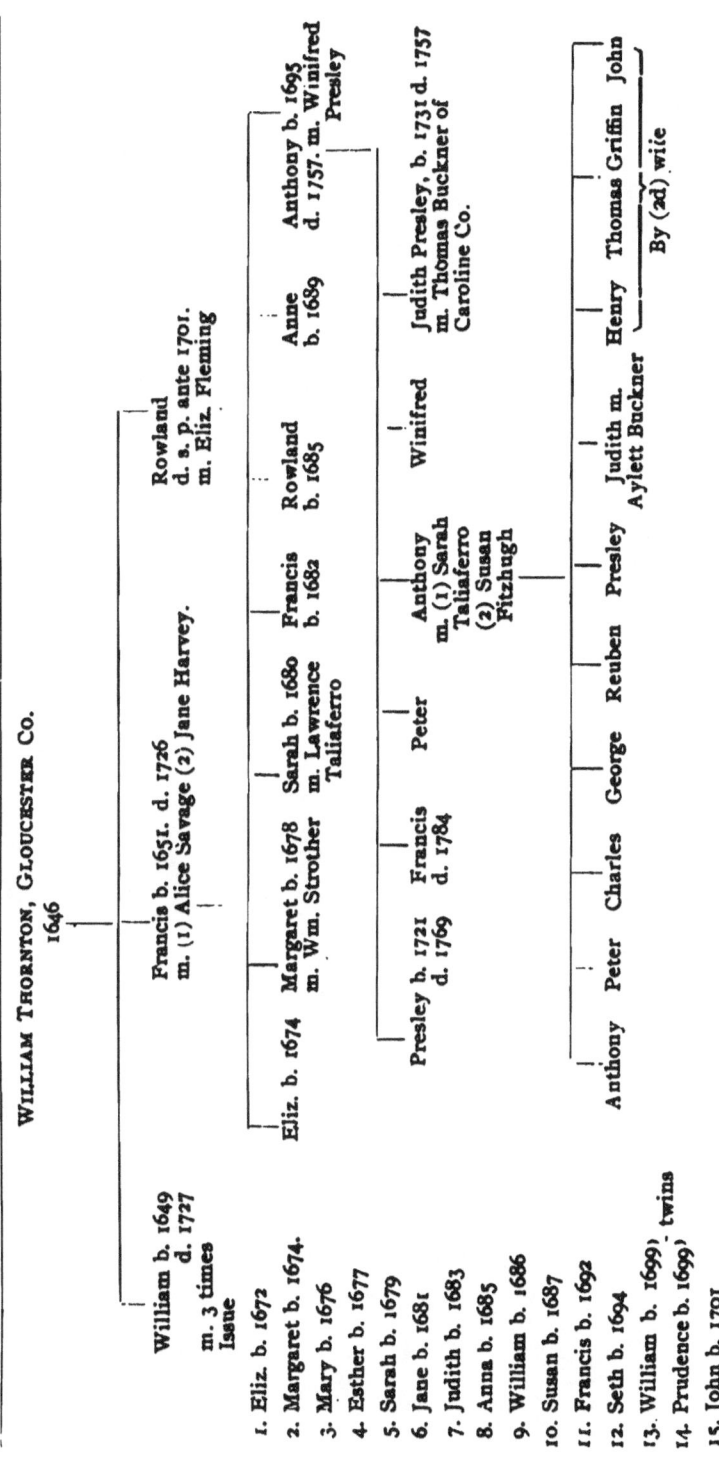

8. Anna Thornton, born June 15, 1685.
9. William Thornton, born Sept. 11, 1686.

ISSUE BY SECOND WIFE.

10. Susan Thornton, born June 11, 1687.
11. Francis Thornton, born June 7, 1692; died Feb. 6, 1737.
12. Seth Thornton, born Oct. 13, 1694.
13 and 14. William and Prudence Thornton (twins), born March 31, 1699.
15. John Thornton, born April 17, 1701.
16. Johanna Thornton, born Dec. 3, 1703.

II. FRANCIS THORNTON, son of William Thornton, Sr., was born Nov. 5, 1651; died 1726; and was a resident of Stafford County previous to 1700. We find his name as a witness to the will of Capt. Symon Miller of Rappahannock, Feb. 16, 1679. His first wife was Alice, daughter of Capt. Anthony Savage of Gloucester County. Capt. Savage was a Justice in 1660, and had considerable landed estates on the Rappahannock river. Francis Thornton's second wife was Jane, widow of John Harvey of Stafford, by whom he had no issue. Children by first marriage:

1. Elizabeth Thornton, born Jan. 3, 1674.
2. Margaret Thornton, born April 2, 1678; married William Strother, who was Sheriff of King George in 1726.
3. Sarah Thornton, born Dec. 17, 1680; married Lawrence Taliaferro.
4. Francis Thornton, born Jan. 4, 1682, of "Fall Hill."
5. Rowland Thornton, born Aug. 1, 1685; died 1748, of "Crowes," King George County.
6. Anne Thornton, born March 22, 1689.
7. Anthony Thornton of St. Paul's Parish, Stafford County, was born in 1695, and died in 1757. He was a Justice of Stafford. He married Winifred, daughter and heiress of Col. Peter Presley of "Northumberland House," Northumberland County. Anthony Thornton's will is dated Jan. 3, 1757, and was proved Nov. 8, in Stafford. In it he names, "son Presley, son Francis, son Anthony, daughter Winifred Bernard a tract of land in Spottsylvania County; son Peter, wife Winifred." Issue:

A. Presley Thornton of "Northumberland House," born 1721; died 1769.
B. Francis Thornton of "Society Hill," King George County; Justice of the Peace and Colonel of Militia; married Sarah Fitzhugh. He died in 1784.
C. Peter Thornton of "Rose Hill," Caroline County, married Ellen Bankhead.
D. Anthony Thornton, of whom presently.
E. Winifred Thornton, married —— Bernard.

F. Judith Presley Thornton, born Oct. 3, 1731; died June 19, 1757, and is buried at Port Royal. She married Thomas Buckner of "Mill Hill" and "Mount Pleasant," Caroline County, and left issue.

Anthony Thornton, above, resided at "Ormesby," Caroline County. This estate was acquired by Anthony Thornton, Sr., who built in 1715, the oldest portion of the present house. Anthony, Jr., was Sheriff of Caroline in 1767, and was alive in 1778. He was married twice, first in 1764 to Sarah Taliaferro, and secondly, to Susannah Fitzhugh. Issue by first wife:

1. Anthony Thornton.
2. Peter Thornton.
3. Charles Thornton.
4. George Thornton.
5. Reuben Thornton.
6. Presley Thornton.
7. *Judith Presley Thornton, married Major Aylett Buckner of Fauquier County, and had issue:
   A. Richard Aylett Buckner, born 1784; died in Greensburg, Ky., in 1849. (See Page 35.)
   B. Col. Thornton Buckner of Fauquier County.
   C. John Buckner.

Issue of Anthony and Susanna (Fitzhugh) Thornton:
8. Henry Thornton.
9. Thomas Griffin Thornton.
10. John Thornton.

III. ROWLAND THORNTON, son of William Thornton, Sr., was a witness to the will of James Yeats of Rappahannock, June 9, 1685-6. There is a deed in Richmond County in 1692, from Rowland Thornton of Rappahannock, planter, and his wife Elizabeth, daughter of Alexander Fleming, to Francis Thornton of same county, gent. Elizabeth, daughter of Capt. Alexander Fleming, sold land in what was afterwards King George, in 1699. In May, 1701, the bond of Elizabeth Thornton as administratrix of Rowland Thornton of Richmond County, deceased, was recorded. It is believed he left no issue.

---

*There is a difference of opinion in regard to the names of the children of Judith Presley Thornton and Major Aylett Buckner. Mr. Stanard in his "History of the Thorntons" states that they were (1) Thornton; (2) Richard; (3) James; (4) Elizabeth, who married —— Taylor of Kentucky; (5) Louisa, who married a Thomas Buckner.

Mr. Wm. Buckner McGroarty, who has made considerable research into the family history, gives the following as the offspring: (1) Thornton; (2) Catherine Taliaferro; (3) Aylett; (4) Elizabeth Aylett; (5) Laura Lightfoot; (6) Richard Aylett; (7) John; (8) Anthony.

Mr. McGroarty has probably confused the last named with the Anthony Buckner and wife Amy, whose daughter, Parthenia, was born Oct. 14, 1758. (Register of St. Pauls, Stafford County.) Of this Anthony, I can find no trace beyond the above mention, neither can I find good evidence that Aylett and Judith (Thornton) Buckner had more than three sons.—(Editor.)

OUTHOUSES AT FAIRFIELD—HOME OF JOHN THORNTON
GEN'L JACKSON DIED IN THE CABIN ON THE LEFT
THE MAIN HOUSE WAS DESTROYED BY FIRE

Claiborne-Buckner

This ancient family is mentioned in Domesday Book, A. D. 1086, Vol. I., 234. The descent of the family from England to Virginia is as follows, the dates named showing they were alive at that period:

I. Hervey de Cliburn, 1134.
II. Hervey de Cliburn, 1174.
III. Alan de Cliburne, 1216-67, married Joan de Ravenswet.
IV. Hervey de Cliburne, 1292-1307.
V. Geoffrey de Cliburne, 1315.
VI. Sir Robert de Cliburne, 1384, Knight of Westmoreland; married Margaret, daughter of Henry, Lord of Cundale and Kyme.
VII. John de Clyburn, 1392; married Margaret ——, whose second husband was John Warthcoppe of Warcup.
VIII. John Cleborne, 1423.
IX. Rowland Clyburne of "Cliborn Hall," 1456.
X. John Cliburne of Westmoreland, died 1489; married Elizabeth, daughter of Sir Thomas Curwen of Workington, County Cumberland.
XI. Thomas Cleburne, born 1467.
XII. Robert Cliborne of Kellerby, Yorkshire, 1533; married Emma, daughter of George Kirkbride of Northumberland.
XIII. Edmund Cleburne of Kellerby; married Anne Layton of Dalemain, County Cumberland.
XIV. Richard Cleburne of Kellerby, Yorkshire, and Cleburne, County Westmoreland; died Jan. 4, 1607.
XV. Edmund Claiborne of Cleburne Hall, married in 1576, Grace, daughter of Alan Bellingham of Helsington and Levins. She was born 1558, and died in 1594. Her tomb is in Catterick Church, Yorks.
XVI. William Claiborne, born 1587; died 1676. Came to Virginia 1621; was Colonial Secretary, and was appointed Surveyor General through the influence of his cousin Anne, Countess of Pembroke.
XVII. Col. Thomas Claiborne, born 1647; died 1683; married Sarah, daughter of Capt. Samuel Fenn.
XVIII. Thomas Claiborne, born 1680; died 1732; married three times and had 27 children. His third wife was Anne, daughter of Henry Fox of King William County.
XIX. Augustine Claiborne, born 1721; died 1787; married Mary Herbert.
XX. Herbert Claiborne, born 1746; married (1) Mary Ruffin; (2) Mary Browne, daughter of William Burnett Browne of "Elsing Green."
XXI. Herbert Augustine Claiborne, born 1784; died at Richmond 1841; married Delia, daughter of James Hayes, and Anne Dent, his wife.
XXII. Major John Hayes Claiborne, C. S. A., married Virginia, daughter of George Washington Bassett of Hanover County.
XXIII. Delia Claiborne, married General Simon Bolivar Buckner of Kentucky.

Unidentified Families

Buckners of South Carolina

BENJAMIN HEAP BUCKNER was born in Beaufort Co., So. Carolina, about 1780, and died at Oakhampton in 1825. The family data in the possession of his various descendants is conflicting. It is presumed that he was married twice, and accepting this hypothesis as correct, his first wife was a Miss Mary Riley, the date of whose death is unknown. His second wife, Margaret Morrison, was born in 1784, and died at Allendale in 1866. Known issue by first wife:

    1. Milton J. Buckner, born at Coosawhatchie, S. C., July 20, 1807. Joined in early life the U. S. Navy, leaving same to join the Confederates at the breaking out of the Civil War. Married July 7, 1855, to Caroline M. Scudder of Westfield, New Jersey, who died at Savannah, Ga., Feb. 17, 1884. Milton J. Buckner engaged in the shoe business at Savannah, in which city he died June 17, 1875. Issue:

      A.. Carrie M. Buckner, born 1864; married Frank L. George of Savannah, Ga.

      B. Elliotte E. Buckner, born Feb. 6, 1865; died May 20, 1898; married Dec. 22, 1887, at Macon, to Hattie McLean, born January 9, 1864, and left issue:

        aa. Elliotte E. Buckner, born Feb. 15, 1889.
        bb. Hugh McLean Buckner, born Oct. 30, 1890.
        cc. Hattie McLean Buckner, born April 26, 1892.
        dd. Caroline Scudder Buckner, born March 15, 1894.

      C. Marian S. Buckner, died Oct. 30, 1887, at Savannah.
      D. Catie A. Buckner, married Charles S. Ellis of Savannah.

By his second wife, Margaret Morrison, Benjamin Heap Buckner had known issue:

    1. Sarah Buckner, deceased.
    2. Mary Buckner, deceased.
    3. Jane Buckner, married ——— Griffin, and had issue a daughter, Florence.
    4. Benjamin Franklin Buckner, M. D., physician and planter, born at Robertville, S. C., April 11, 1818; died at Oakland Oct. 15, 1881; married Jane Harriet Nichols, born June 11, 1821; died at Allendale, 1866. Issue:

      A. Milton Thomas Buckner, born at Robertville, May 17, 1850; died June 22, 1901, at Savannah; married Jan. 3, 1871, to Lavinia Reynolds, born Feb. 12, 1856. Issue, thirteen children, those known being:

        aa. Jane Chaplin Buckner, born May 8th, 1874.
        bb. R. L. Buckner, Vicksburg, Miss.
        cc. Reynold R. Buckner, Waycross, Ga;
        dd. Benj. Franklin Buckner, born Jan. 2, 1880, Savannah.

Claiborne.

The Buckners of Virginia

  ee. M. H. Buckner, Savannah.
  ff. Annie E. Buckner, Savannah.
 B. Benjamin Heap Buckner, Fairfax, S. C.
 C. Henry Nichols Buckner, of Stafford, S. C., born at Hampton Aug. 28, 1855; married at Tillman Jan. 24, 1882, to Agnes Isabel McFail, born Sept. 28, 1856. Issue:
  aa. Franklin C. Buckner, born Jan. 3, 1883.
  bb. Iva Nichols Buckner, born Dec. 6, 1886.
  cc. Montrose Buckner, born Sept. 5, 1889.
  dd. Henry Otis Buckner, born March 22, 1892.
  ee. Benjamin Franklin Buckner, born June 4, 1894.
  ff. George William Buckner, born Sept. 17, 1896.
 D. Sarah Eliza Buckner.
 E. Franklin Pierce Buckner, deceased.
 F. John Moyandollar Buckner, Stafford, S. C.

Buckners of North Carolina

ELISHA BUCKNER of Chatham Co., N. C., was born Jan. 20, 1777, and died in Chatham Co. Feb. 26, 1826. He married———Steele, who died Sept. 22, 1845, at Clarke Co., Ill. Issue:

1. Henry Buckner, born June 10, 1798; died Sept. 28, 1834, near West Yorke, Clarke Co., Ill.
2. Anna Buckner, born May 1, 1800; died ———; married ——— Bailiff and left issue in Clarke Co., Ill.
3. Thomas Buckner, born Feb. 8, 1803; died Sept. 25, 1848.
4. John Buckner, born July 26, 1805; died in Clarke Co., Ill.
5. William Buckner, born Aug. 26, 1808; died in Clarke Co., Ill.
6. Sarah Buckner, born May 18, 1811; died Feb., 1818.
7. Elizabeth Buckner, born Nov. 13, 1816; died March, 1817.
8. Jesse Buckner, born Dec. 29, 1817.
9. Elisha Buckner, born Feb., 1818; died in Clarke Co., Ill.
10. Ruth Buckner, born Feb. 17, 1821.
11. Andrew Buckner, born March 14, 1825, living at Highland Center, Ia.

JESSE BUCKNER of Highland Center, Ia., son of Elisha Buckner, was born Dec. 29, 1817, at Chatham, N. C.; died Feb. 4, 1894, at Highland Center. He married at Sullivan Co., Ind., Elizabeth Osburn, born Feb. 4, 1817, died May 23, 1893. Issue:

1. Silas Buckner, born Oct. 4, 1839.
2. Cyrus Buckner, born Oct. 10, 1841.
3. Elisha S. Buckner, born Oct. 21, 1843.
4. Margaret R. Buckner, born May 11, 1846.
5. James K. Buckner, born July 21, 1849.
6. George W. Buckner, of whom presently.
7. Stephen A. Buckner } Twins, born April 23, 1855.
8. ——— L. Buckner

GEORGE W. BUCKNER, son of Jesse Buckner and Elizabeth, his wife, was born Nov. 25, 1851, at Wapello Co. Iowa, and is engaged in mercantile pursuits at Highland Center, Ia. He married Flora B. Weartham at Kirkville, who was born Feb. 10, 1862. Issue:

1. Minnie E. Buckner.
2. William R. Buckner.

BENJAMIN BUCKNER of Buncombe Co., North Carolina, died April 17, 1848. Of his antecedents nothing is known. He left the following issue:

1. William P. Buckner, Grantville, N. C.
2. Benjamin F. Buckner, Grantville, N. C.
3. Mitchel Buckner, Cletus, N. C.
4. David Buckner, Little Creek, N. C.
5. Squire J. Buckner, born in Buncombe Co., Jan. 18, 1828; died April 4, 1881; married in Henderson Co. Dec. 9, 1858, to Martha S. Drake, born Jan 3, 1837. Issue:

   A. Mary M. Buckner, born Feb. 13, 1860.
   B. James R. Buckner, born Nov. 23, 1861; married Milly L. McVentures.
   C. Richard N. Buckner, born Oct. 31, 1863.
   D. Harriet K. Buckner, born Sept. 23, 1866.
   E. Cletus D. Buckner, born 1877.

Jesse Buckner

Jesse Buckner was one of six or seven brothers who went from Virginia to North Carolina. Not all of their christian names are known, but it is thought that amongst them were Henry, William, John and possibly Aylett. The above named Jesse Buckner settled first in Cabarras County, and afterwards in Buncombe County, where he died at a very advanced age. In the Federal Census of North Carolina, taken in 1790, we find a Jesse Buckner in Chatham County, and in Rowan County, a John, David and Henry Buckner, and in Caswell District, a William Buckner. Jesse Buckner was survived by two children of his first wife.

1. Rebecca Buckner, married —— Harwood, and left descendants.
2. Nimrod Buckner, lived and died at the old homestead. He married Nancy, daughter of Col. Robert Anderson. Issue:

   A. Anderson Buckner.
   B. Jeremiah Buckner.
   C. Robert Buckner.
   D. Marion L. Buckner, died on his return from prison, at the close of the Civil War, leaving a widow and several sons, the eldest, Dallas Buckner, now of Democrat, N. C.
   E. Mary Buckner.
   F. Elizabeth Buckner.
   G. Rebecca Buckner, married Miller Hughey, and moved to Missouri with their family.
   H. Lydia Buckner.
   I. Sarah Buckner.

Of the above sons, Robert Buckner was born Jan., 1824, at the old homestead in Western North Carolina, and died at Alexander, N. C., in 1894. He married Susan A. Chambers, born 1828 at Flat Creek; died at Alexander, aged 70 years. Issue:

1. Rev. Albert Gallatin Buckner of Glasgow, Va., pastor of the Falling Spring Presbyterian Church, was born near Asheville, N. C., Jan. 17th, 1850. He began life as a teacher at an early age and was prepared for college at Newton Academy in

REV. A. G. BUCKNER, D.D.

Asheville. He graduated from Davidson College in June, 1879, and from Union Theological Seminary, Va., in May, 1882. Was licensed to preach in the same month, and was ordained in his first charge at Wadesboro, N. C., in December of the same year. In 1890 he accepted a call as pastor to Cynthiana, Ky., where he served acceptably for nine years. At the end of this period, among other calls, he was elected to the Presidency of King College, at Bristol, Tenn. Under his administration the institution at once revived, was saved to the church and has continued to send young men into the gospel ministry and other callings. While President of the college, Dr. Buckner was also active in church work, supplying churches in the vicinity of the college, and preaching in Presbyteries which control the institution. Finding the work of the pastorate more to his taste, he returned to it, resigning the Presidency two years before his term of office expired. He received his Doctor's degree from Austin College at Sherman, Texas. He was married in Sept., 1891, to Mary McRae of South Carolina, and to them has been born six children, three sons and three daughters.

2. Jas. McMurtry Buckner of Alexander, N. C., the father of a family of eleven living children, and a prosperous farmer.
3. Marion L. Buckner, Justice, Asheville, N. C.
4. Mary E. Buckner, now Mrs. Roberts of Alexander, N. C., a widow with three sons.
5. Rena Buckner, now Mrs. Eller of McKinney, Texas, who has four living sons, her only daughter having died soon after marriage a few years ago.
6. Laura A. Buckner, now Mrs. S. W. Coe of Baltimore, Md., the wife of Rev. Samuel W. Coe, and the mother of five children, four sons and one daughter.
7. Lula M. Buckner, now Mrs. Wm. H. White of Alexander, N. C., who has a large family of children.
8. Lydia J. Buckner, single, of Asheville, N. C.
9. Lillian A. Buckner, single, of Morganton, N. C.

Paschal Buckner

PASCHAL BUCKNER was born in Virginia in 1795, and died in Eastern Tennessee in 1845. He was married in 1830 to Cynthia Rash of North Carolina, who died in Bolivar, Mo., in 1877, aged 66 years. Issue:

1. Jacob Buckner.
2. George Washington Buckner was born in Tennessee April 8, 1833, and was married at Livingston Feb. 8, 1855, to Martha L. Copeland, born June 8, 1839; died Jan. 27, 1893. Issue:
    A. Julia A. Buckner, born Feb. 12, 1857; married April 11, 1875, to W. F. Hutcheson, Huron, Mo.
    B. Mary A. Buckner, born Dec. 1, 1858; married Oct. 20, 1891, to B. F. Kitt, Polk, Mo.

C. Viola L. Buckner, born Aug. 18, 1860; married June 23, 1881, to A. N. List. Both deceased.
D. Alta L. Buckner, born June 8, 1862; married Dec. 11, 1879, to J. F. Payne. Both deceased.
E. James C. Buckner, born Sept. 16, 1866; married June 8, 1886, to Emma Webb, Springfield, Mo.
F. William P. Buckner, twin brother of above, of whom presently.
G. Henry S. Buckner, born Sept. 30, 1868; married 1894, to Maud Grohe, Globe, Arizona.
H. George M. Buckner, born Jan. 20, 1870; married July 4, 1898, to Mertie Davis, San Francisco, Cal.
I. Lela A. Buckner, born Jan. 1, 1872; married July 4, 1893, to Waldo Whitaker, Reed, Mo.
J. Venna A. Buckner, born Oct. 20, 1882, Polk, Mo.

Reverend William P. Buckner of Joplin, Mo., minister of the M. E. Church South, was born at Bolivar, Mo., Sept. 16, 1866; married Sept. 16, 1893, to Dora Lee Vivion, born Oct. 14, 1865. Issue:

aa. Martha Kathryn Buckner, born Sept. 6, 1902.
bb. William Paschal Buckner, born March 13, 1904.

George Buckner

GEORGE BUCKNER, born in Virginia; married Annie Madison Saunders. Issue:

1. Mary Ann Buckner, married ——— Leavitt.
2. Frank Buckner, died.
3. George Buckner, born in King and Queen County, Virginia; died 1878, in Hopkinsville, Ky.; married Jane C. Ratcliffe; died 1888; born in Fairfax County, Virginia. Issue:
A. Annie Buckner.
B. Sue Buckner.
C. Charles Ratcliffe Buckner, born May 8, 1844, Hopkinsville, Ky.; married 1870, at Fayetteville, Ark., to Nannie Walker; born Dec. 24, 1843. Residence, Guthrie, Okla. Issue:
aa. Jane C. Buckner, born Nov. 12, 1871; died Oct. 7, 1896.
bb. George W. Buckner, born May 19, 1873, Guthrie, Okla.
cc. Charles R. Buckner, born April 2, 1876; died Dec. 6, 1891.
dd. David Walker Buckner, born Aug. 12, 1878, Lawton, Okla.

Philip Buckner

PHILIP BUCKNER was born presumably in Kentucky some time during the 1790's; died 1833; married about 1825, at Carmi, Ill., to Sarah Wilson, born in South Carolina, died in 1833. From the christian name Philip, it is conjectured that he belonged to the old Virginia stock of Buckners. Issue:

1. Jane Buckner, married ——— Shelby.

2. Edwin Buckner.
3. Emily Buckner, married James Devere.
4. Laura Buckner, married Col. John Whiting of 87th Illinois Infantry.
5. Josiah Buckner, born Aug. 1, 1833, at Effingham, Ill.; died Oct. 17, 1896; married 1855 at St. Louis, Mo., to Loranna Henry, born Jan. 7, 1840. Issue:
  A. William Edwin Buckner, born Sept. 24, 1856, at Larkinsburg, Ill.; married June 22, 1884, at Effingham, Ill., to Josie Howard, born March 16, 1864. Mr. Buckner's present residence is Chicago, Ill., where he is engaged in the practice of law. Issue:
    aa. William Edwin Buckner, born April 24, 1885.
    bb. Howard Aylett Buckner, born April 27, 1886.
    cc. Ernest Blaine Buckner, born Feb. 15, 1888.
    dd. Philip Horace Buckner, born June 20, 1892.
    ee. Claudius Earl Buckner, born June 20, 1892.
    ff. Kenneth Marion Buckner, born June 12, 1899; died March 11, 1901.
    gg. Paul Bertram Buckner, born Feb. 7, 1890; died Feb. 20, 1890.
    hh. Wallace Ruthven Buckner, born July 7, 1901.
    ii. Bruce Winston Buckner, born Nov. 11, 1902.
    jj. Donald Grant Buckner, born Oct. 15, 1904.
  B. Jemima Jane Buckner, born Sept. 5, 1858; died in infancy.
  C. Leni Leoti Buckner, born Oct. 1, 1860; married Charles P. Hunter, Champaign, Ill.
  D. Henry Clay Buckner, born Dec. 31, 1862; died in infancy.
  E. Franklin Fernando Buckner, born May 20, 1866, Mason, Ill.; married May 14, 1890, Lillian May Simmons, born Jan. 20, 1867. Mr. Buckner in youth was a school teacher, afterwards preparing for the ministry at Lombard College, Galesburg, Ill. Was ordained to the ministry of the Universalist Church Jan. 25, 1889, at Le Roy, Ohio, and has held pastorates in Le Roy, Ohio, Urbana, Ill., Macomb, Ill., Bristol, N. Y., and his present charge at Middleport, N. Y. Issue:
    aa. Marian Loranna Buckner, born Aug. 7, 1891.
    bb. Orello Simmons Buckner, born Aug. 27, 1893.
    cc. Dorothea Aurora Buckner, born Sept. 29, 1896.
    dd. Henry Edward Buckner, born Oct. 8, 1898.
  F. Philip Oscar Buckner, born April 15, 1868. Residing at Seattle, Wash.
  G. Aurora Leigh Buckner, born Sept. 7, 1877. Residing at Chicago, Ill.

Peter Ballard Buckner

PETER BALLARD BUCKNER of Clark County, Ky., born in Virginia; died Feb. 17, 1823; married Alice Catlett; died May 13, 1828. Issue:
  1. Harriet Buckner.
  2. Caroline Gibson Buckner, born March 4, 1804; married (1st) Oct. 4, 1821, John Cloud Hardin; married (2d) Nov. 6, 1855,

James Byars, by whom she had no issue. By first husband she had issue:

A. Mark Washington Hardin of Louisville, Ky., born Shelby County, April 26, 1831; married 1857, Nannie E. Vance, born Nov. 2, 1834; died March 18, 1900. Issue:
    aa. Lily Belle Hardin.
    bb. Charles Catlett Hardin, died.
    cc. Carrie Buckner Hardin.
    dd. Thomas Vance Hardin.
    ee. William Lee Hardin.
    ff. Fanny Sweeney Hardin, died.
    gg. Ernest Mills Hardin.
    hh. George Hayne Hardin.
    ii. Mark Lemon Hardin, died.
    jj. May Oliver Hardin, died.

3. Ballard Buckner, married Lucy Meriwether Anderson near Charlottesville, Va.; she died at Ivy Depot, Va. Issue:

A. Mary Buckner, married, had no issue.
B. Maria Fitzhugh Buckner, married ———— Davidson. Issue: Mrs. N. T. Ragland.
C. Edmund Anderson Buckner, died. Issue:
    aa. Robert Miller Buckner, died.
    bb. E. A. Buckner.

4. Robert Miller Buckner, born July 12, 1824, at Cattletsburg, Ky.; died in Louisville, 1864; married Dec. 23, 1852, Willina J. Abbott, born May 27, 1832; died April 21, 1869. Issue:

A. French Abbott Buckner, born Nov., 1853; died Aug. 1, 1857.
B. Willa L. Buckner, born June 21, 1860, at Paris, Ky.; married Nov. 7, 1882, James Miller Osburn of Louisville, born July 8, 1846. Issue:
    aa. Robert Buckner Osburn, born Sept. 16, 1883.
    bb. Alfred Gibson Osburn, born Oct. 29, 1886; died June 10, 1887.

William Buckner

WILLIAM BUCKNER was born in either Kentucky or Tennessee about 1790. He married Mary Merry, who died about 1842 in Madison County, Miss. Known issue:

1. Homer Buckner.
2. Virgil Buckner.
3. Merry Buckner.
4. William Buckner.
5. James Merry Buckner.
6. Elizabeth Buckner, married Dr. David M. Porter.
7. Harriett Buckner, married Edward Mann.

James Merry Buckner, son of William and Mary (Merry) Buckner, was born in Sumner County, Tenn., in 1811; died Jan. 31, 1840. He was a Baptist minister, and was also engaged in farming. He married in 1830 Minerva B. Cook of Davidson County, Tenn., who was born in 1810 and died July 7, 1857. Issue:

- A. Joseph Samuel Buckner, M.D., of Fredonia, Ky., born in Davidson County, Tenn., April 20, 1832; married (1st) Miss C. V. Nash, born 1846; died Dec. 29, 1870; married (2d) Dollie E. Maxwell, born Nov. 7, 1852; died July 1, 1899.
    - aa. James Milton Buckner, born Aug. 31, 1866; died 1902. (Issue of 1st marriage.)
    - bb. Cora Lee Buckner, born Feb. 24, 1878.
    - cc. Malcom Jeter Buckner, born Nov. 8, 1874; died Jan. 2, 1902.
    - dd. Lena Buckner, born Nov. 26, 1880.
    - ee. Mary M. Buckner, born April 6, 1889; died March 6, 1892.
- B. Sarah Elizabeth Buckner, born April 6, 1834; married —— in 1851; died 1903.
- C. Mary Eliza Buckner, born 1836; died in 187—.
- D. Minerva Affia Buckner, born 1838; married in 1857; died 1880.
- E. James Merry Buckner, born 1840; died 1904, leaving issue.

Elisha Buckner

ELISHA BUCKNER was a resident of Albemarle County, Va., but of his parentage nothing is known. He removed to Green River, Indiana, but died in Albemarle County, whence he had returned on a visit. His known children were:

1. Henry Buckner.
2. William Buckner, who left issue.
3. Elisha Buckner, who left issue.
4. John Buckner, removed to Tennessee. Has a son, Frederick Buckner, living at West York, Ill.
5. Anna Buckner, married —— Bailiff, a prominent Presbyterian minister, the founder of one of the first Churches in Crawford County, Ill. He and his wife are buried on the site of the old log church at West York.

Henry Buckner, eldest son of Elisha Buckner, married a Miss Evans, and had issue:

1. Charles Buckner.
2. William Buckner.
3. Enos Buckner, born July 8, 1832; died near Annapolis, Ill.; married July 5, 1850, to Jane T. Canaday, born Sept. 26, 1832; died Aug. 23, 1882. Issue:
    - A. H. T. Buckner, born 1858, of Orange, Ill.
    - B. William C. Buckner, born 1860; married ——, deceased.
    - C. Charlotte Buckner, married —— McDaniel, Casey, Ill.
    - D. E. M. Buckner, Brazil, Ind.
    - E. John F. Buckner, Attorney-at-Law, born June 5, 1862, resides at Vienna, Ill.; married (1st) to Rosa Martin, March 20, 1892,

died March 20, 1898, by whom he had issue one child, J. Faith Buckner, born May 23, 1896.

John F. Buckner married (2d) April 15, 1900, Anna Hook, by whom he has issue:
    aa. Mary Buckner, born May 5, 1902.
    bb. Ida Jane Buckner, born May 20, 1905.

4. Jemima Buckner, married ―― Bradbury.
5. Sarah Buckner, married ―― Bell.
6. Jesse W. Buckner, married ―― Miller of New York and had issue:
A. Henry Buckner.
B. Richard Buckner.
C. William W. Buckner.
D. Charles C. Buckner.
E. Phylena Buckner, married ―― Allsman of Bourbon Co., Mo.
F. Ellen Buckner, married ―― Hills of Plymouth, O. T.
G. Ivy M. Buckner, married ―― Jackson of Greenland, Mich.
H. Sarah Buckner, married ―― McClure, of Marshall, Ill.
I. F. M. Buckner of Marshall, Ill., born June 6, 1853. Taught school for several years, and was ordained an elder in the M. E. Church in 1879. Married Ellen Plank of Richland Co., Ohio, June 23, 1873. Issue:
    aa. L. Edison Buckner.
    bb. Roscoe Buckner.
    cc. Roy Buckner.
    dd. Lena Buckner.

James Buckner

JAMES BUCKNER was born in Virginia about 1780, and died in Tennessee in 1863. He married Judith Womack, who died in 1856.

1. James Buckner, son of above, was born Oct. 16, 1820, in McMinn County, Tenn., and was killed at Alphareta, Georgia, in 1864. Married in 1838 to Susan Stephenson, born Oct. 17, 1819; died 1858. Issue:
A. Garrett D. Buckner of Petersburg, Tenn., born at Athens, Tenn., March 17, 1839; married at Riceville, Sept. 1, 1858, to Sallie E. Owens, born Sept. 27, 1839; died Aug. 15, 1891. Issue:
    aa. Philip M. Buckner, born Nov. 21, 1860.
    bb. L. C. Buckner, born Sept. 12, 1862.
    cc. E. A. Buckner, born Dec. 13, 1867; died 1889.
    dd. M. O. Buckner, born Oct. 17, 1872; died 1873.
    ee. G. A. Buckner, born Oct. 22, 1874.
    ff. C. L. Buckner, born Sept. 28, 1876.
    gg. S. N. Buckner, born June 13, 1879.
    hh. L. M. Buckner, born March 30, 1882.
B. W. A. Buckner, born 1840; died 1872.
C. J. M. Buckner, born 1842; died 1873.
D. Elizabeth Ann Buckner, born 1844; died 1902.
E. D. L. Buckner, born 1846; living at Maxwell, Tenn.

John Washington Buckner

JOHN WASHINGTON BUCKNER of Clark County, Ky., married in 1794, Mary Ann Martin, born in Albermarle County, Va., in 1778; died in Lexington in 1853. She was a daughter of Major John Martin, who served in the Revolutionary army. John W. Buckner survived his marriage but a few years, his widow marrying secondly, Colonel Richard Taylor, son of Commodore Richard Taylor and a great great grandson of James Taylor, the immigrant ancestor of the family, who is believed to have come to Virginia from Carlisle, England.

Issue by John Washington Buckner:

I. Elizabeth Buckner, born in Clark County, Ky., in 1795; married the Rev. Thomas P. Dudley of Winchester, and had issue:
  1. William Dudley, d. s. p.
  2. John W. Dudley, born in Winchester in 1816; married Harriet McDonald of Lexington. Removed to Missouri in 1855. Issue:
   A. Alice Dudley.
   B. Thomas P. Dudley.
   C. Mary Dudley.
II. John Washington Buckner, Jr., born in Clark Co., Ky., in 1798. He married first, in 1820, Catherine G. Crockett, a daughter of Colonel Anthony Crockett, and niece of the celebrated Colonel David Crockett, who was a Member of Congress from Tennessee. By Catherine Crockett, who died in 1844, he had nine children, and by his second wife, Sarah Margaret Fletcher, whom he married in 1846, he had issue, one child. John W. Buckner, Jr., resided in Arkansas until 1842, when he removed to Mississippi, but returned to Arkansas in 1858, at which time he lived near Barfield Point. Issue:
  1. Mary Ann Buckner, born in 1821; married in 1843, Foster G. Finley, and died in 1844.
  2. Elizabeth M. Buckner, born in Tennessee in 1823; married in 1842, William J. Jones of St. Francis County, Ark., and had issue:
   A. John Jones, born 1843.
   B. Eliza Jones, born 1845.
   C. Sally Jones, born 1848.
   D. Anna Jones, born 1855.
  3. William E. Buckner, born in 1825; married in 1847, Fanny Young of Arkansas, and had issue:
   A. Martha Buckner, born 1848.
   B. James G. Buckner, born 1850.
   C. Bettie Buckner, born 1851.
   D. Helen M. Buckner, born 1854.
  4. Richard T. Buckner, born 1827.
  5. Catherine Crockett Buckner, born 1830.
  6. John Washington Buckner, born 1832.
  7. Anthony Crockett Buckner, born 1834.

8. James Lewis Buckner, born 1836; died 1855.
9. Overton G. Buckner, born 1839.
10. Mary Allen Buckner (by 2nd wife), born 1850.

Buckner-RoBards

WILLIAM BUCKNER of Green County, Ky., was born in Virginia about 1760. He was probably a scion of the Caroline County Buckners, but his parentage is unknown to his descendants. He was Surveyor-General for the State of Kentucky and also represented Green County in the Legislature of 1822. He died in 1843 at the age of 83 years. His wife was Elizabeth Lewis RoBards, and by her he had issue:

I. Elizabeth Lewis Buckner, married Judge Richard Aylett Buckner of Greensburg, Ky., son of Aylett and Judith (Presley Thornton) Buckner of Caroline and afterwards of Fauquier County, Va.
II. Nancy Buckner, married Stanton Buckner.
III. Polly Buckner, married William Winlock.
IV. Louisa Buckner, married Charner Patterson.
V. Sallie Buckner, married Colby B. Cowherd.
VI. Jane Buckner, married John M. McCorkle.
VII. Matilda Buckner, married Thornton Buckner.
VIII. Gabriel Buckner, married —— Hazlewood.
IX. Robert RoBards Buckner, born in Virginia, Dec. 22, 1807; died in Auxvasse, Mo., Feb. 28, 1877; married in 1828 at Green County, Ky., to Mary L. Tate, born in 1810; died in 1864. Issue:
   1. John Tate Buckner, of whom presently.
   2. Margaret Elizabeth Buckner, born 1831; married ——, 1850; died June, 1851.
   3. William G. Buckner, born 1833; died Feb. 6, 1851.
   4. Elijah S. Buckner, born 1835; married ——, 1859.
   5. Sarah Matilda Buckner, born 1837; married ——, 1858.
   6. Frank Thornton Buckner, born 1839; married ——, 1865.

John Tate Buckner, son of Robert RoBards Buckner and Mary L. Tate, was born at Saloma, Green County, Ky., July 13, 1829; married in 1851 to Ellen M. Bernard, born Aug. 21, 1830. Issue:
   1. Robert R. Buckner, born Jan. 2, 1853, of Mexico, Mo.
   2. Thomas Bernard Buckner, Attorney-at-Law, of Kansas City, Mo., born Sept. 8, 1854, in Calloway County, Mo.; married at Elysian Fields, Texas, Jan. 8, 1880, to Effie Hendricks, born March 17, 1857. Issue:
      A. James T. Buckner, born Dec. 23, 1880.
      B. Sterling H. Buckner, born Sept. 24, 1883.
      C. Margaret Buckner, born March 17, 1885.
      D. Thomas Bernard Buckner, born July 12, 1887.
   3. Mary C. Buckner, born Aug. 9, 1856; died Jan. 8, 1898.
   4. William Tate Buckner, born 1858; died Sept. 15, 1881.
   5. John Edward Buckner, born 1860, of Auxvasse, Mo.
   6. Joseph Frank Buckner, born 1864, of Auxvasse, Mo.

The first of the RoBards' line in Virginia, was John RoBards, who died in 1755 in Goochland County. He emigrated from Wales in 1710, and married Sarah, daughter of John Hill. John RoBards' will is dated Dec. 5, 1754, and was probated May 20, 1755, by George Payne, gent., and George Payne, Jr.

William RoBards, son of the above, was married twice, his first wife, whose name is unknown, dying Sept., 1756, leaving the following children:

I. John RoBards, married Sarah Marshall in 1772.
II. William RoBards, Jr., married (1st) Elizabeth Pleasants Cocke, in Jan., 1774; married (2d) Elizabeth Lewis in Sept., 1781.
III. James RoBards, married Mary Massie in 1774.
IV. Jean RoBards, married Samuel Mosby in 1773.

William RoBards, Sr., married (2d) Elizabeth Lewis, Jan. 5, 1758. She was a daughter of Joseph Lewis, Sr., granddaughter of William Lewis, Sr., 1708, who was son of John Lewis, colonist from Wales, testator, 1687, of Henrico County. William RoBards died in 1783. Issue:

1. Lewis RoBards, born Dec. 13, 1758. He served in the Revolutionary War, with the rank of Captain. He obtained a divorce from his first wife, Rachel Donaldson, who eloped with a lawyer, and whom she subsequently married. He married (2d) Hannah, daughter of General James Winn of Lexington, Ky.
2. Capt. George RoBards, born Aug. 5, 1760, enlisted in his sixteenth year in the 14th Virginia Continental Line, under Col. Charles Lewis. His Captain, Moses Hawkins, was killed at Brandywine, and he was promoted to Orderly Sergeant, his Company consolidating with the 10th Va. Regt. In 1780, he was commissioned Lieutenant in the 4th Va. State Line. He participated in the battle of Camden, in which engagement his half-brother, James, was severely wounded. In 1781 he was commissioned Captain, and served until the end of the war. He married in 1785, Elizabeth Barbara, daughter of Charles Sampson and his wife Ann Porter.
3. Jesse RoBards, born April 7, 1762; married —— Perkins; lived in Gerrard County, Ky.
4. Sally RoBards, born Jan. 25, 1765; married Capt. John Jouett; she was the mother of Matthew Jouett, the distinguished Kentucky artist, and grandmother of James E. Jouett, Rear Admiral, U. S. Navy.
5. Joseph RoBards, born Dec. 11, 1766; married —— Harris; lived in Breckenridge County, Ky.
6. Elizabeth Lewis RoBards, born April, 1771; married William Buckner, Surveyor-General of Kentucky.
7. Robert RoBards, born Dec. 7, 1773; died unmarried.

Henry Buckner

According to family tradition, Henry Buckner settled in Virginia shortly before the Revolution. His wife's name was Catherine. Beyond this nothing further can be ascertained in regard to them. Issue:

I. Burrow Buckner, Baptist minister, born June 30, 1796, in Virginia; died Aug. 31, 1861, Dade County, Mo.; married Matilda Maddox, born Feb. 4, 1798; died March 17, 1875. Known issue:
  1. William George Buckner of San José, Cal., Evangelist, born Aug. 27, 1828, Munroe County, Tenn.; married (1st) 1850, Sarah Frances Butts, born April 5, 1832; (2nd) June 23, 1861, Nancy Butts, sister of first wife; (3rd) May 29, 1870, Mrs. Rosa C. L. Rollins née Rees; (4th) 1902, Theresa Steiner, a native of Copenhagen, Denmark. Mr. Buckner served at the age of 18 years as private in the Mexican War. After his discharge he settled in Kansas during the stormy period which occurred after the Kansas-Nebraska Act of 1854. At the commencement of the Civil War he removed with his family to California. In the middle of the '90's he went to Pitcairn Island as a Missionary, and upon his return, after a brief sojourn in Alabama, settled at San José, Cal. Issue:
     A. Henry Freeland Buckner, born May 29, 1851; married twice and resides at Chelan, Wash.
     B. James Burrow Buckner, born Nov. 4, 1852; married Alfa Styles. Both dead.
     C. Andrew Brown Buckner of Lemoore, Cal., born Dec. 7, 1855, at Fort Scott, Kansas; married March 3, 1881, at Modesto, Cal., to Lillie Estella Rees, born Jan. 18, 1862. Issue:
        aa. Delwin Rees Buckner, graduate of University of California, 1905, born Nov. 23, 1882, at Lemoore.
        bb. William Rollo Buckner, born Oct. 21, 1884, at Lemoore.
     D. William J. Van Buckner of Hanford, Cal., born Aug. 31, 1859, at Fort Scott, Kansas; married Nov. 27, 1884, Mary L. Sprague, born Feb. 23, 1862, at Columbus, Wis. When Tulare County, Cal., was divided in 1893, Mr. Buckner was elected Sheriff of the new county—Kings—and was re-elected in 1894, 1898 and 1903. He is a director of the Hanford National Bank, charter member of the Independent Order of Foresters, member of Knights of Pythias Lodge 194, Woodmen of the World and Knights of Maccabees. On March 14, 1900, he was elected 1st Lieutenant of Company I, 6th Regiment, California National Guards, serving two terms of two years each. For several years was Vice-President of the State Sheriffs' Association, becoming President of the same in 1905. Issue:
        aa. Ross William Buckner, born Aug. 5, 1885.
        bb. Vosburg Buckner, born June 21, 1886; died in infancy.
        cc. Hugo James Buckner, born Dec. 4, 1888.
        dd. Frank Leroy Buckner, born Dec. 10, 1891.
        ee. Carroll Van Buckner, born Dec. 25, 1893.
        ff. Harry Sprague Buckner, born Aug. 5, 1895.
     E. Rebecca May Buckner, daughter of William G. and his second wife, Nancy (Butts) Buckner, born June 23, 1866; died Feb. 21, 1877.
  2. Henry DeWitt Buckner, deceased, son of Burrow and Matilda Maddox Buckner. Issue:
     A. Mrs. Nancy Ragsdale, Lemoore, Cal.
  3. James Small Buckner, Ash Grove, Mo. Issue:

ROBERT COOK BUCKNER, D.D., L.L.D.

The Buckners of Virginia

    A. John Buckner, Ash Grove.
  4. Richard Buckner (unheard of for years, probably dead). Issue:
    A. William Buckner, Hanford, Cal.
    B. Mrs. Mary Poland, Hanford, Cal.
    C. Mrs. Rosa Nealey, Memphis, Tenn.
  5. Katherine Buckner, married —— Williams, Lawrenceburg, Mo. Issue:
    A. Mrs. Kate Harsbarger, Long Beach, Cal.
  6. Nancy Buckner, married —— Gillmore, Willard, Mo. Issue:
    A. James Beckley Gillmore, Willard, Mo.
  7. Elizabeth Buckner, married —— Darrel. Issue:
    A. Stephen Darrel, Leadville, Col.
  8. Parmalia Buckner, married —— Roundree. No issue.

II. Rev. Daniel Buckner, Baptist minister, son of Henry and Susanna Buckner, was born in South Carolina in 1801; died in Dallas, Texas, Sept., 1883; married Mary Hampton, born 1799; died Clarkesville, Texas, 1861. Issue:

  1. Rev. Henry F. Buckner, born 1818; died in Eufaula, I. T., after serving as Missionary for 37 years. Left issue, three sons.
  2. Harriet Buckner, born 1827; died in infancy.
  3. Bennett Burrow Buckner, born 1826. Served with General Taylor in Mexican War, and died from wounds and exposure. No issue.
  4. Miriam Buckner, born 1831; married Aaron Holt. Issue:
    A. Rev. A. J. Holt, President of Tennessee College, Knoxville, Tenn.
  5. Rev. Robert Cook Buckner, D.D., L.L.D. Founder, President and General Manager of the Buckner Orphans' Home, Dallas, Texas; is one of the most beloved and respected citizens of the Lone Star State. He was born Jan. 3, 1833, at Madisonville, Tenn.; married July 7, 1854, to Viena Long, born Aug. 6, 1837, and has issue:
    A. Mary Belle Buckner, born Sept. 10, 1855; married Sept. 30, 1875, Rev. L. W. Coleman, Brock, Texas.
    B. Maggie Buckner, born Nov. 22, 1857; married Feb. 1, 1877, James L. Goode, Dallas, Texas.
    C. Samuel Buckner, born and died July, 1860.
    D. Addie Buckner, born Oct. 5, 1862; married May 25, 1881, Dr. A. F. Beddoe.
    E. Robbie Cook Buckner, born Jan. 5, 1867; married June 26, 1860, Dr. Thomas L. Westerfield, Dallas, Texas.
    F. James Dudley Buckner, born April 14, 1871; married Dec. 6, 1893, Sadie McNeil, Dallas, Texas.
    G. Rev. Hal. Freeland Buckner, born Oct. 13, 1878; married Sept. 4, 1901, Bertha Aston, Chapel Hill, Texas.

Buckners of Culpeper County

The Culpeper County Buckners are undoubtedly offshoots from the Caroline County branch. In the Culpeper records we find the will of Horace Buckner, dated March 13, 1820, probated Aug. 21, 1821. Nothing has been learned in reference to the father of Horace, but it is known that he had a brother, George Buckner. The children mentioned in the will are:

I. Frances Buckner.
II. Dr. Horace Buckner, married Fanny, daughter of Francis Thornton and Ann Thompson. Issue:
   1. Archibald Buckner.
   2. Otway Buckner.
   3. Ritchie Buckner.
   4. Walker Buckner.

Taliaferro-Buckner

I. Robin (Robert?) Taliaferro of "Blenheim," Caroline County.
   1. Norborne Taliaferro, married Elizabeth Bankhead Buckner, a niece of President Madison. Issue:
      A. Jane Taliaferro, d. s. p.
      B. Dr. Wm. T. Warren Taliaferro.
      C. Norborne Taliaferro, d. s. p.
      D. Lucy Taliaferro.
      E. James Monroe Taliaferro, d. s. p.
      F. Judith Buckner Taliaferro, d. s. p.

Dr. Wm. Thomas Warren Taliaferro married Fannie Barnes Harrison, daughter of Betsy Harrison, sister of William Fitzhugh of "The Grove," Fauquier County. Issue:
   1. Thomas Dorsey Taliaferro, married his cousin, Eliza Lewis Madison, daughter of Major Ambrose Madison, of Woodbury Forest, Orange County.
   2. William Taliaferro, married Susan, daughter of Col. S. V. Gatewood of Mountain Grove, Bath County, Va. Issue:
      A. Eugenia Massie Taliaferro.
      B. Lucy Mary Taliaferro, d. s. p.
      C. Celia Mouroe Taliaferro.
      D. A son, died in infancy.
      E. Roberta Willis Taliaferro, married her cousin, William Willis Madison, brother of Eliza Lewis Madison.
      F. Cecilia Harrison Taliaferro, married M. V. B. Powell of Texas.
      G. Leslie Sewell Taliaferro, married Abbie Gardner of Texas.
      H. Mary Buckner Taliaferro, married A. W. May of Texas.

Henry William Buckner

Henry William Buckner, married a Miss Boman, and died in Hart County, Ky., at the age of 84 years. Issue:
   1. James Murphy Buckner, born Hart County, Ky.; died in Sullivan County, Mo., in 1893; married in Hart County to Emelia F. Hawkins, who died in 1857. Issue:
      A. Elliott Hartzel Buckner of Sherman, Texas, born in Hart County, Ky., July 22, 1845; married Aug. 10, 1865, to Mary Frances Irelan, born Jan. 14, 1847; died April 6, 1898. Issue:
         aa. Martha Ellen Buckner, born May 16, 1867; died March 12, 1892.
         bb. Mary Catharine Buckner, born April 26, 1868; deceased.
         cc. Daisy Delphine Buckner, born March 20, 1873.

James Madison Buckner

James Madison Buckner, married Elizabeth Bensley, and had the following issue:

1. Charles Grant Buckner.
2. Lewis Penrose Buckner.
3. Elizabeth Neil Buckner.
4. John Simpson Buckner of Ontario, Wis., born at Charleston, Ill., Feb. 14, 1870; married May 5, 1892, at Ridgeway, Mo., to Lydia A. Newlin, born March 13, 1876. Issue:
   A. Leo Fay Buckner, born March 13, 1893.
   B. Hazel Buckner, born March 24, 1895.
   C. James Madison Buckner, born Feb. 28, 1897.

Bucknor of New York

William Goelet Bucknor, born in New York City about 1798; died 1852; was a well-known stock broker. He was married at St. John's Church in 1819, to Emily A. Bulow, born 1803; died 1879. The father of William G. Bucknor was Cornelius Bucknor, but his wife's name is unknown. Catharine, daughter of Cornelius Bucknor, married a Mr. McVicar, but both she and her descendants are deceased. Issue of William G. and Emily A. Bucknor:

I. William Bucknor of Stapleton, Staten Island, born in New York City Feb. 19, 1835. Unmarried.

John F. Buckner

John Farrington Buckner was born at Fayettville, North Carolina, May 12, 1823; died at Greenfield, Iowa, in 1900. His brother, Jackson Buckner, resided at Lincoln, Neb. John F. Buckner married Dec. 21, 1847, Susan V. DeWitt. Issue:

A. Dr. Samuel S. Buckner of Missouri.
B. Henry Jackson Buckner, Clearfield, Ia.
C. Lucretia A. Buckner, married Frank Kobb of Early, Ia.
D. Homer Guy Buckner of Berkeley, Cal., married at Woodbine, Ia., to Nellie DeCou.
E. Arthur G. Buckner, Sioux City, Ia.
F. Carrie May Buckner, Sioux City, Ia.
G. Ethel Blanche Buckner, Sioux City, Ia.
H. George F. Buckner, deceased.
I. Charles W. Buckner, deceased.
J. John Wesley Buckner, D.D., deceased.

Henry S. Buckner

HENRY SULLIVAN BUCKNER, was born in Fauquier Co., Va. and died at New Orleans, La. He was married at Louisville, Ky. to Katherine Allan, who died Oct. 8, 1882. Issue:

1. Ellen Buckner, deceased; married Newton Eustes of New York.
2. Katherine Buckner, deceased.
3. Laura Buckner.

4. Newton Buckner, deceased, who had Mortimer N. Buckner, of New York.
5. James Buckner of New Orleans, born in Louisville, Ky., Oct. 13, 1837; married Jan. 23, 1866 to Julia Rawle, born July 5, 1841. Issue:
   A. Frank Rawle Buckner, born Dec. 16, 1866.
   B. Helen Buckner, born Jan. 7, 1868.
   C. Henry Buckner, born Sept. 14, 1869.
   D. Laura Buckner, born Dec. 25, 1871.
   E. James Buckner, born Feb. 16, 1873.
   F. Frederick Buckner, born Sept. 28, 1874.
   G. Rawle Buckner, born July 24, 1876.
   H. Eustis Buckner, born Feb. 7, 1878.
   I. Archie Allan Buckner, born April 16, 1879.
   J. Julia Rawle Buckner, born March 11, 1881.
   K. Christian Buckner, born Dec. 17, 1884.

James Robinson Buckner

JAMES ROBINSON BUCKNER, was born in Kentucky, and died at Nevada, Mo., Aug. 18, 1878. He married at Lexington, Mo., Oct. 24, 1865, Matilda Donohoe, who was born June 6, 1843. The brothers and sisters of James R. Buckner were, Mary Buckner, William Buckner, Anna Buckner, who married ———— Bean; Martha Buckner and Thomas Buckner, all of whom are now deceased.

Issue of James R. and Matilda Buckner.

1. William Herbert Buckner, born Aug. 11, 1866; died Jan. 17, 1877.
2. Royle Albert Buckner, born Jan. 26, 1869; at Nevada, Mo.
3. Mattie Buckner, born May 26, 1871; married 1891 to H. M. Moffitt of St. Louis, Mo. and has issue a daughter Margorie.
4. Fannie Buckner, born Aug. 26, 1874; married Oct. 19, 1897, P. H. Klinkenberg of Cawker City, Kansas.

Archimedes James Bucknor

Archimedes James Bucknor was born in New Brunswick, Aug. 8, 1805; died Dec. 13, 1877, at Germantown, Pa.; married in 1834, Emeline Levinia Deringer, born Feb. 9, 1814; died Jan. 30, 1887. Issue:

1. Archimedes J. Bucknor, Jr., born 1837; d. s. p. Nov. 2, 1878.
2. Amanda Bucknor, born 1839; died 1843.
3. Marian Young Bucknor, born March 31, 1842; married Oct. 29, 1862, William Ashbridge James, stockbroker of Philadelphia, born Dec. 31, 1832; died April 26, 1886. Issue:
   A. Archimedes John James, born Feb. 22, 1864; married Sept. 12, 1900, Mrs. Minnie Warren.
   B. William Bucknor James, born March 1, 1866; married July 2, 1896, Marie Carleton Wiltbank.
   C. Marion Ashbridge James, born Oct. 12, 1873.

WILLIAM HEALD BUCKNOR

4. Virginia Bucknor, born Oct. 14, 1844; married Carter Landon Wormeley of Richmond, Va.
5. William Heald Bucknor, born March 17, 1846, of Germantown, Pa.; married (1st) Sarah Pearson. Issue:
   A. Mary Pearson Bucknor, born 1872; married John Cochran, who is now deceased.
   B. Florence Bucknor, born 1877; married Samuel Collam.
   C. Ethel P. Bucknor, born 1879.

William Heald Bucknor, married (2d) Elizabeth Weyforth. Issue:
   A. William Archimedes Bucknor.
6. Charles Bucknor, born 1848; died young.
7. Charles Bucknor (2d), born 1850; married Pauline Reaney. Issue:
   A. Pauline R. Bucknor, married Sept. 17, 1901, Charles Barrington.
   B. Laura Jayne Bucknor.
   C. Charles Bucknor, Jr.
8. Ann Eliza Bucknor, born June 27, 1851, married 1871, DeWitt Jayne, died Aug. 27, 1875. Married (2d) Oct. 16, 1879, Henry Chase Starr. Issue by first marriage:
   A. Annie Jayne, born March 18, 1872; married June 1, 1893, Henry Albert Thomas. Issue:
       aa. Laura Jayne Thomas.
       bb. DeWitt Jayne Thomas.
   B. Laura Bucknor Jayne.

New England Buckners

According to *Savage's Genealogical Register*, the name of Buckner is found in New England in 1657, which is earlier than the first mention of the name in Virginia. In 1668 we find a Charles Buckner, schoolmaster, and his wife Mary, described as being of Boston, and who on April 12th of the same year, sold land in Dover to Job Clements. No further trace of them can be found, so that if they did not return to England, they probably left no issue.

In the expedition against Louisbourg in 1745, a Samuel Buckner served under Lieut. Geo. Gerrish, and he is probably the same person as Serg't Samuel Buckner of the 9th Company, 1st Massachusetts Regiment, Capt. William Warner, who was a member of the expedition. As the christian name, Samuel, is well known in the Virginia branch of the family, he may have belonged to that line. The above named are the only Buckners found in the New England records.

Addenda

Page 99. The following detailed information concerning the Blackerby family, was received too late to be inserted in its proper sequence.

I. Ann Whitaker Buckner, daughter of William and Lucy M. T. Buckner of Kentucky, was married at Augusta, Ky., to William Orear Blackerby, born in Fauquier County, Va., and son of Jeduthan Blackerby. They had issue:
   1. Dr. John Marcus Blackerby, born May 21, 1821.
   2. William Buckner Blackerby, born Nov. 30, 1822; deceased.
   3. Dr. Jeduthan Orear Blackerby, of whom presently.
   4. George Washington Blackerby, born Sept. 9, 1826; deceased.
   5. Thornton Taliaferro Blackerby, born Oct. 16, 1829; deceased.
   6. Mary Orear Blackerby, born Oct. 16, 1829; deceased.
   7. Martin Marshall Blackerby, born Oct. 25, 1831; deceased.
   8. Benjamin Franklin Blackerby, born June 28, 1834; deceased.
   9. Matilda Battaille Blackerby, born Aug. 1, 1837; deceased.
   10. Eliza Jane Blackerby, born Aug. 1, 1839; deceased.
   11. Dr. Philip Nicholas Blackerby, born Sept. 9, 1845.
   12. Franklin Battaille Blackerby, born Feb. 15, 1848.

Dr. Jeduthan Orear Blackerby was born in Berlin, Ky., Aug. 4, 1824; died Jan. 13, 1892. He was graduated in law in 1843, but never practised, taking up the profession of medicine, to which science he devoted a long and useful life in his home village. Dr. Blackerby was married at Brookville, Ky., to Sarah Jane Linn, born May 9, 1832. Issue:
   A. William Orear Blackerby, Attorney-at-Law, born Sept. 20, 1853.
   B. Clara Linn Blackerby, born June 8, 1856.
   C. Dr. Jeduthan O. Blackerby, born Dec. 26, 1861.
   D. Emma Lee Blackerby, born July 12, 1863; married at Berlin, Dec. 15, 1887, to Edmund Winston Woolfolk of Ashland, Va., born Feb. 10, 1854. Issue:
      aa. Roper Blackerby Woolfolk, born July 6, 1890.
      bb. Pearl Buckner Woolfolk, born June 11, 1896.
      cc. Edmund Winston Woolfolk, Jr., born Sept. 15, 1899.
   E. Julia Amaretta Blackerby, born March 10, 1865.
   F. Ebenezer Watson Linn Blackerby, born May 30, 1867.

Page 40.
      ee. Marianna Buckner Clark, married June 27, 1904, Hugh Ellmaker Hale of Baltimore, Engineer of Maintenance of Way to the Baltimore and Ohio Railroad. No issue.
      ff. Adah Hawkes Clark, died unmarried.
   J. Augusta Buckner, born Oct. 10, 1835, twin sister of Marianna Buckner, married John White. Issue:
      aa. Marianna Buckner White.
      bb. Elizabeth White, of New Franklin, Mo.

Page 275. C. Sarah Kate Ashby, married in 1855, William Ellis Cocke of Tennessee, and had issue, three boys and four girls.

aa. Maggie Cocke, now deceased, married —— Read of Tennessee, and had issue, two boys.
bb. Mary Ellis Cocke, married S. L. Burdette of Georgia, and has issue, seven children.
cc. Lulie Cocke, married Rev. —— Snow of Oxford, Ga., and has issue, a daughter and two sons.

Page 275.   G. Fanny Ashby, died 1880; married (1st) in 1859, Basil Gordon Taylor.   Issue:
aa. Kate, d. s. p.
bb. Lucie Ashby Taylor, born 1861; married 1889, Charles J. Burroughs of Georgia.   Issue:
1. Robert Archibald Burroughs, born 1890.
2. Marshall Lee Burroughs, born 1892.

Fanny Ashby married (2d) Col. Alexander W. Harris.   Issue:
aa. Ashby Harris, deceased.
bb. Walton Harris, deceased.

Page 275.   II. Laura Ashby, born 1840; married 1865, to Daniel G. Purse of Savannah, Ga.   Issue:
aa. Marshall Ashby Purse, born 1866; married 1898, Josephine Earnest.
bb. Daniel G. Purse.
cc. Thomas Purse, born 1874; married 1898, Elizabeth Morrison.   Issue:
1. Elizabeth Lawton Purse, born 1899.
2. Thomas Purse, born 1902.
dd. Henry Ashby Purse, Naval Cadet at Annapolis, died 1895.
ee. Charles Strong Purse, deceased.
ff. Clayton Purse, born 1882.

Page 276.   J. Eugenie Ashby, born 1844; died 1884; married 1870, Charles J. Burroughs of Savannah, Ga.   Issue:
aa. Lucie Ashby Burroughs, born 1871; married 1897, Basil L. McLaurin of North Carolina.
bb. Ashby Burroughs, born 1873; married Rosa Cecil Berrien.   Issue:
1. Cecil Berrien Burroughs.
2. Eugenia Ashby Burroughs.
cc. Valerian Burroughs.
dd. Laura Ashby Burroughs.
ee. Ella Eugenia Burroughs.
ff. Eugene Ashby Burroughs, born 1880; married 1904, Camille McEachern.   Issue:
1. Camille McEachern Burroughs.
gg. Minnie Green Burroughs.

INDEX I.

BUCKNAR
  John 14
BUCKNER
  Adaline V. 116
  Addie 297
  Addison Walker 162
  Adeline 80
  Agnes 4
  Albert Gallatin 286
  Alexander 184
  Alfred 55
  Alice 13, 116
  Alice Elizabeth 184, 185
  Allen Marion 184
  Almar Washington 184
  Alta L. 288
  Amanda 80
  Amanda J. 55
  Ambrose 78
  Anderson 286
  Anderson Duncan 124
  Andrew 169, 285
  Andrew Brown 296
  Andrew H. 55
  Ann 31, 32, 41, 43, 54, 76, 154, 156, 164, 167, 172, 191
  Ann Elizabeth 118, 123
  Ann Hawes 113, 118, 130, 131, 132
  Ann Timson 157
  Ann Walker 176
  Ann Warren 174
  Ann Whitaker 99, 302
  Anna 181, 285, 291
  Anne Eustace 137
  Anne Roy 120
  Annie 118, 288
  Annie E. 285
  Anthony 1, 3, 7, 169
  Anthony Crockett 293
  Anthony Leach 198
  Anthony Thornton 36
  Arabella 182
  Archibald 298
  Archie Allan 300
  Ariss 125
  Arthur G. 299
  Arthur James 102
  Arthur Presley 36
  Augusta 41, 302
  Augusta Plimley 18
  Aurora Leigh 289
  Aylett 35, 36, 41, 76, 82, 282, 294
  Aylett Hartswell 41, 42, 43
  Aylette Hawes 134, 136, 137, 143, 175

BUCKNER
  Bailey 130, 132, 133, 143, 228
  Bailey Barbour 138
  Baldwin 157
  Baldwin Mathews 155, 156, 160, 162, 168
  Ballard 290
  Benjamin 79, 84, 162, 172, 177, 285
  Benjamin A. 87
  Benjamin F. 111
  Benjamin Forsythe 175
  Benjamin Franklin 162, 284, 285
  Benjamin Hawes 174
  Benjamin Heap 284, 285
  Benjamin Walker 174, 176
  Bennett Burrow 297
  Bernard G. 175
  Bernard Hooe 128
  Bettie 127, 293
  Beverley 114, 115
  Blanche 137
  Blanche Randolph 38
  Bruce Winston 289
  Burrow, Rev. 296
  Burtie 137
  Bushrod 199
  Caldwell Calhoun 88, 139
  Caroline Gibson 289
  Caroline Howard 163
  Caroline June 42
  Caroline Matilda 89, 171
  Caroline Rebecca 128
  Caroline Scudder 284
  Carrie M. 284
  Carrie May 299
  Carroll Van 296
  Catherine 130, 132, 171
  Catherine Bickley 114
  Catherine Crockett 293
  Catherine E. 117, 118
  Catie A. 284
  Charity 157
  Charles 16, 17, 19, 122, 123, 291
  Charles Aylett 136
  Charles Brown 39
  Charles C. 36, 292
  Charles Goddard 18
  Charles Grant 299
  Charles Madison 124
  Charles Montgomery 163
  Charles N. 111
  Charles Philip 102
  Charles Ratcliffe 288
  Charles Smith 39
  Charles T. 102

BUCKNER
- Charles W. 299
- Charlotte 117, 130, 132, 172, 180, 291
- Charlotte Forsythe 175
- Christian 33, 300
- Clara 196
- Clara H. 55
- Clarissa 191
- Clark 138
- Claude 110
- Claudius Earl 289
- Coleman 95
- Colin 114, 117
- Cora 110
- Cora Lee 291
- Cuthbert 39
- Cyrus 285
- Daisy 124
- Daisy Delphine 298
- Dallas 286
- Daniel Rev. 297
- Daniel Turney 175
- David 286
- David Ferguson 181
- David P. 185
- David Pendleton 187
- David Walker 288
- Davis M. 127
- Delwin Rees 296
- Donald Grant 289
- Dora 80
- Dora Adaline 116
- Dorcas 14
- Dorothea Aurora 289
- Dorothy 4, 5, 6, 13, 124, 155, 168
- Dorothy Gordon 163
- Edison 292
- Edmond Sneed 39
- Edmund Anderson 290
- Edmund Garnett 81
- Edna 162
- Edna B. 163
- Edward 181
- Edward Chapman 39
- Edward Everett 175
- Edward Madison 38
- Edwin 289
- Edwin H. 182
- Edwin M. 116
- Edwin Paxton 114
- Elias 39
- Elias Edmonds 39
- Elijah S. 294
- Eliphalet F. 80
- Elisha 285, 291
- Elisha Paxton 114
- Elisha S. 285
- Elizabeth 4, 6, 10, 13, 14, 23, 27, 28, 32, 41, 76, 95, 119, 124, 130, 132, 134, 150, 156, 157, 162, 168, 171, 181, 182, 184, 285, 286, 290, 293, 297
- Elizabeth Ann 43, 292
- Elizabeth Ariss 127, 128, 204, 205
- Elizabeth Aylett 37
- Elizabeth Bankhead 298

BUCKNER
- Elizabeth Beverley 160
- Elizabeth Catherine 162
- Elizabeth Cooke 91
- Elizabeth Ethaline 188
- Elizabeth Giles 181
- Elizabeth Harrison 189
- Elizabeth Hawes 177
- Elizabeth Jane 90, 98
- Elizabeth Lewis 35, 294
- Elizabeth M. 293
- Elizabeth Martin 176
- Elizabeth Merry 162
- Elizabeth M. T. 122
- Elizabeth Neil 299
- Elizabeth Pollard 113
- Elizabeth RoBards 36
- Elizabeth Stith 87
- Elizabeth T. 185
- Elizabeth Walker 172, 173, 174
- Elizabeth Watson 54
- Elizabeth Wyatt 163
- Ella Alice 127
- Ella Simpson 175
- Ellen 39, 111, 131, 183, 292, 299
- Ellen Carmichael 87
- Ellenora E. 186
- Elliott Hartzel 298
- Elliotte E. 284
- Emma Tabitha 124
- Emily 79, 80, 81, 114, 131, 265, 289
- Emily Morehead 42
- Enos 291
- Ernest Blaine 289
- Ethaline Conn 184, 186
- Ethel Blanche 299
- Ethel P. 301
- Ewell E. 81
- Eugene Tunstall 87
- Eugenia 137
- Eustis 300
- F. M. 292
- Faith 292
- Fanny 78, 95, 115, 162, 300
- Fanny Thornton 162
- Florence 301
- Florence Audrey 102
- Frances 13, 102, 124, 184, 298
- Frances Fitzhugh 90, 124
- Frances Gilmore 40
- Frances Thornton 224
- Francis 35, 37, 112, 122, 123, 125, 154, 180
- Francis Philip 108
- Francis T. 123
- Frank 288
- Frank Leroy 296
- Frank M. 38
- Frank Rawle 300
- Frank Thornton 294
- Franklin C. 285
- Franklin Fernando 289
- Franklin Pierce 285
- Frederick 291, 300
- French Abbott 290
- Gabriel 294
- Gabriel Lewis 38

BUCKNER
- Garnett Upshur 38
- Garrett D 292
- Garrett Davis 175
- George 13, 37, 78, 109, 112, 130, 138, 149, 184, 288
- George Aylett 118
- George F. 299
- George Ferguson 181
- George Hubbard 184
- George M. 288
- George Madison 122
- George O. M. 116
- George Phillips 184
- George R. 36
- George W. 111, 138, 285, 288
- George Walker 137
- George Washington 287
- George William 285
- Gertrude Baldwin 163
- Giles Cooke 172
- Hal Freeland, Rev. 299
- Hannah 43
- Harriet 289, 290
- Harriet G. T. 123
- Harriet K. 286
- Harry Alexander 189
- Hattie May 102
- Hattie McLean 284
- Hazel 299
- Helen 116, 300
- Helen M. 293
- Helena 81
- Henry 172, 183, 285, 291, 292, 295, 300
- Henry Aylett 118
- Henry Benjamin 118
- Henry C. 177
- Henry Clay 289
- Henry De Witt 296
- Henry Edward 289
- Henry F. Rev. 297
- Henry Freeland 296
- Henry Jackson 299
- Henry M. 185, 186
- Henry Nichols 285
- Henry Otis 285
- Henry S. 288
- Henry Sprague 296
- Henry Sullivan 299
- Henry Washington 184
- Henry Watson 43, 55
- Henry Willard 40
- Henry William 298
- Hiram 79
- Homer 290
- Homer Guy 299
- Horace 161, 162, 224, 297, 298
- Howard Aylett 289
- Hubbard G. 186
- Hubbard Taylor 184
- Hubbard Thomas 184
- Hugh 5, 6
- Hugh McLean 284
- Hugo James 296
- Humphrey 14
- Ida 110

BUCKNER
- Ida Jane 292
- Iva Nichols 285
- Ivy M. 292
- Jackson 299
- Jacob 287
- James 37, 38, 110, 122, 292, 300
- James Burrow 296
- James C. 288
- James Clark 136
- James Francis 38
- James G. 293
- James H. 127
- James Dudley 297
- James Henry 188
- James K. 285
- James Lewis 294
- James M. 38
- James Madison 299
- James McMurtry 287
- James Merry 290
- James Milton 80, 291
- James Monroe 176
- James Murphy 298
- James R. 286
- James Robinson 300
- James S. H. 143
- James Small 296
- James T. 294
- James W. 55, 176
- Jane 6, 10, 41, 43, 76, 87, 114, 284, 288, 294
- Jane C. 288
- Jane Champe 100
- Jane Chaplin 284
- Jane Ferguson 181
- Jane Richard 87, 139
- Jane White 87
- Jeb Stuart 162
- Jemima 292
- Jemima Jane 289
- Jeremiah 286
- Jesse 285, 286
- Jesse W. 292
- Jessie 128
- Johan 4
- John 1, 2, 3, 4, 5, 6, 10, 13, 16, 17, 20, 22, 23, 27, 31, 35, 43, 55, 76, 91, 95, 107, 109, 157, 172, 181, 285, 291, 297
- John Alexander 186
- John Alan Gardner 18
- John Anthony 191
- John Archer 87
- John Bolling 87
- John Breckenridge 118
- John Catlett 183
- John Chew 160
- John Edward 294
- John F. 291
- John Farrington 299
- John Fitzhugh 128
- John Jay 183
- John Lee 40
- John May 161
- John Moyandollar 285
- John Peyton 198

BUCKNER
John Philip 109, 110
John Simpson 299
John Strother 136, 137, 143
John T. 111
John Tate 294
John Tully 183
John Washington 293
John W. E. 114
John Wesley, Rev. 299
John Willis 183
Jonathan 13
Joseph 55, 82
Joseph Frank 294
Joseph Samuel 291
Joseph Warren 174
Josephine 79, 82
Josiah 289
Judith 39, 119, 172
Judith Ann 39
Judith Thornton 171
Julia 138
Julia A. 287
Julia Rawle 300
Kate 78
Katherine 297, 299
Katherine Gano 183
Katherine Foushee 163
Katherine Louisa 182
Kathryn Alexander 163
Kenneth M. 289
Laura 289, 299, 300
Laura A. 287
Lawrence 6
Leander 79, 81
Leannah 244
Leida 184
Leigh 163
Lela A. 288
Lena 291, 292
Leni Leoti 289
Leo Fay 299
Letitia S. 89
Lewis 37
Lewis Penrose 299
Lewis Probasco 183
Lillian A. 287
Lily 44
Linden Chapman 163
Lizzie 138
Louis 181
Louisa 294
Louisa A. M. 123
Louisa Berryman 127
Louisa C. 143
Louisa Ewing 81
Lucie 137
Lucretia A. 299
Lucy 38, 119, 144, 172, 187
Lucy A. T. 185
Lucy Ann 131
Lucy Clare 128
Lucy Fitzhugh 87
Lucy Madison 38, 122
Lucy Mary 99, 185
Lucy Pendleton 138
Lucy Seignora 157

BUCKNER
Lucy Thornton 124
Lucy Wood 177
Lula M. 287
Luminous 80
Luther Arthur 36
Lyda 138
Lydia 286
Lydia J. 287
Maggie 297
Malcom Jeter 291
Malinda 79
Malinda Madison 124
Mamie M. 111
Margaret 14, 128, 184, 294
Margaret Anderson 136
Margaret Davis 163
Margaret Elizabeth 294
Margaret Ferguson 181
Margaret Hannah 102
Margaret May 102
Margaret R. 285
Margaret Tully 182
Margarie 14
Maria Elizabeth 39
Maria Fitzhugh 290
Maria Lewis 36
Maria Louisa 87
Maria Louise 188
Marian Loranna 289
Marian S. 284
Marianna 40, 302
Marion E. 111
Marion L. 286, 287
Marshall Dulany 143
Marshall Lee 143
Martha 5, 109, 110, 114, 293
Martha A. 109
Martha Ball 137
Martha Ellen 298
Martha H. 111
Martha Jones 38, 107
Martha Kathryn 288
Martha M. B. U. 108
Mary 4, 10, 13, 14, 16, 17, 18, 32, 36, 41, 55, 76, 80, 122, 124, 128, 155, 156, 162, 168, 171, 181, 192, 215, 284, 286, 290, 291
Mary A. 287
Mary Allen 294
Mary Amiss 38
Mary Ann 288, 293
Mary Aylett 38, 180
Mary Belle 297
Mary Blanche 163
Mary C. 294
Mary Carter 143
Mary Catherine 187, 298
Mary D. 157
Mary Dorothy 117
Mary E. 55, 287
Mary Elizabeth 18, 42, 108, 124, 136, 175, 291
Mary Ellen 79, 84, 175, 182
Mary Eppes 114
Mary F. B. 102
Mary Hawes 130, 132

BUCKNER

Mary Helen 184
Mary Hill 123
Mary Horace 162
Mary Louisa 80
Mary Lucy 184
Mary M. 286, 291
Mary Madison 87, 90
Mary Magruder 128
Mary Martha 110
Mary Mildred 123
Mary Monroe 171, 176
Mary Owen 183
Mary Roberta 116
Mary Smith 118
Mary Susan 113
Mary V. 118
Mary Virginia 39
Mary Wilkinson 163
Matilda 294
Matilda B. M. 99
Mattie 127, 300
Melvina E. 55
Merry 290
Mildred 122
Mildred Ann 79, 136
Mildred Charlotte 118, 131
Mildred Hawes 118
Mildred Louise 185
Mildred Matilda 123
Mildred Thomas 184
Milly J. 111
Milton 79, 80, 82
Milton J. 284
Milton Thomas 284
Minerva Affia 291
Minnie E 286
Miriam 297
Mitchel 286
Montgomery Gano 184
Montrose 285
Mordecai, Col. 157
Morelos Aylett 42, 43
Mortimer N. 300
Murphy 55
Murrell 38
Nancy 43, 294, 297
Nancy W. 79, 82
Nanna Richard 36
Nannie H. 136
Nathaniel 1
Nathaniel Chapman 39
Newton 300
Nimrod 286
Orello Simmons 289
Otway 298
Overton G. 294
Parmalia 297
Paschal 287
Paul Bertram 289
Paul C. 38
Pearl 38
Perry 79
Peter Ballard 289
Peyton 157
Phebe 55
Philip Horace 289

BUCKNER

Philip 1, 3, 6, 14, 22, 32, 41, 42, 54, 55, 76, 87, 91, 169, 288
Philip Johnson 98
Philip Oscar 289
Philip T. 128
Phylena 292
Polly 95
Priscilla 79
Priscilla A. 82
Rachel 157
Rachel E. M. 114
Ralph Ruloff 136
Rawle 300
Rebecca 286
Rebecca May 296
Rena 287
Reynold R. 284
Richard 2, 3, 4, 5, 6, 7, 10, 11, 13, 15, 16, 17, 23, 34, 38, 39, 41, 55, 76, 112, 117, 125, 130, 132, 180, 184, 205, 292, 297
Richard A. 127
Richard Aylett 35, 36, 294
Richard Bernard 126
Richard Bolivar 175
Richard Campbell 118
Richard Edward Herbert 18
Richard H. 55, 117
Richard Henry 130, 131, 132, 137
Richard H. W. 117, 118, 130
Richard N. 286
Richard Pratt 127
Richard T. 293
Richard Upshur 37
Ritchie 298
Robert 78, 131, 157, 169, 172, 199, 286
Robert Arthur 162
Robert Cooke, Rev. 297
Robert Henry 115, 175
Robert Miller 290
Robert RoBards 294
Robert W. 55, 108, 116
Robbie Cook 297
Roscoe 292
Rose 6
Ross William 296
Roy 115, 292
Royle Albert 300
Ruth 285
Sally 35, 84, 294
Sallie Diggs 123
Sallie Smith 40
Sallie Thornton 124
Samuel 95, 138, 153, 154, 156, 167, 172, 182, 297
Samuel Glover 80
Samuel Hawes 175, 180
Samuel Owen 182
Samuel S., Dr. 299
Samuel Wilson 137
Sarah 39, 77, 95, 104, 118, 153, 284, 285, 286, 292
Sarah A. 110
Sarah Ann 182, 187
Sarah Ann Amelia 162

BUCKNER
    Sarah Catherine 137
    Sarah Eliza 285, 291
    Sarah Matilda 294
    Sarah Martin 176
    Silas 285
    Simeon 43, 56, 79, 81
    Simon Bolivar 42, 44, 55, 77
    Simon Bolivar, Jnr., 44
    Sophia Belle 184, 185
    Sophia M. 184
    Sophia Mary 98
    Sophie Harrison 189
    Spence Monroe 171
    Spencer Arias 128
    Squire J. 286
    Stanton 294
    Stephen A. 285
    Sterling H. 294
    Stonewall Jackson 136
    Sue 288
    Susan 37, 95, 106, 124
    Susan C. 175
    Susan Covington 185
    Susan D. 175
    Susan Elizabeth 116
    Susan Frances 108
    Susana 171
    Tabitha Ann 38
    Thomas 1, 2, 4, 5, 6, 7, 10, 11, 13, 14, 15, 32, 39, 41, 43, 56, 76, 80, 87, 95, 109, 112, 131, 153, 154, 156, 167, 170, 171, 172, 184, 285
    Thomas Aylette 182, 183
    Thomas Bernard 294
    Thomas Berry 185
    Thomas Griffin Thornton 123
    Thomas Hooe 127
    Thomas Moore 176
    Thomas Robertson 138
    Thornton 35, 122, 294
    Threshley Berryman 38
    Tully Orton 183
    Tully Scott 183
    Turner Hartswell 41, 43
    Venna A. 288
    Viola J., 288
    Virgil 290
    Virginia 39, 80
    Virginia F. 55
    Virginia Teackle 39
    Vosburg 296
    Walker 172, 181, 182, 183, 298
    Walker Hawes 118
    Walker Thornton 183
    Wallace Ruthven 289
    Walter 13, 163
    Warren 171
    Washington 130, 131, 132
    Watson 55
    Willa L. 290
    William 4, 5, 6, 10, 13, 14, 15, 25, 26, 27, 28, 31, 35, 36, 76, 78, 79, 82, 95, 97, 98, 112, 157, 170, 171, 173, 181, 185, 198, 285, 290, 291, 294, 297

BUCKNER
    William Aylett 113, 117, 118, 131, 173, 175, 180, 183
    William C. 291
    William Dickinson 143, 144
    William E. 114, 293
    William Edwin 289
    William Fitzhugh 124
    William Fitzhugh Thornton 123, 124
    William G. 294
    William Garth 162
    William George 296
    William Gilmore 39
    William Henry 87, 183, 184
    William Henry Pierce 18
    William Herbert 300
    William J. Van 296
    William Langhorne 115
    William Moore 116
    William Mordecai 162
    William N. 111
    William P. 286, 288
    William Paschal 288
    William Perry 82
    William Probasco 183
    William R. 286.
    William Rollo 296
    William Smith 113, 118
    William Smith Bickley 131
    William Spence 89, 171
    William Tate 294
    William Taylor 38
    William Thomas 79, 116, 171, 174, 176
    William T. T. 101
    William Thornton Taliaferro 189
    William W. 292
    William Warthon 118
    William West 102
    Willis 109

BUCKNOR
    Amanda 300
    Ann Eliza 301
    Archimedes James 300
    Charles 301
    Cornelius 299
    John 11
    Laura Jayne 301
    Marian Young 300
    Mary Pearson 301
    Pauline R. 301
    Virginia 301
    William 299
    William Archimedes 301
    William Goelet 299
    William Heald 301

BUKENORE
    Sir Thomas 11

BUKNORE
    Robert 12

BYKENORE
    Sir John 12

INDEX II

NAMES OF OTHER PERSONS

ADAMS
  Charles 259
  Elizabeth Thomas 263
  James B. 40
  Sarah 260
  T. M. 174
  Washington 40
ALDRICH
  Lyman D. 127
  Lyman Godfrey 127
  Sarah Davenport 127
ALEXANDER
  A. 115
  Ann 167
ALLAN
  Katherine 299
ALLEN
  C. Tacitus 266
  Ellen Taylor 266
  John R. 36
  Robert Meade 266
  Stuart Ashby 267
ALLENSWORTH
  Mary P. 109
ALMOND
  Elizabeth 246
  Lucy Belle 260
AMBROSE
  William 109
ANDERSON
  Alexander F. 115
  Buckner Wallingford 245
  Clarence 114
  Cora 247
  Davis C. 245
  Elizabeth 208
  Henry 114
  Henry James 264
  John Foster 246
  Larz 245
  Lelia 114
  Mary M. 81
  Pauline Howard 246
  Rebecca 245
ANDREWS
  Landonia A. 160
ANNE
  Dorothy 11
  William 4
ARISS
  Elizabeth 125
  Spencer 125

ARMSTRONG
  Mary 107
ASBURY
  Mary Jane 109
ASHBY
  Adeline T. 264
  Albert Adams 263
  Alexander 248
  Alfred 244
  Alice 260, 264
  Alice Royall 88, 267
  America Henley 248
  Ann 242, 245, 248, 266
  Ann Amanda 263
  Anne 246
  Annie Gillis 264
  Bailey 265, 279
  Belle 261
  Benjamin 241, 248, 257
  Benjamin Thornton 272
  Bernard 264
  Bertrand 268
  Bertrand Wilbur 268
  Bettie 273
  Bettie Scott 272
  Blanche 264
  Buckner 244
  Buckner E. 244
  Caroline 261
  Caroline Elizabeth 260
  Carroll Westwood 270
  Cassandra 248
  Catherine 260
  Charlotte 244, 246
  Charlotte Hawes 265
  Charles 263
  Charles Aylett 265
  Charles Green 272
  Charles Henley 248
  Charles William 88, 267
  Clarkson 260
  Dorothea Green 273
  Dorothy 248, 259
  Edith Turner 269
  Edward 241, 244, 246
  Edwin T. 263, 272
  Eleanor 265
  Elias 279
  Elisha 279
  Elizabeth 242, 244, 246, 267
  Elizabeth Ann 246
  Elizabeth M. 261

ASHBY
- Elizabeth Mildred 266
- Elizabeth Thomas 263
- Elizabeth Todd 265
- Ellen 245
- Emma 260
- Enoch 248
- Estelle 264
- Ethel Irving 265
- Eugenie 276, 303
- Fannie 275, 303
- Fannie Moncure 273
- Frances 279
- Frances Virginia 269
- Francis Westwood 270
- Frank 264
- Frederick 248
- French 267
- Genevive 268
- George 260
- George Strother 267
- Gertrude 268
- Grace 264
- Gregory 269
- Hankisson 279
- Helen 275
- Helen Mary 265
- Henry 241, 275
- Henry Stribbling 260
- Hunter 264
- Irving Gilliss 265
- James 244, 272, 273
- James Samuel 260
- Jamieson 260
- Jane Pollock 88, 267
- Jane Wilson 263
- Janet 269
- Jay Taylor 265
- Jennie 244, 245, 246
- Jess 279
- John 114, 241, 243, 244, 248, 249, 259, 261, 265, 276, 277
- John Jamieson 260
- John Henry 260, 277
- John Marshall 263
- John Moncure 272
- John R. 246, 264
- John Turner 260
- John Washington 275
- John William 270
- Joseph 245, 263
- Julian 260
- Julian Warrington 265
- Kate 137, 244, 267
- Laura 275, 303
- Lesbia Turner 263
- Lewis 244
- Lloyd Browning 248
- Logan 245
- Louise 263
- Lucy 266, 268, 276
- Lucy Dickinson 88, 267
- Lucy S. 261, 268
- Lulie 269
- Luther Rice 260
- Mae 268
- Margaret 245, 246, 270

ASHBY
- Maria 259
- Maria Louisa 275
- Marshall 275
- Martha 260, 277
- Martha Ann 259
- Martha Clarkson 260
- Martha Turner 266
- Martin 248
- Mary 245, 260, 274, 277
- Mary Ann 248
- Mary Arthur 263
- Mary Elizabeth 263, 275
- Mary Ellen 270
- Mary Louisa 88, 267
- Mary Sweetser 265
- Mary Turner 261
- Mary Wade 267
- Mary Wallace 273
- Mattie Chunn 264
- Mauzey Q. 245
- Meriwether 269
- Mildred 244
- Millie 279
- Molly 248, 260
- Mortimer W. 263
- Nannie Hull 273
- Nathaniel 244, 245
- Natila 260
- Nellie B. 270
- Nimrod 248, 263, 276, 277
- Nimrod Thomson 263
- Norman 264
- Philip 267
- Rebecca 264
- Rebecca Wood 263
- Richard 261, 274
- Richard Henry 263
- Richard Moncure 273
- Robert 241, 248, 276
- Robert Francis 248
- Robert S. 261
- Robert Stuart 268
- Robert Turner 268
- Roberta 262
- Rose 242
- Sallie 246, 260
- Samuel 259, 260, 277
- Samuel Turner 263, 264
- Sarah, 241, 249, 277
- Sarah Kate 275, 302
- Scott 260
- Shirley 261
- Sidney Lewis 244
- Stuart 269
- Stephen 241
- Strother 267
- Susan 261
- Thomas 241, 242, 279
- Thomas Bryan 248
- Thomas M. 246
- Thomson 226, 268, 270
- Turner 272, 273, 277
- Turner Wade 256, 269
- Vernon 268
- Virginia 260
- Virginia Buchanan 273

ASHBY
    Webb 260
    William 227, 244, 248, 261, 265
    William Aylett 265
    William Richardson 245
    William Samuel 270
    William Todd 265
    Wilmoth 279
    Wilson 263
    Winifred 248, 279
    Wirt M. 261
ATAWAY
    Sarah 125
AYLETT
    Ann 77
    Elizabeth 35
    Jane 41
    John 35, 41, 76
    William 35, 112
BACON
    Charles Francis 265
BALLARD
    Ann 31
    Catherine 27
    Thomas 27
BALLEXSERD
    Camilla 23
BANDER
    Fannie Case 113
BANE
    Charles L., Rev. 163
BARBOUR
    Edmund Pendleton 132
    James 228
    Philip Pendleton 228
    Thomas, Dr. 228
BARKER
    William Musgrave 100
BARNES
    Alexander 195
BARRET
    Anna 37
    Arthur B. 37
    John Allen 37
    Julia Allen 37
    Mary Lee 37
    Richard Aylett 37
    Richard Farril 36
    William Lee 37
    Winston Lee 37
BARRY
    Francis 5, 10
    Vincent 10
BARTON
    James 249
    David Walker 225
BASTABLE
    Elizabeth 261
    Gilbert Moxley 261
    Virginia 261
BATESON
    Richard H. 272
BATTLE
    Turner W. 208
BAYLESS
    Helen 96

BAYLOR
    Richard 121
BAYNE
    Charles 270
    Charles Ashby 272
    Estelle St. Pierre 272
    Frances Scott 272
    Genevieve 269
    Gertrude Ashby 269
    Harriet Addison 269
    Howard R. 270
    Hunter W. 272
    John 268
    John Henry 268
    Joseph Breckenridge 269
    Lloyd Moore 272
    Louise Dudley 269
    Lucy Ashby 268
    Mae Ashby 269
    Mary A. M. 272
    Nannie Thomson 270
    Richard 270
    Robert Ashby 269
    Samuel P. M. 272
BAYTOP
    Anne Walker Carter 165
    Thomas 165
BEAN
    Anna 300
BECK
    Bettie Buckner 128
    George Thornton 128
    James Burnie 128
    Margaret Buckner 128
    Sophia Burnie 128
BECKWITH
    Ann Lewis 97
BEDDOE
    A. F., Dr. 297
BEDFORD
    Benjamin F. 182
BEERBOWER
    Louis 111
BELKNAP
    Morris B. 44
BELL
    Jefferson 97
BENGER
    Dorothea Brayne 150
    Elliott 150
BERNARD
    David Meade 266
    Ella A. 266
    Ellen M. 294
    Fanny C 266
    George S. 266
    Janet M. 266
    Kate E. 2 6
BERRY
    Elizabeth 238
    Ella 127
    Lawrence 4
    Leander 110
    Margaret 239
    Mildred 184
BERRYMAN
    Louisa H. 127

BESSE
    John G. 195
BETHUNE
    George Maximilian 17
    Georgiana 17
BEVAN
    W. C. 261
BEVERLEY
    Elizabeth 158
    Harry Capt. 159
    Robert Gaines 119
BICKLEY
    William Smith 119
BIDWELL
    Leonard 195
BIRDSELL
    John C. 81
BIRNEY
    William 264
BLACKERBY
    William O. 99, 302
BLACKLEY
    Catherine 29
    Mary 29
    William 29
BLACKWELL
    James 120
BLAIR
    Bettie 128
    Elizabeth Saunders 166
    Montgomery 128
BLAKRY
    W. D. 123
BLANCHARD
    Betsy Jane 95
    John 95, 96
    Lee 96
    Molly 95
    Nelson 96
    Samuel Philip 96
    Sarah 95
    Tabie 95
BOARMAN
    Jerome S. 40
    Richard Keith 40
BOND
    Erwin D. J. 197
    Thomas B. 115
BOOKER
    William 23
BOONE
    Mrs. John T. 39
BOOTH
    George 165
    Mary 164, 165
    Sarah 165
    Thomas 164
BOULWARE
    Judith 117
BOWEN
    John W. 123
BOWMAN
    Mary 55
BOYD
    Byrd 151
    John R. 85
    Nettie 85

BOYER
    Samuel H. Rev. 98
BRADFORD
    George A. 247
BRAZIER
    Zachariah 33
BRICKHAM
    Kathryn H. 163
BRIDGES
    Nancy 89
BRIGGS
    Robert 116
BRISTOR
    Frederick Thomas 123
BROCK
    Agnes Frances 160
    Alice Beverley 160
    Ansalem 160
    Ansalem T. 161
    Charles Bolton 161
    Charles W. P. 161
    Elizabeth B. 161
    Elizabeth Tyler 161
    Francis Joseph 160
    Helen Landonia 160
    Joseph Baldwin 160
    Mary Maud 160
    Sarah Ann 160
    Virginia Allen 161
BRONAUGH
    William, Col. 235
BROOKE
    John 275
BROWN
    Barclay 144
    Edith Hamilton 144
    Louise Dickinson 144
    Sarah Julia 39
    William 191
    William G. 144
BROWNING
    Ann 248
    Belle 227
    Charles 227
    Elizabeth 227
    Fannie Lewis 227
    Francis 227
    Frank 227
    George Lewis 227
    John, Capt. 227
    John A. 227
    Mary Ann 227
    Sarah Louise 249
    William Winston 249
    Willis 227
BROWNLOW
    John Bell, Col. 231
BRUNE
    Eleanor 143
BUCK
    Rebecca 245
    William M. 246
BUMGARNER
    Samuel 194
BURGESS
    W. W. 262

BURKE
    Edward G. 151
    George 151
    George W. 151
    Selina 151
    Thomas Henry 151
BURROUGHS
    Charles J. 303
    Lafayette 97
BURT
    Anna 137
BURTON
    Fanny 180
    Hannah 56, 78
BUTTS
    Delaney F. D. 260
BYRNE
    Elizabeth 190
    George 190
    Lydia 190
    Mary 190
    Samuel 191
CALDWELL
    Benjamin 85
    Clara Buckner 123
    George 85
    John G. 123
    Monroe 85
    Temperance R. 84, 85
    Thomas B. 84, 85
CAMP
    Ashby Pendleton 88
    Charles Ashby 88
    Harriotte Peltier 88
    Mary Jeffery 88
    William Henry 88, 267
CAMPBELL
    Courtney 123
    James 117
    John P. 38
CARLISLE
    John 248
CARMICHAEL
    Charles Ashby 88, 267
    Charles Carter 88, 267
    Lucy Ashby 88
    Mary Spottswood 88, 267
CARPENTER
    Andrew 5
    Herbert Sanford 247
CARTER
    Gertrude Miller 270
    Jennie 269
    Joseph M. 269
    Mary 127
    Meriwether Thomson 269
    Nannie Strother 269
    Oscar F. 270
    Turner 269
    Virginia Ashby 226
    Westwood M. 269
CARY
    Arthur 38
    Bessie 38
    Lucele 38
    Miles 155, 167

CASSIDY
    May Elsie 184
CATLETT
    ——— 183
    Alice 289
    Ambrose 244
    Colin 119
    George 119
CAYCE
    A. Boyd 263
CHANCELLOR
    Ashby 259
    George 260
    Samuel 259
    Virginia 259
CHENVERONT
    Edward J. 194
CHEW
    Larkin 158
CHILDS
    Edward 85
    Ellen 85
    Emily 85
    Richard 85
    Sally 85
    Unette S. 84
    Walter 85
    Walter C. 84, 85
    William 85
CHISMAN
    Charles 155
    George 155
    John 155
    John Buckner 155
    Mary 155
    Mathew 155
    Miles 155
    Patty 155
CHITTS
    Sarah 14
CHUNN
    Ada Belle 262
    Andrew 261
    Martha Turner 263
    Mary Meta 261
    Roberta McNish 261
    Taylor D. 262
CHURCHILL
    Priscilla 202
CLAIBORNE
    Delia H. 44, 283
CLAMP
    H. L. 183
CLARK
    Augusta 40
    Charles Buckner 40
    David Branch 270
    Elias Buckner 40
    James 128
    John Bullock 40
    Kate Pearson 40
    Marcellus 196
    Marianna Buckner 41, 302
CLARKSON
    Martha 259

CLAY
    Mary Woodford 177
    Sallie 177
CLEGG
    Elizabeth 116
CLEMENT
    Robert 82
CLEVELAND
    William P. 116
COCHRAN
    Nathan 245
COCKE
    John C. 266
    William Ellis 275
COGHILL
    Elizabeth Ashby 88
    Henry Burns 88, 267
    Laurence L. 88, 267
    William I. D. 88, 267
COLBERT
    Jane Finney 40
    Mary Lee 40
    Thomas M. 40
    Thomas Reuben 40
    William Cecil 40
COLEMAN
    L. W. Rev. 297
    Lucy 237
COLGATE
    Patience 32
COLVIN
    William 110
COMBS
    Catherine 248
    Jane 244
COMSTOCK
    Cyrus B. 128
CONKLING
    W. H. 138
CONN
    Ethaline E. 185
CONNER
    Aylett Buckner 181
    Charlotte Buckner 181
    Jane G. 181
    Mary 181
    Richard Ellis 181
CONNOR
    Lewis 259
CONWAY
    Anne 133
    Aylett Hawes 133
    Charlotte 132
    George 133
    Mary 132
    Sarah 133
    Thomas 132
CHEWNING
    William 133
COOK
    Minerva B. 291
COOKE
    Elizabeth 34, 76
    John 156
    Llewellyn 269
    Mary 164
    Mordecai 34, 164

CORBIT
    Jennie 118
CORBYN
    Almon D. Rev. 39
CORCORAN
    James W. 128
CORNISH
    John 138
COSNAHAN
    Mary Mercer 165
COVINGTON
    Francis 227
    Susan 186
    William 227
COWHERD
    Colby B. 294
COX
    Ellen 122
CRACKPLACE
    Elizabeth 9, 14
CRAIK
    Mary Martin 38
CRANE
    Joseph Minor 234
CRAWLEY
    Charles D. 265
CREEL
    Battelle W. 193, 196
    Bushrod Washington 196
    Charles Pulaski 193, 196
    Clara Kincheloe 197
    Eleanor Sophia 197
    Elias Wickliffe 197
    George 196
    George R. 196
    Hannah Jane 197
    Harriet Ann 36
    Henry A. Wise 198
    John Alexander 197
    John Anthony Buckner 194, 196
    John Buckner 193, 196
    Laura M. 193, 196
    Lucy F. 196
    Mary Eliza 197
    Monroe T. 198
    William H. 198
CRENSHAW
    Anna 36
CROCKETT
    Catherine G. 293
CRUEGER
    Hermann C. 163
CUNNINGHAM
    J. S. 123
DABNEY
    Cornelius 225
DAINGERFIELD
    Catherine 204
DANIEL
    Elizabeth 91
    Tabitha Ann 91
    William, Capt. 91
DARREL
    Stephen 297
DAVIES
    Jeanette 38

DAVIS
    James J. 113
    Rufus C. 117
DAWSON
    Linzy M. 102
DEBROIS
    Charles 32
DEFREES
    Adelaide 79
    Archibald 81
    Jane L. 81
    Lola Amelia 81
DENTON
    Anne 4
DERIEUX
    Ella Dobyns 55
DESSEZ
    Adrienne 113
DEXTER
    Elizabeth 274
DIBRELL
    James A. 82
DICKINSON
    Abram Halsey 89
    Alice Johnson 89
    Anne Mason 89
    Caroline May 89
    Emma Yerby 89
    Fannie Halsey 89
    Harriet Mason 89
    James 88
    James Cooper 89
    James Morton 89
    Jane Hipkins 88
    John 217
    John Yerby 89
    Louisa Fitzhugh 88, 139
    Lucy Fitzhugh 89
    Margaret Gray 88
    Nathaniel 218
    Sally 88
    Sarah Elizabeth 88, 267
    Thomas Buckner 89
    William Bolling 88
    William Bolling, Jnr. 89
    William I. 87, 89
DIMMET
    Amanda 79
DOBYNS
    Annie Baylor 55
    Frederick 55
    George Henry 55
    Lucy Robinson 55
    Thomas Abner 55
DODGE
    Louisa Malvina 182
DOSTER
    Stella 111
DOSWELL
    Martha 114
DOVE
    John 137
    Lucille 137
DUDLEY
    Morris J. 184
    Peter 171
    Thomas P. Rev. 293

DUFFIELD
    Richard 284
DUKE
    Thomas Marshall 246
DULY
    John Z. 97
DUNSTON
    Lewis 157
DURHAM
    David W. 55
EDMONDS
    Edmund S. 262
    Elias 38
    Judith 8
EDMONDSON
    Katherine 83
EGAN
    James 83
ELDRIDGE
    Elizabeth 28
ELLIS
    Charles S. 284
ENGLAND
    Catherine 97
EUSTIS
    Newton 299
EVANS
    John, Col. 237
    Nimrod 237
    Susan 95
EWING
    Joseph 81
EXALL
    Alice Buckner 55
    Colin Stuart 55
    Douglas 55
    John Sizer 55
    Le Roy Randolph 55
FARISH
    Stephen 171
FARROW
    Amanda 249
    Benjamin 248
    George 248
    George Ashby 249
    John F. 249
    Lucy Mildred 249
    Margaret Ann 249
    Mary Louise 249
    Sarah Smith 249
    Thomas 249
FEILD
    Theophilus A. 266
FELTUS
    Abram M. 181
FENDALL
    Arthur 129
FERGUSON
    Charlotte 181
    Mary Allen 84
FERRERS
    Debora 7, 14, 23
FICKLIN
    Benjamin 235
FIELD
    John B. 81

FIELDING
    Frances 202
FINLEY
    Foster G. 293
FINNEY
    Jane Lee 40
    Maria Ragland 40
    Mary 37
    Mary Ann 40
    Sallie Buckner 40
    Thomas 40
    William Barret 40
    William Harper 40
FINNIE
    William 168
FITZHUGH
    George 235
    Helen Stuart 128
    Henry 28, 87
    Lucy 87
    Madison 132
    Summerfield 118
    William, Col. 21
FLETCHER
    William 157
FLOOD
    Maurice B. 182
FLOURNOY
    David 23
    Elizabeth Julia 23
    Gideon 23
    John 23
    John James 23
    Mary 23
    Mathew 23
    Rachel 23
    Samuel 23
    Thomas 23
FOLLANSBEE
    Robert 262
FONTAINE
    Martha 80
    Martha A. 83
    Messina 80
FORBES
    Alfred 261
FORD
    Elizabeth 274
FORSYTHE
    Charlotte 175
FOUGHT
    Orville C. 195
FOUSHEE
    Sarah Catherine 162
FOWKE
    Gerard 235
    Mary 235
FOX
    J. C. 123
FRENCH
    Daniel 236
    Margaret 236
FREWEN
    Anne 17
FRIZZELL
    Mary 96

FROGG
    John 222
GAAR
    Abram W. 162
    Michael Howard 162
GAINES
    Agnes 231
    Ann 231
    Behethland 231
    Edmund Pendleton 231
    Elizabeth Strother 232
    Frances 231
    Francis Thornton 232
    George Strother 231
    Henry 230
    Henry Pendleton 232
    James 230
    James Strother 232
    Lucy 231
    Nancy 231
    Patsy 231
    Philip 2,2
    Richard Thomas 232
    Susan 232
    Thomas 232
GALLAHER
    B. Frank 127
    Louisa Bernard 127
GANO
    Mary 183
    Mary Eliza 183
GARDNER
    Admiral, Lord 18
    Elizabeth 18
    Honl. William Henry 18
GARNER
    Carrie 175
GARNETT
    Henry 37
GARTH
    Bettie L. 162
GASCOYNE
    Augusta Helen 18
    Edith Eliza 18
    Edward Buckner 18
    Frederic Kelly 18
    Gertrude Sarah 18
    George 18
    Marian Louisa 18
    William Walter 18
    William Whitehead 18
GATES
    Eliza 29
GATEWOOD
    Elizabeth 174
    Thomas 172
GAVIN
    Mary 111
GEIGER
    Margaret Jane 97
GEORGE
    Frank L. 284
GIBBENS
    Catherine 198
GIBBS
    C. R. 124
    Thomas Hayden 275

GIBSON
    Lucy Ellen 136
GIDDINGS
    William B. 123
GILL
    James M. 110
GILLMORE
    James Bickley 297
GLOVER
    Betty M. 82
    Clara 82
    Fanny D. 80
    James L. 82
    John Milton 82
    Joseph Albert 82
    Mildred 82
    Robert G. 82
    Samuel Taylor 79, 82
    William Pike 82
GOBLE
    Annie Louisa 96
    Louis 96
GOFF
    Strander Douglas 176
GOLD
    Isabel Ashby 262
    Loyd O. 261
GOODE
    James L. 297
GOODLOE
    Daniel R. 238
    Green Clay 128
GORDON
    Arthur W. 18
    George Loyall 208
    Samuel 88
GOSS
    Anne 13
GRANGER
    Albert H. 81
    Andrew F. 81
    Charles F. 81
    Joseph M. 81
    Walter C. 81
    William 81
GRANT
    Bernard 84
    Betsy 84
    Caroline 84
    John 222
    Oscar 84
GRANTHAM
    Taliaferro P. 260
GRAVES
    Anne 232
    Catherine Ann 183
GRAY
    Anderson 238
    Daniel 237, 238
    French Strother 230, 238
    George 237
    Henry Weedon 238
    James Strother 238
    Margaret Atchison 88
    Maria 274
    Minor 238

GREEN
    Dora 273
    Dorothea 272
    Francis Wyatt 227
    George Mason 273
    Hugh R. 263
    John Cook 273
    Raleigh Travers 137
GRIFFIN
    John 259
GRIGSBY
    Alcinda 260
GROSVENOR
    Sir Robert 10
GRYMES
    Mary E. 38
HALL
    Benjamin E. 186
HALSEY
    Fannie 89
HAMILTON
    George 245
    Richard J. 80
HANCOCK
    George, Col. 232
HANKS
    R. T. 266
HANSBROUGH
    George W. 259
HARBESON
    P. O. P. 96
    William 85
HARDIN
    D. S. 182
    John Cloud 289
    Mark Washington 290
HARRIOT
    Thomas 9
HARRIS
    Belle Overton 163
    Elizabeth 23
    William 5
HARRISON
    Elizabeth Irwin 189
HARTER
    A. W. 102
HARVIE
    Col. John 224
HATCHER
    D. C. 261
HAUCH
    Ernst F. 264
HAWES
    Ann 131, 151
    Ann Walker 172
    Charlotte 113, 130, 131
    Elizabeth 131, 172
    Judith 112
    Mary 131
    Mildred 113, 131
    Samuel 131
    Thomas 114, 131
    Thomas M. 114
    Walker 131
HAWKINS
    Gabriella Lewis 38
    Martha 55

HAWKINS
    Capt. Moses 230
    Narcissa 55
HEARD
    John 124
HENLEY
    Sarah 248
HENRY
    Annie E. 187
    Robert Randolph 266
    Stephen 187
    Susanna 222
HERNE
    Edmund 5
HEWITT
    Edwin L. 161
HIGGINS
    Robert H. 99
HOARD
    Helena 81
HOLLAND
    Carlton 83
    Dora 83
    Helen Irene 83
    Kate 83
HOLT
    Rev. A. J. 297
    Sir John 9
    Susan 177
    Thomas 9
HOOE
    John 119, 132
    Lucy 126
HORD
    Arthur A. 97
    Betsy Taylor 97
    Frank Joyce 97
    Hebe Susan 97
    John Nicholas 97
    John Willis 97
    Laura Agnes 97
    Lucy N. T. 97
    Mary Ann 96
    Mary Catherine 97
    Matilda Bainton 97
    Mildred Lewis 96
    Moses Pendleton 96
    Philip Buckner 97
    Polly Willis 97
    Robert Craddock 97
    Sarah Thomas 97
    Thomas Todd 96
    William Taylor 97
    William Thomas 97
    Willis 96
HOSKINS
    Judith Eliza 55
HOUSTON
    A. S. 124
HOWISON
    Anne Moore 120
    James 249
HUFMAN
    Catherine 244
HUGHES
    Amelia E. 80
    Anne E. 81

HUGHES
    Clara Louisa 81
    Donald B. 81
    Edgar H. 81
    Floyd 161
    George Buckner 80
    Georgie Marie 81
    George R. D. 81
    Henry 14
    Jennie Priscilla 81
    Jesse Hamilton 80
    Joe E. McD. 81
    Lola Amelia 81
    Mabel Lee 81
    Richard D. 80
    Virginia A. 80
    William 227
HUNT
    Theodosia 237
HUNTEMULLER
    Edith 138
HUNTER
    Charles 266
    Elizabeth Pendleton 234
    Mary Elliot 234
IRVING
    Paulus A. 263
JAMES
    John 235
    Mary 233
    William Ashbridge 300
JEFFRIES
    Dudley 108
JENKIN
    Ann 17
JENNINGS
    Sarah 225
JEWETT
    Catherine 274
JOHNSON
    Isaac L. 264
JOHNSTON
    Agnes R. O. 30
    Benjamin 30
    Christopher 29, 30
    Elizabeth 29
    Eliza Yates 30
    Henry Morris 29, 30
    Isabella Marr 29
    Janet 29
    John 29, 30
    John Griffin 29
    Madeline T. T. 30
    Maria Stith 29
    Matilda Price 30
    Robert Clapham 30
    Robert Neilson 29
    Sarah C. S. 30
    Susanna 29
    Susan Stith 30
    Wm. H. de N. 29
JONES
    Albert 83
    Alberta 84
    Bettie Miller 272
    C. L. 118
    Charles Ashby 272

JONES
  Clarence 266
  Edloe 266
  Elizabeth 223, 224
  Elizabeth Overton 163
  Fletcher Platt 272
  Fontaine 84
  Frances 225
  Francis William 266
  French 266
  Gabriel 223, 259
  Harriet 259
  Helen Mary 266
  James Laurence 266
  John 223
  John Ashby 259
  John William 266
  Lucy Marshall 266
  Margaret 224
  Mattie Bernard 266
  May Ellen 272
  Orlando 23
  Pendleton 266
  Robert 259
  Robert Meade 266
  Servant Rev. 157
  Slaughter 259
  Col. William 156
  Sir William 223
  William D. 96
  William J. 293
  Willie Page 266
  William Strother 224
JOUETT
  Admiral James E. 295
KEENE
  Henry 5
KELLAM
  Nellie Mason 186
KELLY
  Edward Emilius 17
  Walter 17
  Walter William 17
KENNERLY
  Catherine 238
KENYON
  Frances 233
KING
  Robert 4
KINGSBURY
  Mary 44
KIRK
  Alice Virginia 138
  Anne Strother 138
  Edith Buckner 138
  Lydia Hemsworth 138
  Henry Child 138
  Henry Child, Jnr. 138
  May Huntemuller 138
  Mildred Buckner 138
  Olivia Hardesty 138
KLINKENBERG
  P. H. 300
KNOX
  Virginia 249
  William James 249

LAMBERT
  John 90
  Maurice Washington 264
  Nannie P. 90
  William B. 90
LANGHORNE
  Betsy A. 115
  Beverley R. 115
  Daniel A. 115
  Devereux A. 115
  Fannie B. 115
  Kent 115
  Lucy McG. 115
  Martha D. 115
  Maud B. 115
  Maurice B. 114
  Mary P. 115
  Robert C. 115
  Sallie Carey 115
  William A. 115
  William Henry 114
LANSDOWNE
  Andrew Jackson 96
  Daisy 96
  George 96
  Helen 96
  Herman 96
  John C. 96
  Juliet 96
  Lucy 96
  Mary 96
  Rosa 96
  Therese 96
  Underwood 96
  Wallace 96
LANTZ
  Emma 83
  Florence 83
  Simon 83
LAWLER
  John 227
LEACH
  Louisa C. 199
LEACHMAN
  Thomas 260
LEIGH
  Philip 120
LEWIS
  Andrew Genl. 222
  Daingerfield 227
  Fielding 202, 203, 205, 224
  Gabriel Jones 224
  George Washington 204
  John 201, 202, 224, 225
  Myrtie 182
  Samuel 129, 204, 205
  Thomas 225
  Warner 224
LIGHTBURN
  Alvin 84
  Anna T. 85
  Sarah E. 84
LIMERICK
  John A. 181
LINDSAY
  Rosa 173

LIONBERGER
  Isaac 267
LITTLE
  Gray 102
LOCKRIDGE
  Hollis A. 115
LONG
  Viena 297
LONGWORTH
  Annie Rives 245
  Catherine 245
LUCAS
  Orval M. 102
LYON
  James 231
MACKALL
  Robert McGill 264
MACKEEN
  Mary 15
MACKLIN
  George B. 85
  Mary 85
MACNAR
  Alexander James 194
MADDOX
  Cabell 249
MADISON
  George 222
  George Thomas 222
  James 222
  Pres. James 36
  James Catesby 222
  John 222
  Lucy 122
  Margaret 223
  Maria 87
  Roland 222
  Susan 222
  William Strother 222
MANDEVILLE
  Sarah 81
MANSELL
  Elizabeth 184
MANSON
  Ashby 265
  Charlotte 266
  Henry 265
  John E 266
  Joseph Richard 265
  Lucy Strother 265
  Matilda F. 265
  Thomas J. 265
  William Buckner 265
MARSH
  Steele 90
MARSHALL
  Ann Maria 225
MARTIN
  Emily 198
  Helen B. 176
  Mary Ann 293
  Polly 131
MARQUESS
  Eliza Buckner 136
  William Hoge 136

MASON
  Maria 120
  Mary 235
MATHEWS
  Baldwin 154
  Sarah 154
MAUZEY
  Margaret 245
MAWSON
  Edward 83
MAYES
  Hugh 266
MAYFIELD
  Cates B. 105
McCABLE
  Louisa 175
McCAY
  Mildred Buckner 138
  William T. W. 138
McCORKLE
  John M. 294
McCRANE
  Elizabeth 227
McDOWELL
  William 223
McELWAIN
  John N. 116
McGROARTY
  Alma Letitia 98
  Catherine Elizabeth 98
  Charles Neil 98
  Lucina Frances 98
  Patrick 98
  William Buckner 98, 282
McINTOSH
  Charles Fleming 120
McKAY
  George Albert 137
McKEE
  Samuel 245
McLEAN
  William 120
MEADE
  Lucy Ashby 266
  Robert E. 266
  Robert Turner 266
MEDLICOTT
  Elizabeth 165
MEDBY
  Mildred 227
MENEFEE
  Ann Stuart 226, 268
  Benjamin Strother 227
  John 226
  Mildred Johnston 226
  Sarah Strother 227
  William 226
MERRILL
  Ayres P. 181
MERRY
  Mary 290
MILES
  Winifred Price 18
MILLER
  Ashby 272
  Elisha J. 272
  Gertrude 272

MILLER
　James Richard 126
　Julian 272
　Lucy Roy 126
　Sarah Ataway 129, 204, 205
　Thomas 129
　Thomas Roy 129, 204, 205
　Virginia 129
　William 129
MILLS
　A. N. 174
MILLSPAUGH
　M. L. 138
MINOR
　Eliza L. 134
　Malinda 122
MITCHELL
　Douglas 270
　William C. 97
MOFFETT
　Daniel 263
　La Viga 263
MONCURE
　Bettie Ashby 274
　Dora Ashby 89, 274, 275
　Fannie 272
　George V. 274
　James A. 274
　John 274
　Mary Buchanan 273
　Powhatan 274
　Robert S. 274
　Turner Ashby 274
MONROE
　Elizabeth 171
　William W. 171
MOORE
　Cato 234
　Lizzie S. 271
　Nancy 115
MOREHEAD
　Amanda 244, 245
　Bettie 263
　Eliza Ann 41, 43
　Joel 244
　Mary 41
　Mildred 263
　Turner 41
MORGAN
　Capt. Francis 153
　Sarah 153
MORRIS
　Dickinson 102
MORRISON
　Jane Elizabeth 116
MORTIMER
　Hugh de 12
MORTON
　Charles Bruce 89
　Elizabeth B. 234
　Ella 85
　Emma 85
　Fanny 85
　George 223
　Juliet 85
　Mary 85
　Netty 85

MORTON
　Powhatan Moncure 89
　Sallie 85
　William 85
　William J. 275
　William Jackson 89
MURRAY
　Sterling 129
MURRELL
　Elizabeth 38
　Lewis E. 181
　Samuel 38
　William 37
NALLE
　Edmund Cary 266
NEAL
　Richard H. 261
NEALEY
　Rosa 297
NELSON
　Deborah 15
　William J. 115
NEWKIRK
　Josephine 111
NEWTON
　Elizabeth 234
NICHOLS
　Joane 14
NORTON
　Juliet 84
　William 84
OCTERLONG
　Kate A. 81
OGILVIE
　John T. 260
OLINGER
　James 263
　John 263
ORR
　William 107
ORTON
　Eva May 183
OSBORN
　Charles J. 272
　Robert O. 123
OSBURN
　James Miller 290
OSENTON
　Blanche 96
　Charles 96
　George 96
　Juliet 96
　Lansdowne 96
OWEN
　James T. 55
PADDON
　Emily H. 116
PAGE
　Alice 13
　Camm Temple 249
　Granville 260
PALMER
　Charles A. 116
PANNILL
　Laura 143
　Sarah Bayly 229

PARKE
    Rev. John 17
PARKER
    Ann Eliza 247
    Belviard 247
    Elizabeth Clarkson 247
    Howard S. 247
    Mary B. 247
    Montgomery H. 247
    Sarah Moore 247
    Warren Ashby 247
    Warren O. 247
    William Moore 247
    Wilson 246
PARSONS
    Ida M. 81
PATTERSON
    Charner 294
PAXTON
    Rachel Eleanor 114
PAYNE
    Catherine 109
    Daniel 152
    Elizabeth 152
    William 249
PEAKE
    William 87
    William Buckner 87
PEASE
    Georgiana Fee 98
PENDLETON
    Ann Stuart 227
    Benjamin 234
    Edward 227
    Henry 230
    Isabella 230
    Nannie S. 237
    William 227
PENNE
    William 5
PERRY
    Caroline 184
PETERS
    James 248
    John 246
PHELPS
    Ezra C. 197
PHILLIPS
    James Harney 188
    Lida 184
PICKETT
    John 104
    Julia Ann 97
    Mary 261
PIERCE
    Emma Roberta 17
    Mary Marsh 17
PIERSON
    Anne Fitzhugh 89
    Charles Herbert 89
    John Bolling 89
    Leonard Forster 89
    Victor Randolph 89
PIPER
    Helen 227
PLIMLEY
    Rev. Henry 18

PLUMMER
    Sue 114
POLAND
    Mary 297
POPE
    George R. 263
POTTER
    Daisy 124
POTTS
    Thomas S. 187
POWER
    Frank 96
PRATT
    William Livingston 128
PRESTON
    Elizabeth 222
PRIBBLE
    Byron 111
    Laura 111
PRICE
    Kittie 234
PRUITT
    Mary Elizabeth 102
PURSE
    Daniel G. 275, 303
PURVIS
    William R. 270
PURYEAR
    Juliet 80
PUTNAM
    Richard Fletcher 160
RAGLAND
    John K. 39
    Nellie Corbyn 39
    N. T. 290
    Thomas B. 122
RAGSDALE
    Frank V. 124
    Nancy 296
RALEIGH
    Annie L. 82
    Sir Walter 9
RAMSEY
    Jane Oliver 188
RANDOLPH
    Judith 208
RATCLIFF
    Ann M. 108
RAUNCE
    Robert 13
RAWLINGS
    Nellie P. 55
RAY
    Prosser 82
READY
    Williamette 84
    William 84
REARDON
    Annie L. 82
    Priscilla Aylette 56
    Lallie 82
    Lambert J. 82
    Simeon B. 82
REECE
    Jacob C. 196
REINHART
    Joseph 161

RHODES
  Cecil B. 40
  Charles Ross 40
  Mark Finney 40
RICE
  James W. 269
RICHARDS
  Hugh Nelson 97
RICHARDSON
  James 108
RIGG
  Anna 109
RoBARDS
  Elizabeth Lewis 294
  Jane DuTois 36
  John 295
ROBB
  Anna 127
  Florence 127
  Jesse Buckner 127
  Joseph H. 127
  Helen 127
  Ida 128
  Joseph H. 128
ROBERTS
  George 97
ROBERTSON
  Fannie 137
  L. Buckner 138
  William 138
ROBINSON
  Charles Wickliffe 247
  Christopher 41, 77
ROCKHOLD
  Charles B. 193
RONSHEIM
  I. L. 98
ROSS
  James W. 197
ROUNTREE
  Isabel 15
ROWE
  Thomas 133
ROY
  Dolly 113
  John 113
ROYSTON
  Thomas 22
RUFFIN
  Richard 4
RULOFF
  Ella Nora 136
RUST
  Richard H. 263
RYAN
  William 116
SABOURIN
  Jane Frances 23
SADLER
  Elizabeth 8, 14
SALE
  John Henry 18
SANFORD
  Belle 184
  Lucy M. 184

SAPP
  Bessie 87
  C. J. 87
  John M. 87
  Lucy 87
SATTERWHITE
  Ann 246
  Eliza 246
  Ellen 246
  Florence 247
  Henrietta 246
  John 246
  Mann 244, 246
  Mann William 247
  Maurice Langhorne 247
  Theodore Brooke 246
  Victoria Virginia 246
SAUNDERS
  Abner 192
  Alfred Pulaski 195
  Anthony G. W. 196
  Britannia J. 194
  Charles Abner 194
  Charles Robinson 194
  George Buckner 194
  Gustavus Buckner 193
  James Emmett 194
  John Franklin 194
  John Peyton 195
  Lamont L. 196
  Lermine Louise 195
  Lucy Eliza 194
  Mary 16
  Mary Lauretta 194
  Ophelia B. 195
  Parmelia A. J. 193
  Peyton Buckner 194
  William Isaiah 194
SAVAGE
  Anthony 221
  Elizabeth 13
SCARBOROW
  Richard 13
SCHROFFE
  Charles M. 260
SCOTT
  Margaret Julian 163
SCROOPE
  Sir Richard 10
SCROSBY
  Dorothy 157
SECOLE
  William 4
SEMPLE
  Robert B. 39
SHARPE
  Thomasine Elizabeth 2
SHIPP
  Amanthus 81
  Dudley 185
SHIVERS
  Thomas 227
SIDNER
  Martin 123
SIZER
  Lucy Allen 55

SLADE
  Ethel 18
SLAUGHTER
  Maria 117
  Philip 237
SMITH
  Anne Mason 89
  Charles C. 263
  Edward Jaquelin 127
  Edward Warren 127
  Elizabeth 157
  Frances Elizabeth 127
  George William 262
  James Gordon 127
  Jane 222
  John 22
  Lewis A. 244
  Lyman Aldrick 127
  Maria Henrietta 39
  Philip 127, 154
  Richard Bernard 127
  Richard Buckner 127
  Rose 5
  Sallie 261
  Sarah Lucretia Clay 30
  Thomas Turner 127
  William E. 266
SMYTH
  Thomas 5, 6
SNOWDEN
  Hubert 269
SPANGLER
  Edith 97
SPEAR
  Sallie Woodford 177
  Mary 177
SPEED
  James Buckner 38
  Mary Whitney 38
  Thomas 38
SPENCER
  Thomas 23
SPIERS
  Helen Strother 137
  Mary Dandridge 137
  Richard Parham 136
  Winfield Buckner 137
SPOTTSWOOD
  Govnr. Alexander 150
STANARD
  Beverley 158
STAPLES
  Susan 14
STARKE
  Behethland 233
STEEL
  Brice 173
STEPHENS
  John 172
STEVENS
  Sidney B. 265
  Thomas 13
STEWART
  Charlotte Pauline 181
  Clement 107
  Walter Monteith 181

STITH
  Albert 209
  Ann 207
  Bassett 208
  Bathurst 28
  Buckner 28, 207
  Catherine 29, 207
  Drury 28, 29, 206
  Dudley 28, 87
  Elizabeth 28, 209
  Elizabeth Buckner 29
  Frances W. 209
  Griffin 28, 29, 207
  Janet Carson 29
  John 28, 206, 209
  John Buckner 29
  Lavinia 209
  Lucy 29
  Maria 208
  Maria Long 208
  Martha 209
  Nicholas Long 209
  Richard 207
  Robert 207
  Susanna 29, 207
  Thomas 28
  Virginia P. 209
  William 29, 207
STROTHER
  Agatha 222
  Alice 234, 235
  Anne 225, 227, 229, 235, 238
  Anthony 221, 232, 233, 234
  Behethland 232, 234
  Benjamin 221, 227, 232, 234, 235, 239
  Betty 234, 235
  Catherine 234, 238
  Charles 237, 238
  Charles R. 232
  Christopher 238
  Daniel French 237
  David Hunter 234
  Dorothy 221, 239
  Eleanor 236
  Elizabeth 222, 227, 228, 230, 234, 237, 238, 239
  Elizabeth Nicholas 239
  Emily 234
  Enoch 239
  Francis 221, 225, 229, 232, 234, 239
  French 227, 236
  George 229, 232, 234, 239
  George French 237
  Gilley 237
  James 221, 234, 235, 236, 237
  James French 237
  Jane 225
  Jeremiah 221, 227, 236, 238
  John 227, 228, 232, 233, 234, 239
  John Dabney 226
  John F. 227, 238
  John H. 229
  John Hunt 237
  John Robert 237
  Joseph 221, 226, 236, 239
  Kate 228

STROTHER
    Lawrence 238
    Lewis Harvie 237
    Lucy 226, 227, 237, 265
    Margaret 221, 223, 228, 232, 234, 235, 236, 239
    Margaret French 237
    Mary 226, 227, 232, 234, 235, 237, 239
    Mary Wade 226
    Mildred 133, 227, 228
    Nancy 226, 227
    Nicholas 239
    Philip 232
    Philip W. 237
    Polly 227
    Richard 239
    Robert 221, 226, 232, 233, 238, 239
    Sallie 228
    Sallie Williams 237
    Samuel 233, 239
    Sarah 227, 230
    Sarah Catherine 228
    Starke 234
    Susannah 227, 229, 230
    Thomas 238, 239
    William 220, 221, 222, 227, 229, 233, 234, 237, 238, 281
    William Dabney 230
    William Johnson 237
STUART
    Ann 226
    David 132
    Gibbons 132
    Harriet 132
    John 132
    Lucy 132
    Mary 132
    Robert 226
STUBBS
    Jefferson W. 165
    Thomas Jefferson 165
    William Carter 165
SUMNER
    George J. 266
SUTTON
    Cordelia 79
    Cordelia Frances 84
    Demetrius 84
    Elizabeth 84
    Henry 84, 151
    James M. 84, 85
    John 84
    Judith Ann 150
    Juliet 84
    Mary 84
    Norborne E. 152
    Oscar 151
    Paulina V. 84
    Pendleton L. 84
    Philip 84
    Robert 150
    Ruth Ellen 84
    Susan Maria 151
    Unetta S. 85
    William 78, 84

TALBOT
    D. Clay 115
TALIAFERRO
    Elizabeth 171
    Hay B. 134
    John C. 106
    Lawrence Hay 134
    Lucy Mary 98
    Mildred 134, 238
    Nicholas 98
    Norbonne 171, 298
    Robin 298
    Sarah 35
    William 152
TATE
    Sarah 222
TAYLOR
    Anna W. L. 262
    Bessie Revely 263
    Edmund Pendleton 262
    Edward G. 104
    Elizabeth Lee 230
    Emily 230
    Erasmus 262
    George 230
    Hancock 230
    Isabel McN. 262
    James 230
    James Longstreet 262
    Jaquelin Plummer 262
    John Ashby 262
    John Gibson 230
    Joseph Pannill 230
    Lucy Allen 263
    Mary Edwina 262
    Richard 230
    Sally B. 90
    Sara Patton 263
    Sarah 230
    William Dabney 230
    Zachary 230
TENNANT
    David B. 269
THEALL
    Elisha S. 268
THOMAS
    Edmund 77
    Sallie 77
THOME
    Margaret N. 102
THOMPSON
    Fannie 237
    James 39
    John 228, 237
    Mildred 238
    William 228
THORBURN
    Charles Edmondson 120
    Helen Moore 120
    Isabella Donaldson 120
    James 120
    James Donaldson 120
THORNLEY
    Aaron 90
    Allen 90
    Charles 90
    Edwin 87, 90

THORNLEY
    Ella 60
    Francis 90
    Lewis 90
    Mary 90
    Thomas 90
THORNTON
    Annie 132
    Anthony 35, 282
    Aylett 132
    Bickley B. 113
    Charles 176
    Edmund Taylor 132
    Ella 133
    Ellen Rootes 119
    Elizabeth 122
    Francis 221, 281
    George Washington 128
    Jackson 162
    James B. T. 113
    Jane Augusta 128
    Judith 171
    Judith Presley 35, 282
    Margaret 281
    Mary Susan 114
    Mildred Hawes 113
    Nannie R. 114
    Richard Ewell 114
    Richard M. 157
    Rowland 280
    Susan Elizabeth 123
    Thomas Conway 132
    William 280
    William H. 113
    William Willis 113
THRALKILL
    Joseph 111
THROCKMORTON
    Elizabeth 156
THRUSTON
    Charles Mynn 168, 213, 215
    Edward 211
    John 156, 210, 211, 212
    Malachias 210
TILGHMAN
    Madeline Tasker 30
TIMMS
    Clarissa Pulaski 196
    John Abner 195
    Margaret Jane 195
    Mary F. 195
    Nancy E. 195
    William D. 195
TIMSON
    Mary 154, 168
    Samuel 154
TINSLEY
    Henry 246
TOBIN
    L. D. 184
TODD
    L. L. 246
    Thomas 31
TOMKIES
    Elizabeth 156

TOOKE
    Aylett Buckner 42
    Edwin Arthur 42
    John A. 42, 43
    Mary E. 42, 43
TRICE
    Stephen E. 107
TROWBRIDGE
    Alfred 40
    Herbert 40
    Sallie 40
TULEY
    Coatney Melmouth 80
    Katharine Edmondson 56
    Murray F. 56, 80, 83
    Theodore 80
    Virginia 80, 83
TULLY
    Charlotte 183
    Margaret Ann 182
TUNSTALL
    Alexander 121
TURNER
    Mary 259
    Thomas H. 127
TURPIN
    Thomas J. 184
TUTT
    Betsey 226
    Dorothea 268
    Gabriel 226
    John 267
    Julia 268
    Martha 268
    Mary Ann 267
    Philip 226, 260
    Robert 268
    Samuel 268
    Virginia 268
    William 226
TWEED
    Evangeline 98
    Thomas M. 99
TYLER
    Elizabeth 161
    Francis 225
    Henry 235
UPSHUR
    James 37
    Martha 37
VICKERS
    Thomas 22
VIVION
    Sally Ann 123
WADE
    Ida 90
    John B. 90
    Mary Willis 226
    Melia 90
    Robert 90
    Thomas B. 90
WADSWORTH
    Mary J. 116
WALKER
    Amelia Frances 162
    Ann 131
    Frances 157

WALKER
    J. Brisben 234
    Lulu V. 114
    Mary Clarissa 161
WALL
    Elizabeth Ethaline 188
    Garrett B. 188
    Garrett S. 188
    Henry Buckner 188
WALLACE
    Frederick R. 265
    G. M. 273
WALLINGFORD
    Annie 245
    Buckner Ashby 245
    Joel 245
    John 245
    Joseph 244
    Kate 245
WALTERS
    Ann 248
WARDEN
    Arthur Hills 267
    Arthur Lee 267
    Charles William 267
    Eugene French 267
    Herbert P. 267
    Mary Ashby 267
    Mary Pauline 267
    Turner Ashby 267
    William 267
WARE
    William W. 108
WARNER
    Elizabeth 201
WASHINGTON
    Ann 151
    Augustine 151
    Caroline 152
    Catherine 150, 202
    Clement 151
    Cora 151
    Dollie Buckner 151
    Dorothea 151, 152
    Elizabeth 152
    Eugene 151
    Fannie Prior 151
    George 150, 151, 202
    Henry 151
    John 150, 151
    Col. John 131, 151
    J. Boyd 114, 151
    Lund 235
    Mary 151
    Richard 151
    Robert 152, 235
    Roberta Boyd 151
    Selina 152
    Susan E. K. 151
    Thomas 151
    Walker 151
    Walker Hawes 151
    William 151, 152
WATTS
    Margaret 222, 235

WATSON
    Elizabeth 42
    William 42
WAY
    James Clark 80
WAYLAND
    Benjamin 162
WEBB
    Arthur S. 18
WELLS
    Homer 138
    Joseph Estes 138
    Samuel 138
    Terry T. 137
    Thomas Cust 138
WEST
    James 157
WESTERFIELD
    Thomas L. 297
WHITE
    Elizabeth 227
    Harriet Buckner 40
    Paul 40
WHITING
    Major Henry 22
WHITNEY
    W. F. 136
WILKINS
    Edward Pugh 160
WILKINSON
    Mary Ann 162
WILLIAMS
    Arabella A. 175
    James 23
    Sarah Green 237
    Winifred 13
WILLIS
    James Morrison 90
    John T. 90
    Lucy Woodford 90
    Mary Lewis 227
WILLOCK
    David 123
WILTHITE
    Jane 81
WINDER
    Edward Lloyd 120
WINFIELD
    Courtland S. 137
    Edith S. 137
    Gladys G. 137
    John Buckner 137
    Richard M. 137
    William I. 137
    William Meade 137
WINLOCK
    William 294
WINN
    Jesse D. 185
WITHERS
    Eliza 259
    Edward 151
    Evadne 151
    Ezekiel D. 151
    Martha 259
    Mary 259

WITHERS
 Rolla M. 151
 Samuel 259
 William 259
WIRT
 Agnes W. 152
 Daniel Washington 152
 Elizabeth 152
 William 152
 William Washington 152
WISE
 Frederick 185
 Mildred Washington 184
WITHINGTON
 Zaidee Eddy 182
WOFFENDALL
 Mary 239
WOLFE
 Thruston 260
WOLFF
 Ann D. 234
WOOD
 Edith 18
 Jane 14
 John S. 182
WOODE
 Thomas 4
WOODFORD
 Buckner 177
 Catesby 171
 John Thornton 177
 Lucy Archer 176
 Lucy Catesby 171
 Sally Taliaferro 173
 Thomas Catesby 180

WOODS
 Elizabeth M. 124
WOODSON
 Charles Edward 269
 Samuel H. 245
WORNALL
 Clay 176
WRIGHT
 Robert Moseley 117
WURTS
 Rebecca 245
WYNNE
 Thomas G. 265
YANCEY
 Charles 259
YANDELL
 Susan 38
YEATMAN
 Meredith 171
YELTON
 Millie 111
YERBY
 Alice Dickinson 88
 Arthur Bernard 88
 Emma 88
 Gordon Wallace 88
 Jennie Dickinson 88
 Lelia Fauntleroy 88
 Patsy Gordon 88
 Thomas Pratt 88
 William Dickinson 88
YORKE
 Edward 124
ZIMMERMAN
 W. J. 197

www.ingramcontent.com/pod-product-compliance
Lightning Source LLC
Chambersburg PA
CBHW021812300426
44114CB00009BA/150